**W9-CCX-315**

# Discover
# San Francisco

## Experience the best
## of San Francisco

This edition written and researched by

Mariella Krause,
Alison Bing, John A Vlahides

# Discover
# San Francisco

### The Marina & Fisherman's Wharf (p47)

Some of San Francisco's biggest attractions are located here.

**Don't Miss**: Alcatraz, Fisherman's Wharf, Golden Gate Bridge

### Downtown & Civic Center (p77)

Downtown has all the urban amenities: galleries, hotels, dining, theaters and shopping galore.

**Don't Miss**: Ferry Building

### North Beach & Chinatown (p101)

Steep yourself in culture in bohemian North Beach and the largest Chinatown outside of Asia.

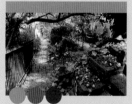

### Nob Hill, Russian Hill & Fillmore (p125)

Cable cars deliver visitors to hilltop bars and high-fashion boutiques.

### The Mission, SoMa & the Castro (p147)

Where's the party? Here, amid killer burritos, rainbow flags and the creative class.

**Don't Miss**: San Francisco Museum of Modern Art (SFMOMA)

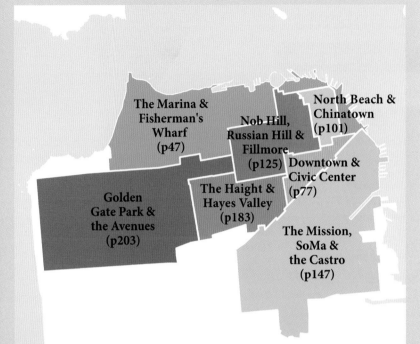

The Marina & Fisherman's Wharf (p47)

North Beach & Chinatown (p101)

Nob Hill, Russian Hill & Fillmore (p125)

Downtown & Civic Center (p77)

Golden Gate Park & the Avenues (p203)

The Haight & Hayes Valley (p183)

The Mission, SoMa & the Castro (p147)

### The Haight & Hayes Valley (p183)

Two chill 'hoods that are home to skateboarders, fashionistas, hippies and Zen monks.

### Golden Gate Park & the Avenues (p203)

Sunny days bring picnics, paddleboats and croquet. Foggy afternoons are spent exploring museums.

**Don't Miss:** Golden Gate Park

# Contents

**Plan Your Trip**  Discover San Francisco

Welcome to San
Francisco ......................6

Highlights Map ...........8

San Francisco's
Top 25
Experiences ...............10

Top Days in
San Francisco ...........32

Month by Month .......40

What's New .............42

Get Inspired .............43

Need to Know ..........44

## The Marina & Fisherman's Wharf  47
Highlights .....................48
Walking Tour ...............50
**Alcatraz** ................**52**
**Fisherman's Wharf** ...**54**
**Golden Gate Bridge** ...**58**
Sights ..........................60
Eating............................65
Drinking & Nightlife......70
Entertainment ..............71
Shopping.......................72
Sports & Activities.......73

## Downtown & Civic Center  77
Highlights......................78
Walking Tour ................80
**Ferry Building**............**82**
Sights ..........................84
Eating............................85
Drinking & Nightlife......93
Entertainment ..............96
Shopping.......................98

## North Beach & Chinatown  101
Highlights.....................102
Walking Tour ...............104
Sights ..........................106
Eating............................115

Drinking & Nightlife.... 118
Entertainment ............120
Shopping......................121

## Nob Hill, Russian Hill & Fillmore  125
Highlights.....................126
Walking Tour ...............128
Sights ..........................130
Eating............................133
Drinking & Nightlife....138
Entertainment ............140
Shopping......................142
Sports & Activities.....145

## The Mission, SoMa & the Castro  147
Highlights.....................148
Walking Tour ...............150
**San Francisco Museum
of Modern Art............152**
Sights ..........................154
Eating............................165
Drinking & Nightlife....170
Entertainment ............175
Shopping......................178
Sports & Activities.....180

## The Haight & Hayes Valley  183
Highlights.....................184
Walking Tour ...............186

Sights ..........................188
Eating...........................189
Drinking & Nightlife....196
Entertainment ...........198
Shopping.....................198

**Golden Gate Park
& the Avenues  203**
Highlights...................204
Walking Tour..............206
**Golden Gate Park.....208**
Sights .........................212
Eating...........................217
Drinking & Nightlife....221
Entertainment ..........222
Shopping....................222
Sports & Activities....224

**Day Trips  227**

San Francisco Today 240
History.......................242
Family Travel.............248
Food & Drink.............250
Arts & Architecture... 254
Hills & Fog ................259
GLBT SF ....................263
Cable Cars ................265

Sleeping ....................270
Transport .................278
Directory .................283

**Behind the
Scenes** ......................**288**
**Index** .........................**292**
**Map Legend** .......... **303**

# Welcome to San Francisco

Quick, name the main attractions in San Francisco. Even if you've never been here before, you can probably rattle off Fisherman's Wharf, Alcatraz, the cable cars and the Golden Gate Bridge without much thought. And while those places do sell the most postcards, San Francisco is equally famous for the unscripted moments that exist in between.

**San Francisco has always been one to set itself apart.** A climb to the top of one of San Francisco's 47 hills yields a unique panorama of Victorian houses, monumental bridges, funny-shaped skyscrapers and stairway gardens, all surrounded by a glittering bay. The city is naturally rebellious, shrugging off typical California stereotypes with fog that turns a warm summer day into an excuse to buy outerwear and enough hills to give the feeling of a slow-moving roller coaster. With a population of free thinkers, crafty inventors and weirdos passing as normal, this city stubbornly refuses to be brought down to earth.

**Did we mention the food?** With an abundance of ultrafresh, locally grown ingredients and the most restaurants per capita anywhere in North America, San Francisco is spoiled for choice. And it's not just lavish, multicourse meals with wine pairings. From burrito joints and food trucks to every sort of ethnic food imaginable, cheap eats are not just plentiful but fabulous.

**If you're bored in SF, you're not doing it right.** Even people who live here stick to a rigorous schedule of year-round farmers markets, free concerts in Golden Gate Park and what seems like an endless supply of street fairs. The city has a way of bending to your will, becoming whatever you want it to be. Child friendly? Gay friendly? Pet friendly? All that and more. So consider permission granted to indulge in whatever you want: that just means you've gotten the hang of San Francisco.

66

**The city is naturally rebellious**

99

California St Cable Car (p267)

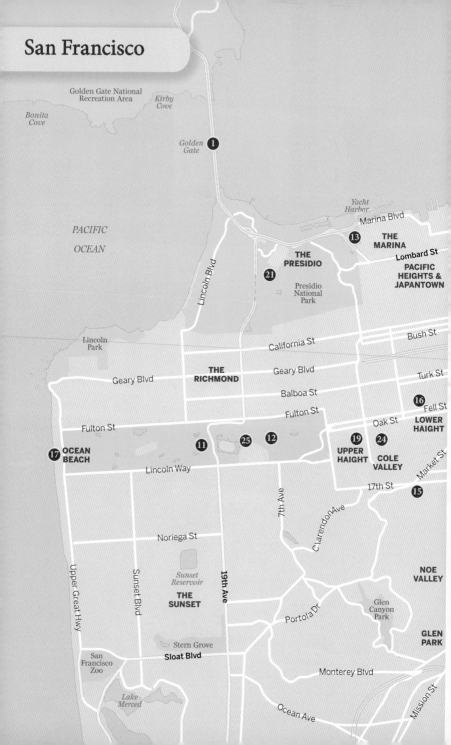

# San Francisco

Golden Gate National
Recreation Area

*Kirby
Cove*

*Bonita
Cove*

*Golden
Gate* **1**

*Yacht
Harbor*

Marina Blvd

**13** **THE
MARINA**

**PACIFIC
OCEAN**

Lombard St

**THE
PRESIDIO**

**PACIFIC
HEIGHTS &
JAPANTOWN**

Lincoln Blvd

**21**

*Presidio
National
Park*

Bush St

*Lincoln
Park*

California St

Geary Blvd

Turk St

Geary Blvd

**THE
RICHMOND**

Geary Blvd

Balboa St

**16**

Fell St

Fulton St

**LOWER
HAIGHT**

Oak St

Fulton St

Fulton St

**11**

**25**

**12**

**19**

**24**

**17**

**OCEAN
BEACH**

**UPPER
HAIGHT**

**COLE
VALLEY**

Lincoln Way

Market St

17th St

**15**

7th Ave

Clarendon Ave

Noriega St

**NOE
VALLEY**

Upper Great Hwy

Sunset Blvd

*Sunset
Reservoir*

19th Ave

**THE
SUNSET**

Glen
Canyon
Park

Portola Dr

**GLEN
PARK**

*Stern Grove*

Sloat Blvd

San
Francisco
Zoo

Monterey Blvd

Mission St

*Lake
Merced*

Ocean Ave

# 25
# Top Experiences

1 Golden Gate Bridge (p58)
2 Ferry Building (p82)
3 Alcatraz (p52)
4 Cable Cars (p265)
5 Pier 39 (p55)
6 Asian Art Museum (p86)
7 The Mission (p154)
8 SFMOMA (p152)
9 Dragon's Gate (p113)
10 Lombard St (p132)
11 Golden Gate Park (p208)
12 California Academy of Sciences (p209)
13 Exploratorium (p63)
14 Coit Tower (p107)
15 Gay Life, the Castro (p164)
16 Alamo Square (p193)
17 Ocean Beach (p213)
18 Telegraph Hill (p107)
19 The Haight (p188)
20 Hayes Valley Boutiques (p200)
21 The Presidio (p61)
22 Symphony and Opera (p96)
23 Drinking in Speakeasies (p96)
24 San Francisco's Hilltops (p188)
25 Japanese Tea Garden (p210)

# 25 San Francisco's Top Experiences

# Golden Gate Bridge (p58)

Other suspension bridges impress with engineering, but none can touch the Golden Gate Bridge for showmanship. On sunny days it transfixes crowds with a radiant glow – a feat pulled off by 25 daredevil painters who maintain the bridge's luminous complexion by applying 1000 gallons of International Orange paint every week. When afternoon fog rolls in, the bridge puts on a magic show that's positively riveting: now you see it, now you don't and, abracadabra, it's sawn in half. Tune in tomorrow for its dramatic unveiling.

## Ferry Building (p82)

This monument to food stands tall and proud on Saturdays, when star chefs trawl farmers market stalls for rare heirloom varietals and foodie babies blissfully teethe on organic peaches. Local farmers and food trucks have dedicated followings any rock star would envy; you'll wait for organic Dirty Girl tomatoes and Namu's Korean steak tacos. Bide your time exchanging recipe tips, then haul your picnic to Pier 2 with sparkling bay and culinary bounty in hand.

## Alcatraz (p52)

From its 19th-century founding – to hold Civil War deserters – to its closure by Bobby Kennedy in 1963, Alcatraz was America's most notorious prison. No prisoner is known to have escaped alive – but after spending even a minute in D-Block solitary, listening to the sounds of city life across the bay, the 1.25-mile swim through riptides may seem worth a shot. For maximum chill factor, book the popular night tour to check out the gloomy jailhouse. On the return ferry to San Francisco, freedom never felt so good.

## The Best...
# Dining Discoveries

**FERRY BUILDING**
The historic port reinvented as a dining destination, with award-winning chefs and year-round farmers markets. (p86)

**DELFINA**
Maverick California cuisine takes on big, ultrafresh flavors with casual finesse. (p165)

**NAMU**
Chef Dennis Lee makes killer Korean tacos with organic ingredients and savory barbecue flavors. (p217)

**COI**
With dishes that are inventive verging on startling, the 11-course dinner doesn't seem like such a splurge. (p115)

# The Best...
# Urban Wildlife

**GOLDEN GATE PARK**
Buffalo roam, carnivorous plants belch and goldfish chase paddleboats. (p208)

**CRISSY FIELD**
Pipers and herons hang out at a reclaimed army airstrip. (p61)

**SEA LIONS AT PIER 39**
The class clowns of the Bay Area are SF's best free attraction. (p55)

**CALIFORNIA ACADEMY OF SCIENCES**
Penguins cuddle upstairs, a white alligator stalks downstairs. (p209)

**WILD PARROTS**
SF's official birds are the renegade parrots of Telegraph Hill. (p107)

## Cable Cars (p265)

White-knuckle grips on worn wooden benches give away the novices. Lurching uphill, you can exhale when the bell finally signals the summit. But don't look now: what goes up all 338ft of Nob Hill must come down. Maybe now is not the best time to mention that the brakes are still hand-operated, or that this Victorian steampunk invention has hardly changed since 1873. Once you reach the terminus, you're ready to take the next giddy ride standing, with nothing between you and eternity but a creaky hand strap.

## Pier 39 Sea Life (p55)

Sea lions have lived the California dream since 1989, when they took to the Pier 39 docks. After disappearing in 2009, their return in 2010 was greeted with cheers and a brass band. Sharks circle nearby at Aquarium of the Bay (p56), where the only barrier between visitors and bay waters is a glass tube. A less ominous underwater world is glimpsed at the newly restored Aquatic Park Bathhouse (p56), where jellyfish flutter across 1930s mosaics.

## Asian Art Museum (p86)

The museum's 18,000-piece collection brings together 6000 years of art history from China, Taiwan, Tibet, Japan, Korea, Pakistan, India and more, all under one roof. Exhibits include Buddha statues, ceremonial relics, lacquerware and even puppets. Given the city's 150-year history as North America's gateway to Asia, the collection is also quintessentially San Franciscan.

## The Mission (p154)

Bragging about Mission finds is a competitive sport in San Francisco, whether it's spotting a mural in progress in Clarion Alley (p159) or discovering pirate treasure at 826 Valencia (p155). But some secrets are meant to be shared: burritos from La Taqueria (p165) are too massive for one, and adults read their teenage journal entries onstage at the Make-Out Room (p176). Clarion Alley (p159)

# SFMOMA (p152)

The San Francisco Museum of Modern Art (SFMOMA) has collected new media art since before anyone knew what to call it and, with art-star discoveries such as Matthew Barney, the museum seems audaciously gifted. But wait until you see what the museum has in store for the future: with the recent windfall of 1100 works donated by the Fisher family (founders of the Gap) and a $480-million expansion in the works, the museum is set to triple in size. San Francisco Museum of Modern Art (p152), designed by Mario Botta

## The Best...
## Museums

**SAN FRANCISCO MUSEUM OF MODERN ART (SFMOMA)**
Big, bold exhibitions push artistic boundaries into an entirely new wing. (p152)

**MH DE YOUNG MUSEUM**
A 27,000-piece collection of art and craft masterworks from around the world. (p209)

**ASIAN ART MUSEUM**
Sightsee halfway across the globe in an hour, from Persian miniatures to Chinese installation art. (p86)

**LEGION OF HONOR**
Iconic Impressionists and a sensational modern collection set amid Rodin sculptures. (p212)

## Dragon's Gate (p113)

There are other ways to enter Chinatown – it's not like it's walled off – but the green-tiled roof of the dragon-bedecked archway that stretches over Grant Ave lets you know you've officially arrived in one of the largest Chinatowns in North America. Pass from the gates to explore 21 blocks that have made and lost fortunes, survived earthquakes and changed history. Fortunes are still made fresh daily at Golden Gate Fortune Cookie Company (p122), and you'll find no shortage of Chinese tchotchkes to take home as souvenirs.

## The Best...
# Hidden Alleyways

**BALMY ALLEY**
*Muralistas* have covered this alley in art since the 1970s. (p159)

**JACK KEROUAC ALLEY**
This byway named after the Beat author is inscribed with his poetry. (p106)

**BOB KAUFMAN ALLEY**
Named for the spoken-word artist who kept a 12-year vow of silence. (p111)

**ROSS ALLEY**
Former home to brothels, now the home of fortune cookies. (p114)

**MACONDRAY LANE**
The setting for Armistead Maupin's *Tales of the City*. (p133)

## Lombard St (p132)

Though there's plenty of debate about whether it's really the crookedest street in the world, Lombard is almost certainly the most comely of the contenders. Paved in red brick, its eight hairpin turns are flanked by colorful, well-tended landscaping that make it a classic SF photo op. If you're not driving, take the Powell-Hyde cable car, which will drop you right at the top, check out the view of Coit Tower, then walk down: the best pictures are from the bottom of the hill looking up.

## Golden Gate Park (p208)

You may have heard that San Francisco has a wild streak a mile wide, but it also happens to be 4.5 miles long. Golden Gate Park lets San Franciscans do what comes naturally: roller-discoing, drum-circling, petting starfish, sniffing orchids and racing bison toward the Pacific. It's hard to believe these 1017 acres of lush terrain were once just scrubby sand dunes and that San Franciscans have successfully preserved this stretch of green since 1866, ousting casinos and a theme-park igloo village. Conservatory of Flowers (p211), Golden Gate Park

SABRINA DALBESIO/LONELY PLANET IMAGES ©

## California Academy of Sciences (p209)

Adorable tree frogs, flirty butterflies, an albino alligator and a giant, bashful pink octopus: even the most worldly visitor is sure to gasp at the California Academy of Sciences. The views inside and outside Renzo Piano's acclaimed LEED-certified green building are sublime: you can stare into infinity in the Planetarium or ride the elevator to the blooming wildflower rooftop for park panoramas. On Thursday nights, come for sunset cocktails on the ingenious roof, just as the penguins are dozing off.

## Exploratorium (p63)

No theory is too far-out to test at the Exploratorium. Can skateboards defy gravity? What can your eyes see in total darkness? Do puffy cheeks automatically make people cuter? The freaky hands-on displays here earned a MacArthur Genius Grant. If science class were always this cool, we'd all have PhDs. Plan ahead to get reservations for the Tactile Dome, a crawl-through experience where you feel your way around in utter darkness. (Was that someone's ankle, or part of the experience?)

## Coit Tower (p107)

Go ahead and snicker at the wacky concrete projectile jutting up from Telegraph Hill – you wouldn't be the first. Eccentric Lillie Hancock Coit left a third of her considerable fortune to build the monument. But the climb is no joke, the tower's dedication to firefighters is heartfelt and the views inside the tower will win you over to Lillie's point of view. From the top of the tower, you can take in panoramic views and spot colorful flocks of parrots turning the treetops red and blue. Coit Tower (p107), designed by Arthur Brown Jr and Henry Howard

14

HOLGER LEUE/LONELY PLANET IMAGES ©

## The Best...
## Quirks

### 826 VALENCIA
A Fish Theater and pirate supplies, for all your buccaneering needs. (p155)

### EXPLORATORIUM
Hair-raising exhibits and a pitch-black Tactile Dome. (p63)

### CARTOON ART MUSEUM
Where Fantastic Mr Fox hangs out with R Crumb. (p158)

### HAIGHT FLASHBACKS
Home to hippies and retail for rebels. (p188)

### WAVE ORGAN
A new way to listen to waves. (p60)

### MUSÉE MÉCANIQUE
Vintage arcade games make Pac-Man look like a newcomer. (p55)

# The Best...
## GLBT Landmarks

**PRIDE**
Crowds roar as 500,000 paraders strut down Market St. (p41)

**THE CASTRO**
The trailblazing, good-time, gay neighborhood gives new meaning to party politics. (p164)

**HARVEY MILK PLAZA**
An enormous rainbow flag is waiting to greet you. (p164)

**WOMEN'S BUILDING**
Murals wrap around this landmark, home to women's nonprofit organizations. (p159)

## Gay Life in the Castro (p164)

Head over the rainbow and into the Castro where, if party boys and political activists have their way, a good time and civil rights will be had by all. For anyone who left their rainbow flag at home, there's a giant one greeting arrivals at the intersection of Castro and Market Sts in Harvey Milk Plaza – otherwise known as the epicenter of gay SF. This a good place to take in local color – on warm days several oddball nudists congregate to shock tourists. Left: Castro Street Fair; Top: Castro Theatre (p177)

LEFT: RICK GERHARTER/LONELY PLANET IMAGES © TOP: LEE FOSTER/LONELY PLANET IMAGES ©

# Alamo Square (p193)

You've probably already seen them: few homes have reached the same celebrity status as the six matching Victorians known as Postcard Row. And while there may be more heavily ginger-breaded Victorians with more fanciful paint selections, Alamo Square gives you the perfect vantage point from which to line them up with downtown SF in the background. So photogenic are these Painted Ladies, they've appeared in dozens of movies and TV shows, as well as countless vacation photos and, you guessed it, postcards.

ROBERTO GEROMETTA/LONELY PLANET IMAGES ©

# Ocean Beach (p213)

Heading to the beach? Don't forget to pack a hoodie, and don't even think about jumping in without a wet suit. In the frigid surf, ankle-deep is about how much most people can stand, although a stroll along the shore is lovely on sunny days. When surfers clear out and fog rolls in, even the air will give you goose bumps, as firewood-wielding locals build bonfires. Ships fade into ghostly silhouettes, and an orange glow stretches across the horizon until you can't take the cold anymore.

## Telegraph Hill (p107)

The chattering and squawking flock of green-and-red parrots made famous in the documentary *The Wild Parrots of Telegraph Hill* surely don't expect to keep scenery like this to themselves. Yet still they seem to mock your progress every step of the way up Telegraph Hill's Filbert St Steps and Greenwich St Stairway. Your reward for taking the scenic route up to Coit Tower – besides your well-defined calf muscles – includes hidden gardens and sweeping views of the waterfront and Golden Gate Bridge. Filbert St Steps (p107), Telegraph Hill

18

## The Best...
## Giddy Views

**GOLDEN GATE BRIDGE**
Fog sneaks between orange cables and tickles deco towers, then runs away. (p58)

**COIT TOWER**
Step through Works Progress Administration (WPA) murals into the elevator – head up for 360-degree SF views. (p107)

**ALAMO SQUARE PARK**
Painted Lady Victorian houses pose for pictures with Downtown backdrops. (p193)

**STERLING PARK**
Bay vistas to inspire poetry or tennis, whichever comes first. (p131)

## The Haight (p188)

**19**

Groovy is a permanent state of mind in Haight-Ashbury, where hippies became rock stars and vintage stores keep suede fringe in fashion, where head shops stay open but the Gap goes out of business. The Summer of Love may be over, but the former neighborhood of Janis Joplin, the Grateful Dead and Hunter S Thompson (who called the area 'Hashbury') still holds on to its hippie roots, and many a pilgrimage has been made to the intersection of Haight and Ashbury to relive a different time. Haight St (p188)

ANTHONY PIDGEON/LONELY PLANET IMAGES ©

# The Best...
# Shows

### SAN FRANCISCO SYMPHONY
See why the Grammys keep coming for conductor Michael Tilson Thomas. (p96)

### SAN FRANCISCO OPERA
See Puccini and Verdi reinvented, plus world premieres of daring new operas. (p97)

### CASTRO THEATRE
Show tunes on the mighty Wurlitzer introduce films at this deco movie palace. (p177)

### BEACH BLANKET BABYLON
This long-running musical review featuring ridiculously large hats is good, campy fun. (p120)

SABRINA DALBESIO/LONELY PLANET IMAGES ©

**(20)** ## Hayes Valley Boutiques (p200)

Break out of the rut with fashion-forward finds in the boutiques of Hayes Valley. Although SF has spawned megaretailers – Levi Strauss, Pottery Barn and the Gap are all headquartered Downtown – zoning restrictions limit chain retailers in the city's neighborhoods. So where other cities might plunk another Walmart or Ross Dress For Less, here you'll find Victorian storefronts where killer sale racks put mall markups to shame. More boutiques can be found on Haight St, Fillmore St and in the Mission. Flight 001 (p201)

## The Presidio (p61)

Salute the military for leaving San Francisco nearly 1500 acres of relatively undeveloped land that includes forests, hills, meadows and beaches. The behavior you'll see nowadays – lollygagging on Crissy Field (p61) and public nudity at Baker Beach (p61) – would've earned soldiers reprimands. Today the only commanding presence is the Yoda statue near the LucasArts offices, and he seems mildly amused.

Crissy Field (p61)

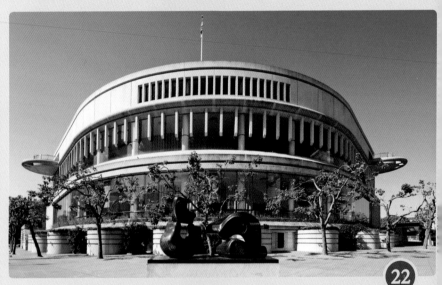

## Symphony & Opera (p96)

Opera brought SF back to its feet after the 1906 earthquake; it's been earning standing ovations ever since at San Francisco Opera – the second-largest opera company in the US. At the Grammy-winning San Francisco Symphony, the air is electric whenever Michael Tilson Thomas raises the baton. Wooed away from the London Symphony Orchestra in 1995, Thomas' innovative programming combines US and Russian composers, full-throttle Mahler and Beethoven, and experimental music. Louise M Davies Symphony Hall (p96), designed by Skidmore, Owings & Merrill and Pietro Belluschi

# Drinking in Speakeasies (p96)

A brief flirtation with respectability in 1906 convinced City Hall to ban dancing in bars, driving the action underground into speakeasies. Everything's back out in the open, but you can still slake your thirst for illicit tippling at the secretive and sign-free Bourbon & Branch (p96), where you'll need a password and an address to get in. Other aficionados of the speakeasy style include Café du Nord (p178) and Smuggler's Cove (p197) – or you can dispense with all the secrecy in the cocktail-friendly areas of SoMa (p173), the Tenderloin (p95) and the Mission (p170). Café du Nord (p178)

## The Best...
## Saloons

**COMSTOCK SALOON**
Vintage Victorian watering hole with lantern lighting. (p118)

**ELIXIR**
Serving spur-shaking cocktails since the Gold Rush. (p170)

**HOMESTEAD**
Front-parlor dive bar complete with stamped-tin ceiling. (p171)

**BLOODHOUND**
Antler chandeliers and cocktails in Mason jars. (p173)

**RICKHOUSE**
Bartenders pour vicious punch bowls and whiskey straight from the barrel. (p93)

**MADRONE**
Victorian art bar with an absinthe fountain and saloon showdowns like Michael Jackson versus Prince. (p196)

23

## San Francisco's Hilltops (p188)

Gravity seems unkind as you scale SF's steepest hills, with calf muscles and cable car wheels groaning. But all grumbling ends once you hit the summit of Buena Vista Park (p188) or any of the city's other peaks, with wind-bent trees, Victorian turrets and the world at your feet. San Francisco has 47 peaks in all, with hilltop parks like Sterling Park (p131) and Ina Coolbrith Park (p129) as its crowning glories.

**24**

# The Best...
# Urban Hikes

**GOLDEN GATE PARK**
Three miles of wilderness and weirdness. (p208)

**FORT FUNSTON**
Hang gliders leap from fortifications at the beginning of the 9-mile Coastal Trail. (p216)

**LINCOLN PARK**
Rugged coastlines give you end-of-the-world views and low-tide shipwreck sightings. (p213)

**OCEAN BEACH**
Pacific waves take on sandcastle condos and hard-core surfers; leave your footsteps temporarily in the sand. (p213)

**25**

# Japanese Tea Garden (p210)

Bridges arch steeply over koi-filled ponds, crooked paths help you evade evil spirits, and a five-tiered pagoda looms over manicured trees. Built in 1894 for the California Midwinter International Exposition, the Japanese gardens are the oldest in the United States. Every spring, a burst of cherry blossoms pay tribute to Makoto Hagiwara, who oversaw the gardens for 30 years and imported the cherry trees from Japan. While you're there, stop for tea at the teahouse, said to be the place where fortune cookies made their crunchy US debut.

# Top Days in
# San Francisco

# San Francisco Must-Sees

*On your first day, check off some of the big, famous San Francisco attractions that everyone will ask you about when you get home. Ride a cable car, do Pier 39, tour Alcatraz and get a glimpse of the Golden Gate Bridge.*

### ① Hop a Cable Car (p265)

Start with a ride on the Powell-Mason cable car line – a quintessential SF experience and the best way to get to Pier 39.

**CABLE CAR ➡ PIER 39**

🚶 From the last cable car stop, walk north on Taylor St, turn right on Beach St and walk three blocks to the waterfront.

### ② Pier 39 (p55)

Check out the shops, ride the carousel, but whatever you do, don't miss the sea lions who hang out on the adjacent docks.

**PIER 39 ➡ BOUDIN BAKERY**

🚶 You won't have far to go: the Boudin Bakery is located at the foot of Pier 39.

### ③ Lunch at Boudin Bakery (p67)

Warm up with some clam chowder served in a sourdough bread bowl – it's cheap, tasty and a Pier 39 tradition.

**BOUDIN BAKERY ➡ FISHERMAN'S WHARF**

🚶 Walk west along the waterfront towards the Golden Gate Bridge.

San Francisco Maritime National Historical Park (p55)
PHOTOGRAPHER: ROBERTO GEROMETTA/LONELY PLANET IMAGES ©

### ④ Fisherman's Wharf (p54)

Check out historical ships along the waterfront, including those at the San Francisco Maritime National Historical Park (p55), USS *Pampanito* (p55) and the SS *Jeremiah O'Brien* (p55).

**WATERFRONT ➡ FORBES ISLAND**

🚶 🚤 Walk back to Pier 39 and catch Forbes Island's private shuttle from the H dock.

### ⑤ Dinner at Forbes Island (p65)

Stick with the waterfront theme and have dinner under the lighthouse at this over-the-top houseboat restaurant.

**FORBES ISLAND ➡ ALCATRAZ**

🚶 🚤 Walk east along the waterfront (away from Golden Gate Bridge) and catch the ferry to Alcatraz from Pier 33.

### ⑥ Alcatraz (p52)

Make reservations in advance for the Alcatraz night tour, when you can see the former prison at its most mysterious. When the sun starts to go down, the views of San Francisco from across the water will make you glad you waited.

## Asian Influences

*Food, shopping and Asian culture are the highlights of day two. After a
morning exploring Chinatown, hit the foodie-friendly Ferry Building, then
look for more Eastern influences at the Asian Art Museum. Save some energy
for boutique shopping, followed by dinner and rum-soaked tiki drinks.*

## 1 Chinatown (p111)

Wander Grant Ave for souvenirs and head into Chinatown's famous alleys for a little bit of history. Duck into the Golden Gate Fortune Cookie Company (p122) to see how the ubiquitous treats are made.

### CHINATOWN ⊙ FERRY BUILDING
🏃 Head east on California, then turn right on Market and look for the clock tower.

## 2 Ferry Building (p82)

Shop, gawk and forage at this foodie empire on the water. Formerly a transit hub, this landmark building from 1898 is now famous as a gastronomic center where you can shop for gifts and food, and graze to your heart's content.

### FERRY BUILDING ⊙ SLANTED DOOR
🏃 Slanted Door is at the northwestern end of the Ferry Building.

## 3 Lunch at Slanted Door (p89)

Stop for upscale Vietnamese food at this popular Ferry Building restaurant. Can't wait for a table? No problem: with all the other delicious options within these walls, you never have to worry about going hungry.

### SLANTED DOOR ⊙ ASIAN ART MUSEUM
Ⓜ Catch any outbound Muni train at the Embarcadero station and get off at the Civic Center stop.

## 4 Asian Art Museum (p86)

Now that you've tackled Chinatown and Vietnamese food, continue the theme at the Asian Art Museum. Start at the top and wind your way down through centuries'

worth of cultural, spiritual and artistic artifacts from nearly every corner of Asia.

### ASIAN ART MUSEUM ⊙ HAYES VALLEY
🏃 Walk south on Larkin St towards Market St and turn right on Hayes. Shopping starts past Franklin St.

## 5 Hayes Valley Shopping (p200)

Wander the boutiques on Hayes St between Franklin and Laguna Sts, and be prepared for spontaneous stops along Gough, Linden and Octavia Sts.

### HAYES VALLEY ⊙ ZUNI CAFE
🏃 From Hayes St, walk south until you hit Market St. Zuni Cafe is between Franklin St and Van Ness Ave.

## 6 Dinner at Zuni Cafe (p195)

Treat yourself with dinner at Zuni Cafe. With a dramatic space on Market St and unique takes on traditional menu items, you can't go wrong.

### ZUNI CAFE ⊙ SMUGGLER'S COVE
🏃 Half a block west of Zuni is Gough St – turn right and walk about half a mile (or hop in a cab if stamina demands).

## 7 Drinks at Smuggler's Cove (p197)

The tiki theme keeps the mood light, but the flaming rum drinks are dead serious. Come see what all the fuss is about.

---

Grant Ave, Chinatown (p111)
PHOTOGRAPHER: LEE FOSTER/LONELY PLANET IMAGES ©

# Museums & Golden Gate Park

*Golden Gate Park is more than just a green space, and day three proves it. You can spend an entire day in and around the park, visiting museums, wandering formal gardens and watching the sun set over the ocean at the end of it all.*

# ① Golden Gate Park (p208)

Take your pick of activities: with over 1000 acres, Golden Gate Park has something to catch your interest, whether it's cycling, bison watching, paddleboating or just strolling the Botanical Gardens.

GOLDEN GATE PARK ⊙ ACADEMY OF SCIENCES

🏃 The Academy of Sciences is an easy walk from anywhere in the east end of the park.

# ② California Academy of Sciences (p209)

With an aquarium, a planetarium, animal exhibits, a rainforest dome and an award-winning building to showcase it all, the California Academy of Sciences packs in a lot of natural wonder.

ACADEMY OF SCIENCES ⊙ SAN TUNG

🏃 Take Music Concourse Dr to MLK Dr, turn left, exit the park, then turn right on Irving.

# ③ Lunch at San Tung (p220)

Pop over to Irving St to wander the shops and nosh on dim sum at this popular and affordable neighborhood restaurant.

SAN TUNG ⊙ DE YOUNG MUSEUM

🏃 Walk back into the park up MLK; the de Young is right across from the Academy of Sciences.

# ④ MH de Young Museum (p209)

Don't let its low-key park location fool you: the de Young is one of SF's top museums, with a 27,000-piece collection that runs the gamut from African art to Oceanic treasures to American decorative arts.

DE YOUNG MUSEUM ⊙ JAPANESE TEA GARDEN

🏃 Coming out of the museum, turn right. The Japanese Tea Garden is just next door.

# ⑤ Japanese Tea Garden (p210)

Take a well-deserved break from museum-going to wander 5 acres of formal Japanese gardens; the five-tiered red pagoda provides a colorful photo op. Stop for afternoon tea if the timing is right.

JAPANESE TEA GARDEN ⊙ OCEAN BEACH

🏃🚗🚲🚌 It's 2.5 miles west on John F Kennedy Dr to get to the ocean; if that sounds daunting, drive, bike or bus.

# ⑥ Ocean Beach (p213)

Take a detour all the way to the western edge of the park for a late-afternoon stroll along the beach, or to watch the sun sink over the Pacific. Be sure to bring a sweater – it can get chilly.

OCEAN BEACH ⊙ AZIZA

🚗 Drive east on Fulton and turn left on 22nd St.

# ⑦ Dinner at Aziza (p217)

Just a few blocks north of the park, in the Richmond, Chef Mourad Lahlou will fulfill your craving for Moroccan-Californian cuisine, whether or not you realized you were having one.

---

California Academy of Sciences (p209)

# Neighborhoods

*Day four is the day to get out and see some of San Francisco's favorite neighborhoods. Start with the Mission for a truly eclectic adventure, head to SoMa to hit SFMOMA, then finish your evening in bohemian North Beach, sipping your beverage of choice.*

## ① The Mission (p154)

Admiring alleyway murals, shopping on Valencia St, sunning in the park or visiting the actual 18th-century mission – whatever brings you to the Mission, here's your chance to explore. Not sure where to start? Try our Mission walking tour (p150).

THE MISSION ➡ LA TAQUERIA
🏃🚌 Walk from wherever you are to 25th and Mission Sts, or hop on an outbound BART at 16th and Mission.

## ② Lunch at La Taqueria (p165)

Mexican food aficionados swear by this hole in the wall, and you know it's not because of the atmosphere. Almost no one can agree on the best burrito in town, but it's definitely in the running.

LA TAQUERIA ➡ SFMOMA
🚌 Catch BART at 24th and Mission, then ride inbound to the Montgomery stop.

## ③ SFMOMA (p152)

From tacos to modern art – why not? Work off your lunch with a stroll around the San Francisco Museum of Modern Art (SFMOMA), where you'll find an eclectic mix of contemporary works from top artists.

SFMOMA ➡ NORTH BEACH
🚌 Catch a 30 or an 8X bus at 3rd and Mission Sts. Either will take you directly to Washington Square.

## ④ North Beach (p106)

Take your time wandering North Beach. The main preoccupations include lingering in sidewalk cafes, browsing poetry selections at City Lights (p121) and having philosophical discussions while watching parrots do fly-bys.

NORTH BEACH ➡ RISTORANTE IDEALE
🏃 The restaurant is on Grant Ave, just north of the intersection of Broadway and Columbus Ave.

## ⑤ Dinner at Ristorante Ideale (p115)

When in North Beach, do as the Romans do: this is the neighborhood for stunningly authentic Italian food, and Ristorante Ideale is our pick.

RISTORANTE IDEALE ➡ BEACH BLANKET BABYLON
🏃 Go north one block and turn right on Green St, cross Columbus and you're there.

## ⑥ Beach Blanket Babylon (p120)

This long-running musical revue has been skewering pop culture since 1974 in ridiculously large headdresses that are bigger than the person they're wearing.

BEACH BLANKET BABYLON ➡ NORTH BEACH NIGHTCAP
🏃 Head back down Columbus Ave; all three bars listed below are just south of City Lights.

## ⑦ North Beach Nightcap (p118)

Finish your night in the style of a Beat poet – with a strong cocktail in a dimly lit bar. You really shouldn't have to choose between Vesuvio (p119), Specs' (p118) or Tosca Cafe (p118); hit all three and call it a lit crawl.

Beach Blanket Babylon (p120)
PHOTOGRAPHER: RICK MARKOVICH ©

# Month by Month

## February

### ⭐ Noise Pop

Winter blues, be gone: discover your new favorite indie band and catch rockumentary premieres and rockin' gallery openings at get-to-know-you venues, all part of the Noise Pop Festival (www.noisepop.com); last week of February.

### ❄ Lunar New Year Parade

Chase the 200ft dragon, lion dancers, toddler kung fu classes and frozen-smile runners-up for the Miss Chinatown title through town, as lucky red envelopes and fireworks fall from the sky during Chinese New Year celebrations (www.chineseparade.com).

## April

### ❄ Perpetual Indulgence in Mission Dolores Park

Easter Sunday is an all-day event (www.thesisters.org) at Mission Dolores Park: there's a morning Easter egg hunt for the kids, followed by the extravagant Bonnet Contest and the Hunky Jesus Contest, for those who prefer their messiahs muscle-bound.

### ❄ Cherry Blossom Festival

Japantown blooms and booms when the Cherry Blossom Festival (www.nccbf.org) turns out *taiko* drums, homegrown hip-hop and street shrines – plus food-stall yakitori and tempura galore.

### ⭐ San Francisco International Film Festival

The nation's oldest film festival (www.sffs.org) is still looking stellar after more than 50 years, with 325 films, 200 directors and star-studded premieres; held late April to early May at Sundance Kabuki Cinema (p142).

## May

### 🕐 Bay to Breakers

Run costumed or naked from Embarcadero to Ocean Beach for Bay to Breakers (www.bay to breakers.com), while joggers dressed as salmon run upstream. Race registration costs $44 to $48; held third Sunday in May.

### ❄ Carnaval

Brazilian or just faking it with a wax and a tan? Get headdressed to impress, shake your tail feathers in the Mission and conga through the inevitable fog during Carnaval (www.car navalsf.com); last weekend of May.

Bay to Breakers

# June

### Haight Ashbury St Fair

Free music on two stages, plus mac-ramé, tie-dye and herbal brownies sur-reptitiously for sale: all that's missing is the free love. Held every mid-June since 1978 (www.haight ashburystreetfair.org).

### San Francisco International Lesbian & Gay Film Festival

We're here, we're queer and we're ready for a pre-miere. The oldest and big-gest gay/lesbian/bisexual/transgender (GLBT) film fest (www.frameline.org) anywhere screens 250 films from 25 countries over two weeks in June.

### Pride Parade

Come out wherever you are: SF goes wild for GLBT pride (www.sfpride.org) on the last Sunday of June, with 1.2 million people, seven stages, tons of glit-ter and ounces of thongs.

# July

### Independence Day

Summer fog doesn't stop the fireworks that celebrate San Francisco's dedication to life, liberty and the pursuit of hap-piness no matter the climate – economic, politi-cal or meteorological.

### AIDS Walk

Until AIDS takes a hike, you can: this 10km fund-raiser hike (www.aidswalk.net /sanfran), held the third Sunday in July, benefits 47 AIDS organizations.

### Stern Grove Festival

Summertime brings free music among the redwood and eucalyptus trees. Con-certs (www.sterngrove .org) include world music and jazz, but the biggest events are performances by the SF Ballet, Sym-phony and Opera.

# September

### Fringe Festival

More outrageous theatri-cal antics than usual hit the stage in late Septem-ber, at discount prices. Book ahead (www.sffringe .org) or chance it at the Exit Theater box office.

### Folsom St Fair

Bondage enthusiasts emerge from dungeons worldwide for a wild street party (www.folsomstreet fair.com), with public spankings for charity, leather, nudity and beer; held the last Sunday of September.

### SF Shakespeare Festival

The play's the thing in the Presidio. Enjoy the Bard outdoors and free of charge on sunny Sep-tember weekends during the Shakespeare Festival (www.sfshakes.org).

# October

### Litquake

Stranger-than-fiction liter-ary events take place the second week of October during SF's literary festival (www.litquake.org), with authors leading lunchtime story sessions and spilling trade secrets over drinks at the legendary Lit Crawl.

### Hardly Strictly Bluegrass Festival

The west goes wild for free bluegrass and rock with a twang at Golden Gate Park (www.strictlybluegrass .com), with three days of concerts and three stages; held early October.

### SF Jazz Festival

Minds are blown by jazz greats and upstarts alike during the SF Jazz Festival (www.sfjazz.org), held late September through November.

# November

### Día de los Muertos

On November 2, zombie brides and Aztec dancers march through the streets of the Mission during the Day of the Dead proces-sion (www.dayofthedeadsf .org), culminating at Gar-field Park where shrines honor the dearly departed.

# What's New

*For this new edition of Discover San Francisco, our authors have hunted down the fresh, the transformed, the hot and the happening. These are some of our favourites. For up-to-the-minute recommendations, see lonelyplanet.com/San Francisco.*

## 1 URBAN FARMING

Recent reports rank San Francisco the greenest city in North America – but you could probably guess that with a glance at SF's Green Festival urban farming programs or the beehive-covered freeway on-ramp at Hayes Valley Farm (p195). For tips on growing your own organic food, farming for kids and urban composting (now mandated by law in SF), check out workshops at SF's nonprofit sustainable gardening program, Garden for the Environment (www.garden fortheenvironment.org).

## 2 OLD-TIMEY SALOONS

The Barbary Coast is roaring back to life with historically researched whiskey cocktails and staggering absinthe concoctions in San Francisco's great saloon revival (p29).

## 3 SFMOMA EXPANSION

SF is more artistically gifted than ever, thanks to a donation of 1100 modern masterworks and a half-billion-dollar expansion in the works at the San Francisco Museum of Modern Art (SFMOMA; p152).

## 4 AQUATIC PARK BATHHOUSE RESTORATION

Maintenance of this 1930s landmark uncovered long-lost deco wood carvings and WPA murals. With its Sargent Johnson mosaics gleaming and ocean-liner structure finally shipshape, this maritime monument is a must-see (p56).

## 5 OUTER SUNSET COOL

The Ocean Beach chill factor brings pro surfers and hipsters alike to the Sunset for artist-designed hoodies at Mollusk (p223), soul-warming organic food at Outerlands (p221) and beachcomber-architect decor at General Store (p223).

## 6 VALENCIA GALLERY SCENE

Downtown is where the money is, but the Mission is where street artists and MFA students live – so arts nonprofits and upstart galleries around Valencia St spot emerging talent first (p154).

## 7 FORAGED FINE DINING

No local chef's tasting menu is complete without wild chanterelles found beneath California oaks, miner's lettuce from Berkeley hillsides or SF-backyard nasturtium flowers. Daniel Patterson sets the standard at Coi (p115).

## 8 PERMANENT POP-UP RESTAURANTS

When pop-up restaurants settle down, they establish regular hours at local bars, cafes and the Corner (p167), a venue that hosts different pop-ups most nights.

## 9 ACOUSTIC TWANG

Gunshots begin races, but most SF events begin with guitars. Lyrics including 'lonesome' and 'cowboy' recall SF's Western longitude, though there's latitude for authenticity at Hardly Strictly Bluegrass (p41).

## 10 DANDIES

Dapper gents are setting trends and throwing off SF's gaydar. Straight and gay men alike spiff up at Sui Generis (p180) and Revolver (p200), and step out at Churchill (p175).

# Get Inspired

## 📖 Books

**• The Maltese Falcon**
(Dashiell Hammett, 1930)
Sam Spade gumshoe
caper best read aloud
over martinis at John's
Grill (p94).

**• Howl and Other Poems**
(Allen Ginsberg, 1956)
Free verse that trumped
censors, inspiring
'angelheaded hipsters
burning for the ancient
heavenly connection.'

**• Slouching Toward
Bethlehem** (Joan
Didion, 1968) Revealing
essays expose the itchy
underside of the Summer
of Love (p245).

**• A Heartbreaking
Work of Staggering
Genius** (Dave Eggers,
2000) Gen X memoir
of innocence lost and
purpose found in SF.

## 🎞 Films

**• City Lights** (1931,
directed by Charlie
Chaplin) This silent
classic, filmed in SF, was
the namesake for the
famous bookstore (p121).

**• Harold and Maude**
(1971, directed by
Hal Ashby) A May-to-
December romance
blooms in the
Conservatory of
Flowers (p211) and Sutro
Baths (p213).

**• Milk** (2008, directed
by Gus Van Sant) Oscar-
winner Sean Penn stars
in this Harvey Milk biopic
shot in SF.

## 🎵 Music

**• Lights** Journey's 1978
hit, 'When the Lights
Go Down in the City,'
('and the sun shines on
the Bayayyy...') is a SF
karaoke staple.

**• San Francisco Anthem**
San Quinn remixes The
Mamas and the Papas'
1967 hit 'San Francisco'
with 2008 rap: 'roll in like
fog/the battle's uphill...'

**• Right On** The Roots'
2010 riff on SF indie
favorite Joanna Newsom
loops the '50s jazz-cat
phrase that has become
SF's mantra.

## 🌐 Websites

**• Craigslist** (http://
sfbay.craigslist.org) The
SF community site lists
events, rentals, cooking
classes and more.

**• SFist** (http://sfist.com)
This blog captures SF's
definitive quirks; see the
'7 Reasons to Love SF'
photo essays.

## ⏱ Short on time?

This list will give you an
instant insight into the city.

**Read** The ultimate Beatnik
road trip to San Francisco,
*On the Road,* was written by
Jack Kerouac in Russian Hill.

**Watch** Views of the Golden
Gate Bridge from Fort Point
(p62) stole scenes in the
Hitchcock mystery *Vertigo*.

**Listen** Jazz pianist Dave
Brubeck defined West Coast
jazz with the virtuoso track
'Blue Rondo à la Turk.'

**Log on** Get the scoop on
food, drink and shop-
ping from *7x7* magazine
(www.7x7.com).

---

Vesuvio (p119) and City Lights (p121), Jack Kerouac Alley
PHOTOGRAPHER: THOMAS WINZ/LONELY PLANET IMAGES ®

# Need to Know

Currency
US dollar ($)

Language
English

## Visas

The USA Visa Waiver Program allows nationals of 36 countries to enter the US without a visa; see p287.

## Money

ATMs widely available; credit cards generally accepted. Farmers markets, food trucks and some bars are cash only.

## Cell Phones

Most US cell phones operate on CDMA, not the European standard GSM; check compatibility with your service provider.

## Time

Pacific Standard Time (GMT/UTC minus eight hours)

## Wi-Fi

Listings marked with 🛜 offer free wi-fi, as do most cafes and hotel lobbies. Find more hotspots at www.openwifispots.com.

## Tipping

In restaurants, 15% of the bill is the minimum (unless service was bad).

For more information, see Survival Guide (p278).

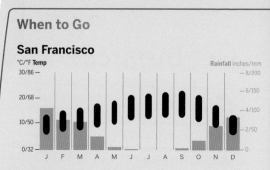

## When to Go

**San Francisco**

Early fall is best for warm weather, street fairs and harvest cuisine
Summer brings fog and chilly 55°F (13°C) weather to San Francisco.

## Advance Planning

**Two months before** Start making dinner reservations, especially if you're going to French Laundry (p230); start walking to build stamina for Mission gallery tours or bar crawls.

**One month before** Book an Alcatraz night tour (p52), Chinatown alleyways tour (p115) or Precita Eyes mural tour (www.precitaeyes.org).

**One week before** Search for tickets to American Conservatory Theater, SF Symphony or SF Opera, and find out what else is on next weekend.

## Your Daily Budget

### Budget Under $100

- Dorm bed $25–30
- Food-truck dishes $5–10
- Mission galleries & murals free
- Live music at Hotel Utah/Bottom of the Hill $5–12
- Castro Theatre show $10

### Midrange $100–250

- Motel/downtown hotel $80–180
- Ferry Building meal $15–35
- SFMOMA $18/9 after 6pm Thursdays
- Symphony rush tickets $20–25
- Muni Passport $14

### Top End Over $250

- Boutique hotel $150–380
- Chef's tasting menu $65–140
- City Pass (Muni plus five attractions) $69
- Alcatraz night tour $33
- Opera orchestra seats $30–90

## Arriving in San Francisco

**San Francisco Airport (SFO)** Fast rides to downtown SF on BART cost $8.10; door-to-door shuttle vans cost $17; express bus fare to Temporary Transbay Terminal is $5; taxis cost $35 to $50.

**Oakland International Airport (OAK)** Take the AirBART shuttle ($3) to Coliseum station to catch BART to downtown SF ($3.80); take a shared van to downtown SF for $30 to $35; or pay $50 to $60 for a taxi to SF destinations.

**Temporary Transbay Terminal** (Map p155) Greyhound buses arrive and depart downtown SF's temporary depot (until 2017) at Howard & Main Sts.

**Emeryville Amtrak station (EMY)** Located outside Oakland, this depot serves LA–Seattle Coast Starlight, Chicago–Emeryville California Zephyr and other trains; Amtrak runs free shuttles to/from San Francisco's Ferry Building and Caltrain.

## Getting Around

Public transportation is easy and accessible all around the Bay Area. To find out how to get where you're going, call ☎511 or check www.511.org, where you can find out what your transit options are or get arrival and departure times. A detailed Muni Street & Transit Map is available for free online and at the Powell Muni kiosk ($3).

○ **Prepay** All-in-one Clipper Cards can be used on Muni, BART, AC Transit, Caltrain and even the Golden Gate Ferry.

○ **Cable cars** Frequent, slow and scenic, from 6am to 1am daily. Single rides cost $6; for frequent use, get a Muni Passport.

○ **Muni streetcar & bus** They're reasonably fast but schedules vary wildly by line; stops are infrequent after 9pm. Fares cost $2, and exact change is required. Transfers are good for 90 minutes.

○ **BART** High-speed transit to East Bay, Mission St, SFO and Millbrae, where it connects with Caltrain.

○ **Taxi** Easy to find in busy Downtown areas, less so in the nontouristed neighborhoods. Fares cost about $2.25 per mile; meters start at $3.50.

○ **On foot** San Francisco is a big walking city, so once you get to your neighborhood, join the throng of pedestrians.

## Sleeping

San Francisco is the birthplace of the boutique hotel, offering stylish rooms at a price: $100 to $200 midrange, plus 15.5% hotel tax (hostels exempt) and $35 to $50 for overnight parking. Some Downtown hotels cost less, but proceed with caution: west of Mason is the sketchy Tenderloin. Motels are better options for parking; hostels offer value for solo travelers but no privacy.

### Useful Websites

○ **B&B San Francisco** (www.bbsf.com) Privately owned B&Bs and neighborhood inns.

○ **SF Visitor Information Center Reservations** (www.onlyinsanfrancisco.com) Vacancies and deals; indispensible in high season and during major conventions.

○ **Lonely Planet** (http://hotels.lonelyplanet.com) Expert author reviews, user feedback, booking engine.

## What to Bring

○ **Coat or jacket** Even in the summer (*especially* in the summer), when you can expect 55–70°F (13–21°C) by day.

○ **Comfortable shoes** San Francisco is a walking city; be prepared.

○ **Camera** Have you seen the Golden Gate Bridge (p58)? Enough said.

○ **Dog** For SF hotels that will make your pooch feel welcome, see www.dogfriendly.com.

○ **Thirst** Across the Golden Gate Bridge, Wine Country awaits (p228).

○ **Hunger** San Francisco is foodie Nirvana (p250).

## Be Forewarned

○ **Taxes** Factor San Francisco city taxes into your dining, sleeping and shopping budget (p286).

○ **Overbooking** To avoid overbooking and high-season premiums, check the convention calendar at www.sfcvb.org/convention/calendar.asp and book around those dates.

○ **Use street smarts** Especially at night in the Tenderloin, South of Market (SoMa) and the Mission, as well as around parks after dark.

○ **Panhandling** Expect to be asked for spare change, but don't feel obliged. Your donation will stretch further at nonprofit organizations.

# The Marina & Fisherman's Wharf

**Since the Gold Rush, the waterfront has welcomed new arrivals.** In 1849, ships full of foolhardy optimists arrived, hoping to find their fortune in gold. Today, enthusiastic crowds rush here to find barking sea lions, wharfs lined with shops and restaurants, views of the Golden Gate Bridge, tours of Alcatraz and centuries' worth of maritime history.

To the west, the Marina has chic boutiques in a former cow pasture and organic dining along the waterfront. The neighborhood is strictly top-drawer and dry-cleaned, with sales reps and ad execs in all their front-office finery at happy hour.

Out near the bridge, the wooded Presidio coastline is dotted with kites, surfers and nudists where once there were fighter planes, gunboats and cannons. For many years now, the only wars going on here have been of the interstellar variety, in George Lucas' Presidio screening room.

Sea lions at Pier 39 (p55), Fisherman's Wharf

# The Marina & Fisherman's Wharf Highlights

## Exploratorium (p63)

Put your theories about the physiology of cuteness, the physics of skateboarding and the emotional life of robots to the test in this hands-on discovery museum, with displays that earned its designers a MacArthur Genius grant. Reserve ahead for the Tactile Dome, where you'll grope your way to enlightenment in total darkness. Although it's a huge hit with kids, inquisitive adults join in the fun with equal enthusiasm.

## Nautical Culture (p55)

From yachts to ferries, sailboats to tugs, you'll find all manner of seafaring vessels along the waterfront. Historical craft including an 1891 schooner and a paddle-wheel tugboat are the stars of the Maritime National Historical Park, and just down the way you can tour the USS *Pampanito*, a WWII-era navy submarine. If you're feeling inspired, boat tours abound around the Fisherman's Wharf area. USS Pampanito (p55)

STEPHEN SAKS/LONELY PLANET IMAGES ©

## Walt Disney Family Museum (p64) ③

Mad about Mickey? Want to know more about the man who created him? Explore the fascinating archives of the Walt Disney Family Museum. If Disneyland is all magic and illusion, the Disney museum is a peek behind the curtain at how that magic was created. It's the more intellectual side of Disney, but aficionados of his work will appreciate this grown-up look at his legacy.

## ④ Crissy Field (p61)

This former airfield was once where generals and world leaders zoomed in for a landing. It's now a grassy gathering place where kids fly kites and bowlegged herons perch meditatively. If the weather is nice, join the locals in picnicking, boat watching or just hanging out with a Frisbee. The view of the Golden Gate Bridge demands a camera.

## ⑤ Marina Boutiques (p72)

No one ever packs correctly for San Francisco. Not only do you have to dress for everything from day hikes to fancy dinners out, you have to be able to switch instantly from summer clothes to winter when the fog rolls in. Not to worry: the stores along Union, Fillmore and Chestnut Sts have your back stylishly covered with local designers, sporting gear, Napa wines and, yes, antique steamer trunks.

# The Marina & Fisherman's Wharf Walk

*Fisherman's Wharf, Pier 39 and Ghirardelli Square have long been staples of the San Francisco tourist scene. There's plenty to see along the bustling waterfront – all set against the backdrop of one spectacularly orange bridge.*

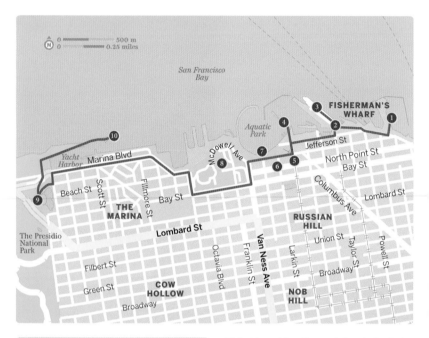

## WALK FACTS
- **Start** Pier 39
- **Finish** Crissy Field
- **Distance** 2.9 miles
- **Duration** Three hours

### ❶ Pier 39

Start your tour at this famed tourist attraction (p55) if for no other reason than to ride the vintage carousel and watch sea lions take over the yacht marina, an ongoing performance that's the city's best free entertainment.

### ❷ Musée Mécanique

You don't have to be a kid to appreciate the vintage amusements at this emporium of old-fashioned fun. Formerly located out at **Cliff House** (p213), the collection is now in a cavernous building on Pier 45 and ranges from hundred-year-old parlor curiosities to more modern arcade games. (p55)

### ❸ SS Jeremiah O'Brien

Even if you don't take the tour, wander Pier 45 to gawk at this massive gray Liberty ship (p55), launched during WWII after being built in 56 days. Of all the WWII Liberty ships, this is the only one that's still fully operational.

### ❹ Hyde St Historic Ships

The vessels on display at the **San Francisco Maritime National Historical Park** (p55) include steamers, ferryboats, tugboats and schooners from the turn of the 20th century. Walk out on to the pier for a free photo op or pay $5 for permission to board.

### 5 Buena Vista Cafe

The **Buena Vista** (p70) serves up to 2000 Irish coffees a day, concocting them in assembly-line fashion for a never-ending throng of shivering, fog-chilled tourists. They do serve other drinks, but almost everyone comes for the special mixture of coffee, frothed cream and Irish whiskey.

### 6 Ghirardelli Square

Famous as a chocolate factory, **Ghirardelli Square** (p57) is now just a shopping area, but you can still pick up your requisite Ghirardelli souvenirs to bring back for your chocolate-deprived pet-sitter at home.

### 7 Aquatic Park Bathhouse

Check out the Streamline Moderne exterior of the **Maritime Museum** (p56), built in 1939 as part of the Works Progress Administration (WPA), and be sure to duck inside to see the colorful, Depression-era murals.

### 8 Fort Mason Center

Wander through this former military complex (p60), which was once the embarkation point for WWII troops. The warehouses are now filled with noncombative businesses, like the **Magic Theatre** (p71), **Mexican Museum** and vegan-friendly **Greens** restaurant (p68).

### 9 Palace of Fine Arts

Not to be confused with an actual palace, this domed structure (p63) was reconstructed from the 1915 Panama-Pacific International Expo. Pose for photos under the Greco-Roman arches reflected in the pond. Until 2013, it sits right next door to the kids-of-all-ages-friendly **Exploratorium** (p63).

### 10 Crissy Field

At Crissy Field (p61) enjoy an unobstructed view of the **Golden Gate Bridge** (p58), and watch windsurfers and kiteboarders attempt one of SF's windiest beaches. For extra credit, hike the extra half mile down Yacht Rd to ponder the mysteries of the **Wave Organ** (p60).

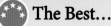 **The Best…**

**PLACES TO EAT**

**Gary Danko** Fabulous multicourse meals. (p65)

**Greens** So hearty, you won't miss the meat. (p68)

**A16** Neapolitan pizza with housemade mozzarella. (p67)

**Friday-night food trucks** A moveable feast at Fort Mason. (p68)

**PLACES TO DRINK**

**Buena Vista Cafe** Warm up with Irish coffee. (p70)

**Pier 23** Live music on the waterfront. (p71)

**Betelnut** Top marks for the restaurant lounge.(p68)

**California Wine Merchant** Sip a glass, take home what you love. (p70)

**PLACES FOR WATERFRONT VISTAS**

**Golden Gate Bridge** Walk across for sweeping views of the bay. (p58)

**Crissy Field** Best for unobstructed bridge views. (p61)

**Pier 39** The busy side of the bay, with sea lions for comic relief. (p55)

Wendy M Ross' Phillip Burton statue, Fort Mason (p60)
RICHARD CUMMINS/LONELY PLANET IMAGES ©

# ✓ Don't Miss
## Alcatraz

For almost 150 years, the name has given the innocent chills and the guilty cold sweats. Over the years Alcatraz has been the nation's first military prison, a forbidding maximum-security penitentiary and disputed territory between Native American activists and the FBI. So it's no surprise that the first step you take off the ferry and onto 'the Rock' seems to cue ominous music: dunh-dunh-dunnnnh!

Alcatraz Cruises
☎ 415-981-7625

www.nps.gov /alcatraz for park info, www.alcatraz cruises.com for ferry reservations

admission daytime adult/child/family $26/16/79; night tours adult/child $33/19.50

⊙ ferry departs Pier 33 every half hour 9am-3:55pm, night tours 6:10pm & 6:45pm

## Early History

It all started innocently enough back in 1775, when Spanish lieutenant Juan Manuel de Ayala sailed the *San Carlos* past the 12-acre island that he called Isla de Alcatraces (Isle of the Pelicans). In 1859 a new post on Alcatraz became the first US West Coast fort, and it soon proved handy as a holding pen for Civil War deserters, insubordinates and those who had been court-martialed.

## Prison Life

In 1934 the Federal Bureau of Prisons took over Alcatraz as a prominent showcase for its crime-fighting efforts. The Rock averaged only 264 inmates, but its roster read like America's Most Wanted. Criminals doing time on Alcatraz included Chicago crime boss Al 'Scarface' Capone, dapper kidnapper George 'Machine Gun' Kelly and hot-headed Harlem mafioso and sometime poet 'Bumpy' Johnson. Today, first-person accounts of daily life in the Alcatraz lockup are included on the excellent self-guided audio tour.

Alcatraz was considered escape-proof, but in 1962 the Anglin brothers and Frank Morris floated away on a makeshift raft and were never seen again. Security and upkeep proved prohibitively expensive, and the island prison was finally abandoned to the birds in 1963.

## Occupation

Native Americans claimed sovereignty over the island in the '60s, noting that Alcatraz had long been used by the Ohlone people as a spiritual retreat. On the eve of Thanksgiving, 1969, 79 Native American activists broke a Coast Guard blockade to enforce their claim. Over the next 19 months, some 5600 Native Americans would visit the occupied island. Public support eventually pressured President Richard Nixon to restore Native territory and strengthen self-rule for Native nations in 1970. After the government regained control of the island, it became a national park, and by 1973 it had already become a major tourist draw.

# ✓ Don't Miss
# Fisherman's Wharf

Where fisherman once snared sea life, San Francisco now traps tourists. Clam chowder in a sourdough bowl? Check. 'I escaped Alcatraz' T-shirts? Check. The Wharf may not be the 'real San Francisco,' but it's always lively and still retains some authenticity, and even a few surprises. Stick near the waterfront, where sea lions bray, street performers scare unsuspecting passersby, and an aquarium and carousel entice wide-eyed kids. Once you've explored the tall ships at Pier 45, consult mechanical fortune-tellers at Musée Mécanique, then hightail it away to discover the real SF.

Map p66

www.fishermans
wharf.org

Embarcadero
& Jefferson St
waterfront, from
Pier 39 to Van Ness
Ave

admission free

🚋 Powell-Mason,
Powell-Hyde

## Pier 39

The focal point of Fisherman's Wharf isn't the waning fishing fleet, but the carousel, carnival-like attractions, shops and restaurants of **Pier 39** (Map p66; www.pier39 .com; Beach St & the Embarcadero; 🚶; Ⓜ Embarcadero & Stockton St; 🚋 Powell-Mason). Developed in the 1970s to revitalize tourism, the pier draws thousands of tourists daily, but it's really just a big outdoor shopping mall.

By far the best reason to walk the pier is to spot the famous sea lions, who took over this coveted waterfront real estate in 1989. They've been making a public display ever since – canoodling, belching, scratching their backsides and gleefully shoving one another off the docks. These unkempt squatters became San Francisco's favorite mascots. However, because California law requires boats to make way for marine mammals, yacht owners have had to relinquish valuable slips to accommodate as many as 1300 sea lions who 'haul out' onto the docks between January and July. They gather on the west side of the pier; follow the signs.

## Musée Mécanique

A flashback to penny arcades, the **Musée Mécanique** (Map p66; www.museemechanique .org; Shed A, Pier 45; 🕙10am-7pm; 🚶; Ⓜ Jefferson & Taylor Sts; 🚋 Powell-Mason, Powell-Hyde) houses a mind-blowing collection of vintage mechanical amusements. Sinister, freckle-faced Laughing Sal has creeped out kids for over a century, but don't let this manic mannequin deter you from the best arcade west of Coney Island. Prices have spiked in the last century: a quarter, not a penny, lets you start brawls in Wild West saloons, peep at belly dancers through a vintage Mutoscope and even learn a cautionary tale about smoking opium.

## San Francisco Maritime National Historical Park

Four Bay Area ships are currently open as museums at the **Maritime National Historical Park** (Map p66; www.nps.gov /safr; Hyde St Pier, 499 Jefferson St; adult/child $5/free; 🕤9:30am-5pm Oct-May, to 7pm Jun-Sep; 🚋 Powell-Hyde). Moored along the Hyde St Pier, standouts include the elegant 1891 schooner *Alma* and the steamboat *Eureka*, the world's largest ferry c 1890. For more mariner action, check out the steam-powered paddle-wheel tugboat *Eppleton Hall* and the magnificent triple-masted, iron-hulled *Balclutha*, an 1886 British vessel, which brought coal to San Francisco and took grain back to Europe via the dreaded Cape Horn.

## USS Pampanito

The **USS Pampanito** (Map p66; www .maritime.org/pamphome.htm; Pier 45; adult/ child/family $9/5/20; 🕘9am-8pm Thu-Tue, to 6pm Wed; 🚋 Powell-Hyde), a WWII-era US navy submarine, completed six wartime patrols, sunk six Japanese ships, battled three others and lived to tell the tale. Submariners' stories of tense moments in underwater stealth mode will have you holding your breath – beware, claustrophobics – and all those cool brass knobs and mysterious hydraulic valves make 21st-century technology seem overrated.

## SS Jeremiah O'Brien

It's hard to believe the historic 10,000-ton **SS Jeremiah O'Brien** (Map p66; www .ssjeremiahobrien.org; Pier 45; adult/child $10/5; 🕘9am-4pm; Ⓜ Jefferson & Taylor Sts; 🚋 Powell-Hyde) was turned out by San Francisco's ship builders in under eight weeks. It's harder still to imagine how she dodged U-boats on a mission delivering supplies to Allied forces on D-Day. Of the

### What the...?

Keep your eyes peeled for the notorious 'Bushman' of Pier 39, who lurks behind branches of eucalyptus trees, then leaps out and shouts 'Ugga bugga!' to scare the bejeezus out of unsuspecting tourists, then (even more shocking) hits them up for change. If you spot him first, stick around and watch how others react. Things don't always go as planned.

TODD BANNOR/ALAMY ©

SABRINA DALBESIO/LONELY PLANET IMAGES ©

2710 Liberty ships launched during WWII, this is the only one still fully operational. Visit on 'steaming weekends' (usually the third weekend of each month), or check the website for upcoming four-hour cruises.

## Aquarium of the Bay

Sharks circle overhead, manta rays sweep shyly by and seaweed sways all around at **Aquarium of the Bay** (Map p66; www.aquariumofthebay.com; Pier 39; adult/child $17/8; ⏱9am-8pm summer, 10am-6pm winter; 👫; Ⓜ49, F), where a series of conveyer belts guide you through glass tubes surrounded by sea life from San Francisco Bay. Not for the claustrophobic, perhaps, but the thrilling fish-eye view leaves kids and parents wide-eyed and humming *Little Mermaid* tunes.

## San Francisco Carousel

A chariot awaits to whisk you and the kids past the Golden Gate Bridge, Alcatraz and other SF landmarks hand-painted onto this Italian **carousel** (Map p66; www

.pier39.com; Pier 39; admission $3; ⏱11am-7pm; 👫; Ⓜ Embarcadero & Stockton St), twinkling with 1800 lights at the bayside end of Pier 39. The carnival music is loud enough to drown out the screams of a tiny tot clinging for dear life to a high-stepping horse.

## Aquatic Park Bathhouse (Maritime Museum)

The quirky **Maritime Museum** (Map p62; www.maritime.org; 900 Beach St; admission free; 👫; Ⓜ Beach & Polk Sts; 🚋 Powell-Hyde) was a casino and public bathhouse when built in 1939 by the Depression-era Works Progress Administration (WPA). Beautifully restored murals depict the mythical lands of Atlantis and Mu, and the handful of exhibits include maritime ephemera and cool dioramas. Notice the entryway slate carvings by celebrated African American artist Sargent Johnson and the back veranda's toad and seal sculptures by SF's own Beniamino Bufano.

## Ghirardelli Square

Willy Wonka would tip his hat to Domingo Ghirardelli (gear-ar-*del*-ee), whose business became the West's largest chocolate factory in 1893. After the company moved to the East Bay, developers reinvented the factory as a mall and landmark ice-cream parlor in 1964. Today, **Ghirardelli Square** (Map p66; www.ghirardellisq.com; 900 North Point St; ⊗10am-9pm; Ⓜ Beach & Polk Sts; ◻Powell-Hyde) has entered its third incarnation as a boutique, luxury timeshare/spa complex with wine-tasting rooms – care for a massage and a merlot with your Ghirardelli chocolate sundae? The square looks quite spiffy, with local boutiques, the charming tearoom Crown & Crumpet and a branch of the ever-tempting Kara's Cupcakes. And, of course, there's still Ghirardelli Ice Cream for chocolate souvenirs.

## Aquatic Park

Eccentricity along Fisherman's Wharf is mostly staged, but at **Aquatic Park** (Map p62; northern end of Van Ness Ave; admission free; 👫; ◻Powell-Hyde), it's the real deal: extreme swimmers dive into the bone-chillingly cold waters of the bay in winter, eccentrics mumble conspiracy theories at panoramic Victoria Park and wistful tycoons contemplate sailing far away from their Blackberries. To get perspective on the Wharf, wander out onto the municipal pier, at the foot of Van Ness Ave.

### Fishermen at Pier 47

A few third- and fourth-generation fishermen remain in the bay, but to survive the drop in salmon and other local stocks some captains now use their boats for whale-watching and bay tours, making a living off the city's new lifeblood: tourism. Find the remaining fleet around Pier 47.

# Don't Miss
# Golden Gate Bridge

The city's most spectacular icon towers 80 stories above the roiling waters of the Golden Gate, the narrow entrance to San Francisco Bay. Hard to believe SF's northern gateway lands not into a tangle of city streets but the Presidio, an army base turned national park, where forested paths and grassy promenades look largely as they have since the 19th century.

Map p70

www.goldengate bridge.org/visitors

off Lincoln Blvd

southbound toll $6, northbound free; carpools (three or more) free 5-9am & 4-6pm

M Golden Gate Bridge parking lot, all Golden Gate Transit buses

# Engineering & Aesthetics

San Francisco's famous suspension bridge, painted a signature shade called International Orange, was almost nixed by the navy in favor of concrete pylons and yellow stripes. Joseph B Strauss rightly receives a lot of praise as the engineering mastermind behind this iconic marvel, but without the aesthetic intervention of architects Gertrude and Irving Murrow and the incredibly quick work of daredevil workers, this 1937 landmark might have been just another traffic bottleneck.

# How It Came to Be

It wasn't until the early 1920s that the City of San Francisco began to seriously investigate the possibility of building a bridge over the treacherous, windblown strait. The War Department owned the land on both sides; safety and solidity were its primary goals, but the green light was given to a suspension span that harmonized with the natural environment. Before the War Department could insist on an eyesore, laborers dove into the treacherous riptides of the bay and got the bridge underway. Just four years later, in 1937, workers balanced atop swaying cables to complete what was then the world's longest suspension bridge – nearly 2 miles long, with 746ft suspension towers.

# Viewpoints

Cinema buffs believe Hitchcock had it right: seen from below at Fort Point, the bridge induces a thrilling case of *Vertigo*. Fog aficionados prefer the lookout at Vista Point in Marin, on the sunnier north side of the bridge, to watch gusts of clouds rush through the bridge cables. Crissy Field is a key spot to appreciate the span in its entirety, with windsurfers and kite-fliers adding action to your snapshots. Unlike the Bay Bridge, the Golden Gate Bridge can be accessed by cyclists and pedestrians (see p281).

(see p281)

## Local Knowledge

# Don't Miss List

BY CARLEIGH ARNOLD,
TOUR GUIDE

1 **FORT BAKER**
Just before the end of the bridge, there's this really touristy vista point, and it's always jam-packed. People get off there because they want a close-up of the bridge, but they don't realize that if they just keep going down toward Fort Baker, they can get an amazing view and there are not nearly as many people.

2 **FIRE ENGINE TOUR**
This tour is a great way to experience the Golden Gate Bridge. You're in a shiny red fire truck with the wind in your hair, and you're up a little higher than a regular vehicle so you can really see everything. It's very exhilarating. Plus, you get the history of the bridge and a sense of where it began.

3 **PAINTING CREWS**
Look for the painting crew that's constantly on the bridge; they paint daily because of the rust. They're not actually painting it gold; the colour is called 'International Orange.' The reason they call it the Golden Gate Bridge is that it was the gateway to the gold that everyone came for during the Gold Rush.

4 **THE PRESIDIO**
Another wonderful place right before the bridge is the Presidio, an old military base. It's a beautiful wooded area, very pristine, and there are lots of beautiful hidden spots. A lot of the trees there are eucalypts that were brought here from Australia, where they're called blue gum trees.

5 **SUSPENSION CABLES**
One thing that's really cool about the bridge is the cables. It's a suspension bridge, so there's nothing down below; the only thing holding it up is the tension from the cables. It took 80,000 miles of wire to create the cables that hold up the roadway.

# Discover the Marina & Fisherman's Wharf

##  Getting There & Away

○ **Streetcar** Historic F Market streetcars run along Market St, then up the Embarcadero waterfront to Fisherman's Wharf.

○ **Cable car** The Powell-Hyde and Powell-Mason lines run up Powell St to the Wharf; the Mason line is quicker, but the hills are better on the Hyde line.

○ **Bus** Major routes to the Wharf and/or the Marina from downtown include the 19, 30, 47 and 49.

○ **Parking** At the Wharf, there are garages at Pier 39 and Ghirardelli Square (enter on Beach St, between Larkin and Polk Sts). At the Marina, there's parking at Crissy Field and Fort Mason. The Presidio is the only place where it's easy to park – and free.

Forbes Island (p65)
STEPHEN SAKS/LONELY PLANET IMAGES ©

## ◉ Sights

The Marina generally refers to everything north of busy Lombard St, west of Van Ness Ave. Cow Hollow refers to the area around Union St, just south of Lombard St, on the slope below Pacific Heights.

## The Marina

### Fort Mason Center
Cultural Buildings

Map p62 ( ☎415-441-3400; www.fortmason .org; Marina Blvd & Laguna St; Ⓜ Marina Blvd & Laguna St) San Francisco takes subversive glee in turning military installations into venues for nature, fine dining and out-there experimental art. Evidence: Fort Mason, a former shipyard and the embarkation point for WWII troops shipping out for the Pacific. The military mess halls are gone, replaced by vegan-friendly **Greens**, a restaurant run by a Zen community. Warehouses now host cutting-edge theater at **Magic Theatre**, the home base of Pulitzer Prize–winning playwright Sam Shepard, and improvised comedy workshops at **BATS Improv**.

### FREE Wave Organ
Monument

Map p62 (www.exploratorium.edu; Marina Small Craft Harbor jetty; ☉daylight hours; 👫) An Exploratorium project worth investigating, the Wave Organ is a sound system of PVC tubes and concrete pipes capped with found marble from San Francisco's old cemetery, built right into the tip of the yacht harbor jetty. Depending on the waves, winds and tide, the tones emitted by the organ can sound like nervous humming from a dinnertime

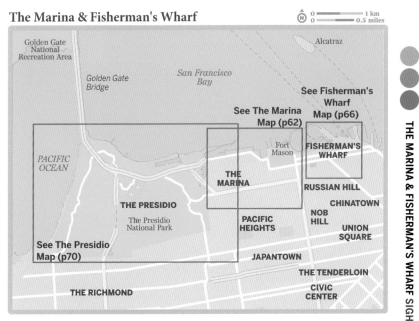

line chef or spooky heavy breathing over the phone in a slasher film. Access to the organ is free but a bit of a hike from the Exploratorium.

### Church of St Mary the Virgin
Church

Map p62 (📞415-921-3665; www.smvsf.org; 2325 Union St; ⏱9am-5pm Sun-Fri; Ⓜ Union & Steiner Sts) You might expect to see this rustic Arts and Crafts building on the slopes of Tahoe instead of Pacific Heights, but this Episcopal church is full of surprises. The structure dates from 1891, but the church has kept pace with its progressive-minded parish, with homeless community outreach and 'Unplugged' all-acoustic Sunday services led by hip young reverend Jennifer Hornbeck.

## Fisherman's Wharf

### Fisherman's Wharf
Landmark

Fisherman's Wharf includes the following sights: Pier 39 (p55), Musée Mécanique (p55), San Francisco Maritime National Historical Park (p55), USS *Pampanito* (p55), SS *Jeremiah O'Brien* (p55),

Aquarium of the Bay (p56) and San Francisco Carousel (p56).

### Alcatraz
Historical Site

See p52.

## The Presidio

### Golden Gate Bridge
Landmark

See p58.

### Crissy Field
Nature Reserve

Map p70 (www.crissyfield.org; btwn Mason St & Golden Gate Promenade; Ⓜ Broderick & Jefferson Sts) War is for the birds in this military airstrip turned waterfront nature preserve with knockout views of the Golden Gate. On foggy days, stop by the certified-green Warming Hut (p69) or **Crissy Field Center** (603 Mason St; ⏱9am-5pm) to browse regional nature books and thaw out over fair-trade coffee.

### Baker Beach
Beach

Map p70 ( ⏱sunrise-sunset; Ⓜ Baker Beach) Picnic amid wind-sculpted pines, fish from craggy rocks or frolic nude at the mile-long sandy Baker Beach, with spectacular views of the Golden Gate Bridge.

# The Marina

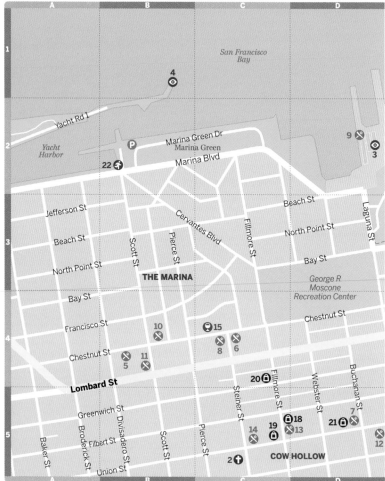

Crowds come on weekends, especially on fog-free days; get here early. For nude sunbathing (mostly straight girls and gay boys), head to the north end. Families in clothing stick to the south end, nearer to the parking lot. Mind the currents and the c-c-cold water.

### Fort Point
Historical Site

Map p70 (📞415-556-1693; www.nps.gov/fopo; Marine Dr; admission free; ⏰10am-5pm Fri-Sun; Ⓜ Golden Gate Bridge Parking Lot) Fort Point came about after an eight-year makeover from a small Spanish fort to a triple-decker, brick-walled US military fortress. Fort Point was abandoned in 1900 and became neglected once the Golden Gate Bridge was built over it – engineers even added an extra span to preserve it.

Alfred Hitchcock saw deadly potential in Fort Point, and shot the trademark scene from *Vertigo* here of Kim Novak leaping from the lookout to certain death into the bay...or not, as it turned out. Fort Point has since given up all pretense of being deadly, and now has a gift shop,

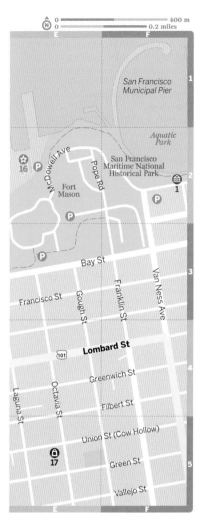

0 —————— 400 m
0 —————— 0.2 miles

San Francisco
Municipal Pier

Aquatic
Park

San Francisco
Maritime National
Historical Park

San Francisco
Maritime National

Fort
Mason

McDowell Ave

Pope Rd

Bay St

Francisco St

Gough St

Franklin St

Van Ness Ave

Lombard St

Greenwich St

Octavia St

Laguna St

Filbert St

Union St (Cow Hollow)

Green St

Vallejo St

## The Marina

### ◎ Sights
1 Aquatic Park Bathhouse
  (Maritime Museum) ........................ F2
2 Church of St Mary the Virgin ............. C5
3 Fort Mason Center ............................. D2
4 Wave Organ ..................................... B1

### ✦ Eating
5 A16 ................................................. B4
6 Barney's Burgers .............................. C4
7 Betelnut ............................................ D5
8 Blue Barn Gourmet ........................... C4
9 Greens ............................................. D2
10 Judy's Cafe ...................................... B4
11 Kara's Cupcakes .............................. B4
12 La Boulange ..................................... D5
13 Real Food ........................................ C5
14 Rose's Café ...................................... C5

### ◉ Drinking & Nightlife
15 California Wine Merchant .................. C4

### ◈ Entertainment
BATS Improv ............................ (see 16)
16 Magic Theatre .................................. E2

### ⓐ Shopping
17 Mingle ............................................. E5
18 My Roommate's Closet ..................... C5
19 Past Perfect ..................................... C5
20 PlumpJack Wines ............................ C4
21 Uko ................................................. D5

### ◎ Sports & Activities
22 Oceanic Society Expeditions
   Boat Departure ............................. B2

Civil War displays and panoramic viewing decks.

### Exploratorium — Museum

Map p70 (☎415-561-0360; www.exploratorium.edu; 3601 Lyon St; adult/child $15/10, 1st Wed of month free; ☺10am-5pm Tue-Sun; ❸; Ⓜ28, 30, 43) Is there a science to skateboarding? Do robots have feelings? Do toilets really flush counterclockwise in Australia? Head to the Exploratorium to get fascinating scientific answers to all the questions you always wanted to ask in science

class. Try out a punk hairdo courtesy of the static-electricity station, and feel your way – in darkness – through the maze of the highly recommended **Tactile Dome** (☎415-561-0362); admission to the Tactile Dome is extra on top of general admission, patrons must be over seven years old, and advance reservations are required. Note: in 2013 the Exploratorium is slated to move to Pier 13.

### FREE Palace of Fine Arts — Monument

Map p70 (www.lovethepalace.org; Palace Dr; Ⓜ28, 30, 43) Like a fossilized party favor, this romantic, ersatz Greco-Roman ruin is the memento San Francisco decided

**63**

to keep from the 1915 Panama-Pacific International Exposition. The original was built in wood, burlap and plaster as a picturesque backdrop by celebrated Berkeley architect Bernard Maybeck, but by the 1960s it was beginning to crumble. The structure was recast in concrete, so that future generations could gaze up at the rotunda relief to glimpse 'Art under attack by materialists, with idealists leaping to her rescue.' Further renovations in 2010 restored the palace to its former glory. Plan to pose for pictures by the swan lagoon.

### Swedenborgian Church    Church

Map p70 ( ☏415-346-6466; www.sfsweden bor gian.org; 2107 Lyon St; ☉hours vary; Ⓜ Jackson & Presidio Sts) Radical ideals in the form of distinctive buildings make beloved SF landmarks; this standout 1894 example is the collaborative effort of 19th-century Bay Area progressive thinkers, such as naturalist John Muir, California Arts and Crafts leader Bernard Maybeck and architect Arthur Page Brown. Enter the church through a modest brick archway, and pass into a garden, sheltered by trees from around the world. Inside, nature is

everywhere – in the hewn-maple chairs, the mighty madrone trees supporting the roof and scenes of Northern California that took muralist William Keith 40 years to complete.

### Walt Disney Family Museum    Museum

Map p70 ( ☏415-345-6800; www.disney.go.com /disneyatoz/familymuseum; 104 Montgomery St; adult/child $20/12; ☉Wed-Mon 10am-6pm; Ⓜ Presidio Blvd & Simonds Loop) An 1890s military barracks houses 10 galleries that tell the exhaustively long story of Walt Disney. Opened in 2009, the museum gets high marks for design, integrating 20,000 sq ft of contemporary glass-and-steel exhibition space with the original 19th-century brick building, but it's definitely geared toward grown-ups and will bore kids after an hour (too much reading). In typical Disney style, the exhibits are impeccably presented, with lavish detail in a variety of media, including a jaw-dropping scale model of Disneyland that will delight die-hard Mouseketeers, but budgeteers may prefer to save their $20 toward a trip to Anaheim.

Palace of Fine Arts (p63)

# How to Know if It's Foggy at the Coast

San Francisco is famous for its summertime microclimates (p261). Downtown may be sunny and hot while the Golden Gate is fogged in and 20°F (10°C) colder. Thanks to satellite imagery, you can get a view of the fog line over the California coast (during daylight hours only) and immediately know if clouds are hugging the shoreline and – most importantly – how many layers to pack before trekking to the Golden Gate Bridge. Go to the **National Oceanic & Atmospheric Administration** (NOAA; www.wrh.noaa .gov/mtr) website for San Francisco, navigate to the 'Satellite imagery' page, and click on the '1km visible satellite' for Monterey, California. SF is the thumb-shaped peninsula, surrounded by bays to its right. Voilà!

# Eating

Fisherman's Wharf is where the fishing fleet unloads its morning catch. From mid-November to June, the local specialty is fresh-caught Dungeness crab. Look for roiling cauldrons in front of restaurants near the docks at the foot of Taylor St. Though Wharf restaurants are fine for a quick bowl of chowder or a crab Louis, most are overpriced and there's nothing groundbreaking about the cooking. Major Marina dining destinations are on Chestnut St from Fillmore to Divisadero Sts, and Union St between Fillmore St and Van Ness Ave. There's fun, funky fare on Lombard St.

## Fisherman's Wharf

### Gary Danko
Californian $$$

Map p66 ( ☎415-749-2060; www.garydanko .com; 800 North Point St; 3-/5-course menus $68/102; ☺dinner; Ⓜ North Point & Hyde St; Ⓟ Powell-Hyde) Smoked-glass windows prevent passersby from tripping over their tongues at the sight of exquisite roasted lobster with trumpet mushrooms, blushing duck breast with rhubarb compote, trios of crème brûlée and the lavish cheese cart. Take your server's seasonal recommendations of three to five courses and prepare to be impressed. Gary Danko has won multiple James Beard Awards for providing impeccable dining experiences, from inventive salad courses like oysters with caviar and lettuce cream to the casually charming server who hands you tiny chocolate cakes as a parting gift. Reservations essential.

### Forbes Island
Grill $$$

Map p66 ( ☎415-951-4900; www.forbesisland .com; Pier 41; mains $28-40; ☺5-10pm Wed-Sun; ⛟; Ⓜ Jefferson & Powell St) No man is an island, except for an eccentric millionaire named Forbes Thor Kiddoo. A miniature lighthouse, thatched hut, waterfall, sandy beach and swaying palms transformed his moored houseboat into the Hearst Castle of the bay. Today this bizarre domicile is a restaurant strong on grilled meats and atmosphere. Reserve in advance and catch boat shuttles from Pier 39; landlubbers dining below deck should bring their motion-sickness meds.

### Eagle Café
American $$

Map p66 ( ☎415-433-3689; www.eaglecafe .com; Pier 39, 2nd fl, Suite 103; mains $10-20; ☺7:30am-9pm; ⛟; Ⓜ Embarcadero & Stockton St; Ⓟ Powell-Mason) The best breakfast and lunch spot on Pier 39 is here. The Eagle's food is simple and straightforward – pancakes and omelets, crab-salad sandwiches and juicy burgers. The views are good, the prices right and they even accept reservations, which you should definitely make on weekends to save yourself a long wait.

### Crown & Crumpet
Cafe $$

Map p66 ( ☎415-771-4252; www.crownand crumpet.com; 207 Ghirardelli Sq, North Point & Larkin St; dishes $8-12; ☺10am-9pm Mon-Fri, 9am-9pm Sat, to 6pm Sun; ⛟; Ⓜ North Point & Larkin St; Ⓟ Powell-Hyde) Designer style

# Fisherman's Wharf

## Fisherman's Wharf

### ◎ Top Sights
Fisherman's Wharf ...............................B1

### ◎ Sights
1 Aquarium of the Bay.............................D2
2 Ghirardelli Square................................A3
3 Musée Mécanique................................C2
4 Pier 39..................................................D1
5 San Francisco Carousel........................D1
6 San Francisco Maritime National
   Historical Park....................................A2
7 SS Jeremiah O'Brien............................B1
8 USS Pampanito.....................................B1

### ✕ Eating
9 Boudin Bakery.......................................C2
10 Crown & Crumpet................................A3

11 Eagle Café.............................................D2
12 Forbes Island.........................................C1
13 Gary Danko...........................................A3
14 Ghirardelli Ice Cream............................A3
   Grandeho's Kamekyo II ................(see 19)
15 In-N-Out Burger....................................B2

### 🍷 Drinking & Nightlife
16 Buena Vista Cafe...................................A3

### 🛍 Shopping
17 elizabethW.............................................A3

### 🏄 Sports & Activities
18 Adventure Cat........................................D2
19 Blazing Saddles.....................................A3
20 Red & White Fleet..................................C2

and rosy cheer usher tea time into the 21st century: girlfriends rehash hot dates over scones with strawberries and champagne, and dads and daughters clink porcelain cups after choosing from 38 kinds of tea. Weekend reservations recommended.

## Grandeho's Kamekyo II
Japanese $$

Map p66 (☎415-673-6828; 2721 Hyde St; mains $10-20; ⏱lunch & dinner Mon-Fri, dinner Sat & Sun; Ⓜ North Point & Hyde St; 🚡Powell-Hyde) A reliable spot to slurp udon and nosh sushi while touring the Wharf. This storefront Japanese satisfies for friendly service and reasonable lunchtime prices (considering the neighborhood), and makes a good pit stop before hopping on the Powell-Hyde cable car out front.

## Boudin Bakery
Bakery $

Map p66 (www.boudinbakery.com; Jefferson St at Mason St; dishes $7-15; ⏱11am-9:30pm) Dating to 1849, Boudin was one of the first five businesses in San Francisco, and still uses the same yeast starter in its sourdough bread. Though you can find better bread elsewhere these days, Boudin's food court remains a Wharf staple for clam chowder in a hollowed-out bread bowl.

## In-N-Out Burger
Burgers $

Map p66 (☎800-786-1000; www.in-n-out.com; 333 Jefferson St; meals under $10; ⏱10:30am-1am Sun-Thu, to 1:30am Fri & Sat; Ⓜ Jones & Beach Sts; 🚡Powell-Hyde) Gourmet burgers have taken SF by storm, but In-N-Out has had a good thing going for 60 years: prime chuck beef, processed on site, plus fries and shakes made with ingredients you can pronounce, all served by employees paid a living wage.

## Ghirardelli Ice Cream
Ice Cream $

Map p66 (☎415-771-4903; www.ghirardellisq.com; 900 North Point St, West Plaza; dishes $4-8; ⏱10am-11pm; 👶; Ⓜ North Point & Larkin St; 🚡Powell-Hyde) Mr Ghirardelli sure makes a swell sundae. The legendary Cable Car comes with Rocky Road ice cream, marshmallow topping and enough hot fudge to satisfy a jonesing chocoholic.

# The Marina
## A16
Italian $$

Map p62 (☎415-771-2216; www.a16sf.com; 2355 Chestnut St; pizza $12-18, mains $18-26; ⏱lunch Wed-Fri, dinner daily; Ⓜ Divisadero & Chestnut Sts) Like a high-maintenance date, this Neapolitan pizzeria demands reservations and then haughtily makes you wait in the foyer. The housemade mozzarella *burrata* (cheese shell containing cream) and chewy-but-not-too-thick-crust pizza makes it worth your while. Skip the spotty desserts and concentrate on adventurous appetizers, including house-cured *salumi* platters and delectable marinated tuna.

Boudin Bakery
LEE FOSTER/LONELY PLANET IMAGES ©

## Food Truck Fridays

The most happening Friday-night food scene occurs at **Off the Grid** (www.offthegridsf.com), in the parking lot of Fort Mason Center (Map p62). Scores of Bay Area food trucks gather here for an appreciative crowd of local eaters, who graze from truck to tent, sampling everything from coconut curry to crème brûlée. The hours are from 5pm to 10pm, but we recommend arriving before 6:30pm to avoid long waits. Cash only. After dinner, stroll the waterfront and watch the sun slip behind the Golden Gate.

### Betelnut
Asian $$

Map p62 ( ☎415-929-8855; www.betelnut restaurant.com; 2030 Union St; dishes $10-20; ⏰11:30am-11pm Sun-Thu, to midnight Fri & Sat; Ⓜ Union & Laguna Sts) Palm-frond ceiling fans whirl overhead at high-energy Betelnut, a Marina District spin on the Chinese beer house. It serves fiery pan-Asian street foods designed to pair with house-label brews and fresh-fruit cocktails. Best dishes: Szechuan string beans, Celia's lettuce cups and succulent glazed pork ribs. Plan to share. Up-tempo lounge beats set a party mood, making this a great spot to start a night on the town. Make reservations.

### Greens
Vegetarian, California $$

Map p62 ( ☎415-771-6222; www.greensrestau rant.com; Fort Mason Center, Bldg A; mains lunch $15-17, dinner $17-24; ⏰lunch Tue-Sat, dinner Mon-Sat, brunch Sun; Ⓜ Marina Blvd & Laguna St) Career carnivores won't realize there's no meat in the hearty black-bean chili with crème fraîche and pickled jalapeños, or that roasted eggplant panino, packed with hearty flavor from ingredients mostly grown on a Zen farm in Marin. On sunny days, get yours to go so you can enjoy it on a wharfside bench, but if you're planning a sit-down weekend

dinner or Sunday brunch you'll need reservations.

### Rose's Café
Californian $$

Map p62 ( ☎415-775-2200; www.rosescafesf .com; 2298 Union St; mains lunch $10-17, dinner $17-28; ⏰8am-10pm; Ⓜ Union & Fillmore Sts) Follow your salads and house-made soups with rich organic polenta with gorgonzola and thyme, or a simple grass-fed beef burger, then linger over espresso or tea. Shop if you must, but return to this sunny corner cafe from 4pm to 6pm for half-priced wine by the glass. Great breakfasts, too.

### Judy's Cafe
Breakfast $

Map p62 ( ☎415-922-4588; www.judyscafesf .com; 2268 Chestnut St; mains $9-13; ⏰7am-4pm; Ⓜ Chestnut & Scott Sts) Locals queue up for giant breakfasts at Judy's, a storefront diner with standouts like sourdough French toast, enormous omelets and great pumpkin bread. Expect to wait. Cash only.

### Barney's Burgers
Burgers $

Map p62 ( ☎415-563-0307; www.barneys hamburgers.com; 3344 Steiner St; dishes $8-12; ⏰11am-10pm Mon-Sat, to 9:30pm Sun; Ⓜ Chestnut & Fillmore Sts) Don't let the name fool you. Yes, its many varieties of all-natural beef and turkey burgers are great, but Barney's also makes big, healthy salads and even serves organic tofu for vegetarians. And, yum, those milkshakes.

### Blue Barn Gourmet
Sandwiches, Salads $

Map p62 ( ☎415-441-3232; www.blue barngourmet.com; 2105 Chestnut St; dishes $9-12; ⏰11am-8:30pm Sun-Thu, to 7pm Fri & Sat; Ⓜ Chestnut & Fillmore Sts) Toss aside thoughts of ordinary salads. For $8.75, build a mighty mound of organic produce, topped with six fixings: artisan cheeses, caramelized onions, heirloom tomatoes, candied pecans, pomegranate seeds, even Meyer grilled sirloin. For something hot, try the toasted panini oozing with Manchego cheese, fig jam and salami.

## La Boulange
Sandwiches, Bakery $

Map p62 ( ☎415-440-4450; www.laboulange
bakery.com; 1909 Union St; dishes $7-11; ☽7am-
6pm; ♿☝; Ⓜ Union & Laguna Sts) Even the
most die-hard boutique trawler needs to
refuel sometime, and La Boulange offers
caffeine and house-baked carbo-loading
in the middle of the Union St strip. La
Combo is a $7.25 lunchtime deal to justify
your next Union St boutique purchase:
half a *tartine* (open-faced sandwich) with
soup or salad, plus all the Nutella and
pickled *cornichons* (gherkins) you desire
from the condiments bar.

## ✒ Real Food
Groceries $

Map p62 ( ☎415-567-6900; www.realfoodco
.com; 3060 Fillmore St; ☽8am-9pm; Ⓜ Union
& Lyon Sts) The deli cases at this organic
grocery are packed with housemade prepared foods, including respectable sushi,
roasted-eggplant-and-tomato salad,
free-range herb-turkey sandwiches and
organic gingerbread. On sunny days, grab
a seat on the patio.

## Kara's Cupcakes
Bakery, Dessert $

Map p62 ( ☎415-563-2253; www.karascupcakes
.com; 3249 Scott St; cupcakes $3; ☽10am-8pm

Mon-Sat, to 6pm Sun; Ⓜ Chestnut & Scott Sts)
Proustian nostalgia washes over fully
grown adults as they bite into cupcakes
that recall childhood magician-led
birthday parties. Varieties range from
yummy chocolate marshmallow to classic
carrot cake with cream-cheese frosting,
all meticulously calculated for maximum
glee.

# The Presidio

## ✒ Warming Hut
Cafe, Sandwiches $

Map p70 ( ☎415-561-3040; 983 Marine Dr;
dishes $4-6; ☽9am-5pm; Ⓜ Richardson Blvd
& Francisco St) Wet-suited windsurfers
and Crissy Field kite-fliers thaw out with
fair-trade coffee, organic pastries and
organic hot dogs at Warming Hut, while
browsing an excellent selection of field
guides and sampling honey made by
the Presidio honeybees. This ecoshack
below the Golden Gate Bridge has walls
ingeniously insulated with recycled
denim and a heartwarming concept: all
purchases fund Crissy Field's ongoing
conversion from US army airstrip to
wildlife preserve.

Crown & Crumpet (p65)

# The Presidio

### Presidio Social Club
American $$

Map p70 (📞415-885-1888; www.presidio socialclub.com; 563 Ruger St; mains $12-24; 🕑11:30am-10pm Mon-Fri, 10am-10pm Sat & Sun; Ⓜ Lombard & Lyon Sts) Inside an atmospheric converted army building within the Presidio, this is a good spot for weekend brunch before hiking, or a lingering afternoon meal with classic cocktails. The comfort-food menu includes dishes like crab sandwiches, mac-n-cheese, and flat-iron steak with French fries.

## 🍷 Drinking & Nightlife

Marina District watering holes – which author Armistead Maupin called 'breeder bars' – cater to frat boys and bottle blonds. The epicenter of the scene is at Fillmore and Greenwich Sts.

### Buena Vista Cafe
Bar

Map p66 (📞415-474-5044; www.thebuenavista .com; 2765 Hyde St; 🕑9am-2am Mon-Fri, 8am-2am Sat & Sun; 🚋Powell-Hyde) Warm your cockles with a prim little goblet of bitter-creamy Irish coffee, introduced to the US at this destination bar that once served sailors and cannery workers. The creaky Victorian floor manages to hold up carousers and families alike, served community-style at round tables overlooking the Wharf.

### California Wine Merchant
Bar

Map p62 (www.californiawinemerchant.com; 2113 Chestnut St; 🕑10am-midnight Mon-Wed, to 1:30am Thu-Sat, 11am-11pm Sun; Ⓜ Chestnut & Fillmore Sts) Part wine store, part wine bar,

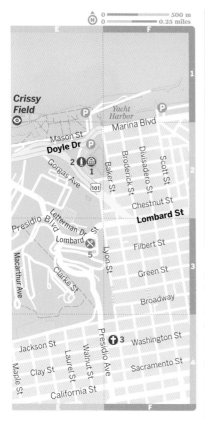

## The Presidio

### ◎ Top Sights
Baker Beach .......................................A3
Crissy Field ......................................E1
Fort Point ........................................B1
Golden Gate Bridge ........................B1

### ◎ Sights
1 Exploratorium ..............................E2
2 Palace of Fine Arts......................E2
3 Swedenborgian Church ..............F4
4 Walt Disney Family Museum.............D2

### ✕ Eating
5 Presidio Social Club......................E3
6 Warming Hut ................................C1

### ✦ Sports & Activities
7 House of Air ..................................C2
8 Presidio Golf Course.....................D4

menu and performers are refreshed quarterly. Reservations essential.

### Pier 23        Live Music

off Map p66 ( ☏ 415-362-5125; www.pier23cafe
.com; Pier 23; admission $10; ◷ shows 5-7pm
Tue, 6-8pm Wed, 7-10pm Thu, 10pm-midnight Fri &
Sat, 4-8pm Sun; Ⓜ Embarcadero & Greenwich St)
It looks like a surf shack, but this old
waterfront restaurant on Pier 23 regularly
features R&B, reggae, Latin bands, mellow rock and the occasional jazz pianist.
Wander out to the bayside patio to soak
in views. The dinner menu features pier-worthy options like batter-fried oysters
and whole roasted crab.

### Magic Theatre        Theater

Map p62 ( ☏ 415-441-8822; www.magictheatre
.org; 3rd fl, Bldg D, Fort Mason Center; tickets
$25-55; Ⓜ Marina Blvd & Laguna St) The Magic
is known for taking risks and staging provocative plays by playwrights such as Bill
Pullman, Terrence McNally, Edna O'Brien,
David Mamet and longtime playwright-in-residence Sam Shepard.

### BATS Improv        Theater

Map p62 ( ☏ 415-474-8935; www.improv.org;
3rd fl, Bldg B, Fort Mason Center; admission $15;
◷ weekend shows 8pm; Ⓜ Marina Blvd & Laguna
St) Bay Area Theater Sports explores all
things improv, from audience-inspired

this little shop on busy Chestnut St caters
to grey-at-the-temples professionals
and neighborhood wine aficionados, and
serves half-glasses. Arrive early to score a
table, or stand and gab with the locals.

## ✪ Entertainment

### Teatro Zinzanni        Theater

( ☏ 415-438-2668; www.zinzanni.org; check
website for location; admission $117-145; ◷ dinner
Wed-Sun, lunch Sun) Inside a 19th-century
*Spiegeltent* (an opulent Belgian traveling-circus tent) top circus talent flies over-head, a celeb-diva croons and clowns pull
wacky stunts as you dig into a surprisingly
good five-course dinner or Sunday lunch.
This ain't no B-grade dinner theater: a
'clown-wrangler' seeks out world-class
talent in Europe and Asia, and the acts,

71

themes to wacked-out musicals at completely improvised weekend shows.

# 🔒 Shopping

**elizabethW**  Beauty Products
Map p66 (www.elizabethw.com; 900 North Point St; ⏰10am-9pm Mon-Sat, to 7pm Sun; Ⓜ North Point & Larkin St; 🚋 Powell-Hyde) Local scent-maker elizabethW supplies the tantalizing aromas of changing seasons without the sweaty brows or frozen toes. 'Sweet Tea' smells like a Georgia porch in summertime; 'Vetiver' like autumn in Maine. For a true SF fragrance, 'Leaves' is as audaciously green as Golden Gate Park in January.

**Mingle**  Clothing, Accessories
Map p62 (www.mingleshop.com; 1815 Union St; ⏰11am-7pm; Ⓜ Union & Laguna Sts) To break up the khaki monotony of the Gap and wrest free of H&M trends, get out there and mingle with SF designers. Local designers keep this boutique stocked with hot Cleopatra-collar dresses, mod ring-buckled bags and plaid necklaces, all for less than you'd pay for Marc Jacobs on megasale. Men emerge from Mingle date-ready in dark tailored denim and black Western shirts with white piping – the SF version of a tux.

**My Roommate's
Closet**  Clothing, Accessories
Map p62 (www.myroommatescloset.com; 3044 Fillmore St; ⏰11am-6pm, noon-5pm Sun; Ⓜ Union & Fillmore Sts) All the half-off bargains and none of the clawing dangers of a sample sale. You'll find cloud-like Catherine Malandrino chiffon party dresses, executive Diane Von Furstenburg wrap dresses and designer denim at prices approaching reality.

**Past Perfect**  Antiques, Housewares
Map p62 (📞415-929-7651; 2224 Union St; ⏰11am-7pm; Ⓜ Union & Fillmore Sts) So this is how Pacific Heights eccentrics fill up

those mansions: Forna-setti face plates, Danish teak credenzas and Lucite champagne buckets. The store is a collective, so prices are all over the place – some sellers apparently believe their belongings owe them back rent, while others are happy just to unload their ex's mother's prized spoon collection.

### Uko                    Clothing, Accessories
Map p62 ( ☎ 415-563-0330; 2070 Union St; ⏰11am-6:30pm Mon-Sat, noon-5:30pm Sun; Ⓜ Union & Buchanan Sts) Laser-cut, draped and micropleated are the fashion-forward signatures of Uko's inventive garments for men and women. Get bonus fashion IQ points for clever jackets with hidden pockets-within-pockets, Cop-Copine wrap skirts with oddly flattering flaps, and silver drop earrings that add an exclamation point to your look.

### PlumpJack Wines              Wine
Map p62 (www.plumpjack.com; 3201 Fillmore St; ⏰11am-8pm Mon-Sat, to 6pm Sun; Ⓜ Fillmore & Lombard Sts) Discover a new favorite California vintage under $30 at the distinctive wine boutique that won partial-owner and former-mayor Gavin Newsom respect from even Green Party gourmets. A more knowledgeable staff is hard to find anywhere in SF, and they'll set you up with the right bottles to cross party lines.

## 🏃 Sports & Activities

### Blazing Saddles              Cycling
Map p66 ( ☎ 415-202-8888; www.blazingsaddles .com; 2715 Hyde St; bike hire per hour $8-15, per day $32-88; ⏰8am-7:30pm, weather permitting; 🚴; 🚋 Powell-Hyde) Blazing Saddles is tailored to visitors, with a main shop on Hyde St and five rental stands around

# Finding Waterfront Addresses

When searching for addresses on the waterfront, remember that even-numbered piers lie *south* of the Ferry Building and odd-numbered piers *north* of the Ferry Building. All even-numbered piers are south of Market St.

Fisherman's Wharf, convenient for cycling the Embarcadero or to the Golden Gate Bridge. Reserve online for a 10% discount; rentals includes all extras (bungee cords, packs etc).

## Oceanic Society Expeditions
Whale Watching

Map p62 ( 415-474-3385; www.oceanic-society.org; trips per person $100-120; office 8:30am-5pm Mon-Fri, trips Sat & Sun; M Broderick & Jefferson Sts) The Oceanic Society runs top-notch, naturalist-led, ocean-going weekend boat trips – sometimes to the Farallon Islands – during both whale-migration seasons. Cruises depart from the yacht harbor (Scott St and Marina Blvd) and last all day. Kids must be 10 years or older. Reservations required.

## Adventure Cat
Sailing

Map p66 ( 415-777-1630; www.adventurecat.com; Pier 39; adult/child $35/15, sunset cruise $50; M Embarcadero & Stockton Sts) There's no better view of San Francisco than from the water, especially at twilight on a fogless evening aboard a sunset cruise. Adventure Cat uses catamarans, with a windless indoor cabin for grandmums and a trampoline between hulls for bouncy kids. Three daily cruises depart March through October; weekends-only November through February.

## Red & White Fleet
Bay Cruise

Map p66 ( 415-673-2900; www.redandwhite.com; Pier 43½; adult/child $24/16; M Jefferson & Powell Sts) A one-hour bay cruise gives you perspective on San Francisco's geography and the chance to see the Golden Gate Bridge from water level. Brave the wind and sit on the outdoor upper deck. Audio tours in multiple

PlumpJack Wines (p73)

languages provide narrative. On-board alcohol subdues naysayers.

### House of Air
Trampoline Park

Map p70 ( 415-345-9675; www.houseofairsf .com; 926 Old Mason St, Crissy Field; adult/child $14/10; 10am-10pm Mon-Thu, to 11pm Fri, 9am-9pm Sun; ; Broderick & Jefferson Sts) If you ever resented your gym teacher for not letting you jump as high as you wanted on the trampoline, you can finally get your way at this incredible trampoline park, with multiple areas to jump, including the Matrix, where you can literally bounce off the walls on 42 attached trampolines the size of a basketball court. Little kids have dedicated play areas.

Reservations strongly recommended, especially for weekends.

### Presidio Golf Course
Golf

Map p70 ( 415-561-4661; www.presidiogolf .com; Arguello Blvd & Finley Rd; 18 holes SF resident $65-85, nonresident $125-145; sunrise-sunset; Sacramento & Cherry Sts) Whack balls with military-style precision on the course once reserved exclusively for US forces. The Presidio course, now operated by the Arnold Palmer company, overlooks the bay and is considered one of the country's best. Book up to 30 days in advance on the website, which sometimes lists specials, too. Rates include cart.

# Downtown & Civic Center

**Downtown restaurants and stores can't hide San Francisco's colorful past.** This was once a notorious dock area, where saloon owner Shanghai Kelly conked new arrivals on the head and delivered them to ships as crew. Today, only your attention gets shanghaied – by art galleries, swanky hotels, first-run theaters, boutiques and a mall full of brand names.

The Ferry Building at the foot of Market St was erected as a transit hub in 1898; you can spot its clock tower in pictures from the 1906 earthquake. Today it lures in anyone who likes food – which seems to be pretty much everybody – with its many opportunities to taste, shop and forage.

Farther down Market, the Civic Center area is a zoning conundrum: on one side of City Hall are Asian art treasures, the symphony and the opera, and on the other are dive bars, XXX theaters and soup kitchens.

# Downtown & Civic Center Highlights

## Asian Art Museum (p86)

The curatorial concept is to follow the geographical path of Buddhism through Asia from the top floor down, beginning on the 3rd floor with India, then – wait, isn't that Iran, followed by Sikh kingdoms, then Indonesia? By the time you've cruised past 3000-plus Zoroastrian artifacts and splendid Balinese shadow puppets, all theological quibbles will yield to astonishment – and possibly exhaustion.

## Riding Cable Cars (p265)

Take a leap onto the baseboard and grab a strap: you're in for the ultimate urban carnival ride on one of San Francisco's vintage cable cars. Burly operators work that hand brake and bell as though their lives depend on it, and little else prevents these restored 1870s contraptions from careening downhill into traffic. When climbs yield glimpses of the Golden Gate, public transit never seemed so poetic.

## Union Square (p84)

It's mind-boggling that an entire block of prime real estate in the heart of San Francisco has managed to remain undeveloped since it was a pro-Union meeting place during the Civil War. Before the addition of paved terraces during a massive renovation in 2002, the park was little more than a patch of grass with a monument in the middle, but today it's a popular downtown outdoor space.

## San Francisco Symphony & Opera (p96)

Since conductor Michael Tilson Thomas took the baton, the San Francisco Symphony has racked up 13 Grammys. Pick up last-minute tickets for $20 – never mind what's on. From summer Mozart through stormy winter Berlioz, this is heart-racing, mind-expanding classical music. At the SF Opera, megatalents command the stage in celebrated productions, as well as free Stern Grove performances.

## Transamerica Pyramid & Redwood Park (p81)

William Pereira's pyramid cleverly maximizes sunshine in the streets below, drawing lunchtime lollygaggers to the redwood grove that thrives in its pointy shadow. Unfortunately, the observation deck has been closed since September 11, so it's more landmark than attraction, but you can amuse yourself by asking passersby if they knew that the hull of a Gold Rush–era whaling vessel is embedded in the ground below.

# Downtown & Civic Center Walk

*With its compact layout and dearth of parking, SF's Downtown is best explored on foot. Get acquainted with some of the city's top historical sites. Don't miss the Ferry Building, a transit hub that's been reinvented as a foodie mecca.*

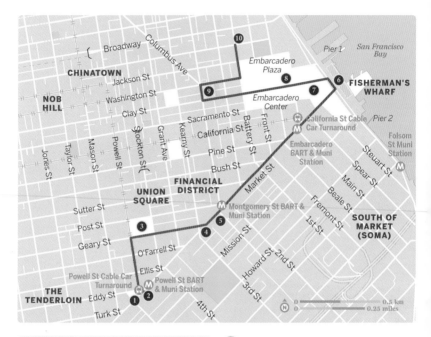

## WALK FACTS

- **Start** Union Square
- **Finish** Old Ship Saloon
- **Distance** 2 miles
- **Duration** 1½ hours

## ① Cable Car Turnaround

Where Powell St meets Market St, cable cars take a break on a circular platform while they get turned around and pointed back toward **Fisherman's Wharf** (p54). Street performers and megaphone-wielding cranks proclaiming the end to be near complete the scene. (p84)

## ② Flood Building

This 1904 building retains much of its original character. Upstairs are long, labyrinthine halls lined with frosted-glass doors, just like in a noir movie. Dashiell Hammett worked there as a private investigator for the Pinkerton National Detective Agency before writing *The Maltese Falcon*.

## ③ Union Square

During the Civil War, **Union Square** (p84) was the site of pro-Union rallies; it's been a popular gathering place ever since. A 2002 renovation made it more paved plaza than grassy park, but the 97ft column in the middle, topped by a 1903 statue of Victory, gives a nod to its past.

### 4 Lotta's Fountain

Opera diva Lotta Crabtree commissioned this cast-metal pillar as a gift to SF's people. It was useful during the 1906 fire, when it became the sole source of water downtown.

### 5 Palace Hotel

The city's most storied hotel opened in 1875 and was gutted during the 1906 earthquake and fire. The current building opened in 1909; President Warren Harding died upstairs in 1923. Stop in to peek at the opulent **Garden Court** and its luminous stained-glass dome, as well as the Maxfield Parrish mural at the **Pied Piper Bar**.

### 6 Ferry Building

The long-vacant 1898 ferry hub (p82) was gutted and spiffed up in 2001 to become a gourmet-food emporium and upscale farmers market, housing acclaimed restaurants such as **Slanted Door** (p89).

### 7 Justin Herman Plaza

Where Market St meets the Ferry Building, skaters, vendors and protesters do their best to distract visitors from a fountain that looks like an industrial accident. (p84)

### 8 Sue Bierman Park

Stop by this diminutive patch for a daily air show put on by the parrots of Telegraph Hill. Around dusk you can catch them at their most raucous, as they have one last noisy hurrah before settling down for the night.

### 9 Transamerica Pyramid & Redwood Park

Alongside the **Transamerica Pyramid**, the distinguishing feature of SF's skyline, is a grove of redwoods, where there are kitschy/creepy statues of cackling children and frogs leaping from lily pads in the fountain.

### 10 Old Ship Saloon

In 1851, enterprising Joseph Anthony built a bar around the good ship *Arkansas* at 298 Pacific Ave. The bar was notorious for drugging customers, who woke up miles from shore, shanghaied into service on a crew.

## ⭐ The Best...

### PLACES TO EAT

**Ferry Building** Restaurants, kiosks and farmers markets keep you satisfied. (p82)

**Gitane** A sexy little Union Square bistro. (p90)

**Slanted Door** Superpopular Vietnamese restaurant in the Ferry Building. (p89)

**Cotogna** Rustic Italian – plan ahead, and try the prix fixe. (p87)

### PLACES TO DRINK

**Rickhouse** Creative whiskey drinks, always crowded. (p93)

**Barrique** Small-batch wines directly from the vineyard. (p94)

**Edinburgh Castle** Darts and trivia keep this Scottish pub lively. (p95)

**Bix** A swanky, old-school martini bar for sophisticated tastes. (p95)

### PLACES FOR LIVE PERFORMANCES

**San Francisco Symphony** Grammy-winning conductor. (p96)

**San Francisco Opera** Second-largest opera company in the US. (p97)

**Rrazz Room** The city's premier cabaret theater. (p97)

**Café Royale** Artsy and cool, with eclectic performances. (p97)

## ☑

## Don't Miss
# Ferry Building

Other towns have gourmet ghettos, but San Francisco puts its love of food front and center at the Ferry Building. The once-grand port was overshadowed by a 1950s elevated freeway until 1989, when it turned out to be less than earthquake-proof. The freeway above the waterfront was demolished and the Ferry Building again emerged as the symbol of San Francisco. Now it has become its own destination, marking your arrival onto America's most happening food scene.

Map p87

www.ferrybuilding
marketplace.com

Market St & the
Embarcadero

⊙10am-6pm Mon-
Fri, 9am-6pm Sat,
11am-5pm Sun

Ⓜ & ℝEmbarcadero

# History

Like a grand salute, the Ferry Building's trademark 240ft tower greeted dozens of ferries daily after its 1898 inauguration. But with the opening of the Bay and Golden Gate Bridges, ferry traffic subsided in the 1930s. Then the new overhead freeway obscured the building's stately facade and car fumes turned it black. Only after the 1989 earthquake did city planners snap to and realize what they'd been missing: with its grand halls and bay views, this was the perfect place to develop a new public commons.

# Renovations

Even before building renovations were completed in 2003, the Ferry Plaza Farmers Market began operating out front on the sidewalk. While some complained that the prices were higher than at other markets, there was no denying that this one offered seasonal, gourmet treats and local specialty foods. Artisanal goat cheese, fresh-pressed California olive oil, wild boar and organic vegetables soon captured the imagination of SF's professional chefs and semiprofessional eaters.

Today the organic gourmet action also continues indoors, where select local shops sell wild-harvested mushrooms, gold-leaved chocolates, sustainably farmed oysters and caviar, as well as myriad other temptations. Standout shops and restaurants provide further reasons to miss your ferry. For restaurants, see p86.

# Justin Herman Plaza

The plaza at the foot of Market St, across the Embarcadero from the Ferry Building, may lack pleasing aesthetics – the Vaillancourt Fountain was intentionally designed to be ugly, mirroring the freeway that once roared above – but Justin Herman Plaza draws big crowds. The wild parrots of Telegraph Hill are the most thrilling sight here. Follow the poplar trees leading north to lush **Sue Bierman Park (Map p87; Clay & Drumm Sts)**, a patch of green where you can picnic and watch squawking birds zip through the branches.

# Don't Miss List

BY AMY SHERMAN,
FOOD WRITER

### 1 FARMERS MARKET
The Saturday farmers market is one of the best in the country, but the crowds are large unless you come early. For a more leisurely experience, visit Tuesday or Thursday between 10am and 2pm. You'll find a smaller but pristine selection of produce, plus plenty of food stalls where you can make a meal out of Korean tacos from Namu, fresh noodles from Hapa Ramen or a mean cheeseburger from 4505 Meats.

### 2 OUT THE DOOR
Slanted Door is one of the most well-known and best-loved Vietnamese restaurants, but it's hard to get a table if you don't plan ahead. For a fantastic lunch, grab a refreshing and juicy grapefruit and jicama salad from the Out the Door window around the corner from the restaurant, and grab a seat on one of the benches outside with a sparkling view of the bay.

### 3 COWGIRL CREAMERY & SIDEKICK
Cowgirl Creamery is the perfect place to find cheese to bring home or take on a picnic. The staff are patient and always willing to make suggestions or offer samples. If you're hungry, Cowgirl Creamery Sidekick offers cheese-centric breakfast and lunch specialties. The grilled cheese of the day is always a good bet.

### 4 HODO SOY
If you're interested in something a little different, Hodo Soy has a kiosk where they sell different grab-and-go meals, including salads, wraps and sandwiches all made from fresh soy. Even nonvegetarians will enjoy the spicy yuba salad that tastes like noodles but is really soy skin.

### 5 RECCHIUTI
Recchiuti is a local chocolate shop where you can find gifts like a s'mores kit or the signature chocolate, burnt caramel truffles. The chocolate bars studded with fruit and nuts, including mulberries, currants and almonds, are a particularly affordable luxury. Different products are constantly being added so be sure to ask what's new.

# Discover Downtown & Civic Center

## 🔄 Getting There & Away

- **Streetcar** Historic F-Market line streetcars run above Market St, then along the Embarcadero to Fisherman's Wharf.

- **Cable car** The Powell-Hyde and Powell-Mason lines link Downtown with the Wharf (the Mason line is shorter, the Hyde line more scenic); the California St line runs west up Nob Hill.

- **Bus** Market St–bound Muni lines serve downtown: 2, 5, 6, 14, 21, 30, 31, 38, 41, 45 and 71.

- **Metro** The J, K, L, M and N metro lines run under Market St.

- **BART** Downtown stations are Embarcadero, Montgomery and Powell.

## 👁 Sights

### Financial District & Jackson Square

**Ferry Building**　　　　Landmark
See p82.

**Justin Herman Plaza**　　Square
See p83.

### Union Square

**Union Square**　　　　　Square
Map p88 (intersection of Geary, Powell, Post & Stockton Sts; Ⓜ & Ⓡ Powell St; 🚡 Powell-Mason, Powell-Hyde) Louis Vuitton is more top-of-mind than the Emancipation Proclamation, but Union Square – bordered by department stores and mall chains – was named after pro-Union Civil War rallies held here 150 years ago.

**Powell St Cable Car Turnaround**　　Landmark
Map p88 (cnr Powell & Market Sts; Ⓜ & Ⓡ Powell St) Stand awhile at Powell and Market Sts and you'll spot arriving cable-car operators leaping out, gripping trolleys and slooowly turning them around by hand on a revolving wooden platform. Cable cars can't go in reverse and this terminus is where the Powell-Mason and Powell-Hyde lines end and begin. Riders line up late morning to early evening for the city's famous moving historic landmarks – so do panhandlers, street performers and preachers on megaphones.

Shoppers in the Ferry Building (p82)
JUDY BELLAH/LONELY PLANET IMAGES ©

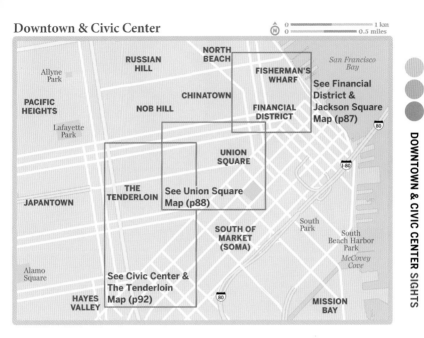

# Civic Center
# & the Tenderloin

**FREE** **City Hall**        Historical Building

Map p92 ( 🖋 tour info 415-554-6023, art exhibit
line 415-554-6080; www.ci.sf.ca.us/cityhall;
400 Van Ness Ave; ⏱8am-8pm Mon-Fri, tours
10am, noon & 2pm; 🚹; Ⓜ & ℞ Civic Center)
That mighty beaux arts dome pretty
much covers San Francisco's grandest
ambitions and fundamental flaws. Free
docent tours of City Hall meet at the tour
kiosk near the Van Ness Ave entrance, but
City Hall is best seen in action. The Board
of Supervisors meets Tuesdays at 2pm;
check the agenda and minutes online.

## Glide Memorial United
## Methodist Church        Church

Map p92 ( 🖋 415-674-6090; www.glide.org; 330
Ellis St; ⏱celebrations 9am & 11am Sun; Ⓜ &
℞ Powell St) The 100-member Glide gospel
choir kicks off Sunday celebrations, and
the welcome is warm for whoever comes
through the door – the diverse, 1500-plus
congregation includes many who'd once
lost all faith in faith. After the celebration

ends, the congregation keeps the inspiration coming, providing a million free
meals a year and housing for formerly
homeless families – now that's hitting a
high note.

# 🍴 Eating

**The sustainable-food temple known
as the Ferry Building (see p82) houses
several foodie shrines under one roof.
At dinnertime, Downtown is best
known for its high-end houses, but at
lunchtime most eateries cater to office
workers, with meals around $10. The
Financial District is quiet at night, when
only midrange and top-end restaurants
stay open. The Tenderloin – west of
Powell St, south of Geary St, north of
Market St – feels sketchy and sometimes rough but, as always in San
Francisco, superior dining rewards the
adventurous. Note that some cheap
eats in the 'Loin close earlier than their
posted hours.**

BLOOMBERG/GETTY IMAGES©

## ✓ Don't Miss
## Asian Art Museum

The largest viewable collection of Asian art outside Asia covers 6000 years and thousands of miles of terrain. A trip through the galleries is a treasure-hunting expedition, from racy Rajasthan palace miniatures and the largest collection of Japanese sculptural baskets outside Japan to the jewel-box gallery of lustrous Chinese jade – just don't bump into those priceless Ming vases.

The Asian Art Museum has amassed 18,000 prime examples of the region's ingenuity and artistry. Consider the diplomatic backbends curators had to perform to put such a diverse collection into proper perspective. Where the UN falters, this museum succeeds in bringing Taiwan, China and Tibet together, uniting Pakistan and India, and striking a harmonious balance between Japan, Korea and China.

### NEED TO KNOW

Map p92; ☏415-581-3500; www.asianart.org; 200 Larkin St; adult/child $12/free, 1st Sun of month free; ⏱10am-5pm Tue-Sun, to 9pm Thu Feb-Sep; Ⓜ & Ⓡ Civic Center

## Financial District & Jackson Square

**Michael Mina**  Californian $$$

Map p87 (☏415-397-9222; www.michaelmina.net; 252 California St; lunch $49-59, dinner $35-42; ⏱lunch Mon-Fri, dinner daily; Ⓜ & Ⓡ Montgomery St, Ⓒ California St) San Francisco's favorite culinary son and winner of the James Beard Award has reinvented his posh namesake restaurant, which spawned an empire of 16 others around the country. Gone is the multicourse, silver-service European luxe, in favor of more lighthearted, á la carte French-Japanese cooking that blurs the lines between formal and casual. Reservations essential.

# Financial District & Jackson Square

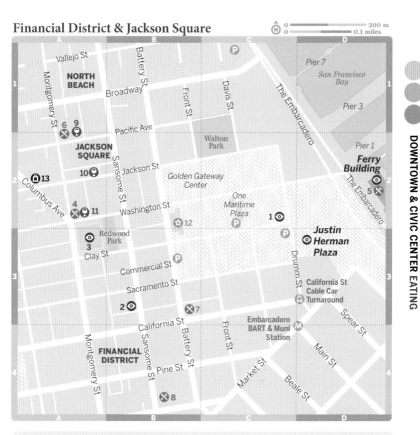

## Financial District & Jackson Square

### ◎ Top Sights
Ferry Building ......................................... D2
Justin Herman Plaza ............................. D3

### ◎ Sights
1 Sue Bierman Park.................................... C2
2 Sun Terrace............................................. B3
3 Transamerica Pyramid & Redwood
  Park.......................................................... A3

### ✖ Eating
4 Bocadillos ................................................ A2
5 Boulette's Larder .................................... D2
6 Cotogna...................................................... A2
  Hog Island Oyster Company ..........(see 5)

7 Michael Mina............................................ B3
  Mijita.................................................... (see 5)
8 Mixt Greens .............................................. B4
  Slanted Door ..................................... (see 5)

### ◎ Drinking & Nightlife
9 Barrique..................................................... A1
10 Bix.............................................................. A2
11 Taverna Aventine ................................... A2

### ✪ Entertainment
12 Punch Line............................................... B2

### ◎ Shopping
13 Eden & Eden............................................ A2

**Cotogna**                    Italian $$
Map p87 ( ☎ 415-775-8508; www.cotognasf.com;
470 Pacific Ave; mains $14-24; ☺ lunch & dinner
Mon-Sat; ☕; Ⓜ Pacific Ave & Montgomery St)

Chef-owner Michael Tusk won the 2011
James Beard Award for best chef. Ever
since, it's been hard to book a table at
Cotogna (and its fancier big sister Quince,

next door), but it's worth planning ahead to be rewarded by his authentic *rustica* Italian cooking that magically balances a few pristine flavors. Pastas are outstanding, and pizzas have tender-to-the-tooth crusts. The $24 prix-fixe menu is a steal.

### Bocadillos · Basque $$

Map p87 ( ☎415-982-2622; www.bocasf.com; 710 Montgomery St; dishes $9-15; ⏰7am-10pm Mon-Fri, 5-10:30pm Sat; Ⓜ Clay & Montgomery Sts) Forget multipage menus and giant portions, and have your choice of two small sandwiches on toasted rolls, with a green salad, for just $10 at this Downtown favorite for tapas and small plates. The juicy lamb burgers, snapper ceviche with Asian pears, and Catalan sausages are just-right Basque bites, made better with wine by the glass.

### 🌿 Mixt Greens · Salads $

Map p87 (www.mixtgreens.com; 120 Sansome St; salads $8-11; ⏰10:30am-3pm Mon-Fri; 🖋; Ⓜ & 🚇 Montgomery St) Stockbrokers line up out the door for generous organic salads, like

## Union Square

### ◎ Sights

| | | |
|---|---|---|
| 1 | Fairmont Hotel | B1 |
| 2 | One Montgomery Terrace | F2 |
| 3 | Orchard Garden Hotel | D1 |
| 4 | Powell St Cable Car Turnaround | C5 |
| 5 | Union Square | C3 |

### ✖ Eating

| | | |
|---|---|---|
| 6 | Bio | D4 |
| 7 | Boxed Foods | E2 |
| 8 | Cafe Claude | E2 |
| 9 | Emporio Rulli | D3 |
| 10 | Gitane | E2 |
| 11 | Johnny Foley's | C4 |
| 12 | Lefty O'Douls | C3 |
| 13 | Mocca on Maiden Lane | D3 |
| 14 | Rotunda | D3 |
| 15 | Sons & Daughters | C2 |

### 🍷 Drinking & Nightlife

| | | |
|---|---|---|
| 16 | Irish Bank | E1 |
| 17 | John's Grill | D4 |
| 18 | Le Colonial | A3 |
| 19 | Rickhouse | E1 |
| 20 | Ruby Skye | C3 |
| 21 | Tunnel Top | D2 |

### 🎭 Entertainment

| | | |
|---|---|---|
| 22 | Rrazz Room | C4 |
| 23 | Starlight Room | C2 |

### 🛍 Shopping

| | | |
|---|---|---|
| 24 | Barneys | D4 |
| 25 | H&M | C4 |
| 26 | Original Levi's Store | D2 |
| 27 | Westfield San Francisco Centre | D5 |

humanely raised, herb-marinated chicken with chipotle dressing or mango, jicama and roasted peanuts with tangy Thai vinaigrette. Grab a stool or get yours to go in a compostable corn container to enjoy bayside near the Ferry Building.

**Slanted Door**     Vietnamese $$$
Map p87 ( ☎ 415-861-8032; www.slanteddoor .com; 1 Ferry Bldg; lunch $13-24, dinner $18-36; ⊙ lunch & dinner; Ⓜ & Ⓡ Embarcadero) San Francisco's most effortlessly elegant restaurant harmonizes California

ingredients, continental influences and Vietnamese flair. Book two weeks ahead for lunch, one month for dinner – or call at 5:30pm for last-minute cancellations.

**Hog Island Oyster Company**     Seafood $$
Map p87 ( ☎ 415-391-7117; www.hogisland oysters.com; 1 Ferry Bldg; 6 oysters $15-17; ⊙ 11:30am-8pm Mon-Fri, 11am-6pm Sat & Sun; Ⓜ & Ⓡ Embarcadero) Slurp the bounty of the North Bay, with a view of the East Bay, at this Ferry Building favorite for sustainably farmed oysters. Mondays and Thursdays between 5pm and 7pm

are happy hours indeed for shellfish fans, with half-priced oysters and $4 pints.

### Boulette's Larder
French $$

Map p87 ( 415-399-1155; www.bouletteslarder.com; 1 Ferry Bldg; mains $18-23; 9am-3pm Mon-Fri, noon-3pm Sat, 11am-3pm Sun; M & Embarcadero) Dinner theater doesn't get more literal than brunch at Boulette's communal table, strategically placed inside a working kitchen, amid a swirl of chefs preparing fancy French take-out dinners for commuter gourmands.

### Mijita
Mexican $

Map p87 ( 415-399-0814; www.mijitasf.com; 1 Ferry Bldg; dishes $4-5; 10am-7pm Mon-Wed, to 8pm Thu-Sat, to 4pm Sun; ; M & Embarcadero) At this order-at-the-counter taco shop, owner-chef Traci Des Jardins puts her signature stamp on her Mexican grandmother's standbys. Expect fresh local produce for the tangy-savory jicama and grapefruit salad with pumpkin seeds, and sustainably harvested fish cooked with the minimum of oil in seriously addictive Baja fish tacos.

## Union Square

### Gitane
Basque, Mediterranean $$

Map p88 ( 415-788-6686; www.gitane restaurant.com; 6 Claude Lane; mains $15-25; 5:30pm-midnight Tue-Sat, bar to 1am; ; M & Montgomery St) Slip out of the Financial District and into something more comfortable at this sexy jewel-box bistro – a dimly lit mash-up of French boudoir and '70s chic, with lipstick-red lacquered ceilings reflecting tasseled silks, tufted leather and velvet snugs. Make reservations and dress sharp. Or drop by for craft cocktails at the swank little bar.

### Sons & Daughters
Californian $$$

Map p88 ( 415-391-8311; www.sonsand daughterssf.com; 708 Bush St; 4-course menu $58; dinner; Powell-Hyde, Powell-Mason) Sons & Daughters is a breath of culinary fresh air in a city that can get haughty about food. The young chefs here incorporate unusual elements in their

## Old-School Tourist Favorites

Downtown is chockablock with tourist joints that fit the bill under certain circumstances – like, when you're traveling with screaming, hungry kids and you just want to have a couple of cocktails and be left alone, but realize you're on vacation and should go somewhere atmospheric. Fear not: we've got you covered.

**Tommy's Joynt** (Map p92; 415-775-4216; www.tommysjoynt.com; 1101 Geary St; mains $4-9; 11am-2am; ; M Geary St & Van Ness Ave) Open and unchanged since 1947 – with enough ephemera and animal heads on the walls to prove it – Tommy's is the classic for *hof brau* (cafeteria-style) meals of turkey, corned beef and buffalo stew.

**Johnny Foley's** (Map p88; 415-954-0777; www.johnnyfoleys.com; 243 O'Farrell St; mains $14-24; 11:30am-1:30am; ; M & Powell St) Great-looking vintage bar and grill, with tile floors and gorgeous woodwork, live music nightly and passable Irish pub grub.

**Lefty O'Douls** (Map p88; 415-982-8900; www.leftyodouls.biz; 333 Geary St; mains $7-11; 7am-2am; ; M & Powell St) Floor-to-ceiling kitsch, baseball memorabilia, sports on TV, live music and *hof brau* – Lefty's is tourist central and reliably fun on game nights.

# Alfresco Dining on Warm Nights

During the odd heat wave in SF, when it's too hot to stay indoors without air-con (which nobody in SF has) and warm enough to eat outside, two Downtown streets become the go-to destinations for dining alfresco: **Belden Place** (www .belden-place.com) and **Claude Lane**. Both are pedestrian alleyways lined with restaurants, which set up side-by-side tables in the street, creating scenes remarkably like Paris in summertime. The food is better on Claude Lane, notably at sexy Gitane and Cafe Claude. But the scene on Belden is more colorful, especially at restaurants Plouf, Tiramisu and Café Bastille – which are otherwise not outstanding, but a lot of fun.

### Boxed Foods                         Sandwiches, Salads $

Map p88 (www.boxedfoodscompany.com; 245 Kearny St; dishes $8-10; ⏱8am-3pm Mon-Fri; 🍴; Ⓜ & ℝMontgomery St) Organic, local, seasonal ingredients make outrageously flavorful lunches, whether you choose the zesty strawberry salad with mixed greens, walnuts and tart goat cheese or the Boxed BLT, with crunchy applewood-smoked bacon. Get yours to go to the **Transamerica Pyramid and Redwood Park** (Map p87), or grab one of the tables out back.

## Civic Center & the Tenderloin

### Millennium               Vegetarian $$$

Map p92 (🕿415-345-3900; www.millennium restaurant.com; 580 Geary St; set menu $39-72; ⏱dinner; 🍴; Ⓜ & ℝPowell St) If all vegetarian food could be this satisfying and opulent, there could be cattle roaming the streets of SF and no one would give them a second glance. Seasonal first courses include grilled semolina flatbread topped white-tablecloth, farm-to-table cooking, but manage to keep the food accessible, with dishes like potato-skin consommé and black-truffle ice cream.

### Cafe Claude                          French $$

Map p88 (🕿415-392-3505; www .cafeclaude.com; 7 Claude Lane; mains $10-20; ⏱11:30am-10:30pm Mon-Sat, 5:30pm-10:30pm Sun; Ⓜ & ℝMontgomery St) Hidden on a little alleyway, Cafe Claude is the perfect French cafe, with zinc bar, umbrella tables outside and staff chattering en français. Lunch is served till a civilized 5pm, and a jazz combo plays during dinner Thursday to Saturday, when regulars dine on classics like coq au vin and steak tartare.

Boulette's Larder

## Civic Center & The Tenderloin

### ◎ Top Sights
Asian Art Museum ................................. C5

### ◎ Sights
1 City Hall ............................................. B5
2 Glide Memorial United
    Methodist Church .............................. D2

### ✘ Eating
3 Brenda's French Soul
    Food .................................................. B3
4 Millennium ......................................... C2

5 Shalimar ............................................. D2
6 Tommy's Joynt .................................... A2

### ⊙ Drinking & Nightlife
7 Edinburgh Castle ............................... B2
8 Lush Lounge ...................................... A1
9 Rickshaw Stop ................................... A6

### ⊕ Entertainment
10 Café Royale ...................................... C2
11 San Francisco Opera ......................... A5
12 San Francisco Symphony ................... A5

with caramelized onions, wilted spinach and a flourish of almond *romesco* (sauce).

### Brenda's French Soul Food
Creole, Southern $

Map p92 ( 415-345-8100; www.frenchsoul food.com; 652 Polk St; mains $8-12; 8am-3pm Sun-Tue, to 10pm Wed-Sat; Van Ness Ave) Chef-owner Brenda Buenviaje blends New Orleans–style Creole cooking with French technique to create 'French soul food.' Expect updated classics like red beans and rice, serious biscuits and grits, amazing Hangtown fry (eggs scrambled with salt pork and fried oysters), good shrimp-stuffed po' boys, and fried chicken served with collard greens and hot-pepper jelly.

### Shalimar
Indian $

Map p92 ( 415-928-0333; www.shalimarsf .com; 532 Jones St; dishes $5-10; noon-midnight; Geary & Jones Sts) Follow your nose to tandoori chicken straight off the skewer and naan bread still bubbling from the oven at this fluorescent-lit, linoleum-floored Downtown Indian dive. Watch and learn as foodies, who demand five-star service elsewhere, meekly fetch their own water pitchers and tamarind sauce from the fridge.

## ⊙ Drinking & Nightlife

The only downside to Downtown drinking is the Downtown crowd. For more texture and grit, head to the Tenderloin to drink with 20-something hipsters. Drinks are cheapest in the 'Loin and get increasingly pricey as you move towards the Financial District. Most Downtown bars have good happy-hour specials; otherwise drinks cost upwards of $10 (or more) east of Powell St, but drop in price in the Tenderloin.

## Union Square

### Rickhouse
Bar

Map p88 (www.rickhousebar.com; 246 Kearny St; Mon-Sat; & Montgomery St) Rickhouse is lined floor to ceiling with repurposed whiskey casks imported from Kentucky and backbar shelving from an Ozark Mountains nunnery that once secretly brewed hooch. The emphasis is (naturally) on whiskey, including some killer hard-to-find bourbons.

### Tunnel Top
Bar

Map p88 (www.tunneltop.com; 601 Bush St; Mon-Sat; Sutter & Stockton Sts) You can't tell who's local and who's not in this happening, chilled two-story bar, with exposed beams, beer-bottle chandelier and little mezzanine where you can spy on the crowd below. The owners are French, and their Gallic friends throng the place, tapping their toes to community-conscious hip-hop (think Common, not Little Wayne) and boom-boom house music, the SF soundtrack. Cash only.

### Irish Bank
Pub

Map p88 (www.theirishbank.com; 10 Mark Lane; 11:30am-2am; California St) Perfectly pulled pints and thick-cut fries with malt vinegar, plus juicy burgers, brats and anything else you could possibly want with lashings of mustard, are staples at this cozy Irish pub. There are tables beneath a big awning in the alley out front, ideal for smokers – even on a rainy night.

### Le Colonial     Nightclub

Map p88 (www.lecolonialsf.com; 20 Cosmo Pl; Ⓜ Montgomery St; ⬚ Powell-Mason, Powell-Hyde) Time travel to colonial French-Vietnam at this sexy downtowner with attentive service and tasty, if overpriced, southeast Asian cooking. The draw is the scene: after 10pm Friday and Saturday, the 2nd-floor lounge becomes a nightclub and everyone dances. Make a night of it with dinner, or head directly upstairs to the pink-lit bar, with its rattan decor and low-slung stools, and order a Singapore sling.

### Ruby Skye     Nightclub

Map p88 (www.rubyskye.com; 420 Mason St; admission $10-25; ⊗9pm-late Fri & Sat, sometimes Thu & Sun; Ⓜ & ⬚ Powell St) The city's premier-name nightclub occupies

a vintage theater reminiscent of classic NY clubs, with reserveable balcony boxes. The who's-who of the world's DJs play here – think Danny Tenaglia, Dimitri from Paris, Christopher Lawrence and Paul Van Dyk. The very mainstream crowd sometimes gets messy (hence gruff security), but when your fave DJ's playing, who cares? The Funktion-One sound system is state of the art.

### John's Grill     Bar

Map p88 (www.johnsgrill.com; 63 Ellis St; ⊗11am-10pm; Ⓜ & ⬚ Powell St; ⬚ Powell-Mason, Powell-Hyde) It could be the martinis, the low lighting or the *Maltese Falcon* statuette upstairs, but something about Dashiell Hammett's favorite bar lends itself to hard-boiled tales of lost love and true crimes, confessed while chewing toothpicks.

# Financial District & Jackson Square

### 🖊 Barrique     Bar

Map p87 (☎415-421-9200; www.barriquesf .com; 461 Pacific Ave; ⊗3-10pm Tue-Sat; Ⓜ Pacific Av & Montgomery St) Here your glass of high-end, small-batch vino comes straight from the cask, directly from the vineyard, sans label. Though there's a bottle list, stick to barrel tastings for the full experience. Sitting up front in the brick-walled space provides better people watching, but we prefer the white-leather sofas out back, near the casks, to watch blending in action. Cheese and charcuterie plates – artisanal and organic, natch – keep your buzz in check.

### Taverna Aventine     Bar

Map p87 (☎415-981-1500; www.aventinesf.com; 582 Washington St; ⊗11:30am-

Edinburgh Castle
SABRINA DALBESIO/LONELY PLANET IMAGES ©

# Downtown Rooftop Gardens

Above the busy sidewalks, there's a serene world of public rooftop gardens that provide perspective on Downtown's skyscraper-canyons. Here's a short list of favorites.

**One Montgomery Terrace** (Map p88; 50 Post St/1 Montgomery St; ⊙10am-6pm Mon-Sat) Great Market St views of old and new SF. Enter through Crocker Galleria, take the elevator to the top, then ascend stairs or enter Wells Fargo at One Montgomery and take the elevator to 'R.'

**Sun Terrace** (Map p87; 343 Sansome St; ⊙10am-6pm Mon-Fri) Knockout vistas of the Financial District and Transamerica Pyramid from atop a slender art deco skyscraper. Take the elevator to level 15.

**Orchard Garden Hotel** (Map p88; 466 Bush St; ⊙7am-9pm) Green space above the Chinatown Gate, with south-facing, big-sky Downtown views.

**Fairmont Hotel** (Map p88; 950 Mason St; ⊙24hr) Traverse the lobby toward the Pavilion Room, then out glass doors to a deliciously kitsch rooftop courtyard – our favorite.

midnight Mon-Fri, 8:30pm-2am Sat; MClay & Montgomery Sts) In the days of the Barbary Coast, the 150-year-old building that houses the Aventine fronted on the bay, and you can still see saltwater marks on the brick walls in the parlor downstairs. But the main action happens upstairs, where the high ceilings, brick-walled space and creative reuse of wood lends a vintage vibe and bartenders whip up bourbon and Scotch cocktails in the old-new fashion. The place packs for happy hour, from 3pm to 7pm Monday to Friday.

**Bix**  Bar
Map p87 (☎415-433-6300; www.bixrestaurant .com; 56 Gold St; MPacific Av & Montgomery St) Down a little alleyway at Jackson Square, Bix evokes 1930s supper clubs, with mahogany paneling and white-jacketed barmen shaking cocktails. This was one of the bars that jump-started the martini craze of the 1990s, and it's as swank as ever. The restaurant is solid, but the bar is great, with nightly live piano and some-times a jazz trio. Look sharp and swagger.

# Civic Center & the Tenderloin

### Edinburgh Castle  Bar
Map p92 (☎415-885-4074; www.castlenews .com; 950 Geary St; MGeary & Polk Sts) SF's finest old-school monument to drink comes complete with dart boards, pool tables, rock bands, occasional literary readings and locals acting out (as is their habit). Photos of bagpipers, the *Train-spotting* soundtrack on the jukebox and a service delivering vinegary fish and chips in newspaper are all the Scottish authen-ticity you could ask for, short of haggis.

### Lush Lounge  Bar
Map p92 (☎415-771-2022; www.thelushlounge sf.com; 1221 Polk St; MPolk & Post Sts) Snag a wooden table by the steel-front fireplace and order anything in stemware – martinis are the specialty (15 different varieties) at this industrial-cool bar, but we also recommend the lemon drops and cosmos. Lush Lounge marks the line on Polk St where grit ends and hip begins. Ideal for couples and small groups of all sexual persuasions.

### Rickshaw Stop
Nightclub

Map p92 ( ☎ 415-861-2011; www.rickshawstop
.com; 155 Fell St; admission $5-35; ⏱6pm-2am
Wed-Sat) DIY-looking, red-velvet curtains
line the black-box walls of this former TV
studio, which hosts a changing lineup
that appeals to alterna-20-somethings
who style life on a shoestring. Thursday's
Popscene (18 plus) is always happening.
Other nights range from Bollywood to
lesbian. Check the calendar online.

### Bourbon & Branch
Speakeasy

Psst – keep a secret? Speakeasies, those
Prohibition-era underground gin joints,
still exist in SF. We're not telling how, but
once you've found the phone number or
website for Bourbon & Branch, you can
make a reservation to get the location (an
unmarked door in the Tenderloin) and
password for entry. Inside, studded leather
banquettes, mirrored oak tables and red-
velvet walls evoke the roaring 1920s. The
original speakeasy basement – complete
with bullet holes and secret escape
routes – and the room hidden behind the
fake bookcase are perfect for superprivate
parties. Keep it under your hat.

## ⭐ Entertainment

### San Francisco Symphony
Live Music

Map p92 ( ☎ 415-864-6000; www.sfsymphony
.org; tickets $30-125; Davies Symphony Hall, 201
Van Ness Ave; Ⓜ Van Ness Ave) The SF Symphony often wins Grammys, thanks to
celebrity-conductor and musical director
Michael Tilson Thomas, the world's fore-
most Mahler impresario. When he's not
on the podium, other famous conductors
take the baton. The best sound is in the
cheap seats in the center terrace, but the
loge is most comfy and glam, and it has
the best sight lines. Call the **rush-ticket
hotline** ( ☎ 415-503-5577) after 6:30pm
to find out whether the box office has
released $20 next-day tickets.

**Left:** Opera House interior; **Below:** The Kopecky Family Band, Rickshaw Stop
(LEFT) RICK GERHARTER/LONELY PLANET IMAGES ©; (BELOW) TIM MOSENFELDER/GETTY IMAGES ©

### San Francisco Opera
Live Music

Map p92 ( ☎ 415-864-3330; www.sfopera
.com; War Memorial Opera House, 301 Van Ness
Ave; tickets $10-350; Ⓜ Van Ness Ave) The gor-
geous 1932 hall is cavernous and echoey,
but there's no more glamorous seat
in SF than the velvet-curtained boxes,
complete with champagne service. The
best midrange seats for sight lines and
sound are in the front section of the dress
circle. Or you can hang in the back of the
hall alongside die-hard opera buffs with
standing-room-only tickets.

### Café Royale
Lounge

Map p92 ( ☎ 415-441-4099; www.caferoyale-sf
.com; 800 Post St; admission free; ☺3pm-
midnight Sun-Thu, to 2am Fri & Sat; Ⓜ Post &
Leavenworth Sts) A Parisian tiled floor and
semicircular fainting couches lend atmosphere and acoustics to this artsy-cool
lounge, which hosts live jazz, film screen-
ings, theatrical presentations, readings
by local writers and sometimes even belly
dancing.

### Rrazz Room
Live Music

Map p88 ( ☎ 415-394-1189; www.therrazzroom
.com; 222 Mason St; tickets from $30; Ⓜ &
Ⓡ Powell St; Ⓡ Powell-Mason, Powell-Hyde)
The city's premier cabaret theater hosts
a variety of jazz, pop and comedy acts,
ranging from Broadway divas like Betty
Buckley and Pia Zadora to local celebs
like Connie Champagne and Wesla Whit-
field. Great for a night on the town.

### Starlight Room
Live Music

Map p88 ( ☎ 415-395-8595; www.harrydenton
.com; 21st fl, 450 Powell St; cover varies, often
free; ☺8:30pm-2am Tue-Sat; Ⓜ & Ⓡ Powell St;
Ⓡ Powell-Mason, Powell-Hyde) Views are
mesmerizing from the 21st floor of the
Sir Francis Drake Hotel, where khaki-clad
tourists let down their hair and dance
to live bands on weekends and DJs on
weekdays. On Sundays, there's a kooky
drag-show brunch (make reservations).

97

### Punch Line
Comedy

Map p87 (📞415-397-4337; www.punchline comedyclub.com; 444 Battery St; admission $12-23 plus 2-drink minimum; ⏰shows 8pm Tue-Thu, Sun, 8pm & 10pm Fri & Sat; 🅼 & 🆁Embarcadero) Known for launching promising talent (think Robin Williams, Chris Rock, Ellen DeGeneres and David Cross), this historic stand-up venue is small enough for you to see into performers' eyes.

# 🔒 Shopping

### Westfield San Francisco Centre
Department Store

Map p88 (www.westfield.com/sanfrancisco; 865 Market St; ⏰most shops 10am-8:30pm Mon-Sat, 11am-7pm Sun; 👶; 🅼 & 🆁Powell St; 🆁Powell-Mason, Powell-Hyde) This glittering tribute to commercialism is about as aesthetically pleasing as a mall can be, with natural light supplied by an enormous glass dome that has sat atop the building for more than 100 years. Anchored by Bloomingdale's and Nordstrom, the mall includes 400 stores – mostly chains – plus a movie theater. The basement food court has better dining options than most small towns.

### H&M
Clothing, Accessories

Map p88 (www.hm.com; 150 Powell St; 🅼 & 🆁Powell St; 🆁Powell-Mason, Powell-Hyde) What IKEA is to home furnishing, H&M is to fashion: suspiciously affordable, perpetually crowded, not really made for the long haul and perfect for parties. With limited-edition runs and special collections by designers like splashy British colorist Matthew Williamson (and lesser ones like, oof, Madonna) you won't have to worry that your closet looks exactly like everyone else's – unless you bought it at IKEA.

### Original Levi's Store
Clothing, Accessories

Map p88 (📞415-501-0100; www.us.levi.com; 300 Post St; 🅼 & 🆁Powell St; 🆁Powell-Mason, Powell-Hyde) The flagship store in Levi Strauss' hometown sells classic jeans that fit without fail, plus limited-edition pairs made of tough Japanese selvage and eco-organic cotton denim. Start with the impressive discount racks (30% to

Westfield San Francisco Centre

# Quick Bites while Shopping

A few of our favorite places to recharge between boutiques:

**Emporio Rulli** (Map p88; ☎415-433-1122; www.rulli.com; Union Sq; ⏰7:30am-7:30pm; Ⓜ & Ⓡ Powell St) Artisanal Italian pastries, powerful espresso and prosciutto sandwiches at outdoor tables in Union Square.

**Mocca on Maiden Lane** (Map p88; ☎415-956-1188; 175 Maiden Lane; ⏰8am-6pm Mon-Fri, 8:30am-4pm Sat; Ⓜ & Ⓡ Powell St) Order steak sandwiches, seafood salads and cheesecake inside, then carry outside to umbrella tables in a chic pedestrian alley. Cash only.

**Rotunda** (Map p88; ☎415-362-4777; www.neimanmarcus.com; 150 Stockton St; ⏰11am-5pm Mon-Sat; Ⓜ & Ⓡ Powell St) Favored by ladies in Chanel suits, who come for lobster club sandwiches and proper afternoon tea beneath the gorgeous stained-glass dome at Neiman Marcus.

**Bio** (Map p88; ☎415-362-0255; 75 O'Farrell St; ⏰8am-6pm; Ⓜ & Ⓡ Powell St) Healthful sandwiches, vegan salads, gluten-free quiches and multiple varieties of kombucha, but no seating (picnic at Union Square).

60% off), but don't hold out for sales. They'll hem your jeans for $10.

## Barneys
Department Store

Map p88 (www.barneys.com; 77 O'Farrell St; Ⓜ & Ⓡ Powell St; ᗡ Powell-Mason, Powell-Hyde) The high-end New York fashion staple known for its inspired window displays and up-to-70%-off sales has hit the West Coast. Barneys showcases emerging designers; well-priced, well-fitted sportswear on its co-op label; and exclusive ecoconscious lines by Philip Lim, Theory and its own affordable Green Label, focusing on clean lines with a clean conscience.

## Eden & Eden
Boutique

Map p87 (www.edenandeden.com; 560 Jackson St; Ⓜ Kearny St) Detour from reality at Eden & Eden, a Dadaist design boutique, where anchors float on silk dresses, clouds rain on pillows, architectural blueprints serve as placemats and Ozzy Osbourne has been transformed into a stuffed mouse wearing bat wings. Prices are surprisingly down to earth for far-out, limited-edition finds from local and international designers.

# North Beach & Chinatown

**Two historic neighborhoods – one Italian, one Chinese – come together here.** Once the land of the Beat poets, North Beach still embraces a bohemian lifestyle reflected in its sidewalk cafes and dimly lit bars, many of which were frequented by Jack Kerouac himself. The Beat Museum and City Lights are stops on many a Beat pilgrimage.

Staircases and garden-lined boardwalks up steep Telegraph Hill yield great rewards that include historic murals, 360-degree views from Coit Tower and a flock of wild parrots that makes the hill their home.

On the main streets of Chinatown, dumplings and rare teas are served under pagoda roofs; in its historic back alleys you'll find temple incense, mah-jong-tile clatter and distant echoes of revolution. The annual lunar new year parade is the largest outside of Asia, and the streets are filled with dancing lions, gold-and-red dragons and exploding firecrackers.

Grant Ave, Chinatown (p111)

# North Beach & Chinatown Highlights

## North Beach Cafes (p118)

To experience North Beach properly, don't charge through it with an agenda and a timetable. Slow your sightseeing to a leisurely pace and linger over an afternoon cappuccino at one of North Beach's many neighborhood cafes. You'll be following in the footsteps of decades of Beatniks, bohemians, poets and dreamers – all of whom would surely approve if afternoon coffee turned into evening cocktails. Caffe Trieste (p118)

## City Lights (p121)

Unlike its namesake – a Charlie Chaplin movie shot in San Francisco – this bookstore just wouldn't stay silent. After his arrest for 'willfully and lewdly' publishing Allen Ginsberg's epic *Howl and Other Poems*, founder and Beat poet Lawrence Ferlinghetti fought the law and won the right to free speech. These three floors are a literary landmark, creatively organized into sections such as Muckraking and Stolen Continents.

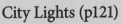

DIANA MAYFIELD/LONELY PLANET IMAGES ©

### Coit Tower (p107)

**3**

Coit Tower, eccentric monument, showcases the historic WPA murals lining the lobby. For decades after their completion, the murals and the 25 artists who worked on them were denounced as communist. But the accusations backfired: for the controversy they ignited as well as the artistic effort involved, the murals and tower have been embraced by SF as a beloved landmark. Coit Tower, designed by Arthur Brown Jr and Henry Howard

**4**

### Grant Ave (p113)

It's hard to picture how this cheerfully inauthentic attraction looked a century ago when it was notorious, brothel-lined Dupont St. In the 1920s, Chinatown merchants built pagoda-topped buildings to attract curiosity seekers and souvenir shoppers – and their plan worked like a charm. Start at the Dragon's Gate at Grant Ave and Bush St, duck into historic alleyways and be sure to stop for dim sum. Li Po (p119)

**5**

### Telegraph Hill & Filbert St Steps (p107)

In the 19th century, a ruthless entrepreneur began quarrying Telegraph Hill and blasting away roads – much to the distress of his neighbors – and the Filbert St Steps became the main uphill route. City Hall eventually stopped the quarrying, but the view from the boardwalk is still (wait for it) dynamite. As an added bonus, you'll get your cardio in for the day.

# North Beach & Chinatown Walk

*Poetry is in the air and on the sidewalk on this literary tour of North Beach. You'll want at least a couple of hours to see the neighborhood as On the Road author Jack Kerouac did – with drinks at the beginning, middle and end.*

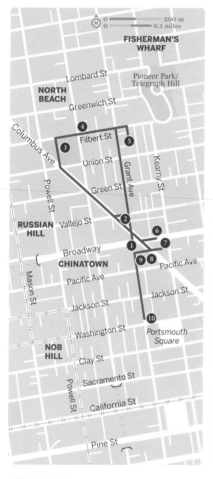

### WALK FACTS
- **Start** City Lights
- **Finish** Li Po
- **Distance** 1.5 miles
- **Duration** Two hours

### ❶ City Lights

At one of the most famous bookstores (p121) in the US, the home of Beat poetry and free speech, pick up something to inspire your journey into the heart of literary North Beach – Lawrence Ferlinghetti's *San Francisco Poems* is a good bet. Take a load off in the **Poet's Chair**.

### ❷ Caffe Trieste

Order a potent espresso, check out the opera on the jukebox and slide into the back booth where Francis Ford Coppola allegedly wrote his first draft of *The Godfather*. This place (p118) has been beloved since 1956, with the local characters and bathroom-wall poetry to prove it.

### ❸ Washington Square

Pause to admire parrots in the treetops and octogenarians' smooth tai chi moves below: pure poetry in motion. **Saints Peter & Paul Church** (p110) – backdrop of Marilyn Monroe and Joe DiMaggio's wedding photos, and star of the movie *Sister Act* – sits on the northern edge.

### ❹ Liguria Bakery

Focaccia hot from a 100-year-old oven makes a worthy pit stop (p116) for ravenous readers – though you might have to hustle a little: they close at 1pm and often run out long before that.

### ❺ Bob Kaufman Alley

This quiet alley (p111) was renamed for the legendary street-corner poet, who broke a 12-year vow of silence when he walked into a North Beach cafe and recited his poem 'All Those Ships That Never Sailed': 'Today I

bring them back/Huge and transitory/And let them sail/Forever.'

### 6 Beat Museum

Don't be surprised to hear a Dylan jam session by the front door or see Allen Ginsberg naked in documentary footage screened inside the museum (p106): the Beat goes on here in rare form.

### 7 Specs'

Dimly lit and tucked away in an alley, there's something that feels a little illicit about **Specs' Twelve Adler Museum Cafe** (p118). What better place to begin the bar crawl portion of your walk, amid merchant-marine memorabilia, choice words worthy of a sailor and a glass of Anchor Steam beer.

### 8 Vesuvio

Over the past 60-plus years, this former Beat haunt (p119) has earned its colorful atmosphere. Jack Kerouac once blew off Henry Miller to go on a bender here; try the house brew and see if you have the will to continue this walking tour...

### 9 Jack Kerouac Alley

It's poetic justice that this mural-covered byway (p106) is named for the Beat Generation's most famous author. Not only are his words from *On the Road* embedded in the alley, this is where he was tossed after a raucous night at **Vesuvio** (p119).

### 10 Li Po

Follow the literary lead of Kerouac and Ginsberg and end your night in a vinyl booth at **Li Po** (p119), with another beer beneath the gold Buddha's forgiving gaze.

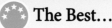 The Best...

#### PLACES TO EAT

**Jai Yun** No menu, just whatever's fresh. (p119)

**City View** Get your dim sum fix. (p117)

**Ristorante Ideale** Look no further for authentic Italian. (p115)

**Molinari** Step up to the counter for old-school sandwiches. (p116)

#### PLACES TO DRINK

**Specs'** Part bar, part museum. (p118)

**Caffe Trieste** North Beach's cafe of choice. (p118)

**Comstock Saloon** A holdover from the Barbary Coast. (p118)

**Tosca Cafe** Sip drinks to the tune of jukebox opera. (p118)

#### PLACES FOR ARTISTIC INSPIRATION

**City Lights** A true Beat-poet bookstore. (p121)

**Bob Kaufman Alley** Pay tribute to a silenced spoken-word artist. (p111)

**Li Po** Chinatown bar and former Beat-poet haunt. (p119)

**Jack Kerouac Alley** A pedestrian way inscribed with Kerouac's poetry. (p106)

Li Po (p119)

# Discover North Beach & Chinatown

## 🔄 Getting There & Away

○ **Bus** The key routes passing through Downtown, Chinatown and North Beach are 1, 30, 41 and 45.

○ **Cable car** From Downtown or the Wharf, take the Powell-Mason and Powell-Hyde lines through Chinatown and North Beach. The California St cable car passes through the southern end of Chinatown.

## ◎ Sights

Standing atop the Filbert St Steps, you can understand what Italian fishermen, Beat poets and wild parrots saw in North Beach: tough climbs and giddy vistas, a place with more sky than ground, an area that was civilized but never entirely tamed. Across Columbus Ave is Chinatown, survivor of gold booms and busts, anti-Chinese riots and bootlegging wars, and trials by fire and earthquake. Yet Chinatown repeatedly made history, providing labor for America's first cross-country railroad, creating original Chinatown deco architecture and leading the charge for civil rights.

### North Beach

**Jack Kerouac Alley**    Street
Map p108 (btwn Grant & Columbus Aves; M Columbus Ave) Fans of *On the Road* and *Dharma Bums* will appreciate how fitting it is that Kerouac's namesake alleyway offers a poetic and slightly seedy shortcut between Chinatown and North Beach via favorite Kerouac haunts City Lights (p121) and Vesuvio (p119). Kerouac took his books, Buddhism and drink to heart.

**Beat Museum**    Museum
Map p108 ( 📞 800-537-6822; www.thebeat museum.org; 540 Broadway; admission $5; 🕙10am-7pm Tue-Sun; M Columbus Ave) The Beat goes on and on – OK, so it rambles a little – at this truly obsessive collection of SF literary-scene ephemera c 1950–69. The banned edition of Allen Ginsberg's *Howl* is the ultimate free-speech trophy,

Jack Kerouac Alley
RICHARD CUMMINS/LONELY PLANET IMAGES ©

KRIS DAVIDSON/LONELY PLANET IMAGES ©

## Don't Miss
# Coit Tower & Telegraph Hill

The exclamation point on San Francisco's skyline is Coit Tower, which punctuates the pinnacle of North Beach's Telegraph Hill. The stark white deco shaft was built in 1933 with funds bequeathed by eccentric heiress Lillie Hancock Coit, who left a third of her estate 'for the purpose of adding to the beauty of the city which I have always loved.'

The main route up Telegraph Hill is the **Filbert St Steps** (Map p108). The climb is steep, but it leads past sculpture gardens, hidden cottages along a wooden boardwalk called **Napier Lane** and colorful wild parrot flocks that have claimed the trees of Telegraph Hill. When you reach the top, you're rewarded with sweeping views of the city and the bay. Still not bird's-eye enough for you? Take the elevator up to the tower's panoramic open-air platform, 210ft above San Francisco.

In addition to the views, Coit Tower is known for its colorful, provocative 1930s Works Progress Administration (WPA) murals that are grounded in the realities of California's Great Depression. The murals show San Franciscans at work and play, lining up at soup kitchens and organizing dockworkers' unions, partying despite Prohibition and reading library books in Chinese, Italian and English. If the murals in the rotunda leave you wanting more, you can find more hidden inside the stairwell by taking the free tour at 11am on Saturdays.

### NEED TO KNOW
Map p108; Telegraph Hill Blvd; adult/child $4.50/2; ⊙10am-6pm; **M**39

and the 1961 check for $10.08 that Jack Kerouac wrote to a liquor store has a certain dark humor, but those Kerouac bobblehead dolls are the real headshakers.

Enter the museum through a turnstile at the back of the museum store, grab a ramshackle reclaimed theater seat, redolent with the accumulated odors

# North Beach & Chinatown

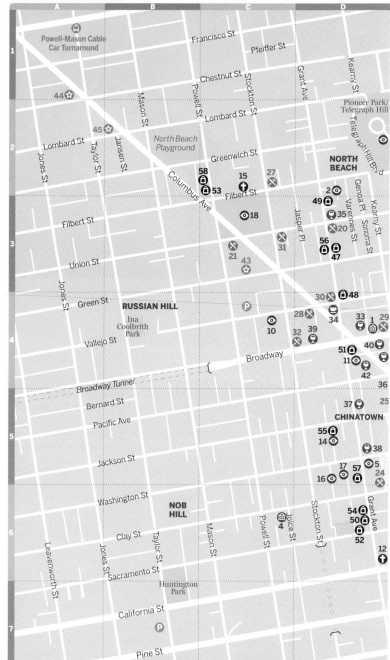

NORTH BEACH & CHINATOWN SIGHTS

of poets, pot and pets, and watch fascinating films about the Beat era's leading musicians, artists, writers, politicos and indefinable characters. Upstairs there are shrines to individual Beats with firsthand remembrances and artifacts, including first editions of books that expanded the US outlook to include the margins. Downstairs in the museum store you can buy poetry chapbooks and obscure Beat titles you won't find elsewhere.

### Columbus Tower  Historical Building

**Map p108 (916 Kearny St; M Kearny St)** Like most SF landmarks worthy of the title, this one has a seriously checkered career. Built by shady political boss Abe Ruef in 1905, the building was finished just in time to be reduced to its steel skeleton in the 1906 earthquake and fire. The new copper cladding was still shiny in 1907 when not-so-honest Abe was convicted of bribing city supervisors. By the time he emerged bankrupt from San Quentin State Prison, the cupola was oxidizing green.

Towering artistic aspirations found a home here, too. Grammy-winning folk group The Kingston Trio bought the tower in the 1960s, and the Grateful Dead recorded in the basement. Since the 1970s, Columbus Tower has been owned by Francis Ford Coppola, and film history has been made here by Coppola's American Zoetrope filmmaking studio, *The Joy Luck Club* director Wayne Wang and Academy Award–winning actor and director Sean Penn.

### Washington Square  Park

**Map p108 (Columbus Ave & Union St; M Columbus Ave)** Wild parrots, tai chi masters, nonagenarian churchgoing *nonnas* (grandmothers) and Ben Franklin are the company you'll keep on this lively patch of lawn. The parrots keep their distance in the treetops, but like anyone else in North Beach, they can probably be bribed into friendship with a focaccia from Liguria Bakery (p116) on the square's northeast corner.

**109**

# North Beach & Chinatown

## ◎ Top Sights
Coit Tower ............................................. D2

## ◎ Sights
1 Beat Museum .................................... D4
2 Bob Kaufman Alley ......................... D2
3 Chinese Culture Center ................. E5
4 Chinese Historical Society of
   America ........................................... C6
5 Chinese Telephone Exchange ......... D5
6 Columbus Tower ............................... E5
7 Commercial St .................................. E6
8 Dragon's Gate ................................... E7
9 Filbert St Steps ................................ E2
10 Good Luck Parking Garage ............. C4
11 Jack Kerouac Alley ........................... D4
12 Old St Mary's Cathedral ................. D6
13 Portsmouth Square .......................... E5
14 Ross Alley .......................................... D5
15 Saints Peter & Paul Church ............ C2
16 Spofford Alley ................................... D5
17 Tien Hau Temple ............................... D5
18 Washington Square .......................... C3

## ◎ Eating
19 Brioche Bakery ................................. E4
20 Café Jacqueline ................................ D3
21 Cinecittá ........................................... C3
22 City View ........................................... E6
23 Coi ...................................................... E4
24 Golden Star ....................................... D5
25 House of Nanking .............................. E5
26 Jai Yun ............................................... E5
27 Liguria Bakery .................................. C2
28 Molinari .............................................. D4
29 Naked Lunch ...................................... D4
30 Ristorante Ideale .............................. D4

31 Tony's Coal-Fired Pizza &
   Slice House ...................................... C3
32 Yuet Lee ............................................. D4

## ◎ Drinking & Nightlife
33 15 Romolo .......................................... D4
34 Caffe Trieste ..................................... D4
35 Church Key ........................................ D3
36 Comstock Saloon ............................. E4
37 EZ5 ...................................................... D5
38 Li Po .................................................... D5
39 Rosewood ........................................... D4
40 Specs' ................................................. D4
41 Tosca Cafe ........................................ D4
42 Vesuvio ............................................... D4

## ◎ Entertainment
43 Beach Blanket Babylon .................... C3
44 Bimbo's 365 Club ............................. A1
45 Cobb's Comedy Club ........................ B2
46 Purple Onion ..................................... E4

## ◎ Shopping
47 101 Music ........................................... D3
48 Al's Attire ......................................... D4
49 Aria ..................................................... D3
50 Chinatown Kite Shop ....................... D6
51 City Lights ......................................... D4
52 Clarion Music Center ...................... D6
53 Double Punch .................................... C2
54 Far East Flea Market ....................... D6
55 Golden Gate Fortune
   Cookie Company ............................. D5
56 Lola of North Beach ......................... D3
57 Red Blossom Tea Company ............. D5
58 Rock Posters &
   Collectibles ..................................... C2

The 1897 statue of Ben Franklin is a non sequitur, and the taps below his feet falsely advertise mineral water from Vichy, France. This is yet another example of a puzzling public artwork courtesy of a certifiable SF eccentric, Henry D Cogswell, who made his fortune fitting miners with gold fillings.

## Saints Peter & Paul Church
Church

Map p108 ( ☎415-421-0809; www.stspeterpaul.san-francisco.ca.us; 666 Filbert St; ⊙7:30am-4pm; M Columbus Ave) Wedding cake was the apparent inspiration for this 1924 triple-decker cathedral with its lacy white towers, and in its downtime among Catholic masses in Italian, Chinese and Spanish, the church pulls a triple wedding shift on Saturdays. Joe DiMaggio and Marilyn Monroe had their wedding photos taken here, though they weren't permitted to marry in the church because both had been divorced (they got hitched at City Hall instead).

True to North Beach literary form, there's poetry by Dante in a glittering mosaic inscription over the grand triple entryway that brings to mind Beat poets and Beatles alike: 'The glory of Him who

## Detour:
# Bob Kaufman Alley

What, you mean your hometown doesn't have a street named after an African American Catholic Jewish voodoo anarchist Beat poet who refused to speak for 12 years? The man revered in France as the 'American Rimbaud,' and who helped found the legendary *Beatitudes* magazine in 1959, was a major poet and spoken-word bebop jazz artist. Kaufman was never at a loss for words, yet he felt compelled to take a Buddhist vow of silence after John F Kennedy's assassination, which he kept until the end of the Vietnam War.

Kaufman's life was hardly pure poetry: he was a teenage runaway, periodically found himself homeless, was occasionally jailed for picking fights in rhyme with police, battled methamphetamine addiction with varying success and once claimed that his goal was to be forgotten. Like the man himself, the hidden **Bob Kaufman Alley** (Map p108; off Grant Ave near Filbert St; M Columbus Ave) is offbeat, streetwise and often profoundly silent.

moves all things/Penetrates and glows throughout the universe.'

# Chinatown

### Chinese Culture Center   Art Gallery
Map p108 ( 415-986-1822; www.c-c-c.org; 3rd fl, Hilton Hotel, 750 Kearny St; gallery admission free, donation requested, tours adult/child $30/25; 10am-4pm Tue-Sat; M Kearny St) You can see all the way to China on the 3rd floor of the Hilton inside this cultural center, which hosts exhibits of traditional Chinese arts, including China's leading brush-painters; Xian Rui (Fresh & Sharp) cutting-edge art installations, recently featuring Stella Zhang's ethereal indoor sails and discomfiting toothpick-studded pillows; and a new Art at Night series showcasing Chinese-inspired art, jazz and food. In odd-numbered years, don't miss the Present Tense Biennial, where 30-plus Bay Area artists are invited to give their personal takes on Chinese culture.

For more firsthand experiences of Chinese culture, check the center's schedule for upcoming concerts, hands-on arts workshops for adults and children, Mandarin classes, genealogy services, arts festivals in Chinatown's historic alleyways and Chinatown Heritage Walking Tours.

### Chinese Historical Society of America   Museum
Map p108 (CHSA; 415-391-1188; www.chsa .org; 965 Clay St; adult/child $5/2, 1st Thu of month free; noon-5pm Tue-Fri, 11am-4pm Sat; M Stockton St; California St) Picture what it was like to be Chinese in America during the Gold Rush, the transcontinental railroad construction or the Beat heyday at the nation's largest Chinese American historical institute. Intimate vintage photos, an 1880 temple altar and Francis Wong's mesmerizing miniatures of Chinatown landmarks are seen alongside the Daniel KE Ching collection of thousands of vintage advertisements, toys and postcards conveying Chinese stereotypes. Sleuthing by CHSA historians continues to uncover lost and neglected artifacts, including Jake Lee's fascinating watercolors of Chinese American history, painted in the 1960s for a Chinatown restaurant.

Rotating art and history exhibits are across the courtyard in CHSA's graceful red-brick, green-tile-roofed landmark building. This was built as Chinatown's YWCA in 1932 by Julia Morgan, one of California's first female architects and the chief architect of Hearst Castle. Check CHSA's website for openings and events, including the ever-popular **Chinatown Food Walking Tours**.

### Portsmouth Square   Park

Map p108 (733 Kearny St; **M** Kearny St; 🚋 California St) Since apartments in Chinatown's narrow brick buildings are small, Portsmouth Square is the neighborhood's living room. The square is named after John B Montgomery's sloop, which pulled up near here in 1846 to stake the US claim on San Francisco. Bronze plaques and monuments dot the perimeter of the historic square, and a monument bearing a ship with golden sails is dedicated to adventure author Robert Louis Stevenson, who found inspiration here c 1879. But the presiding deity at this park is the Goddess of Democracy, a bronze replica of the statue made by Tiananmen Square protesters in 1989.

First light is met with outstretched arms by tai chi practitioners. By afternoon toddlers rush the playground slides and tea crowds collect at the kiosk under the pedestrian bridge to joke and dissect the day's news. The checkers and chess played on concrete tables in gazebos late into the evening aren't mere games, but

365-day obsessions, come rain or shine. Chinese New Year brings a night market to the square, featuring Chinese opera, calligraphy demonstrations and cell-phone charms of the goddess Guan Yin (for better reception).

### Old St Mary's Cathedral   Church

Map p108 ( 🕿 415-288-3800; www.oldsaintmarys .org; 660 California St; 🕙 11am-6pm Mon-Tue, to 7pm Wed-Fri, 9am-6:30pm Sat, to 4:30pm Sun; **M** Stockton St; 🚋 California St) Many thought it a lost cause, but California's first cathedral, inaugurated in 1854, tried for decades to give San Francisco some religion – despite its location in brothel central. Hence the stern admonition on the church's clock tower: 'Son, observe the time and fly from evil.'

Eventually the archdiocese abandoned attempts to convert Dupont St whoremongers and handed the church over to America's first Chinese community mission, run by the activism-oriented Paulists. During WWII, the church served 450,000 members

**Left:** City Lights (p121); **Below:** Chinatown souvenir

of the US armed services as a recreation center and cafeteria. The walls of the church miraculously withstood the 1906 earthquake and fire, which destroyed one of the district's biggest bordellos directly across the street, making room for St Mary's Sq. Today, skateboarders do tricks of a different sort in the park, under the watchful eye of Beniamino Bufano's 1929 pink-granite-and-steel statue of Chinese revolutionary Sun Yat-sen.

### Chinese Telephone Exchange
Historical Building

Map p108 (743 Washington St; Ⓜ Stockton St; 🚋 California St) California's earliest adopters of advanced technology weren't in Silicon Valley but right here in Chinatown. This triple-decker tiled pagoda caused a sensation in 1894, not for its looks but its smarts. To connect callers to the right person, switchboard operators had to speak fluent English and five Chinese dialects, as well as memorize at least 1500 Chinatown residents by name, residence and occupation. The switchboard was open 365 days a year, and the manager and assistant managers lived on site.

Since anyone born in China was prohibited by law from visiting San Francisco throughout the 1882–1943 Chinese Exclusion era, this switchboard was the main means of contact with family and business partners in China for 60 years. The exchange operated until 1949, and the landmark was bought and restored by Bank of Canton in 1960.

### Dragon's Gate
Monument

Map p108 (intersection of Grant Ave & Bush St; Ⓜ Stockton St; 🚋 California St) Enter the Dragon archway and you'll find yourself on the once-notorious street known as Dupont in its red-light heyday. Sixty years before the family-friendly overhaul of the Las Vegas Strip, Look Tin Eli and a group of forward-thinking Chinatown businessmen pioneered the approach here in

**113**

RICK GERHARTER/LONELY PLANET IMAGES ©

## ✓ Don't Miss
# Chinatown Alleyways

Forty-one historic alleyways packed into Chinatown's 22 blocks have seen it all since 1849: gold rushes and revolution, incense and opium, fire and icy receptions. These narrow backstreets are lined with towering buildings because there was nowhere to go but up in Chinatown after 1870, when laws limited Chinese immigration, employment and housing.

Off Sacramento St on Waverly Pl are the flag-festooned balconies of Chinatown's historic temples, where services have been held since 1852 – even in 1906 while the altar was still smoldering at **Tien Hau Temple** (125 Waverly Pl; ⊙hours vary).

As sunset falls on nearby **Spofford Alley**, you'll hear clicking mah jong tiles and a Chinese orchestra warming up. But generations ago, you might have overheard Sun Yat-sen and his conspirators at number 36 plotting the 1911 overthrow of China's last dynasty.

A block north, **Ross Alley** (pictured above) was known as Mexico, Spanish and Manila St after the women who staffed its notorious back-parlor brothels. Colorful characters now fill alleyway murals, and anyone can make a fortune the easy way at **Golden Gate Fortune Cookie Company**.

Across Portsmouth Square from San Francisco's City Hall is **Commercial St**, a euphemistically named hot spot that caught fire in 1906. The city banned Commercial St's 25¢ Chinese brothels in favor of 'parlor houses,' where basic services were raised to $3 and watching cost $10.

### NEED TO KNOW

Map p108; btwn Grant Ave & Stockton St, California St & Broadway; Ⓜ Stockton St; 🚋 Powell St, California St

# Chinatown Heritage Walking Tours

Local-led, kid-friendly **Chinatown Heritage Walking Tours** (☎415-986-1822; www.c-c-c.org; adult/child $30/25; ⏰10am, noon & 2pm Tue-Sat) guide visitors through the living history and mythology of Chinatown in two hours, winding through backstreets to key historic sights: Golden Gate Fortune Cookie Company, Tien Hau Temple and Portsmouth Square. All proceeds support Chinatown community programming at the Chinese Culture Center; bookings can be made online or by phone. Groups of four or more should book two days in advance.

Chinatown, replacing seedy attractions with more tourist-friendly ones.

After consultation with architects and community groups, Dupont St was transformed into Grant Ave, with deco-chinoiserie dragon lamps and tiled pagoda rooftops, and police were reluctantly persuaded to enforce the 1914 Red Light Abatement Act in Chinatown. By the time this gate was donated by Taiwan in 1970, grandly proclaiming that 'everything in the world is in just proportions,' Chinatown finally had a main street that did the community greater justice.

### Good Luck Parking Garage
Landmark

Map p108 (735 Vallejo St; Ⓜ Stockton St; 🚃 Mason St) Each parking spot at this garage comes with fortune-cookie wisdom stenciled onto the asphalt: 'The time is right to make new friends' or 'Stop searching forever – happiness is right next to you.' These omens are brought to you by artist Harrell Fletcher and co-conspirator Jon Rubin, who also gathered the vintage photographs of the Chinese and Italian ancestors of local residents

that grace the entry tiles like heraldic emblems.

## 🍴 Eating

When choosing an Italian restaurant in North Beach, use this rule of thumb: if a host has to lure you inside with 'Ciao, bella!,' keep walking. Try smaller neighborhood restaurants on side streets off Grant Ave and Washington St, where staff gossip in Italian. Ignore menus in Chinatown, where the best dishes are loaded onto dim sum carts or listed in Chinese. Try dim sum places along Stockton St, and wander off Grant Ave to find basement eateries long beloved by starving artists, including Jack Kerouac and Allen Ginsberg.

## North Beach

### Coi
Californian $$$

Map p108 (☎415-393-9000; www.coirestaurant.com; 373 Broadway; set menu $145; ⏰5:30-10pm Wed-Sat; Ⓜ Columbus Ave) Chef Daniel Patterson's wildly inventive, 11-course menu is a Hwy 1 road trip, all unexpected curves and giddy heights. With skillful handling, California's specialty produce wows at every turn – especially black-and-green noodles made from Manilla clams and seaweed. Wild foods top it all: purple ice-plant petals are strewn atop warm duck's tongue, and wild abalone makes a positively salacious salad course. With a wink at the Broadway strip joint next door, Coi's interior seems borrowed from a '70s Big Sur nudist colony, with shaggy cushions, grass-cloth walls, terrariums and framed moss – but the seasonal flavors and intriguing wine pairings ($95; generous enough for two to share) will have you living for the moment.

### Ristorante Ideale
Italian $$

Map p108 (☎415-391-4129; 1315 Grant Ave; pasta $11-18; ⏰5:30-10:30pm Mon-Sat, 5-10pm Sun; Ⓜ Columbus Ave) Italian regulars are stunned that a restaurant this authentic borders the Pacific, with Roman chef Maurizio Bruschi's *bucatini ammatriciana*

# North Beach Parking

Wild hawks and parrots circle above North Beach as though looking for a parking spot. The weekend parking situation is so dire that locals tend to avoid North Beach and Chinatown – forgetting there's public parking underneath Portsmouth Square. You may also luck into a spot at Good Luck Parking Garage, where bays are stenciled with fortune-cookie wisdom: 'You are not a has-been.'

(Roman tube pasta with savory tomato-pancetta-pecorino sauce) served properly al dente. There's also ravioli and ricotta gnocchi made by hand in-house, and a well-priced selection of robust Italian wines served by wisecracking Tuscan waitstaff. Portions are lavishly American, but seafood and meat preparations remain strictly Italian to highlight freshness and flavors released in cooking – unlike North Beach's many sundried-tomato-pesto-on-everything imposters.

### Liguria Bakery                    Bakery $
Map p108 ( ☎415-421-3786; 1700 Stockton St; focaccia $2-4; ⏰8am-1pm Mon-Fri, from 7am Sat & Sun; Ⓜ Columbus Ave; 🚊 Mason St) Bleary-eyed art students and Italian grandmothers are in line by 8am for the cinnamon-raisin focaccia hot out of the 100-year-old oven, leaving 9am dawdlers a choice of tomato or classic rosemary and 11am stragglers out of luck. Take what you can get, and don't kid yourself that you're going to save it for lunch.

### Café Jacqueline          French $$$
Map p108 ( ☎415-981-5565; 1454 Grant Ave; soufflés $16-25; ⏰5:30-11pm Wed-Sun; Ⓜ Columbus Ave) The secret terror of top chefs is the classic French soufflé: only when the ingredients are in golden-mean proportions, whipped into perfect peaks, baked at the right temperature and removed from the oven not a second too early or late will a soufflé rise to the occasion. Chef Jacqueline's soufflés float across the tongue like fog over the Golden Gate Bridge, and with the right person across the tiny wooden table to share that seafood soufflé, dinner could hardly get more romantic – until you order the chocolate for dessert.

### Cinecittá                          Pizza $
Map p108 ( ☎415-291-8830; 663 Union St; pizzas $9-15; ⏰noon-10pm Sun-Thu, to 11pm Fri & Sat; 🖋🚻; Ⓜ Columbus Ave; 🚊 Mason St) That tantalizing aroma you followed into this 22-seat eatery is thin-crust Roman pizza, probably the ever-popular Travestere (fresh mozzarella, arugula and prosciutto), served with sass by Roman owner Romina. Vegetarians prefer the Funghi Selvatici, with wild mushrooms, zucchini and sun-dried tomato, but that saliva-prompting aroma that elicits exclamations from Italian regulars is the O Sole Mio, with capers, olives, mozzarella and anchovies. Go local with drinks – Anchor Steam is on tap or Claudia Springs Zin (bottles are half price on Mondays and Tuesdays) – and save room for housemade tiramisu.

### Brioche Bakery          Bakery, Sandwiches $
Map p108 ( ☎415-765-0412; www.briochecafe .com; 210 Columbus Ave; pastries $2-6; ⏰7am-8pm; 🛜🖋🚻; Ⓜ Columbus Ave) When Gold Rush miners found gold here they treated themselves to 'Frenchy food,' on what was once San Francisco's Barbary Coast. Now you too can start your day striking it rich with flaky cinnamon twists and not-too-sweet pain au chocolat (chocolate croissants). You'll be back later for the decadent North Beach–inspired tartine with prosciutto, pear, and herbed ricotta, drizzled with honey.

### Molinari                              Deli $
Map p108 ( ☎415-421-2337; 373 Columbus Ave; sandwiches $5-8; ⏰9am-5:30pm Mon-Fri, 7:30am-5:30pm Sat; Ⓜ Columbus Ave) Grab a number and a crusty roll, and when your number rolls around, the guys behind the counter will stuff it with translucent

sheets of prosciutto, milky buffalo mozzarella, tender marinated artichokes or slabs of the legendary house-cured salami (the city's best). While you wait, load up on essential Italian groceries for later, like truffle-filled gnocchi, seasoned *pecorino* (sheep's cheese) and aged balsamic vinegar.

### Tony's Coal-Fired Pizza & Slice House
Pizza $

Map p108 ( 📞 415-835-9888; www.tonys pizzanapoletana.com; 1556 Stockton St; slices $4-5; 🕐 noon-11pm Wed-Sun; M Columbus Ave; 🚋 Powell St) Fuggedaboudit: this may be San Francisco, but you can still grab a cheesy, thin-crust slice to go in a New York minute from nine-times-world-champion-pizza-slinger Tony Gemignani. What? You were expecting meatball subs and Kosher saltshakers? Done. Difference here is you can take that slice to sunny Washington Square and watch tai chi practice and wild parrots in the trees year-round. Sorry, Manhattan – whaddayagonnado?

### Naked Lunch
Sandwiches $

Map p108 ( 📞 415-577-4951; www.naked lunchsf.com; 504 Broadway; sandwiches

$8-12; 🕐 11:30am-2pm Tue-Sat; M Columbus Ave; 🚋 Powell St) Unpredictable, utterly decadent cravings worthy of a William S Burroughs novel are satisfied by the ever-changing menu at this lunch stall tucked between XXX entertainment venues. Foie gras, duck prosciutto and black truffle salt are liable to sprawl across a sandwich, keeping company with naughty salty-sweet, artisan-made *chicharrones* (fried pork rinds) and sweet-talking Southern cinnamon iced tea.

# Chinatown

### City View
Dim Sum $

Map p108 ( 📞 415-398-2838; 662 Commercial St; dishes $3-5; 🕐 11am-2:30pm Mon-Fri, 10am-2:30pm Sat & Sun; M Kearny St; 🚋 California St) Dim sum aficionados used to cramped quarters and surly service are wowed by impeccable shrimp-and-leek dumplings, tender asparagus, crisp Peking duck and coconut-dusted custard tarts, all dished up from carts with a flourish in a spacious, sunny room. Try to arrive on the early or late side of lunch, when your server has the time to explain what exactly it is that smells so good in those bamboo steamers.

Molinari

### Yuet Lee
Chinese, Seafood $$

Map p108 (☎415-982-6020; 1300 Stockton St; mains $11-18; ⏱11am-3am Wed-Mon; ⊞; ⓂStockton St; ⓇPowell St) With a radioactive-green paint job and merciless fluorescent lighting, this Chinese seafood diner isn't for first dates – it's for drinking buddies and committed couples who have nothing to hide and are willing to share outstanding batter-dipped, salt-and-pepper calamari and tender roast duck.

### House of Nanking
Chinese $$

Map p108 (☎415-421-1429; 919 Kearny St; mains $9-15; ⏱11am-10pm Mon-Fri, noon-10pm Sat, to 9pm Sun; ⓂKearny St) Meekly suggest an interest in seafood, nothing deep-fried, perhaps some greens, and your brusque server nods, snatches the menu and, within minutes, returns with Shanghai specialties: melt-away scallops, fragrant sautéed pea shoots, garlicky noodles and a tea ball that blossoms in hot water. Expect bossy service, a wait for a shared table and a strict cash-only policy – but also bright, fresh flavors at reasonable prices.

### Golden Star
Vietnamese $

Map p108 (☎415-398-1215; 11 Walter Lum Pl; noodles $5-8; ⏱10am-9pm; ⓂKearny St) Elementary school cafeterias could outclass the Golden Star for atmosphere – but if you know *pho* (Vietnamese noodle soup), this is the place to go. Five-spice chicken *pho* is the house specialty that warms the bones on a foggy day, but on a hot day, branch out and get the *bun* (rice vermicelli) topped with thinly sliced grilled beef, imperial rolls, mint and ground peanuts. Except in understandable cases of extreme noodle gluttony, your bill will be under $8. Cash only.

## 🍷 Drinking & Nightlife

## North Beach

### Specs'
Bar

Map p108 (12 William Saroyan Pl; ⏱5pm-2am) If you've ever wondered what you do with a drunken sailor, here's your answer: march that sailor down this hidden pedestrian alley and stow him away in the back of the bar, where he can wax nostalgic over Seven Seas mementos. With all the merchant-marine memorabilia on the walls, your order is obvious: one pint of Anchor Steam, coming right up.

### Caffe Trieste
Cafe

Map p108 (601 Vallejo St; ⏱6:30am-11pm Sun-Thu, to midnight Fri & Sat; 🛜; ⓂColumbus Ave) Poetry on bathroom walls, opera on the jukebox, live Italian and gypsy folk music weekly, and regular sightings of Beat poet laureate Lawrence Ferlinghetti: this is North Beach at its best, as it's been since the 1950s. Linger over a legendary espresso, join aging anarchists debating how best to bring down the government or scribble your screenplay under the Sicilian mural, just as young Francis Ford Coppola did. Perhaps you've heard of the movie: it was called *The Godfather*.

### Comstock Saloon
Bar

Map p108 (155 Columbus Ave; ⏱11:30am-2am Mon-Fri, 2pm-2am Sat; ⓂColumbus Ave) Welcome to the Barbary Coast, where fortunes were made and squandered, burlesque dancers had hearts (or at least teeth) of gold, and well-researched cocktails at Victorian Comstock Saloon remain period-perfect: the Pisco Punch is made with real pineapple gum, and the Hop Toad with Jamaican rum, bitters and apricot brandy would make sea captains abandon ship. The adjacent restaurant is the kind of place where you might take a madam gone respectable for a 'pig in a blanket' (sausage in a fluffy biscuit), beef shank and bone marrow pot pie, or decadent maple bourbon cake.

### Tosca Cafe
Bar

Map p108 (www.toscacafesf.com; 242 Columbus Ave; ⏱5pm-2am Tue-Sun; ⓂColumbus Ave) Sean Penn, Bobby DeNiro and Sofia Coppola might lurk in the VIP room, but they'll probably be basing their next character study on regulars sipping *caffe corretto* (espresso 'corrected' with liquor) in the retro red-vinyl booth next to yours. Opera

# Detour:
## Jai Yun

There's no need to worry about what to order at **Jai Yun** (Map p108; ☎415-981-7438; www.menuscan.com/jaiyun; 680 Clay St; ☯by reservation only 11am-2pm Mon-Wed & Fri, 6:30-9:30pm Fri-Wed; Ⓜ Kearny St; 🚋 California St): there's no menu, since chef Ji Nei creates the market-inspired, Shanghai-style bill of fare based on what's fresh that day (mention any food allergies or aversions when you book). Fingers crossed, the day's specialties will include tender abalone, translucent housemade rice noodles with cured pancetta, and addictive, paper-thin marinated lotus root. Lunches are a better deal for six to 10 small plates ($18 to $35 per person prix fixe), while dinners are proper feasts of 20-plus, tiny, sensational dishes ($55 to $70 per person). Never mind that servers often rely on hand gestures with non-Mandarin speakers – the sophisticated, fascinating flavors will leave you assured of your impeccable taste. Cash only, and the wine selection is limited – bring your own riesling for $20 corkage.

on Tosca's jukebox (with genuine 45rpm platters) sometimes has to compete with the thump-thump of Larry Flynt's Hustler Club next door, but Tosca wins for classic movie-star sex appeal.

### 15 Romolo
Bar

Map p108 ( ☎415-398-1359; www.15romolo .com; 15 Romolo Pl; ☯5pm-2am; Ⓜ Columbus Ave) Strap on your spurs and prepare for an adventure: finding this Western saloon tucked inside an alleyway wedged between North Beach burlesque joints calls for a stiff drink. Arrivals are swiftly rewarded at the dark-wood bar with Victorian-inspired cocktails that stay on the manly side of dainty – the Pimm's Cup strikes a rigorous gin/cucumber/ bitters ratio, and the honey vodka and basil-spiked Track 42 has just a dab of egg white. Happy hour runs from 5pm to 7:30pm daily, and if the mood and menu strikes you, stick around for spiffed-up pub grub like smoked pulled-pork sliders and fries with Madras curry ketchup – but bear in mind bathrooms are limited.

### Church Key
Bar

Map p108 (1402 Grant Ave; ☯5pm-midnight; Ⓜ Columbus Ave) Foggy North Beach nights call for a beer, but warm ones deserve two – ideally from the selection of 55 international craft brews at Church Key.

Whether your favorite beer is Brazilian or Kiwi, bacon-flavored or pomegranate-scented, look for the discreet white key sign over the door and head on back to the copper-topped bar for a consultation with well-versed bartenders. There are only a couple of wines on the menu and no cocktails – but with potent 10% to 12% beer, you won't miss them. Cash only.

### Vesuvio
Bar

Map p108 (www.vesuvio.com; 255 Columbus Ave; ☯6am-2am; Ⓜ Columbus Ave) Guy walks into a bar, roars and leaves. Without missing a beat, the bartender says to the next customer, 'Welcome to Vesuvio, honey – what can I get you?' It takes a lot more than a barbaric yawp to get Vesuvio's regulars to glance up from their microbrewed beer and anesthetizing absinthe. Kerouac blew off Henry Miller to go on a bender here, and after knocking back his namesake drink (a small bucket of rum, tequila and OJ) with neighborhood characters, you'll understand why.

## Chinatown

### Li Po
Bar

Map p108 ( ☎415-982-0072; 916 Grant Ave; ☯2pm-2am; Ⓜ Stockton St) Beat a hasty retreat from Grant Ave souvenir shops to the retro red booths where Allen Ginsberg and Jack Kerouac debated the meaning of life and literature under the patient gaze of the golden Buddha by the bar. Enter the faux-grotto doorway and try not to bump your head on the red lanterns as you place your order: beer or Chinese mai tai, made with *baiju* (rice liquor), better known as white lightning.

### Rosewood
Bar

Map p108 ( 📞 415-951-4886; 732 Broadway; 🕐 5:30pm-2am Wed-Fri, 7pm-2am Sat; Ⓜ Stockton St) This unmarked bar delivers on its name with sleek floor-to-ceiling, rosewood-paneled walls, dim lighting and low-slung tufted black-leather sofas. Basil gimlets and crafty DJs drum up dance-floor action and intrigue on the bamboo-enclosed smokers' patio – arrive before 10pm if you're here for casual conversation.

### EZ5
Bar

Map p108 ( 📞 415-362-9321; www.ez5bar.com; 684 Commercial St; cover free; 🕐 4pm-2am Mon-Fri, 8pm-2am Sat; Ⓜ Kearny St) Need a day off? EZ5 obliges happy hour from 4pm to 8pm weekdays, offering sweet deals on Day Off sweet-sour lemon vodka cocktails. The '80s are in the house, with cherry-red vinyl seating and classic video games like Ms Pac-Man – which comes in handy on a slow night. Karaoke and Jell-O shots take the edge off Monday nights, and Fi-Di ties loosen once DJs start spinning house and hip-hop around 9pm or 10pm.

## ✪ Entertainment

### Beach Blanket Babylon
Live Music

Map p108 (BBB; 📞 415-421-4222; www.beach blanketbabylon.com; 678 Green St; admission $25-100; 🕐 shows 8pm Wed, Thu & Fri, 6:30pm & 9:30pm Sat, 2pm & 5pm Sun; Ⓜ Stockton St; 🚋 Mason St) Since 1974, San Francisco's longest-running musical-cabaret Beach Blanket Babylon has spoofed current events with topical comedy that changes so often that stagehands giggle along with the audience. Heads of state and pop-culture figureheads alike are played by actors in campy giant wigs and hats,

and no subject is above mockery: Queen Elizabeth, Prince Charles and Duchess Camilla saw the show, but that didn't stop one of BBB's resident drag queens from satirizing the royal wedding. Spectators must be over 21 to handle the racy humor, except at cleverly sanitized Sunday matinees. Reservations essential; arrive one hour early for best seats.

### Cobb's Comedy Club
Comedy

Map p108 ( 📞 415-928-4320; www.cobbscomedy club.com; 915 Columbus Ave; admission $18-33, plus 2-drink minimum; 🕐 shows 8pm & 10:15pm; Ⓜ Columbus Ave) There's no room to be shy at Cobb's, where bumper-to-bumper shared tables make for an intimate (and vulnerable) audience. The venue is known for launching local talent and giving big-name acts from HBO's Dave Chapelle to NBC's Tracy Morgan a place to try risky new material. Check the website for shows.

### Purple Onion
Comedy

Map p108 ( 📞 415-956-1653; www.caffe macaroni.com; 140 Columbus Ave; admission $10-15; Ⓜ Columbus Ave) Legendary comics including Woody Allen, Robin Williams and Phyllis Diller clawed their way up from underground at this grotto nightclub. Recently, comics have been taking back the stage from lackluster lounge acts, and the club's enjoying a renaissance – Zach Galifianakis shot an excruciatingly funny comedy special here. Bookings are sporadic; see online event calendar for shows and opening hours.

### Bimbo's 365 Club
Live Music

Map p108 ( 📞 415-474-0365; www.bimbos 365club.com; 1025 Columbus Ave; tickets from $20; 🚋 Powell-Mason) This vintage-1931 speakeasy still plays it fast and loose with strong drinks, a polished parquet dance floor where Rita Hayworth once kicked up her heels in the chorus line and live shows by the likes of Cibo Matto, Ben Harper and Coldplay. Cash only, and bring something extra to tip the powder-room attendant – this is a classy joint. Check the website for shows and opening hours.

# 🔒 Shopping

## North Beach

### City Lights
Bookstore

Map p108 ( 📞 415-362-8193; www.citylights.com; 261 Columbus Ave; 🕙 10am-midnight; Ⓜ Columbus Ave) 'Abandon all despair, all ye who enter,' orders the sign by the door to City Lights bookstore, written by founder and San Francisco poet laureate Lawrence Ferlinghetti. This commandment is easy to follow upstairs in the sunny **Poetry Room**, with its piles of freshly published verse, a designated **Poet's Chair** and literary views of laundry strung across Jack Kerouac Alley. Poetic justice has been served here since 1957, when City Lights won a landmark free speech ruling over Allen Ginsberg's incendiary epic poem *Howl,* and went on to publish Lenny Bruce, William S Burroughs, Angela Davis and Zapatista Subcomandante Marcos, among others. When you abandon despair, you make more room for books.

### Aria
Antiques, Collectibles

Map p108 ( 📞 415-433-0219; 1522 Grant Ave; 🕙 11am-6pm Mon-Sat, noon-5pm Sun; Ⓜ Columbus Ave) Find inspiration for your own North Beach epic poem under Nelson lamps on Aria's battered shelves, piled with anatomical drawings of starfish, love-potion bottles, castle keys lost in gutters a century ago and even a bucket of paint-spattered brushes (not for sale). Hours are erratic whenever owner-chief scavenger Bill Haskell is out treasure hunting.

### 101 Music
Music

Map p108 ( 📞 415-392-6369; 1414 Grant Ave; 🕙 10am-8pm Tue-Sat, noon-8pm Sun; Ⓜ Columbus Ave) You'll have to bend over those bins to let DJs and hardcore collectors pass (and, hey, wasn't that Tom Waits?!), but among the $3 to $10 discs are obscure releases *(Songs for Greek Lovers)* and original recordings by Nina Simone, Janis Joplin and San Francisco's own anthem-rockers, Journey. At the sister shop at 513 Green St, don't hit your head on the vintage Les Pauls, and check out the sweet turntables that must've cost some kid a year's worth of burger-flipping c 1978.

### Al's Attire
Clothing, Accessories

Map p108 (www.alsattire.com; 1314 Grant Ave; 🕙 11am-7pm Mon-Sat, noon-5pm Sun; Ⓜ Columbus Ave) Hepcats and slick chicks get their duds at Al's, where vintage styles are reinvented in noir-novel twill, dandy high-sheen cotton and midcentury flecked tweeds. Prices aren't exactly bohemian, but turquoise wing-tips are custom-made to fit your feet, and svelte hand-stitched jackets have silver-screen star quality. Ask about custom orders for weddings and other shindigs.

101 Music

### Rock Posters & Collectibles
Antiques

Map p108 (www.rockposters.com; 1851 Powell St; ⏰10am-6pm Tue-Sat; Ⓜ Columbus Ave; 🚋 Mason St) Anyone who hazily remembers the '60s may recall long-lost bands (and brain cells) in this trippy temple to the rock gods. Nostalgia isn't cheap, so expect to pay hundreds for first-run psychedelic Fillmore concert posters featuring Jimi Hendrix or the Grateful Dead. But you can still find deals on handbills for 1970s local acts like Santana, Dead Kennedys, and Sly and the Family Stone.

### Double Punch
Toys, Art

Map p108 (www.doublepunch.com; 1821 Powell St; ⏰11am-7pm Mon-Sat, to 6pm Sun; Ⓜ Columbus Ave; 🚋 Mason St) Art and collectible toys line these walls, making Double Punch doubly dangerous for collectors with kids. Artworks in the upstairs gallery are originals by emerging local artists (the San Francisco Art Institute is right up the block), and toys are limited edition – though since LucasFilm is based in San Francisco, *Star Wars* action figures are usually in stock. Prices run high for graffiti artist Brian Donnelly's rare KAWS

figurines, but check the $5 bargain bin for kid-friendly finds.

### Lola of North Beach
Gifts, Stationery

Map p108 (www.lolaofnorthbeach.com; 1415 Grant Ave; ⏰11am-6:30pm Mon-Sat, to 5:30pm Sun; Ⓜ Columbus Ave; 🚋 Mason St) Answers to all your SF gifting quandaries, from artsy souvenirs (ticket-stub album for all those cleverly designed SF museum tickets) to Beatnik baby showers (onesies with a typewriter tapping out 'So my story begins...'), plus California-made soy travel candles that smell like sunshine.

## Chinatown

### Golden Gate Fortune Cookie Company
Food, Drink

Map p108 (📞415-781-3956; 56 Ross Alley; ⏰8am-7pm; Ⓜ Stockton St; 🚋 Powell St) You too can say you made a fortune in San Francisco after visiting this bakery, where cookies are stamped out on old-fashioned presses and folded while hot – just as they were back in 1909, when they were invented in San Francisco for the Japanese Tea Garden (p210). You can make your own customized cookies

Vesuvio (p119)

(50¢ each) or pick up a bag of the risqué adult fortune cookies – no need to add 'in bed' at the end to make these interesting. Cash only; 50¢ tip for photo requested.

### Clarion Music Center   Music
Map p108 (www.clarionmusic.com; 816 Sacramento St; ⏱11am-6pm Mon-Fri, 9am-5pm Sat; Ⓜ & 🚃California St) The minor chords of the *erhu* (Chinese string instrument) will pluck at your heartstrings as you walk through Chinatown's alleyways, and here you can try your hand at the bow yourself with a superior student model. With the impressive range of congas, gongs and hand-carved tongue drums, you could become your own multiculti, one-person band. Check the website for concerts, workshops and demonstrations by masters.

### Red Blossom Tea Company   Food, Drink
Map p108 (www.redblossomtea.com; 831 Grant Ave; ⏱10am-6:30pm Mon-Sat, to 6pm Sun; ⓂStockton St; 🚃Powell St) Crook your pinky: it's always teatime at Red Blossom, which features 100 specialty teas imported by brother-sister team Alice and Peter Luong. Make your selection from shiny canisters lining wooden shelves, or go with namesake blossoms – tightly wound balls of tea that unfurl into flowers in hot water – and score a free sample with purchase.

### Chinatown Kite Shop   Gifts
Map p108 (www.chinatownkite.com; 717 Grant Ave; ⏱10am-8.30pm; ⓂKearny St; 🚃Powell St) Be the star of Crissy Field and wow any kids in your life with a fierce 6ft-long flying shark, a surreal set

# Tea Tasting

Several Grant Ave tea importers have tasting bars where you can sample their teas. Places that offer free tastings usually expect you to make a purchase, and the hard sell may begin before you finish sipping. For a more relaxed, enlightening, teatime experience, Red Blossom Tea Company offers half-hour tea classes with freshly brewed tastings from a daily tasting menu – plus a brief immersion course on preparing tea for maximum flavor ($30 for up to four participants). Drop in weekdays or call ahead on weekends; seating is limited.

of flying legs or a flying panda bear that looks understandably stunned. Pick up a two-person, papier-mâché lion dance costume and invite a date to bust ferocious moves with you next lunar new year.

### Far East Flea Market   Gifts
Map p108 (☎415-989-8588; 729 Grant Ave; ⏱10am-10pm; ⓂStockton St; 🚃Powell St) The shopping equivalent of crack, this bottomless store is dangerously cheap and certain to make you giddy and delusional. Of course you can get that $8.99 samurai sword through airport security! There's no such thing as too many bath toys, bobbleheads and Chia Pets! Step away from the dollar Golden Gate snow globes while there's still time...

# Nob Hill, Russian Hill & Fillmore

**Hilltop views are the pride of San Francisco.** But they weren't always such coveted real estate. Nob Hill was inhabited mostly by hermits until the 1870s, when Andrew Hallidie introduced cable cars that made the steep terrain more accessible.

Today, Russian and Nob Hills are the stomping grounds of eccentric millionaires and hardcore urban hikers, with cable cars delivering customers to hilltop bars and high-fashion boutiques. Russian Hill's garden stairway walks remain lined with minuscule playgrounds and hidden cottages with literary merits.

West of Nob Hill is Pacific Heights, known for its Victorian mansions that were spared from the Great Quake of 1906 and the ensuing fire that destroyed Nob Hill's most stately homes. Just south of Pac Heights is where many Japanese San Franciscans relocated after the quake. In Japantown you'll find Japanese stationers, communal bathing at Kabuki Springs, sushi and shabu-shabu.

Macondray Lane (p133)
SABRINA DALBESIO/LONELY PLANET IMAGES ©

# Nob Hill, Russian Hill & Fillmore Highlights

## Lombard St (p132)

Leave it to San Francisco to turn a traffic bottleneck into a joyride. Model Ts careened down the steep slide of Lombard in Russian Hill until 1922, when eight hairpin turns were added to slow speeders. Now drivers patiently wait their turn to slooooowly round these flower-lined bends – saving reckless moves on Lombard for video games such as Tony Hawk's Pro Skater and Grand Theft Auto.

**1**

**2**

## Tonga Room (p139)

The Fairmont Hotel's resident tiki bar brings the kitsch with a Polynesian theme that's legitimately retro: the bar has been in operation since 1945, when it was built around the hotel's indoor pool – now the 'lagoon' over which rain showers predictably occur every half hour. Order a Bora Bora Horror, Tonga Itch or Tematangi Ubangi – or drink from a communal Lava Bowl, which serves four.

OCEAN/CORBIS ©

## Cable Car Museum (p133)

**3**

Each cable car is practically a museum in its own right, but if you really want to go under the hood, you can find out how these mechanical marvels can still make it up the city's steepest hills despite their (ahem) advanced age. You might actually learn a little more about them than you ever wanted to know, but it's a learning experience you can't find anywhere else.

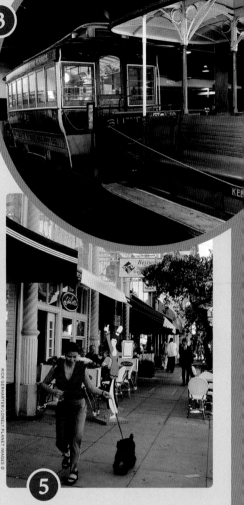

**4**

## Kabuki Springs & Spa (p145)

Summer and winter aren't so different in San Francisco, but at the communal baths, you can change seasons at will, alternating between 170°F (77°C) saunas and 55°F (13°C) cold plunges. Take your time and your choice of free teas and bath products, and relax. Summer fog is no match for treatments that include ginger scrubs, private soaking tubs and steam massages.

**5**

## Fillmore St (p138)

Like the Main St of a small town but exceedingly more interesting, Fillmore St between Geary Blvd and Broadway is 0.7 miles of concentrated local goodness. It elevates the neighborhood from just a cluster of houses to a place you can get lost in for a few hours – it's where you go to wander, nosh, hunt, gather and generally enjoy yourself. Stay past sunset, when the bars and jazz clubs become the main attractions.

# Nob Hill, Russian Hill & Fillmore Walk

*This is our steepest walking tour, taking you from crooked streets and hilltop parks to storied buildings. The stops are geared toward more esoteric interests, covering sites that are cultural, historical, natural, scandalous or just plain delicious.*

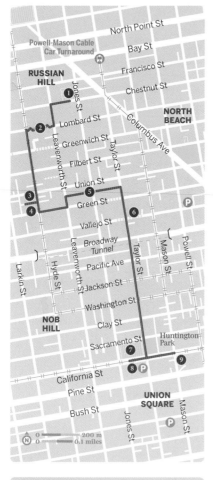

### WALK FACTS
○ **Start** San Francisco Art Institute
○ **Finish** Mark Hopkins Hotel
○ **Distance** 1.5 miles
○ **Duration** One hour

### ❶ San Francisco Art Institute

The graceful mission-style building still operates as an art school, and it's where you'll find **Diego Rivera Gallery** (p131), which contains a magnificent example of the muralist's art. Climb the stairs to the roof for views of the bay.

### ❷ Lombard St

With its famous and meticulously maintained switchbacks, **Lombard St** (p132) isn't technically the most crooked street in the world, but it's surely the kinkiest. It wasn't always so bent; before the automobile the street lunged straight down the hill.

### ❸ Swenson's Ice Cream

One of SF's seriously yummy landmarks: the original **Swenson's Ice Cream**. Traditional faves, such as peppermint stick and rum raisin, are made here, alongside the more exotic mango and Turkish coffee. You might need to come more than once.

### ❹ Jack Kerouac's Love Shack

The modest house at 29 Russell St was the source of major drama from 1951 to 1952, when Jack Kerouac shacked up with Neal and Carolyn Cassady and their baby daughter to pound out his 120ft-long scroll draft of *On the Road*. Jack and Carolyn became lovers at her husband Neal's suggestion, but Carolyn frequently kicked them both out.

### ❺ Macondray Lane

This scenic route via a steep stairway and gravity-defying wooden cottages is so charming that it looks like something out of a novel. And so it is: Armistead Maupin used this as the model for Barbary Lane in his *Tales of the City* series. (p133)

## 6 Ina Coolbrith Park

Named after a former poet laureate from California, this is one of several steep stairway garden parks in the city. Climb past the gardens, decks and flower-framed apartment buildings, and you'll feel the 'cool breath' of the breeze in the trees.

## 7 Grace Cathedral

What's it got that other churches haven't? How about more than 7000 sq ft of stained-glass windows, an **AIDS Memorial Chapel** with a bronze altarpiece by Keith Haring – his last work before he died of AIDS in 1990 – and an inlaid stone labyrinth. (p133)

## 8 Nob Hill Masonic Center

Built as a temple to Freemasonry in 1958, the building features stained-glass mosaic windows depicting the accomplishments of Freemasons in California – if you can decipher the enigmatic symbols. Downstairs a visitors center reveals some of the society's secrets.

## 9 Mark Hopkins Hotel

This Nob Hill hotel was built on the spot where the Mark Hopkins mansion once stood, and on its top floor is the famous **Top of the Mark** (p139), known for its views of the city and the bay. Just across California St is the **Fairmont San Francisco** (p95), opened just after the 1906 earthquake.

## ⭐ The Best...

### PLACES TO EAT

**Acquerello** Cal-Italian in a converted chapel. (p135)

**Tataki** Sustainable sushi delicacies. (p133)

**Out the Door** Less crowded offshoot of the Slanted Door. (p133)

**Pizzeria Delfina** Thin-crust pizza with farm-fresh ingredients. (p134)

### PLACES TO DRINK

**Tonga Room** A tiki staple in the Fairmont Hotel. (p139)

**Amélie** Cool neighborhood wine bar. (p139)

**1300 on Fillmore** Get cozy in the living-room style lounge. (p138)

**Bigfoot Lodge** Rustic, lodge-like atmosphere. (p139)

### PLACES FOR LIVE MUSIC

**Yoshi's** Where to go for jazz. Period. (p140)

**Boom Boom Room** Blues, funk, soul – and dancing. (p141)

**Fillmore Auditorium** Catch big acts in a 1250-seat venue. (p140)

**Rasselas** Live music plus Ethiopian food. (p141)

Boom Boom Room (p141)
ANTHONY PIDGEON/LONELY PLANET IMAGES ©

# Discover Nob Hill, Russian Hill & Fillmore

## Getting There & Away

○ **Bus** The 1, 2, 3 and 38 buses connect Downtown with Japantown and Pacific Heights; the 22 connects Japantown and Pacific Heights with the Marina and the Mission. Bus 10 links Russian and Nob Hills with Pacific Heights. Bus 27 runs from Downtown to Nob Hill. Buses 41 and 45 run from Downtown to Russian Hill.

○ **Cable car** The Powell-Hyde cable car serves Russian and Nob Hills; the Powell-Mason line serves Nob Hill; and the California St line runs among Downtown, Nob Hill and the easternmost edge of Pacific Heights.

○ **Parking** Street parking is hard to find, but possible. Find garages at Japan Center on Fillmore St (between Geary and Post Sts) and Post St (between Webster and Buchanan Sts).

Diego Rivera Gallery
SABRINA DALBESIO/LONELY PLANET IMAGES ©

# ◎ Sights

## Japantown & Pacific Heights

**Japan Center**  Notable Building
Map p134 (www.sfjapantown.org; 1625 Post St; ⊙10am-midnight; Ⓜ Post & Webster Sts) Entering this oddly charming mall is like walking onto a 1960s Japanese movie set – the fake-rock waterfall, indoor wooden pedestrian bridges, rock gardens and curtained wooden restaurant entryways have hardly aged since the mall's grand opening in 1968. If not for the anachronistic Tare Panda cell-phone charms and Harajuku fashion mags displayed at Kinokuniya Books & Stationery (p142), Japan Center would be a total time warp.

**Konko Temple**  Temple
Map p134 (☏415-931-0453; www.konkofaith.org; 1909 Bush St; ⊙8am-6pm Mon-Sat, to 3pm Sun; Ⓜ Sutter & Laguna Sts) Inside the low-roofed, high-modernist temple, you'll find a handsome blond-wood sanctuary with a lofty beamed ceiling, vintage photographs of Konko events dating back 70 years and friendly Reverend Joanne Tolosa, who'll answer questions about the temple or its Shinto-based beliefs, then leave you to contemplation. On New Year's Day, the temple invites visitors to jot down a remembrance, regret and wish on a slip of paper to affix to a tree and to receive a blessing with sacred rice wine.

**Haas-Lilienthal House**  Historic Building
Map p134 (☏415-441-3004; www.sfheritage.org/haas-lilienthal-house; 2007 Franklin St;

# Nob Hill, Russian Hill & Fillmore

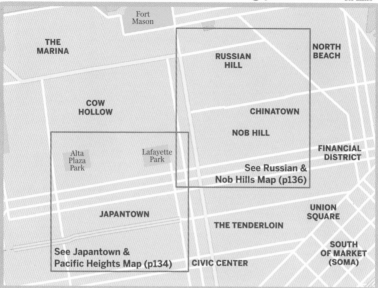

See Russian &
Nob Hills Map (p136)

See Japantown &
Pacific Heights Map (p134)

adult/child $8/5; ⏱noon-3pm Wed & Sat, 11am-4pm Sun; Ⓜ Van Ness Ave & Jackson St) A grand Queen Anne–style Victorian with its original period splendor c 1882, this family mansion looks like a Cluedo game come to life – Colonel Mustard could definitely have committed murder with a rope in the dark-wood ballroom, or Miss Scarlet with a candlestick in the red-velvet parlor. One-hour tours are led by volunteer docents devoted to Victoriana.

**Audium** — Sound Sculpture

Map p134 (☎415-771-1616; www.audium.org; 1616 Bush St; admission $20; ⏱performances 8:30pm Fri & Sat, arrive by 8:15pm; Ⓜ Van Ness Ave & California St; 🚡California St) Sit in total darkness as Stan Shaff plays his hour-plus compositions of sounds emitted by his sound chamber, which sometimes degenerate into 1970s sci-fi sound effects before resolving into oddly endearing Moog synthesizer wheezes. The Audium was specifically sculpted in 1962 to produce bizarre acoustic effects and eerie soundscapes that only a true stoner could enjoy for two solid hours.

## Russian & Nob Hills

**Sterling Park** — Park

Map p136 (www.rhn.org/pointofinterestparks .html; Greenwich & Hyde Sts; 👣; 🚡Powell-Hyde) 'Homeward into the sunset/Still unwearied we go/Till the northern hills are misty/With the amber of afterglow.' Poet George Sterling's *City by the Sea* is almost maudlin – that is, until you watch the sunset over the Golden Gate Bridge from the hilltop park named in his honor.

**FREE** **Diego Rivera Gallery** — Gallery

Map p136 (☎415-771-7020; www.sfai.edu; 800 Chestnut St; ⏱9am-5pm; Ⓜ Stockton St & Columbus Ave; 🚡Powell-Hyde) Diego Rivera's 1931 *The Making of a Fresco Showing a Building of a City* is a trompe l'oeil fresco within a fresco, showing the artist himself as he pauses to admire his work, as well as the work in progress that is San Francisco. The fresco covers an entire wall in the Diego Rivera Gallery at the San Francisco Art Institute, on your left through the entryway courtyard. For a memorable San Francisco vista, head to the terrace

ORIEN HARVEY/LONELY PLANET IMAGES ©

# ✓ Don't Miss
# Lombard St

You've seen its eight switchbacks in 1000 photographs and maybe in a few movies and TV shows, too. Hitchcock used it in *Vertigo,* MTV shot episodes of *The Real World* here, and Barbra Streisand and Ryan O'Neal came flying down the twisty street in the classic cinema car chase in *What's Up, Doc?* Everyone knows Lombard St as the 'world's crookedest street,' but is it really true?

Russian Hill, as it descends Lombard St, has a natural 27% grade – far too steep for automobiles in the 1920s. Property owners in the street came up with the idea to install a series of curves. The result is what you see today: a red-brick street with eight sweeping turns, divided by lovingly tended flower beds and 250 steps rising on either side.

Once the street started appearing on postcards in the 1950s, the tourist board dubbed it the 'world's crookedest street,' which is factually incorrect. Vermont St, on Potrero Hill, between 20th and 22nd Sts, deserves this cred, but don't bother trekking across town: Lombard St is (way) prettier. To avoid throngs of tourists, come early morning, but chances are it'll be foggy; for sun-lit pictures, try timing your visit for midafternoon.

Until 2008, every Easter Sunday for seven years adults had arrived at the crest of Lombard St toting plastic toy tricycles for the annual Bring Your Own Big Wheel Race. But after vehement complaints from residents, the art-prankster organizers moved their toy-joyride to – where else? – Vermont St.

## NEED TO KNOW

Map p136; 900 block of Lombard St; 🚋 Powell-Hyde

cafe for espresso and panoramic bay views.

## Grace Cathedral
Church

Map p136 (📞415-749-6300; www.grace cathedral.org; 1100 California St; except for services, suggested donation adult/child $3/2; ⏰8am-6pm, services 8:30am & 11am (with choir) Sun; 🚃California St) This Episcopal church has been rebuilt three times since the Gold Rush, and the current French-inspired, reinforced concrete cathedral took 40 years to complete. But Grace keeps pace with the times. Its commitment to pressing social issues is embodied in its **AIDS Memorial Chapel**, which has a bronze altarpiece by artist-activist Keith Haring. Here his signature figures are angels taking flight – especially powerful imagery as this was his last work before he died of AIDS in 1990. Day and night you'll notice people absorbed in thought while walking the outdoor, inlaid stone labyrinth, meant to guide restless souls through three spiritual stages: releasing, receiving and returning. Check the website for events at the indoor labyrinth, which include meditation services and yoga.

## Macondray Lane
Street

Map p136 (btwn Jones & Leavenworth Sts; 🚇Union & Jones Sts; 🚃Powell-Mason) *Tales of the City* fans can return to Barbary Lane – or at least visit the inspiration for it. The scenic stairway to and from **Ina Coolbrith Park** was the model for the fictional pedestrian lane made famous by Armistead Maupin. You won't spot Mary Anne Singleton or Anna Madrigal here, but you might find the charming scenery as inspiring as the author did.

## FREE Cable Car Museum
Museum, Historic Site

Map p136 (📞415-474-1887; www.cablecar museum.org; 1201 Mason St; ⏰10am-6pm Apr-Sep, to 5pm Oct-Mar; 🚼; 🚃Powell-Mason, Powell-Hyde) Grips, engines, braking mechanisms...if terms like these warm your gearhead heart, you will be completely besotted with the Cable Car Museum, housed in the city's still-functioning cable car barn. See three original 1870s cable cars and watch as cables glide over huge bull wheels – as awesome a feat of physics now as when the mechanism was invented by Andrew Hallidie in 1873.

# 🍴 Eating

Japan Center is packed with restaurants, but some more intriguing Japanese restaurants lie along Post St and in the Buchanan Mall, across Post St. Upper Fillmore St is lined with restaurants, but many emphasize style over flavor. Along Hyde St on Russian Hill, you'll be glad you climbed to prime picnic spots and neighborhood bistros, but if the walk afterwards seems anticlimactic, hop a cable car.

## Japantown & Pacific Heights

### 🍱 Tataki
Japanese, Sushi $$

Map p134 (📞415-931-1182; www.tatakisushibar .com; 2815 California St; dishes $12-20; ⏰lunch Mon-Fri, dinner daily; 🚇Divisadero & California Sts) Pioneering sushi chefs Kin Lui and Raymond Ho rescue dinner and the oceans with sustainable delicacies: silky Arctic char drizzled with yuzu-citrus and capers happily replaces at-risk wild salmon; and the Golden State Roll is a local hero, featuring spicy, line-caught scallop, Pacific tuna, organic-apple slivers and edible 24-karat gold leaf.

### Out the Door
Vietnamese $$$

Map p134 (📞415-923 9575; www.outthedoors .com; 2232 Bush St; mains lunch $12-18, dinner $18-28; ⏰8am-4:30pm & 5:30pm-10pm Mon-Fri, 8am-3pm & 5:30pm-10pm Sat & Sun; 🚇Fillmore & Pine Sts) Offshoot of the famous Slanted Door (p89). Jump-start early shopping with stellar French beignets and Vietnamese coffee, or salty-sweet Dungeness crab frittatas. Lunchtime's rice plates and noodles are replaced at dinner with savory clay-pot meats and fish. Make reservations.

## Pizzeria Delfina
Pizza **$$**

Map p134 ( 415-440-1189; www.pizzeriadelfina .com; 2406 California St; pizzas $11-17; 5-10pm Mon, 11am-10pm Tue-Thu, 11:30am-11pm Fri, noon-11pm Sat, noon-10pm Sun; M Fillmore & Sacramento Sts) Pizzeria Delfina derives success from simplicity: fresh-from-the-farm ingredients in copious salads, and house-cured meats on tender-to-the-tooth, thin-crusted pizzas – this is one place you actually *want* anchovies on your pizza. Inside gets loud; sit on the side-walk. Expect a wait at peak meal times; come early or late.

## Benkyodo
Japanese **$**

Map p134 ( 415-922-1244; www.benkyodo company.com; 1747 Buchanan St; 8am-5pm Mon-Sat; M Sutter & Buchanan Sts) The

perfect retro lunch counter cheerfully serves an old-school egg-salad sandwich or pastrami for $4. Across the aisle, glass cases display teriyaki-flavored pretzels and $1 *mochi* (Japanese rice cakes) made in-house daily – come early for popular varieties of green tea and chocolate-filled strawberry, but don't be deterred by savory, nutty lima-bean paste.

## Saporro-Ya
Japanese **$$**

Map p134 ( 415-563-7400; 1581 Webster St, Suite 202; noodles $8-11; 11am-11pm Mon-Sat, to 10pm Sun; M Geary Blvd & Webster St) Locals favor this 2nd-floor noodle house for no-fuss meals of homemade ramen, served in big earthenware bowls on Formica tables in a room that's barely changed since the 1970s. Giant-sized combination

NOB HILL, RUSSIAN HILL & FILLMORE EATING

## Japantown & Pacific Heights

### ⊙ Sights
1 Audium.................................................D2
2 Haas-Lilienthal House............................D1
3 Japan Center........................................C3
4 Konko Temple.......................................C2

### ⊗ Eating
5 Benkyodo..............................................C3
6 Bun Mee................................................B2
  Grove..........................................(see 13)
7 Out the Door.........................................B2
8 Pizzeria Delfina.....................................B2
  Saporro-Ya....................................(see 24)
  Sophie's Crepes.............................(see 24)
9 Tataki...................................................A2

### ⊙ Drinking & Nightlife
10 1300 on Fillmore..................................C4
11 Butterfly Bar........................................D2
12 Dosa..................................................B3
13 Harry's Bar.........................................B2
14 Jazz Heritage Center...........................C4
15 Rasellas............................................B3

### ⊙ Entertainment
16 Boom Boom Room................................B3
17 Fillmore Auditorium.............................B3
18 Sheba Piano Lounge............................B4
19 Sundance Kabuki Cinema.....................B3
   Viz Cinema..................................(see 28)
20 Yoshi's...............................................C4

### ⊙ Shopping
21 Clary Sage Organics............................B2
   Crossroads.................................(see 29)
22 Ichiban Kan.........................................C3
23 Jonathan Adler....................................B2
24 Katsura Garden....................................C3
25 Kinokuniya Books &
   Stationery..........................................C3
26 Kohshi................................................C3
27 Nest...................................................B1
28 New People.........................................C3
29 Zinc Details.........................................B2

### ⊙ Sports & Activities
30 Kabuki Springs & Spa...........................B3

NOB HILL, RUSSIAN HILL & FILLMORE EATING

dinners complete the menu, but noodles are the thing here.

**Bun Mee**  Vietnamese, Sandwiches $
Map p134 ( ☏415-800-7698; www.bunmee.co; 2015 Fillmore St; dishes $6-12; ⏱11am-10pm; Ⓜ Fillmore & Pine Sts) The lines out the door are evidence of Bun Mee's perfect Vietnamese sandwiches; five-spice chicken is the classic, but the pork belly is sublime. Rice bowls and salads present alternatives to non-sandwich-lovers. The tiny storefront packs; consider picnicking at nearby Alta Plaza Park.

**Grove**  American $
Map p134 ( ☏415-474-1419; 2016 Fillmore St; dishes $8-12; ⏱7am-11pm; 🛜💺; Ⓜ Fillmore & Pine Sts) Rough-hewn recycled wood, bric-a-brac in the rafters and a stone fireplace lend a ski-lodge aesthetic to this Fillmore St cafe, where Pacific Heights locals recover from hangovers with made-to-order breakfasts, hunch over laptops with salads and sandwiches, and gab fireside with warm-from-the-oven cookies and hot cocoa.

**Sophie's Crepes**  Dessert $
Map p134 (1581 Webster, Suite 275, Japan Center; dishes $4-8; ⏱11am-9pm Sun-Thu, to 10pm Fri & Sat; Ⓜ Geary Blvd & Webster St) Crowds line up for Sophie's made-to-order crepes and sundaes. As interesting as the ice-cream selection (try the red bean) are the posses of Lolita Goth girls eating here, who take their fashion cues from filmmaker Tim Burton.

# Russian & Nob Hills

**Acquerello**  Californian, Italian $$$
Map p136 ( ☏415-567-5432; www.acquerello .com; 1722 Sacramento St; 3-/5-course menu $64/90; ⏱5:30-9:30pm Tue-Sat; Ⓜ Polk & Sacramento Sts; 🚃 California St) A converted chapel is a fitting location for a meal that'll turn Italian culinary purists into true believers in Cal-Italian cuisine. Chef Suzette Gresham's generous pastas and ingenious seasonal meat dishes include heavenly quail salad, devilish lobster *panzerotti* (stuffed dough pockets in a spicy seafood broth) and venison loin chops.

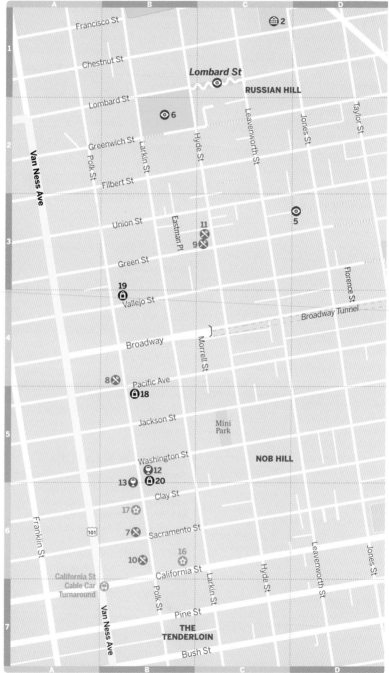

# Russian & Nob Hills

## ◎ Top Sights
Lombard St..............................................C1

## ◎ Sights
1 Cable Car Museum..............................E5
2 Diego Rivera Gallery..........................C1
3 Grace Cathedral.................................E6
4 Ina Coolbrith Park..............................E3
5 Macondray Lane.................................D3
6 Sterling Park......................................B2

## ✖ Eating
7 Acquerello..........................................B6
8 Cheese Plus.......................................B4
9 Frascati..............................................C3
10 Swan Oyster Depot..........................B6
11 Za.....................................................C3

## ◉ Drinking & Nightlife
Amélie.......................................(see 12)
12 Bigfoot Lodge...................................B5
13 Cinch.................................................B5
14 Tonga Room......................................F6
15 Top of the Mark................................F6

## ✪ Entertainment
16 Encore Karaoke Lounge....................B6
17 Red Devil Lounge..............................B6

## ⬤ Shopping
18 Cris...................................................B5
19 Eco Citizen.......................................B4
Hyde & Seek Antiques..............(see 9)
20 Studio...............................................B5

## Swan Oyster Depot  Seafood $$
Map p136 ( ☎415-673-1101; 1517 Polk St; dishes $10-20; ⊙8am-5:30pm Mon-Sat; Ⓜ Polk & Sacramento Sts; 🚃California St) Superior flavor without the superior attitude of most seafood restaurants. The downside is an inevitable wait for the few counter seats, but the upside of the high turnover is unbelievably fresh seafood. On sunny days, place an order to go, browse Polk St boutiques, then breeze past the line to pick up your crab salad with Louie dressing and the obligatory top-grade oysters with mignonette sauce.

## Frascati  Californian, Italian $$$
Map p136 ( ☎415-928-1406; www.frascatisf.com; 1901 Hyde St; mains $20-30; ⊙5:30-9:45pm Mon-Sat, to 9pm Sun; 🚃Powell-Hyde) 'Clang

clang clang went the trolley, zing zing zing went my heartstrings.' That classic Judy Garland tune makes sense after a romantic evening at this hilltop neighborhood charmer, with storefront windows looking out to passing cable cars. The Mediterranean menu skews Italian and French, with flavor-rich dishes like duck confit, pork chops with ratatouille, and a simple roast chicken with lemon-oregano jus. Make reservations.

### Za                                              Pizza $

Map p136 ( ☎415-771-3100; www.zapizzasf.com; 1919 Hyde St; ☺noon-10pm Sun-Wed, to 11pm Thu-Sat; Ⓜ Union & Hyde Sts; 🚋Powell-Hyde) You don't get a gourmet, cornmeal-dusted, thin-crust slice like this every day. Pizza lovers brave the uphill climb for pizza slices piled with fresh ingredients, a pint of Anchor Steam and a cozy bar setting – all for under $10.

### Cheese Plus                                     Deli $

Map p136 (www.cheeseplus.com; 2001 Polk St; ☺10am-7pm; Ⓜ Polk St & Pacific Ave) Foodies, rejoice: here's one deli where they won't blink an eye if you say you'd rather have the aged, drunken goat cheese than provolone on your sandwich. For $8, you get a salad loaded with oven-roasted turkey and sustainable Niman Ranch bacon, but the specialty is the classic $7 grilled cheese, made with the artisan cheese du jour.

# 🍷 Drinking & Nightlife

## Japantown & Pacific Heights

### Butterfly Bar                                   Lounge

Map p134 (www.thehotelmajestic.com; 1500 Sutter St; ☺5-11pm Tue-Sat; Ⓜ Sutter & Gough Sts) The Hotel Majestic's intimate 20-seat lounge resembles an elegant library bar in an English manor house, with a gorgeous collection of rare butterflies adorning the walls. Great martinis. Bring a date.

### 1300 on Fillmore                                Lounge

Map p134 (www.1300fillmore.com; 1300 Fillmore St; ☺4:30-10pm Sun-Thu, to midnight Fri & Sat; Ⓜ Fillmore & Eddy Sts) Reviving swank south of Geary, 1300 on Fillmore's enormous heavy doors open into a double-high living-room space, with oriental rugs, tufted-leather sofas and floor-to-ceiling, black-and-white portraits of jazz luminaries. There's good Southern-inspired food, and gospel brunch on Sundays (reservations required) – big with the after-church crowd.

### Dosa                                            Bar

Map p134 ( ☎415-441-3672; www.dosasf.com; 1700 Fillmore St; Ⓜ Fillmore St & Geary Blvd) Baubled, glittering chandeliers hang from high ceilings at Dosa, an otherwise expensive (and good)

Harry's Bar

Indian restaurant with a happening bar scene of sexy, nonsnooty locals. It's good for snazzy cocktails, but if you're wearing dumpy clothes, you'll feel out of place.

### Harry's Bar
Bar

Map p134 (www.harrysbarsf.com; 2020 Fillmore St; ⊙4pm-2am Mon-Thu, 11:30am-2am Fri-Sun; MFillmore & Pine Sts) Cap off a shopping trip at Harry's mahogany bar with Bloody Marys made properly with horseradish or freshly muddled mojitos. A Pacific Heights mainstay, Harry's appeals to aging debutantes who love getting politely hammered.

## Russian & Nob Hills

### Tonga Room
Lounge

Map p136 (www.fairmont.com; 950 Mason St, lower level, Fairmont Hotel; ⊙5-11:30pm Sun, Wed & Thu, 5:30pm-12:30am Fri & Sat; cover $5-8; California St) Tonight's San Francisco weather: 100% chance of tropical rainstorms every 20 minutes, but only around the top-40 band playing on the island in the middle of the indoor pool – you're safe in your grass hut. For a more powerful hurricane, order one in a plastic coconut. Come before 8pm to beat the cover charge.

### Amélie
Bar

Map p136 (www.ameliesf.com; 1754 Polk St; MPolk & Washington Sts; Powell-Hyde) This très cool neighborhood wine bar, painted to look like red wine splashing, serves well-priced vintages – happy-hour flights of three cost just $10 – with delish cheese and charcuterie plates. Weekends get too crowded, but on weekdays it's an ideal spot to cozy up with your sweetheart.

### Bigfoot Lodge
Bar

Map p136 (www.bigfootlodge.com; 1750 Polk St; MPolk & Washington Sts; California St) Log-cabin walls, antler chandeliers, taxidermied animals everywhere you look – you'd swear you were at a state park visitors center, but for all the giggly-drunk 20-somethings. If you're looking for your gay boyfriend, he's wandered across the street to the Cinch.

### Top of the Mark
Bar

Map p136 (www.topofthemark.com; 999 California St; cover $5-15; ⊙5pm-midnight Sun-Thu, 4pm-1am Fri & Sat; California St) So what if it's touristy? Nothing beats twirling in the clouds in your best cocktail dress to a full jazz orchestra on the city's highest dance floor. Check the online calendar to ensure

## Fillmore St Jazz Bar Crawl

The Fillmore St Jazz District was once the 'Harlem of the West,' back in the '40s and '50s, when Ella Fitzgerald and Duke Ellington played clubs near Fillmore and Geary. The 'hood fell victim to urban blight in the '70s and '80s, but lately has bounced back, particularly since the opening of Yoshi's and the **Jazz Heritage Center** (Map p134; www.jazzheritagecenter.org; 1320 Fillmore St).

Start the evening at Geary and Fillmore and head south, listening at doors of clubs to find what turns you on. John Lee Hooker's Boom Boom Room (p141) marks the gateway to the neighborhood. You can see right onto the stage at Rasselas (p141), but if you don't like the sound, cross the street to the more intimate **Sheba Piano Lounge** (Map p134; www.shebapianolounge.com; 1419 Fillmore St; ⊙5pm-midnight, later on weekends) for piano jazz and a fireplace. Even if you don't catch an act at Yoshi's, pop into the lobby-level Lush Life Gallery to see ephemera of jazz greats. End with drinks on tufted-leather sofas at 1300 on Fillmore, where photos of jazz luminaries line the walls.

**Below:** Top of the Mark (p139); **Right:** Fillmore Auditorium

(BELOW) SABRINA DALBESIO/LONELY PLANET IMAGES ©; (RIGHT) ANTHONY PIDGEON/LONELY PLANET IMAGES ©

a band is playing the night you're coming. Expect $15 drinks.

### Cinch                                    Gay Bar

Map p136 (www.thecinch.com; 1723 Polk St; ⏰9am-2am Mon-Fri, 6am-2am Sat & Sun; Ⓜ Polk & Washington Sts) The last of the old-guard Polk St gay bars still has an old-timey saloon vibe, with pool, pinball, free popcorn and a big smokers' patio where you get yelled at if you spark a joint (but people do it anyway).

## ⭐ Entertainment

### Yoshi's                              Live Music

Map p134 (📞415-655-5600; www.yoshis .com; 1300 Fillmore St; ⏰shows 8pm or 10pm; Ⓜ Fillmore & Eddy Sts) San Francisco's definitive jazz club draws the world's top talent and hosts appearances by the likes of Leon Redbone and Nancy Wilson, along with occasional classical and gospel acts. We suggest buying tickets in advance – if you're with a group, we like the round, high-back booths (table numbers 30 to 40), but there's not a bad seat in the house. Make a night of it with great sushi in the swingin' restaurant up front.

### Fillmore Auditorium        Live Music

Map p134 (📞415-346-6000; www.thefillmore .com; 1805 Geary Blvd; admission $20-40; ⏰box office 10am-4pm Sun, 7:30-10pm show nights; Ⓜ Fillmore St & Geary Blvd) Jimi Hendrix, Janis Joplin, the Doors – they all played the Fillmore. Now you might catch anyone from Devo or The Ting Tings to Snow Patrol in the historic 1250-capacity standing-room theater (if you're polite and lead with the hip, you might squeeze up to the stage). Don't miss the priceless collection of psychedelic posters in the upstairs gallery.

### Boom Boom Room
Live Music

Map p134 (☎415-673-8000; www.boomboom blues.com; 1601 Fillmore St; admission $5-15; ⏰4pm-2am Tue-Sun; Ⓜ Fillmore St & Geary Blvd) Cooking continuously since the '30s, this place is an authentic relic from the jumping post-WWII years of Fillmore St. Blues, soul and New Orleans funk, by top touring talent, play six nights a week. A large dance floor, killer cocktails and cool photos lining the walls may have you lingering till 2am. Shows start around 9pm.

### Rasselas
Live Music

Map p134 (☎415-346-8696; www.rasselasjazz club.com; 1534 Fillmore St; 2-drink minimum; ⏰8pm-midnight Sun-Thu, to 1am Fri & Sat; Ⓜ Fillmore St & Geary Blvd) Doubling as a good Ethiopian restaurant, Rasselas' big windows let you look inside to see (and hear) who's playing before you commit. Live jazz every night (and occasionally salsa on Fridays) make this our favorite Upper Fillmore backup when we're wishy-washy about where to go.

### Red Devil Lounge
Live Music

Map p136 (☎415-921-1695; www.reddevillounge .com; 1695 Polk St; Ⓜ Polk & Washington Sts) The up-and-coming and formerly famous (think Vanilla Ice and Sugar Hill Gang) play this narrow, intimate club. Your once-fave stars may have lost their luster, but the strong drinks haven't. Mondays are movie nights, Tuesdays open mic. Opening hours and cover charges vary.

### Encore Karaoke Lounge
Lounge

Map p136 (☎415-775-0442; www.encore karaokesf.com; 2nd fl, 1550 California St; ⏰3pm-2am; Ⓜ Polk & California Sts; 🚋 California St) Our favorite karaoke bar, Encore is a throwback to 1970s rumpus rooms, with low-slung swiveling chairs of stitched Naugahyde, a pool table to keep you busy and a friendly crowd of raucous regulars who cheer when you nail a number.

### ⬥ Sundance Kabuki Cinema
Cinema

Map p134 ( 📞415-929-4650; www.sundance
cinemas.com/kabuki.html; 1881 Post St; adult/
child $11/8; Ⓜ Geary Blvd & Fillmore St) Cinema
going at its best. Reserve a stadium seat,
belly up to the bar and order from the
bistro, which serves everything from rib-
eye steak to mac-n-cheese. A multiplex
initiative by Robert Redford's Sundance
Institute, Kabuki features big-name
flicks and festivals. It's also green, with
recycled-fiber seating, reclaimed-wood
decor, and local chocolates and booze.
Expect a $1 to $3 surcharge to see a
movie not preceded by commercials.
Validated parking available.

### Viz Cinema
Cinema

Map p134 ( 📞415-525-8600; www.vizcinema
.com; 1746 Post St; tickets $12; Ⓜ Geary Blvd &
Webster St) Catch up on current-release
Japanese films, anime and documen-
taries at this underground 143-seat
theater inside New People (p143) with HD
projection and kick-ass sound. Also hosts
the San Francisco International Asian
American Film Festival.

## 🔒 Shopping

## Japantown & Pacific Heights

### Nest
Housewares, Gifts

Map p134 (www.nestsf.com; 2300 Fillmore St;
Ⓜ Fillmore & Sacramento Sts) Make your nest
cozier with the one-of-a-kind accessories
from this well-curated collection, including Provençal quilts, beaded jewelry, craft
kits and papier-mâché trophy heads for
the kids' room, and mesmerizing century-
old bric-a-brac and toys.

### Clary Sage Organics
Beauty Products

Map p134 (www.clarysageorganics.com; 2241
Fillmore St; Ⓜ Fillmore & Sacramento Sts) To
top off your spa day at Kabuki Springs &
Spa (p145), Clary Sage designs its own
line of yoga-wear and will outfit you
with effortlessly flattering tunics made
from organic California cotton, organic
plant-based cleansers and lotions with
light, delectable scents, and homeopathic
flower-essence stress remedies.

### Kinokuniya Books & Stationery
Bookstore

Map p134 ( 📞415-567-7625; 1581
Webster St; Ⓜ Geary Blvd &
Webster St) Like warriors in a
showdown, the book-
store, stationery and
manga divisions of
Kinokuniya compete
for your attention. Only
you can decide where
your loyalties lie: with
stunning photography
books and Harajuku
fashion mags upstairs,
vampire comics down-
stairs, or the stationery
department's *washi* paper,

Nest
RICK GERHARTER/LONELY PLANET IMAGES ©

SABRINA DALBESIO/LONELY PLANET IMAGES ©

supersmooth Sakura gel pens and pig notebooks with the motto 'what lovely friends, they will bring happy.'

### New People — Clothing, Gifts

Map p134 (www.newpeopleworld.com; 1746 Post St) An eye-popping three-story emporium devoted to Japanese art and pop culture, New People is reason alone to visit Japantown. Get inspired by contemporary artists at **Superfrog Gallery**, then try on Lolita fashions (imagine *Alice in Wonderland*) at 2nd-floor **Baby the Stars Shine Bright** and traditional Japanese clothing emblazoned with contemporary graphics at **Sou-Sou**. At **New People Shop**, find funky *kawaii* (Japanese for all things cute), like origami kits and cute-as-Pikachu Japanimation cards and T-shirts.

### Katsura Garden — Bonsai

Map p134 (☎415-931-6209; 1581 Webster St; Ⓜ Geary Blvd & Webster St) For a little something special, consider a bonsai. Katsura Garden can set you up with a miniature juniper that looks like it grew on a windswept molehill, or a stunted maple that will shed five tiny, perfect red leaves next autumn.

### Ichiban Kan — Gifts

Map p134 (☎415-409-0472; 22 Peace Plaza, Suite 540; Ⓜ Sutter & Buchanan Sts) It's a wonder you got this far in life without penguin soy-sauce dispensers, 'Men's Pocky' chocolate-covered pretzels, extra-spiky Japanese hair wax, soap dishes with feet and the ultimate in gay gag gifts, the handy 'Closet Case' — all for under $5.

### Kohshi — Gifts

Map p134 (www.kohshisf.com; 1737 Post St, Suite 335; ⊗Mon closed; Ⓜ Geary Blvd & Webster St) Fragrant Japanese incense for every purpose, from long-burning sandalwood for meditation to cinnamon-tinged Gentle Smile to atone for laundry left too long. There are also lovely gift ideas: gentle charcoal soap, cups that look like crumpled paper and purple Daruma figurines for making wishes.

### Jonathan Adler — Housewares

Map p134 (www.jonathanadler.com; 2133 Fillmore St; Ⓜ Fillmore & Sacramento Sts) Vases with handlebar mustaches and cookie jars labeled 'Quaaludes' may seem like holdovers from a Big Sur bachelor pad c 1974, but they're snappy interior inspirations from California pop potter (and

*Top Design* judge) Jonathan Adler. Don't worry whether that leather pig footstool matches your midcentury couch – as Adler says, 'Minimalism is a bummer.'

### Zinc Details
Housewares

Map p134 (www.zincdetails.com; 1905 Fillmore St) Pacific Heights chic meets Japantown mod at Zinc Details, with items like orange lacquerware salad-tossers, a sake dispenser that looks like a Zen garden boulder, and bird-shaped soy dispensers. If you can't find what you need here, try up the street at Zinc's 2410 California St location.

### Crossroads
Clothing, Accessories

Map p134 (www.crossroadstrading.com; 1901 Fillmore St; M Fillmore & Pine Sts) Pssst, fashionistas: you know those designers you see lining Fillmore St? Many of their creations wind up at Crossroads for a fraction of retail, thanks to Pacific Heights clotheshorses who tire of clothes fast and can't be bothered to hang onto receipts. That's why this Crossroads store is better than the other ones in the city (including Market and Haight Sts). For even better

deals, trade in your own old stuff and browse the half-price rack.

# Russian & Nob Hills

### Eco Citizen
Clothing, Accessories

Map p136 (www.ecocitizenonline.com; 2255 Polk St; M Polk & Green Sts) Idealism meets street chic in this boutique of ecofriendly, fair-traded fabulousness, from artisanal-made Afghani gold charm message necklaces, to Vivienne Westwood T-strap heels made of nontoxic PVC (recyclable on site). Prices are reasonable and sales a steal – $50 could get you a fair-trade cashmere dress or SF-made Turk+Taylor recycled hot-air-balloon windbreaker.

### Studio
Gifts

Map p136 (www.studiogallerysf.com; 1815 Polk St; 11am-8pm Wed-Fri, to 6pm Sat & Sun, by appointment Mon & Tue; M Polk & Washington Sts; California St) Spiff up your pad with locally made arts and crafts at bargain prices, such as Chiami Sekine's collages of boxing bears and Monique Tse's fat-free cupcakes made of blown glass. For a visual remembrance of your visit to SF,

Grace Cathedral (p133)

ROBERTO GEROMETTA/LONELY PLANET IMAGES ©

Studio is the place, with small prints of local haunts by Elizabeth Ashcroft and architectural etchings by Alice Gibbons.

## Cris
Clothes, Accessories

Map p136 ( 📞415-474-1191; 2056 Polk St; 🚇Polk St & Broadway; 🚋Powell-Hyde) The best-looking windows on Polk St are consistently at Cris, a consignment shop specializing in contemporary high-end fashion by big-name designers like Balenciaga, Lanvin, Marni, Alexander Wang and Chloé, all in beautiful condition, at amazing prices, carefully curated by an elegant Frenchwoman with an eagle's eye and duchess' taste. Also great for handbags by Prada, Dolce & Gabbana, yada-yada-yada...

## Hyde & Seek Antiques
Antiques

Map p136 ( 📞415-776-8865; 1913 Hyde St; 🕐noon-6pm Wed-Sat; 🚇Union & Hyde Sts; 🚋Powell-Hyde) Like the home of a long-lost eccentric aunt, this tiny storefront is full of surprises: a briefcase that opens to reveal a full tartan bar, a Danish-design silver calla lily, a Native American basket more tightly wound than your boss – all at reasonable prices.

# 🏃 Sports & Activities

## Kabuki Springs & Spa
Spa

Map p134 ( 📞415-922-6000; 1750 Geary Blvd; admission $22-25; 🕐10am-9:45pm, coed Tue, women only Wed, Fri & Sun, men only Mon, Thu & Sat; 🚇Geary Blvd & Fillmore Sts) Our favorite urban retreat is a spin on communal, clothing-optional, Japanese baths. Scrub yourself down with salt in the steam room, soak in the hot pool, then the cold plunge and reheat in the sauna. Rinse and repeat. The look befits the location – slightly dated Japanese modern, with vaulted lacquered-wood ceilings, tile mosaics and low lighting. Men and women alternate days, except on Tuesdays, when bathing suits are required (arrive before 5pm to beat the line). Plan two hours' minimum, plus a 30-to-60-minute wait at peak times (add your name to the wait-list, then go next door to slurp noodles or catch a movie; when you return, breeze right in). Communal bathing gets discounted with massage appointments; book ahead and come on the gender-appropriate day.

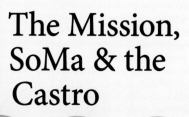

# The Mission, SoMa & the Castro

**Diversity rules in the city's hippest 'hoods.** When you visit the Mission, people are itching for you to ask: what kind of neighborhood is this, anyway? This is a trick question. Latinos, lesbians, star chefs, street artists, designers, activists, punks and suits all play featured roles in this avant-garde ensemble act.

Wander South of Market St (most everyone calls it 'SoMa') to find a neighborhood that's enjoying a rowdy, experimental second adolescence. If cutting-edge art shows in Yerba Buena Arts District strike you as risqué, wait until you see the nightlife around Folsom St.

The Castro is where the Mission ends, SoMa club kids settle down and a giant rainbow flag flies over Harvey Milk Plaza – named for the Castro entrepreneur who became the first openly gay man elected to US public office. Today there's no better place than the Castro to be out, proud and thirsty.

Medjool Sky Terrace (p172)
SABRINA DALBESIO/LONELY PLANET IMAGES ©

# The Mission, SoMa & the Castro Highlights

## Castro Theatre (p177)

Arrive early, because the show at the Castro begins even before the red-velvet curtains part. As you gape at the chinoiserie-deco dome, the mighty Wurlitzer suddenly rises from the orchestra pit below and strikes up classic show tunes. The crowd hums along but bursts into hoots and roars at the anthem that signals the start of every movie: the theme from the film *San Francisco*.

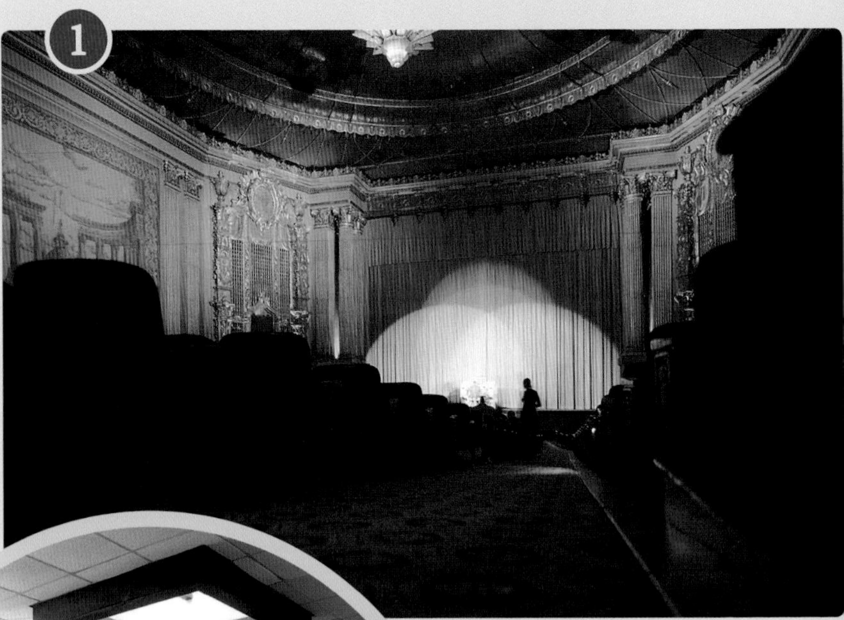

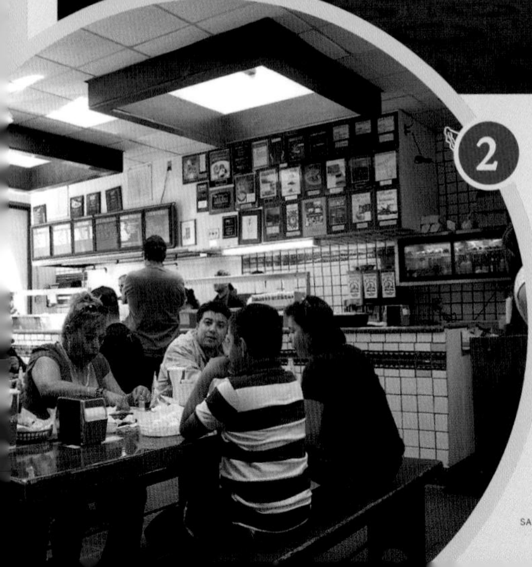

## Taquerías (p165)

Get your Mexican-food fix in the Mission; it's the real deal. Dozens of taquerías offer all sorts of hangover-soothing combinations of meat (usually chicken or beef), beans (pinto, black or refried), salsa (red, green or chunky *pico de gallo*) and cheese, served inside a corn or flour tortilla. Tacos are smaller and simpler, while burritos involve stuffing all the ingredients you can into an enormous, tasty package. La Taqueria (p165)

SABRINA DALBESIO/LONELY PLANET IMAGES ©

## Club Hopping (p170)

Decisions, decisions. Eighties dancing in SoMa? Drunken debauchery in the Mission? Getting your gay on in the Castro? All three neighborhoods offer copious opportunities for carousing, so whatever scene you're looking for, this is where you'll find it. Around the Mission and the Castro, bars and clubs are clustered close together. Find one you like and there are probably 10 more to choose from in close proximity. El Rio (p171)

RICHARD CUMMINS/LONELY PLANET IMAGES ©

## Mission Murals (p159)

Yet more proof that beauty can be found in the most unlikely places: colorful murals that turn buildings into works of art and otherwise unglamorous alleyways into unexpected, grassroots galleries. Look for them throughout the Mission, and don't miss the Women's Building, Balmy Alley and Clarion Alley. For a more in-depth experience, take a tour with **Precita Eyes** (☎415-285-2287; www.precitaeyes .org; adult $12-15, child $5; ⏰11am, noon, 1:30pm Sat & Sun). Balmy Alley (p159)

## Yerba Buena Center for the Arts (p176)

San Francisco loves its spectacles, and YBCA keeps them coming in vast galleries and theaters built for big thinking and grand gestures – indoor Ferris wheels, video art and acrobatic dance are all on the bill. At openings and fund-raisers here, San Francisco freak levels hit new highs. At the very least, stop by to check out provocative contemporary art during regular gallery hours.

# The Mission, SoMa & the Castro Walk

*Two neighborhoods bookend this colorful walking tour, which features murals, mosaics and rainbow flags. Along the way, you'll pass unique local shops and get a glimpse of how San Franciscans really live, from the glam to the gritty.*

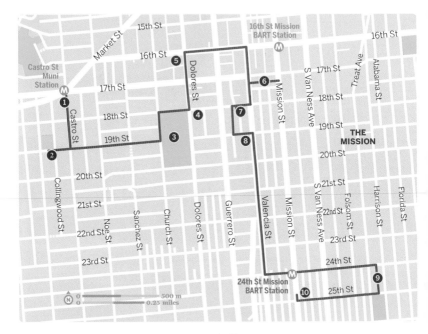

## WALK FACTS
- **Start** Harvey Milk Plaza
- **Finish** La Taqueria
- **Distance** 3.4 miles
- **Duration** Two hours

### ❶ Harvey Milk Plaza

Why, hello, enormous rainbow flag! Harvey Milk, San Francisco's first openly gay city supervisor, who was assassinated in 1978, would be proud to see this big whopping salute to diversity and tolerance flapping in the wind over the plaza (p164) that bears his name.

### ❷ Harvey Milk Civil Rights Academy

Look closely at the trio of glittering mosaics that graces the outer walls of an alternative elementary school on 19th St: the students' drawings and poems are embedded under bits of glass, adding extra depth to the themes of literacy, math and science, and civil rights and equality.

### ❸ Mission Dolores Park

The sunny microclimate of this park (p155), paired with views of SF and the Bay Bridge, make it the place to spend warm afternoons. Sometimes the crowds make you think a free concert is about to start, but no, that's just the locals getting their vitamin D.

### 4 Bi-Rite Creamery

Ready to stop for some ice cream? Sunny summer days see lines that stretch around the corner, but you don't have to wait for that meteorological anomaly to enjoy the creamy goodness of **Bi-Rite** (p168) – it's a treat even when the fog has rolled in.

### 5 Mission Dolores

While the impressive basilica will first catch your eye, the smaller adobe structure to its left is what you should really focus your attention on: the original church is San Francisco's oldest surviving building. (p154)

### 6 Clarion Alley

Since the Clarion Alley Mural Project (p159) was founded in 1992, almost every inch here has been covered with art – some by San Francisco street artists who have gone on to exhibit in museums. Only the strong art survives peeing, tagging and overpainting here and in neighboring **Sycamore Alley**.

### 7 Women's Building

Stop to gawk at the elaborate *Maestrapeace* that covers two sides of this four-story structure (p159). The elaborate mural was created in 1993–94 by seven local *muralistas* with a team of community collaborators.

### 8 826 Valencia

Stop by the **Pirate Supply Store** (p155) – a front for a writing-skills nonprofit started by author Dave Eggers – to browse the selection of glass eyes, peg-leg oil and publications by local authors. Walk south and browse the shops of Valencia St.

### 9 Balmy Alley

Following the lead of Mexican muralists Diego Rivera and José Clemente Orozco, local *muralistas* address current social and political themes in styles that range from social realism to hallucinogenic. (p159)

### 10 La Taqueria

Your reward for all that walking? A huge burrito at one of our favorite taquerías (p165), in a neighborhood that's known for them.

## ⭐ The Best...

### PLACES TO EAT

**Benu** Pacific Rim fine dining. (p167)

**La Taqueria** Down-and-dirty burritos. (p165)

**Commonwealth** Farm-to-table in a dive format. (p165)

**Delfina** Simple, seasonal, sensational Cal-Ital. (p165)

### PLACES TO DRINK

**Bar Agricole** Traditional mixed drinks in a modern space. (p173)

**Zeitgeist** Sunny afternoons call for a patio. (p170)

**Elixir** Open since 1858, but it's also a green business. (p170)

**Bloodhound** Crows, antlers – it's all about the atmosphere. (p173)

### REASONS TO STAY UP LATE

**Bottom of the Hill** Pogoing and live music. (p176)

**EndUp** 'Ghettodisco' on Saturdays. (p173)

**Cat Club** Thursday is '80s night. (p173)

**AsiaSF** Get down with drag queens. (p177)

Statue, Mission Dolores (p154)
RAY LASKOWITZ/LONELY PLANET IMAGES ©

# ✓ Don't Miss
# San Francisco Museum of Modern Art

From its start in 1935, the San Francisco Museum of Modern Art (SFMOMA) dared to differ from other museums. Instead of ignoring the Great Depression, SFMOMA made a point of addressing the issues through its contemporary art collection, featuring Diego Rivera's poignant paintings and Dorothea Lange's haunting Works Progress Administration (WPA) photographs. Since photography had flourished in Northern California since early in the Gold Rush days, SFMOMA got a head start on other museum collections with groundbreaking photography by local pioneers.

Map p160

📞 415-357-4000

www.sfmoma.org

151 3rd St

adult/child $18/free, half price Thu after 6pm, 1st Tue of month free

🕙 11am-6pm Fri-Tue, to 9pm Thu

Ⓜ & Ⓡ Montgomery St

# New Media, New Directions

When SFMOMA moved to architect Mario Botta's light-filled brick box in 1995, it became clear just how far this museum was prepared to push the art world. The new museum showed its backside to New York and leaned full tilt toward the western horizon, taking risks on then-unknown SF artist Matthew Barney and his poetic videos involving industrial quantities of Vaseline, and Larry Sultan's revealing photographs of bored porn stars between takes in suburban California homes. The 1995 reopening coincided with the tech boom, and new-media art took off in the SFMOMA galleries at roughly the same time as new technologies in the Bay Area.

## Ongoing Expansion

Collectors took notice of SFMOMA's bold direction, and since 1995 donations have doubled SFMOMA's holdings – which now include over 1100 major modern works gifted by the Fisher family (founders of SF-based clothiers the Gap, Old Navy and Banana Republic). A $480-million expansion is currently under way with Norway-based Snøhetta architects to accommodate the museum's expanded collection of paintings and photography, alongside emerging niches: video art, conceptual architecture, wall-drawing installations and relational art.

## Museum Itinerary

There are regular, free gallery tours, but exploring on your own gives you the thrill of discovery. Begin with the 3rd-floor photography galleries, then head up through the 4th- and 5th-floor rotating contemporary exhibits. The rooftop sculpture garden offers extraordinary views of the city, plus there's reviving Blue Bottle cappuccino and color-blocked Mondrian Cake at the rooftop cafe.

From here, work your way down through the galleries via the dramatic stairwell for vertiginous perspectives over the rotating atrium installation. Tack on additional time to browse in SFMOMA's shop.

## Local Knowledge

# Don't Miss List

BY CJ FEINBERG,
SFMOMA DOCENT
SINCE 1993

### 1 ROOFTOP SCULPTURE GARDEN
The open-air sculpture garden is a wonderful place to visit, a real urban oasis. The sculptures are rotated to show off a diversity of artists, techniques and materials – as well as ideas about what sculpture is. In the little cafe they serve Blue Bottle coffee and confections that mimic the art.

### 2 WALKWAY MURAL
On the walkway that goes out to the sculpture garden, notice the mural on your right by Rosana Castrillo-Diaz. It takes up the whole wall, but a lot of people miss it. It was inspired by the way Renaissance drapery was sculpted in marble, and the artist used mica in the paint to reflect the light. What's fascinating is how it changes as you walk.

### 3 ATRIUM
The architect of SFMOMA, Mario Botta, incorporated cathedral-like features within the museum to mimic a town piazza, where the main feature is often a church. At the top of the atrium there's a bridge right under the skylight – very typical of Mario Botta – and from there you can see all the way down into the lobby. It's four stories up, so it can invite a little vertigo.

### 4 MUSEUM STORE
The museum store is a nice place to buy a gift for yourself or someone else. They sell contemporary jewelry designed by artists, fun housewares and a wonderful selection of art books and children's books.

### 5 REVOLVING EXHIBITS
What we have is always rotating, but you can almost always count on finding something wonderful. The 2nd floor features pieces from our permanent exhibit; the 3rd is photography and works on paper; the 4th floor has media arts; and the 5th houses larger, more contemporary pieces. There are all different kinds of media, so we invite people to leave their preconceptions about what art should be at the coat check.

# Discover the Mission, SoMa & the Castro

## Getting There & Away

○ **Bus** In SoMa, the 30 and 45 lines run down 4th St from Union Square and the 14 runs through SoMa to the Mission District along Mission St. The 27 runs from the Mission to Nob Hill via SoMa, the 47 runs along Harrison through SoMa and up Van Ness to Fisherman's Wharf, while the 19 runs up 8th and Polk Sts to the Wharf. In the Mission, bus 49 follows Mission St and Van Ness Ave to the Wharf, while the 33 links the Mission to the Castro, the Haight and Golden Gate Park.

○ **Metro** K, L and M trains run beneath Market St to Castro Station.

○ **Streetcar** All of the Market St streetcars serve the upper part of SoMa, as well as the Castro. The N line heads south along the Embarcadero and connects SoMa to the Haight and Golden Gate Park. The J streetcar heads from Downtown through the Mission.

○ **BART** Stations at 16th and 24th Sts serve the Mission.

Mission Dolores Park
THOMAS WINZ/LONELY PLANET IMAGES ©

## ⊙ Sights

The Mission is a crossroads of contradictions, and at its heart is Mission St, San Francisco's faded 'miracle mile' of deco cinemas now occupied by 99¢ stores and shady characters, surrounded by colorful murals and trendsetting restaurants. Wander South of Market St (SoMa) and discover corporate HQs from the Embarcadero to 3rd St, museums and galleries from 2nd to 4th, Skid Row between 6th and 8th, and nightclubs from 9th to Van Ness.

### The Mission

**Mission Dolores**          Church
Map p156 ( 📞 415-621-8203; www.mission dolores.org; 3321 16th St; adult/child $5/3; ⊙ 9am-4pm Nov-Apr, to 4:30pm May-Oct; Ⓜ & 🚇 16th St Mission) The city's oldest building and its namesake, the whitewashed adobe Misión San Francisco de Asis was founded in 1776 and rebuilt in 1782 with conscripted Ohlone and Miwok labor in exchange for a meal a day.

The building's nickname, Mission Dolores (Mission of the Sorrows), was taken from a nearby lake, but it turned out to be tragically apt. With harsh living conditions and little resistance to introduced diseases, some 5000 Ohlone and Miwok died in measles epidemics in 1814 and 1826. In the cemetery beside the adobe mission, a replica Ohlone hut commemorates their mass burial in the graveyard, among early Mexican and European settlers. Hitchcock fans looking for the grave of Carlotta Valdes will be disappointed: the tomb was only a prop for the film *Vertigo*.

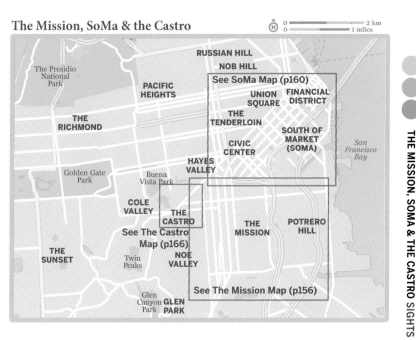

Today the modest adobe mission is overshadowed by the adjoining ornate Churriguera-esque basilica, built in 1913 after an 1876 brick Gothic cathedral collapsed in the 1906 earthquake. The front doors are usually only open during services, so you'll need to pass through the original mission structure and cross a courtyard to enter a side door.

## Mission Dolores Park — Park

Map p156 (Dolores St, btwn 18th & 20th Sts; M 18th St; R 16th St Mission) The site of quasi-professional Castro tanning contests, a small kids' playground (currently under reconstruction), free movies on summer nights and a Hunky Jesus Contest (p40) every Easter, this sloping park is also beloved for its year-round political protests and other favorite local sports. Flat patches are generally reserved for soccer games, candlelight vigils and ultimate Frisbee, and the tennis and basketball courts are open to anyone who's got game.

## Creativity Explored — Art Gallery

Map p156 (☎ 415-863-2108; www.creativity explored.org; 3245 16th St; donations welcome; ☺ 10am-3pm Mon-Fri, to 7pm Thu, 1-6pm Sat; M & R 16th St Mission) Brave new worlds are captured in celebrated artworks that have appeared in museum retrospectives, in major collections from New York to New Zealand and even on Marc Jacobs handbags – all by the local developmentally disabled artists who create at this nonprofit center. Intriguing themes range from superheroes to architecture, and openings are joyous celebrations with the artists, their families and their rock-star fan base.

## 826 Valencia — Cultural Site

Map p156 (☎ 415-642-5905; www.826valencia .com; 826 Valencia St; ☺ noon-6pm; M 18th St) 'No buccaneers! No geriatrics!' warns the sign above the vat of sand where kids rummage for buried pirates' booty. The treasures are theirs for the taking, if they barter for it at the front counter – a song, perhaps, or a knock-knock joke.

The eccentric **Pirate Supply Store** selling eye patches, message bottles,

# The Mission

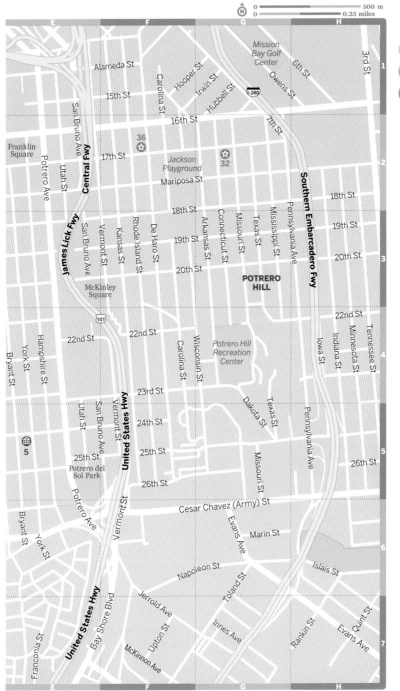

N

0 — 500 m
0 — 0.25 miles

Mission Bay Golf Center

Alameda St

Hooper St
Irwin St
Hubbell St

6th St

3rd St

Carolina St

15th St

Owens St

I-280

San Bruno Ave

16th St

7th St

Franklin Square

Central Fwy

17th St

36

Jackson Playground

32

Mariposa St

Southern Embarcadero Fwy

18th St

Potrero Ave

Utah St

18th St

Mississippi St
Pennsylvania Ave

19th St

James Lick Fwy

San Bruno Ave

Vermont St

Kansas St

Rhode Island St

De Haro St

19th St

Arkansas St

Connecticut St

Missouri St

Texas St

20th St

20th St

POTRERO HILL

McKinley Square

101

22nd St

22nd St

Carolina St

Wisconsin St

Potrero Hill Recreation Center

22nd St

Iowa St

Indiana St

Minnesota St

Tennessee St

Hampshire St

York St

Bryant St

23rd St

Dakota St

Texas St

Pennsylvania Ave

24th St

5

25th St

Potrero del Sol Park

United States Hwy

San Bruno Ave

Vermont St

Utah St

25th St

26th St

Missouri St

26th St

Bryant St

York St

26th St

Cesar Chavez (Army) St

Potrero Ave

Vermont St

Evans Ave

Marin St

Napoleon St

Toland St

Islais St

United States Hwy

Bay Shore Blvd

Jerrold Ave

Upton St

Innes Ave

Rankin St

Evans Ave

Quint St

Franconia St

McKinnon Ave

# The Mission

## ◎ Sights

| | | |
|---|---|---|
| 1 | 826 Valencia | B3 |
| 2 | Balmy Alley | D5 |
| 3 | Clarion Alley | B2 |
| 4 | Creativity Explored | B2 |
| 5 | Galería de la Raza | E5 |
| 6 | Mission Dolores | A2 |
| 7 | Mission Dolores Park | A3 |
| 8 | Women's Building | B3 |

## ⊗ Eating

| | | |
|---|---|---|
| 9 | Bi-Rite | B3 |
| 10 | Bi-Rite Creamery | B3 |
| 11 | Commonwealth | C3 |
| 12 | Corner | C3 |
| 13 | Delfina | B3 |
| 14 | Duc Loi | C3 |
| 15 | Humphry Slocombe | D5 |
| 16 | Ichi Sushi | B7 |
| 17 | La Taqueria | C5 |
| 18 | Mission Beach Cafe | B1 |
| 19 | Mitchell's Ice Cream | B7 |
| 20 | Tartine | B3 |
| 21 | Udupi Palace | B4 |

## ⊙ Drinking & Nightlife

| | | |
|---|---|---|
| 22 | Doc's Clock | C4 |
| 23 | El Rio | C6 |
| 24 | Elixir | B2 |
| 25 | Heart | B5 |
| 26 | Homestead | D3 |
| 27 | Latin American Club | C4 |
| 28 | Medjool Sky Terrace | C4 |
| 29 | Ritual Coffee Roasters | B4 |
| 30 | Zeitgeist | B1 |

## ⊙ Entertainment

| | | |
|---|---|---|
| 31 | Amnesia | B3 |
| 32 | Bottom of the Hill | G2 |
| 33 | Dance Mission | C5 |
| 34 | Elbo Room | B3 |
| 35 | Make-Out Room | C4 |
| 36 | Metronome Dance Collective | F2 |
| 37 | Roccapulco Supper Club | C6 |
| 38 | Roxie Cinema | B2 |

## ⓐ Shopping

| | | |
|---|---|---|
| 39 | Adobe Books & Backroom Gallery | B2 |
| 40 | Good Vibrations | B2 |
| 41 | Gravel & Gold | B4 |
| 42 | Mission Statement | B3 |
| 43 | Needles & Pens | B2 |
| 44 | Paxton Gate | B3 |
| 45 | Room 4 | B4 |

scoops from an actual tub o' lard and McSweeney's literary magazines, is the front for a nonprofit offering free writing workshops and tutoring for youth, plus the occasional adult program on starting a magazine or scripting video games (check the website for listings).

### Galería de la Raza
Art Gallery

Map p156 ( ☏415-826-8009; www.galeria delaraza.org; 2857 24th St; donations welcome; ◷noon-6pm Wed-Sat, to 7pm Tue; Ⓜ & Ⓡ24th St Mission) Art never forgets its roots at this nonprofit showcase for Latino art since 1970. Recent standouts include Sayuri Guzman's group portrait of Latinas connected by their long, braided hair, a group show exploring SF's Latin gay culture, and Enrique Chagoya's post–September 11 dinosaurs escaping the TV and rampaging through suburban living rooms.

## SoMa

### San Francisco Museum of Modern Art (SFMOMA)
Art Gallery

See p152.

### Cartoon Art Museum
Museum

Map p160 ( ☏415-227-8666; www.cartoonart .org; 655 Mission St; adult/student $7/$5, 1st Tue of month is 'pay what you wish' day; ◷11am-5pm Tue-Sun; Ⓜ & Ⓡ Montgomery St) Founded on a grant from Bay Area cartoon legend Charles M Schultz of *Peanuts* fame, this bold museum isn't afraid of the dark, racy or political, including R Crumb drawings from the '70s and a retrospective of political cartoons from the *Economist* by Kevin 'Kal' Kallaugher.

### Contemporary Jewish Museum
Museum

Map p160 ( ☏415-344-8800; www.thecjm.org; 736 Mission St; adult/child $10/free, after 5pm Thu $5; ◷11am-5pm Fri-Tue, 1-8pm Thu; Ⓜ &

SABRINA DALBESIO/LONELY PLANET IMAGES ©

## Don't Miss
# Mission Murals

Diego Rivera has no idea what he started. Inspired by the Mexican maestro's Depression-era works in San Francisco, generations of Mission muralists have covered neighborhood alleys and community institutions with some 400 murals to show political dissent, community pride and graffiti-art bravado. Barflys can be merciless in these streets, relieving themselves on notable works by muralists who've gone on to become art stars – but when historic **Balmy Alley** (btwn 24th & 25th Sts; Ⓜ & Ⓡ 24th St Mission) works are tagged, muralists carefully restore them.

When 1970s Mission *muralistas* disagreed with US foreign policy in Latin America, they took to the streets with paintbrushes in hand – beginning with Balmy Alley. Bodegas, taquerías and community centers lining 24th St are now covered with murals of mighty Mayan goddesses and Aztec warriors, honoring the Mission District's combined Native and Mexican origins. At the corner of 24th and Bryant, the Galería de la Raza (p158) has reserved billboard space for its Digital Mural Project, broadcasting messages such as 'Trust your struggle.'

Before Barry McGee and Chris Johansen sold out shows at international art fairs, they could be found at **Clarion Alley** (picture above; btwn 17th & 18th Sts, off Valencia St; Ⓜ & Ⓡ 16th St Mission), gripping spray-paint cans. In 1993–94 an all-star team of seven *muralistas* and local volunteers covered the **Women's Building** (☏ 415-431-1180; www .womensbuilding.org; 3543 18th St; Ⓜ 18th St; Ⓡ 16th St Mission) with *Maestrapeace,* featuring icons of female strength. Atop literary nonprofit 826 Valencia (p155) is a gold-leafed mural celebrating human attempts to communicate by Chris Ware, known for his acclaimed graphic novel *Jimmy Corrigan, Smartest Kid on Earth.*

## NEED TO KNOW
Map p156; 24th St btwn Mission & Potrero, Valencia St btwn 17th & 20th Sts; admission free; Ⓡ 24th St Mission or 16th St Mission

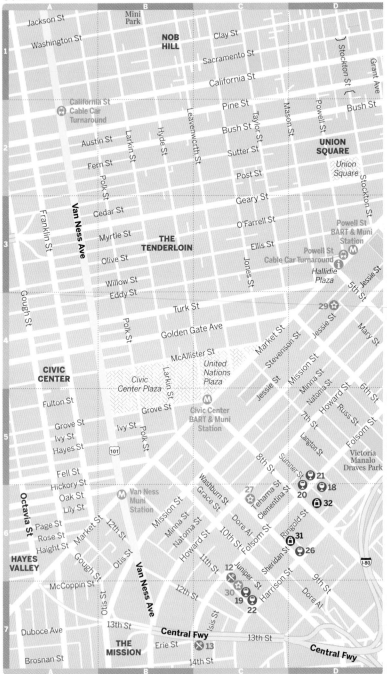

Jackson St

Washington St

Mini Park

**NOB HILL**

Clay St

Sacramento St

California St

Stockton St

Grant Ave

California St Cable Car Turnaround

Pine St

Bush St

Austin St

Larkin St

Hyde St

Leavenworth St

Bush St

Taylor St

Mason St

Powell St

**UNION SQUARE**

Fern St

Sutter St

Union Square

Polk St

Post St

Stockton St

Cedar St

Geary St

Franklin St

Van Ness Ave

Myrtle St

**THE TENDERLOIN**

O'Farrell St

Powell St BART & Muni Station

Gough St

Olive St

Ellis St

Powell St Cable Car Turnaround

Willow St

Jones St

Hallidie Plaza

5th St

Jessie St

Eddy St

Turk St

29

Jessie St

Mary St

Golden Gate Ave

Polk St

Market St

Stevenson St

Jessie St

McAllister St

**CIVIC CENTER**

Civic Center Plaza

Larkin St

United Nations Plaza

Mission St

Jessie St

Minna St

Natoma St

Howard St

6th St

Russ St

Fulton St

Grove St

Ivy St

Polk St

Grove St

Civic Center BART & Muni Station

7th St

Langton St

Folsom St

Victoria Manalo Draves Park

Ivy St

Hayes St

101

8th St

Sumner St

21

Fell St

Hickory St

Oak St

Lily St

Van Ness Muni Station

Washburn St

Grace St

27

Tehama St

Clementina St

20

18

32

Octavia St

**HAYES VALLEY**

Page St

Rose St

Haight St

Market St

12th St

Mission St

Minna St

Natoma St

Dore Al

10th St

Folsom St

Ringold St

31

26

Sheridan St

9th St

I-80

Gough St

Otis St

Howard St

11th St

Juniper St

12

Harrison St

Dore Al

McCoppin St

Van Ness Ave

12th St

Isis St

30

19

22

Duboce Ave

Otis St

13th St

**Central Fwy**

13th St

Central Fwy

**THE MISSION**

Erie St

13

14th St

Brosnan St

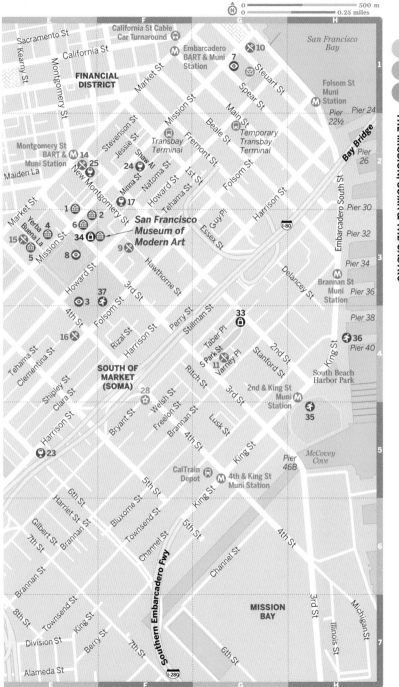

# SoMa

## ◉ Top Sights
San Francisco Museum of Modern Art ........................................F3

## ◉ Sights
1 California Historical Society Museum ..................................E2
2 Cartoon Art Museum ..........................E3
3 Children's Creativity Museum ...............E3
4 Contemporary Jewish Museum ...........E3
5 Museum of Craft & Folk Art ...................E3
6 Museum of the African Diaspora ..........E3
7 US Post Office ......................................G1
8 Yerba Buena Gardens ..........................E3

## ✕ Eating
9 Benu ....................................................F3
10 Boulevard ............................................G1
11 Butler & the Chef ................................G4
   Citizen's Band ..........................(see 20)
12 Juhu Beach Club ..................................C6
13 Rainbow Grocery ..................................C7
14 Sentinel ..............................................E2
15 Tropisueño ...........................................E3
16 Zero Zero ............................................E4

## ◉ Drinking & Nightlife
17 111 Minna ...........................................F2
   Bar Agricole ..............................(see 22)

18 Bloodhound ........................................D6
19 Butter .................................................C7
20 Cat Club ..............................................D6
21 City Beer Store & Tasting Room ............D5
22 DNA Lounge ........................................C7
23 EndUp ..................................................E5
24 Harlot .................................................F2
25 House of Shields .................................E2
26 Stud ....................................................D6

## ◉ Entertainment
27 AsiaSF .................................................C6
28 Hotel Utah Saloon ...............................F4
29 Mezzanine ...........................................D4
30 Slim's ..................................................C7
   Yerba Buena Center for the Arts ... (see 8)

## ◉ Shopping
31 Branch .................................................D6
32 Gama-Go .............................................D6
33 Jeremy's ..............................................G4
34 SFMOMA Museum Store .......................E3

## ◉ Sports & Activities
35 AT&T Park ...........................................H5
36 City Kayak ...........................................H4
37 Yerba Buena Center Ice Skating & Bowling ..............................F3

 Montgomery St) That upended brushed-steel box balancing improbably on one corner isn't a sculpture but a gallery for the Contemporary Jewish Museum, a major new San Francisco landmark that opened in 2008 but has been around since 1984. The exhibits inside are thoughtfully curated, compelling and heavy hitting. Standout recent shows have included *Warhol's Jews: 10 Portraits Reconsidered;* Linda Ellia's *Our Struggle: Artists Respond to Mein Kampf,* for which 600 artists from 17 countries were each invited to alter one page of Hitler's book; and a retrospective of the life and work of audacious author and modern-art instigator Gertrude Stein, raised across the bay in Oakland.

## Museum of the African Diaspora        Museum

Map p160 ( 415-358-7200; www.moadsf .org; 685 Mission St; adult/student $10/5; ⏰11am-6pm Wed-Sat, noon-5pm Sun; Ⓜ &  Montgomery St) A three-faced divinity by Ethiopian icon painter Qes Adamu Tesfaw, a stereotype in silhouette by American Kara Walker, a regal couple by British sensation Chris Ofili: this museum has assembled a standout international cast of characters to tell the epic story of diaspora. Memorable recent shows range from Romare Bearden's graphic riffs on trains, jazz and family, to quilts by India's Siddi community, descended from 16th-century African slaves. Themed interactive displays vary in interest and depth, but don't miss the moving video of slave narratives narrated by Maya Angelou.

## Museum of Craft & Folk Art

Art Gallery

Map p160 (☏415-227-4888; www.mocfa
.org; 51 Yerba Buena Lane; adult/child $5/free;
⏱11am-6pm Wed-Sat; Ⓜ & ⓇMontgomery St)
Vicarious hand cramps are to be expected from a trip to this small but utterly
absorbing museum, where remarkable
handiwork comes with equally fascinating backstories. Recent exhibitions
showcased Korean *bojagi* (hand-pieced
textiles), playful modern takes on iconic
Mexican handicrafts and internationally
acclaimed SF artist Clare Rojas' urban
folklore mural installations.

## California Historical Society Museum

Museum

Map p160 (☏415-357-1848; www.california
historicalsociety.org; 678 Mission St; adult/child
$3/1; ⏱noon-4:30pm Wed-Sat; Ⓜ & ⓇMont-
gomery St) Get the lowdown on California
history at this exhibition space devoted
entirely to the state's history. Galleries
show themed highlights from the
museum's vast collection of more than
half a million photographs, paintings and
ephemera. Recent exhibits have shown
how the Golden State built its reputation
for movies, fresh food and the good life
through silent-movie posters, vintage fruit
labels and tourism brochures – and how
that mythology washes with historical
realities.

## Children's Creativity Museum

Museum

Map p160 (☏415-820-3320; www.zeum.org;
221 4th St; admission $10; ⏱11am-5pm Tue-
Sun; Ⓜ & ⓇPowell St) No velvet ropes or
hands-off attitude here: kids have the
run of the place, with high-tech displays
that double dare them to make their own
music videos, Claymation movies and
soundtracks. Jump right into a live-action
video game, and sign up for workshops
with the Bay Area's superstar animators,
techno-whizzes, robot-builders and belly
dancers. The vintage 1906 **Loof Carousel**
out front operates until 6pm daily, and
one $3 ticket covers two rides.

## Yerba Buena Gardens

Park

Map p160 (☏415-541-0312, 415-820-3550;
www.yerbabuenagardens.com; 3rd & Mission Sts;
⏱sunrise-10pm; Ⓜ & ⓇMontgomery St) A
spot of green in the swath of concrete
South of Market. With Yerba Buena

Cartoon Art Museum (p158)

## Detour:
# WPA Murals at Rincon Annex Post Office

Russian-born painter Anton Refregier won the Works Progress Administration's (WPA) largest commission to depict the history of Northern California in 1941, but WWII intervened. When Refregier began again in 1945, he was lobbied by interest groups to present their version of history, and it took three years and 92 changes to make everyone happy. The murals were deemed 'communist' by McCarthyists in 1953, but they're now protected as a national landmark.

The colorful chronology begins over the old **US Post Office** (Map p160; 101 Spear St; admission free; M & R Embarcadero) window with *Preaching & Farming at Mission Dolores*, where emaciated Native workers do the heavy lifting while a friar expounds. A few scenes later, *Finding Gold at Sutter's Mill* shows the diversity of early Gold Rush arrivals: Latino, Asian and African American '49ers are depicted, plus sundry pirates. The version of history Refregier presents is not all rosy: *Vigilante Days* shows a man pulling a gun while another hangs from a noose, and *Beating the Chinese* shows red-faced attackers perpetrating 1870s anti-Chinese riots, alongside newspaper denunciations. *San Francisco as a Cultural Center* is a cultural collage with a wink: opera flyers, men of letters and burlesque dancers all gather under a glowing moon. The *Waterfront/1934 Strike* shows the history-changing dock-workers' strike, organized just outside Rincon Center, and *War and Peace* concludes the cycle with very pointed (and given the artist's experience, quite personal) anticensorship imagery, moving from Nazi book burning to postwar promises for 'Freedom from fear/want/of worship/speech.'

Center for the Arts and SFMOMA on one side and the Metreon cinema on the other, this is a prime spot for sun and downtime in between art and a movie. Free noontime concerts in the summer feature world music, hip-hop and jazz. The showstopping centerpiece is Houston Cornwell and Joseph De Pace's sleek Martin Luther King Jr Memorial Fountain, a wall of water that runs over the Reverend's immortal words: 'until justice rolls down like waters and righteousness like a mighty stream.'

A pedestrian bridge over Howard St links the popular esplanade to an often overlooked playground and family entertainment complex. Kids with energy and creativity to spare won't want to miss this complex, which includes the hands-on Children's Creativity Museum and carousel, a small bowling alley and an ice rink.

## The Castro

### GLBT History Museum     Museum
Map p166 ( ☎ 415-777-5455; www.glbthistory .org/museum; 4127 18th St; admission $5; M Castro St) America's first gay-history museum cobbles ephemera from the community – Harvey Milk's campaign literature, matchbooks from long-gone bathhouses, the dress Laura Linney wore as Mary Anne Singleton in the TV remake of *Tales of the City* – together with harder-hitting installations, such as audiovisual interviews with Gore Vidal and pages of the 1950s penal code banning homosexuality.

### Harvey Milk Plaza     Square
Map p160 (Market & Castro Sts; M Castro St) A huge, irrepressibly cheerful rainbow flag lords over Castro and Market Sts, officially dubbed Harvey Milk Plaza. Look closer and spot a plaque honoring the man whose lasting legacy to the Castro is civic pride and political clout.

# ⊗ Eating

## The Mission

**La Taqueria**                    Mexican **$**

Map p156 ( 📞415-285-7117; 2889 Mission St;
burritos $6-8; 🕐11am-9pm Mon-Sat, to 8pm Sun;
🚹; Ⓜ & 🚈24th St Mission) Rabble-rouser?
Ask a group of San Franciscans where
to get the best burrito in town, then as
voices rise, quietly slip off to La Taqueria.
There's no saffron rice, spinach tortilla
or mango salsa up for debate here – just
perfectly grilled meats, flavorful beans
and classic tomatillo or mesquite salsa
wrapped in a flour tortilla.

**Commonwealth**               Californian **$$**

Map p156 ( 📞415-355-1500; www.common
wealthsf.com; 2224 Mission St; small plates $5-16;
🕐5:30-10pm Tue-Thu & Sun, to 11pm Fri & Sat;
🚹; Ⓜ & 🚈16th St Mission) California's most
imaginative farm-to-table dining isn't
in some quaint barn, but the converted
cinder-block Mission dive where chef
Jason Fox serves crispy hen with toybox
carrots cooked in hay (yes, hay), and sea
urchin floating on a bed of farm egg and
organic asparagus that looks like a tide
pool and tastes like a dream. Savor the
$65 prix fixe, knowing that $10 is donated
to charity.

**🖊 Delfina**         Californian, Italian **$$$**

Map p156 ( 📞415-552-4055; www.delfinasf
.com; 3621 18th St; mains $18-27; 🕐5:30-10pm
Sun-Thu, to 11pm Fri & Sat; 🚹; Ⓜ18th St;
🚈16th St Mission) Simple yet sensational
seasonal California cuisine with a slight
Italian accent: Sonoma duck with Barolo-
roasted cherries, housemade pasta with
local wild-boar *ragu* (sauce), profiteroles
with coffee gelato and candied almonds.
Since this is the one California-cuisine
restaurant all of SF's picky eaters agree
on, make reservations now, arrive early
and prepare for a wait with a glass of
wine – though when you get a whiff of
the sensational wild-mushroom pizza at
**Delfina Pizza** next door, you might want
to sign up there instead.

---

# SF's Top Three Gourmet Groceries

**Bi-Rite** (Map p156; 📞415-241-9760; www.biritemarket.com; 3639 18th St; 🕐9am-9pm;
🚈16th St Mission) Nemesis of grocery budgets and ally of gourmands whose
cooking repertoire is limited to reheating, Bi-Rite is a San Francisco foodie's
version of breakfast at Tiffany's. Local artisan chocolates, sustainable cured
meats and organic fruit are displayed like jewels, and the selection of California
wines and cheeses is downright dazzling. Across the street is organic Bi-Rite
Creamery (p168).

**Duc Loi** (Map p156; 2200 Mission St; 🕐8am-8pm; Ⓜ18th St; 🚈16th St Mission) Stretch
your culinary imagination with a browse through the refrigerated grocery case
of organic lettuces and pan-Asian herbs fresh from the Central Valley, the wall
of Mayan spices and tropical tree barks, and an entire aisle of international
cookies and Japanese condiments.

**Rainbow Grocery** (Map p160; 📞415-863-0620; www.rainbowgrocery.org; 1745 Folsom St;
🕐9am-9pm) The legendary cooperative attracts masses to buy eco/organic/fair-
trade products in bulk, drool over the bounty of local cheeses and flirt in the
all-natural skin-care aisle. To answer your questions about where to find what
in the Byzantine bulk section, ask a fellow shopper – staff can be elusive. Small
though well-priced wine and craft beer selections; no meat products.

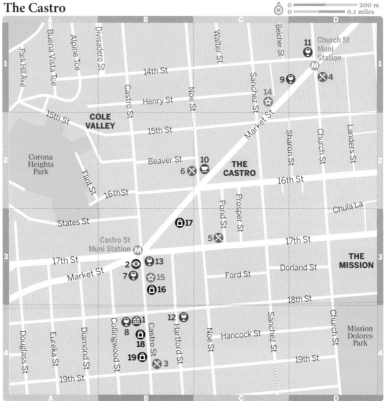

### Ichi Sushi
Sushi $$

Map p156 ( 📞415-525-4750; 3369 Mission St; www.ichisushi.com; ⏰11:30am-10pm Tue-Thu, to 11pm Fri, 5:30-11pm Sun, 5:30-10pm Mon; Ⓜ Mission St; Ⓡ24th St Mission) Alluring on the plate and positively obscene on the tongue, Ichi Sushi is a sharp cut above other fish thanks to clever culinary engineering. Silky, sustainably sourced fish is sliced with a jeweler's precision, balanced atop well-packed rice, and topped with tiny but powerfully tangy dabs of gelled *yuzu* (Japanese citrus fruit) and a microscopic brunoise of spring onion and chili daikon that makes soy sauce unthinkable.

### Udupi Palace
Indian $

Map p156 ( 📞415-970-8000; www.udupi palaceca.com; 1007 Valencia St; mains $8-10; ⏰11am-10pm Mon-Thu, to 10:30pm Fri-Sun; Ⓜ Valencia St; Ⓡ24th St Mission) Tandoori in the Tenderloin is for novices – SF foodies swoon over the bright, clean flavors of South Indian *dosa* (a light, crispy pancake made with lentil flour) dipped in mildly spicy vegetable *sambar* (soup) and coconut chutney. Don't miss the *medhu vada* (savory lentil donuts with *sambar* and chutney) or *bagala bhath* (yogurt rice with cucumber and nutty toasted mustard seeds).

### Tartine
Bakery $

Map p156 ( 📞415-487-2600; www.tartinebakery .com; 600 Guerrero St; pastries $3-6, sandwiches $10-13; ⏰8am-7pm Mon, 7:30am-7pm Tue & Wed, 7:30am-8pm Thu & Fri, 9am-8pm Sat & Sun; 🌐; Ⓜ18th St; Ⓡ16th St Mission) Riches beyond your wildest dreams: butter-intensive *pain au chocolat,* cappuccino with ferns drawn in dense foam and *croque monsieurs* turbo-loaded with ham, two

# The Castro

**◎ Sights**
1 GLBT History Museum..........................B4
2 Harvey Milk Plaza...............................B3

**❌ Eating**
3 Anchor Oyster Bar...............................B4
4 Chow......................................................D1
5 Frances..................................................C3
6 La Méditerranée..................................B2

**◐ Drinking & Nightlife**
7 440 Castro.............................................B3
8 Badlands................................................B4
9 Blackbird................................................D1
10 Cafe Flore............................................C2

11 Churchill...............................................D1
12 Moby Dick............................................B4
13 Twin Peaks Tavern.............................B3

**✪ Entertainment**
14 Café du Nord/Swedish
    American Hall....................................C1
15 Castro Theatre....................................B3

**◓ Shopping**
16 Cliff's Variety.......................................B3
17 Sui Generis...........................................B3
18 Under One Roof...................................B4
19 Worn Out West ...................................B4

kinds of cheese and béchamel. Don't be dismayed by the inevitable line out the door – it moves fast – but be aware that lolling in Mission Dolores Park is the only possible post-Tartine activity.

**Corner**  Pop-Up **$**
Map p156 (☎415-875-9278; 2199 Mission St; dishes $8; ◷hours vary; Ⓜ18th St; Ⓡ16th St Mission) Forget *Top Chef,* the ultimate culinary trial for SF chefs is a night at the Corner. Successful chefs are invited back for command performances and may generate enough buzz to open permanent restaurants – but this is a tough crowd to impress. Recent encores have been granted to Ken Ken Ramen's housemade Japanese noodles with slow-cooked pork and Cat's Head Barbecue's sweet-tea marinated chicken.

**◪ Mission Beach Cafe**  Californian **$$**
Map p156 (☎415-861-0198; www.mission beachcafesf.com; 198 Guerrero St; brunch mains $8-13; ◷9am-2:30pm & 5:30-10pm Mon-Sat, to 11pm Fri & Sat, 9am-3:30pm Sun; Ⓜmarket St) Brunch gets an upgrade to first class with farm-fresh organic ingredients: pancakes come with strawberries and bourbon syrup, while huevos rancheros (ranch-style eggs) are served with heritage beans and sustainably raised pulled pork. The crowning glory is the veggie eggs Benedict with wild mushrooms, caramelized onions and truffle sauce, loaded onto an English muffin made by the in-house pastry chef.

# SoMa

**Benu**  Californian Fusion **$$$**
Map p160 (☎415-685-4860; www.benusf.com; 22 Hawthorne St; mains $25-40; ◷5:30-10pm Tue-Sat; Ⓜ & Ⓡmontgomery) SF has refined fusion cuisine over 150 years, but no one rocks it quite like chef/owner Corey Lee (formerly of Napa's French Laundry), who remixes local, sustainable fine-dining staples and Pacific Rim flavors with a SoMa DJ's finesse. Velvety Sonoma foie gras with tangy, woodsy *yuzu*-sake glaze makes taste buds bust wild moves, while Dungeness crab and black truffle custard bring such outsize flavor to faux–shark's fin soup, you'll swear there's Jaws in there.

**Zero Zero**  Pizza **$$**
Map p160 (☎415-348-8800; www.zero zerosf.com; 826 Folsom St; ◷noon-2:30pm & 5:30-10pm Sun-Thu, to 11pm Fri & Sat; Ⓜ & ⓇPowell St) The name is a throw-down of Neapolitan pizza credentials – '00' flour is used exclusively for Naples' famous puffy-edged crust – and these pies deliver on that promise, with inspired SF-themed toppings. The Geary is an exciting offering involving Manila clams, bacon and chilies, but the real crowd-pleaser is the Castro,

# SF à la Mode: Top Three Local Ice Creams

**Humphry Slocombe** (Map p156; ☎415-550-6971; www.humphryslocombe.com; 2790 Harrison St; ice cream $2.75-5; ◷noon-9pm Mon-Thu, to 10pm Fri-Sun; ⃞24th St Mission) Indie-rock organic ice cream may permanently spoil you for Top-40 flavors: once Thai curry peanut butter and strawberry goat cheese have rocked your taste buds, cookie dough seems so obvious, and ordinary sundaes can't compare to Sonoma olive oil ice cream drizzled with 20-year aged balsamic.

**Mitchell's Ice Cream** (Map p156; ☎415-648-2300; www.mitchellsicecream.com; 688 San Jose Ave; ice cream $3-6; ◷11am-11pm; Ⓜ Mission St) An otherwise nondescript Mission block is thronged with grinning grown-ups and kids doing happy dances as they make their Mitchell's selections: will it be a classic like Kahlua mocha cream or a tropical flavor like *macapuno* (young coconut)?

**Bi-Rite Creamery** (Map p156; ☎415-626-5600; www.biritecreamery.com; 3692 18th St; ice cream $3-7; ◷11am-10pm Sun-Thu, to 11pm Fri & Sat; Ⓜ18th St) Velvet ropes at clubs seem pretentious in laid-back San Francisco, but at organic Bi-Rite Creamery they make perfect sense: as soon as SF temperatures nudge past 70°F (21°C), the line wraps around the corner for legendary salted caramel ice cream with housemade hot fudge.

which, as you might guess, is turbo-loaded with housemade sausage.

### Boulevard
Californian $$$

Map p160 (☎415-543-6084; www.boulevard restaurant.com; 1 Mission St; mains $28-39; ◷11:30am-2pm & 5:30-10pm Mon-Thu, to 10:30pm Fri & Sat; Ⓜ & ⃞Embarcadero) The quake-surviving, 1889 belle epoque Audiffred Building is a fitting locale for Boulevard, which remains one of San Francisco's most solidly reliable and effortlessly graceful restaurants. Chef Nancy Oakes has a light, easy touch with classics like juicy pork chops, finesses Dungeness crab salad with fresh basil, watermelon and yogurt, and ends East-West coastal rivalries with Maine lobster stuffed inside California squid.

### Juhu Beach Club
Indian $

Map p160 (☎415-298-0471; www.facebook .com/juhubeachclub; 320 11th St; dishes $4-8; ◷11:30am-2:30pm Mon-Fri; Ⓜ Folsom St) SoMa's gritty streets are looking positively upbeat ever since reinvented *chaat* (Indian street snacks) popped up inside the **Garage Café**, serving lunchtime pork vin-

daloo buns, aromatic grilled Nahu chicken salad and the aptly named, slow-cooked shredded-steak 'holy cow' sandwich.

### ✐ Citizen's Band
Californian $

Map p160 (☎415-556-4901; www.citizens bandsf.com; 1198 Folsom St; ◷11:30am-2pm & 5:30-11pm Tue-Fri, 10am-2pm & 5:30-11pm Sat, 10am-2pm & 5:30-9:30pm Sun; Ⓜ Folsom St; ⃞Civic Center) The name refers to CB radio, and the menu here is retro American diner with a California difference: mac-n-cheese with Sonoma jack cheese and optional truffle, wedge-lettuce salads with local Point Reyes blue cheese, and local Snake River Kobe beef burgers (the best in town). Don't miss small-production local wines and after-lunch treats from the pop-up cupcake shop on the premises.

### Butler & the Chef
French $

Map p160 (☎415-896-2075; www.thebutler andthechefbistro.com; 155a South Park St; brunch mains $9-12; ◷8am-3pm Tue-Sat, 10am-3pm Sun; Ⓜ Townsend St) All the French classics you'd never expect to find among SoMa warehouses are here, from the *croque monsieur* (pressed ham and cheese) with Niman Ranch ham, Emmenthal cheese and béchamel on organic bread, to light, flaky-crusted quiche lorraine studded with Niman Ranch bacon.

### Sentinel · Sandwiches $
Map p160 ( ☏415-284-9960; www.thesentinelsf .com; 37 New Montgomery St; sandwiches $9; ⏰7:30am-2:30pm Mon-Fri; Ⓜ & Ⓡ Montgomery St) Rebel SF chef Dennis Leary is out to revolutionize lunchtime takeout, taking on the classics with top-notch seasonal ingredients. Tuna salad gets radical with chipotle mayo and the snap of crisp summer vegetables, and corned beef crosses borders with Swiss cheese and housemade Russian dressing.

### Tropisueño · Mexican $
Map p160 ( ☏415-243-0299; www.tropisueno .com; 75 Yerba Buena Lane; ⏰11am-10:30pm; Ⓜ & Ⓡ Powell St) Last time you enjoyed casual Mexican dining this much, there were probably balmy ocean breezes and hammocks involved. Instead, you're steps away from SFMOMA, savoring an *al pastor* (marinated pork) burrito with mesquite salsa and grilled pineapple, and sipping a margarita with a chili-salted rim.

## The Castro

### Frances · Californian $$
Map p166 ( ☏415-621-3870; www .frances-sf.com; 3870 17th St; mains $14-27; ⏰5-10.30pm Tue-Sun) Chef/owner Melissa Perello earned a Michelin star for fine dining, then ditched Downtown to start this market-inspired neighborhood bistro. Daily menus showcase bright, seasonal flavors and luxurious textures: cloud-like sheep's milk ricotta gnocchi with crunchy bread crumbs and broccolini, grilled calamari with preserved Meyer lemon, and artisan wine served by the ounce, directly from Wine Country.

### Anchor Oyster Bar · Seafood $$
Map p166 (www.anchoroysterbar.com; 579 Castro St; mains $15-25; ⏰11:30am-10pm Mon-Sat, 4-9:30pm Sun; Ⓜ Castro St) Since its founding in 1977, Anchor's formula has been simple: seafood classics, like local oysters, crab cakes and Boston clam chowder, and copious salads. The nautical-themed room seats just 24 at shiny stainless-steel tables; you can't

Burrito

make reservations, but you can sit at the marble-top bar to shorten the wait.

### Chow
American $$

Map p166 ( 📞 415-552-2469; www.chowfoodbar .com; 215 Church St; mains $9-14; ⏰ 11am-11pm; 🍴 ; Ⓜ Church St) Chow's diverse menu appeals to all tastes, with everything from pizza and pork chops to Thai-style noodles and spaghetti and meatballs. The wood-floored room is big, loud and always busy. Avoid tables alongside the bar (you'll get jostled); request a table on the back patio for quiet(er) conversations. Call ahead for the 'no-wait' list.

### La Méditerranée
Middle Eastern $$

Map p166 ( 📞 415-431-7210; www.lamediterranee .net; 288 Noe St; mains $12-15; ⏰ 11am-10pm Sun-Thu, to 11pm Fri & Sat; 🍴 👪 ; Ⓜ Castro St) Zesty, lemon-laced Lebanese fare at friendly prices makes La Méd the Castro's neighborhood meet-up spot. Chicken kebabs on rice pilaf are pleasingly plump; the *kibbe* is a harmonious blend of pine nuts, ground lamb and cracked wheat;

and the smoky eggplant in the baba ghanoush was roasted for hours and isn't the least bit bitter about it.

## 🍷 Drinking & Nightlife

### The Mission

#### Zeitgeist
Bar

Map p156 (www.zeitgeistsf.com; 199 Valencia St; ⏰ 9am-2am; 🚆 16th St Mission) You've got two seconds flat to order from tough-gal barkeeps who are used to putting macho bikers in their place – but with 40 beers on draft available by the pint or pitcher, beer lovers are at a loss for words. When it's warm, regulars head straight to the bar's huge, graveled beer garden to sit at long picnic tables and smoke out.

#### 🖊 Elixir
Bar

Map p156 (www.elixirsf.com; 3200 16th St; ⏰ 3pm-2am Mon-Fri, noon-2am Sat & Sun;

**Left:** Elixir; **Below:** The Castro (p164)

(LEFT) SABRINA DALBESIO/LONELY PLANET IMAGES ©; (BELOW) ROBERTO GEROMETTA/LONELY PLANET IMAGES ©

🚊 16th St Mission) Do the planet a favor and have another drink at SF's first certified-green bar in an actual 1858 Wild West saloon, serving knockout cocktails made with seasonal organic fruit juices and local, organic, even biodynamic spirits. Invent your own or consult the resident mixologist – *ayiyi,* those peach margaritas with ancho-chili-infused tequila – and mingle over darts and a killer jukebox.

### El Rio
Nightclub

Map p156 (📞415-282-3325; www.elriosf.com; 3158 Mission St; admission $3-8; ⏱5pm-2am Mon-Thu, 4pm-2am Fri, noon-2am Sun; Ⓜ & 🚊24th St Mission) The DJ mix at El Rio takes its cue from the patrons: eclectic, funky and sexy, no matter your orientation. The club rightly boasts about the back garden, its 'Totally Fabulous Happy Hour' from 5pm to 9pm Tuesday to Friday, and free oysters on the half shell on Fridays at 5:30pm. Sunday afternoons are the busiest, especially when salsa bands rock (lessons at 3pm); check the calendar for Saturday-night events. Drawback: the distance from other bars on slow nights.

### Heart
Bar

Map p156 (www.heartsf.com; 1270 Valencia St; ⏱5pm-11pm Sun, Mon & Wed, to midnight Thu-Sat; Ⓜ & 🚊24th St Mission) Friendly, arty, gourmet: this wine bar is all Heart. Check the website to arrive when Kitchenette pop-up is serving five-star organic, seasonal meals (share plates $4 to $12) – that masala cauliflower *panna cotta* (custard) will have you licking the jam jar it came in (ahem). The pinot noir is entirely too good for dribbly Mason jars, but there's no resisting the wine menu descriptions: one malbec is 'for kids who ate dirt' and a French white shows 'more soul than Marvin Gaye.'

### Homestead
Bar

Map p156 (2301 Folsom St; ⏱5pm-1am; Ⓜ18th St; 🚊16th St Mission) Your friendly Victorian corner dive c 1893, complete

171

with carved-wood bar, roast peanuts in the shell, cheap draft beer and Victorian tin-stamped ceiling. On any given night, SF's creative contingent pack the place to celebrate an art opening, dance show or fashion launch – and when Iggy Pop or David Bowie hits the jukebox, watch out.

### Ritual Coffee Roasters                     Cafe
Map p156 (www.ritualroasters.com; 1026 Valencia St; 6am-10pm Mon-Fri, 7am-10pm Sat, 7am-9pm Sun; ; M & 24th St Mission) Cults wish they inspired the same devotion as Ritual, where lines head out the door for house-roasted cappuccino with ferns in the foam and specialty drip coffees with some genuinely bizarre flavor profiles – believe the whiteboard descriptions claiming certain coffee beans taste like grapefruit or hazelnut. Electrical outlets are limited to encourage conversation instead of IMing, so you can eavesdrop on people plotting their next dates, art projects and political protests.

### Medjool Sky Terrace                        Bar
Map p156 (www.medjoolsf.com; 2522 Mission St; 5-11pm Sun-Thu, to 2am Fri & Sat; M & 24th St Mission) SF's best open-air rooftop bar has knockout views of vintage Mission street marquees, Mediterranean small plates and basic but tasty cocktails (cash only). Go early for sunsets and prime spots by heat lamps; instead of heading into the downstairs restaurant, take the hotel elevator to the top floor.

### Latin American Club                        Bar
Map p156 (3286 22nd St; 6pm-2am Mon-Fri, 2pm-2am Sat & Sun; M Mission St) Margaritas go the distance here – just don't stand up too fast. *Ninja pinatas* and *papel picado* (cut-paper banners) add a festive atmosphere, and rosy lighting and generous

## Top Three Dance Venues

Couples dancing has never gone out of style here. SF was at the forefront of the swing revival, and salsa and tango are perennial favorites. The following host dance nights in most genres, from cha-cha and swing to tango and waltz. Admission ranges between $5 and $10; when bands perform, the price rises to about $25. Swing events tend to move venues; check www.oldtimey.net and www.lindylist.com for the latest.

**Metronome Dance Collective** (Map p156; 415-871-2462; www.metronomedance collective.com; 1830 17th St; M 16th St) Always wished you could tango, swing or ballroom dance? This dancing school has one of the largest floors in the city, and top-ranked dance pros teach classes for beginners, advanced dancers and kids, plus wedding workshops; see the website for details.

**Dance Mission** (Map p156; www.dancemission.com; 3316 24th St; 24th St Mission) Step out and find your niche at this Mission institution, featuring contact improv, dance jams and classes. The 140-seat theater showcases female performers, dance troupes and choreographers.

**Roccapulco Supper Club** (Map p156; www.roccapulco.com; 3140 Mission St; admission $10-15; 8pm-2am; 24th St Mission) Get your salsa, rumba and *bachata* (Dominican dance) on at this high-ceilinged, stadium-sized Latin venue that books sensational touring acts like El Grupo Niche. This is a straight bar, ripe with cologne and hormones; single women new to the scene may feel more comfortable in a group.

pours enable shameless flirting outside your age range.

## Doc's Clock
Bar

Map p156 (www.docsclock.com; 2575 Mission St; 🕐6pm-2am Mon-Thu, 4pm-2am Fri & Sat, 8pm-midnight Sun; Ⓜ Mission St) Follow the siren call of the dazzling neon sign into this mellow, green-certified dive for your choice of 14 local craft brews, free shuffleboard, Pac-Man, tricky old pinball games and easy conversation.

# SoMa

## Bar Agricole
Bar

Map p160 (📞415-355-9400; www.baragricole .com; 355 11th St; 6-10pm Sun-Wed, 6pm-late Thu-Sat; Ⓜ10th St) Drink your way to a history degree with well-researched cocktails: Bellamy Scotch Sour with egg whites passes the test, but Tequila Fix with lime, pineapple gum and hellfire bitters earns honors. And talk about an overachiever – for its modern wabi-sabi design with natural materials and sleek deck, Agricole won a James Beard Award for restaurant design. Bar bites here are a proper pig-out, including pork pâté with aspic and fried farm egg with crispy pork belly.

## Bloodhound
Bar

Map p160 (www.bloodhoundsf.com; 1145 Folsom St; 🕐4pm-2am; Ⓜ Mission St) The murder of crows painted on the ceiling is definitely an omen: nights at Bloodhound often assume mythic proportions. Vikings would feel at home amid these white walls and antler chandeliers, while bootleggers would appreciate the reclaimed barnwood walls and top-shelf booze served in Mason jars.

## Cat Club
Club

Map p160 (www.catclubsf.com; 1190 Folsom St; admission $5 after 10pm; 🕐9pm-3am Tue-Sun; Ⓜ & Ⓡ Civic Center) You'll never really know your friends until you've seen them belt out A-ha's 'Take on Me' at 1984, Cat Club's Thursday-night retro dance party, where the euphoric bi/straight/gay/indefinable scene is like some surreal John Hughes movie. Come back to belt at karaoke Tuesdays, jump to '90s power

pop at Saturday's Club Vogue and shuffle winsomely at Friday and Sunday goth/new-wave nights. The two small rooms get sweaty fast at special theme nights like Bondage-a-Go-Go and queer-strip-core Blowpony; check the online calendar.

## Stud
Gay Club

Map p160 (📞415-252-7883; www.studsf .com; 399 9th St; admission $5-8; 🕐5pm-3am; 🚇10th St) The Stud has rocked the gay scene since 1966, but has branched out beyond the obvious leather daddies and preppy twinks into whole new categories of gay good times. Check the schedule for rocker-grrrl Monday nights, anything-goes Meow Mix Tuesday drag variety shows, raunchy comedy and karaoke Wednesdays, art/drag dance parties on Fridays and drag-disco-performance-art cabaret whenever hostess DJ MC MF Anna Conda gets the notion.

## EndUp
Gay Club

Map p160 (www.theendup.com; 401 6th St; admission $5-20; 🕐10pm-4am Mon-Thu, 11pm-11am Fri, 10pm Sat-4am Mon; Ⓜ Bryant St) Anyone left on the streets of San Francisco after 2am on weekends is subject to the magnetic force of the EndUp's marathon dance sessions. It's the only club with a 24-hour license and though straight people do come here, it remains best known for its gay Sunday tea dances, in full force since 1973. Regulars arrive in time for popular reggae and 'Ghettodisco' sets on Saturdays (check the web) and bring a change of clothes for work Monday.

## 111 Minna
Bar, Club

Map p160 (www.111minnagallery.com; 111 Minna St; admission free-$15; Ⓜ & Ⓡ Montgomery St) A superhero to rescue the staid Downtown scene, 111 Minna is a streetwise art gallery by day (open from noon to 5pm Wednesday to Saturday) that transforms into a happening lounge space and club by night (evening hours vary).

## Harlot
Club

Map p160 (www.harlotsf.com; 46 Minna St; admission free-$20; 🕐5pm-2am Wed-Fri, 9pm-2am Sat; Ⓜ & Ⓡ Montgomery St) Vampire bordello is the vibe here, with intense red lighting, velvet curtains revealing exposed-brick walls and table-sized photos of pinups wearing nothing but boa constrictors (watch where you put down that cocktail). Before 9pm it's a lounge, but after that the killer sound system pumps – especially with house on Thursdays, indie-rock on Wednesdays and monthly women-only Fem Bar parties.

### House of Shields                        Bar

Map p160 (39 New Montgomery St; ◷2pm-2am Mon-Fri, 7pm-2am Sat; Ⓜ & Ⓡ Montgomery St) Flash back 100 years at this recently restored mahogany bar, with original c 1908 chandeliers hanging from high ceilings and old-fashioned cocktails without the frippery. This is the one bar in SF that slumming Nob Hill socialites and Downtown bike messengers can agree on – especially after a few $5 cocktails in dimly lit corners.

### DNA Lounge                        Nightclub

Map p160 (www.dnalounge.com; 375 11th St; admission $3-25; ◷9:30pm-3am Fri & Sat, other nights vary; Ⓜ Market St) One of SF's last megaclubs hosts live bands and big-name DJs, with two floors of late-night dance action just seedy enough to be interesting (the cops keep trying and failing to shut this rowdy joint down). Choose your night from the website – events ranging from seriously silly PopRocks to major drag king competitions – and dress the part. Early arrivals may hear crickets.

### City Beer Store & Tasting Room                        Bar

Map p160 (www.citybeerstore.com; 1168 Folsom St; ◷noon-10pm Tue-Sat, to 6pm Sun; Ⓜ Civic Center) Sample exceptional local and Belgian microbrewed beer from the 300-brew menu (6oz to 22oz, depending on how thirsty you are) at SF's top beer store. Create your own tastings of stouts or red ales, or pick a point on the globe at random and drink your way home via unknown artisan brews. Line your stomach with cheese and salami plates, and assemble your own six-pack to go. Check the website for bottle release parties and tapping events.

### Butter                        Bar

Map p160 (www.smoothasbutter.com; 354 11th St; ◷6pm-2am Thu-Sat, 8pm-2am Sun; Ⓜ 11th St) Lowbrow and loving it: everyone's chasing Tang cocktails with PBR and wailing to rock anthems here, while across the street at VIP clubs they're still politely waiting for the good times to start. You'll never pay $10 for a drink at this tiny, happening bar, leaving plenty of cash for tater tots, mini corn dogs and deep-fried Twinkies...dude, if you want nutrition, what're you doing in a bar called Butter?

## The Castro

### Cafe Flore                        Cafe

Map p166 (☎415-621-8579; www.cafeflore.com; 2298 Market St; ◷7am-midnight

Bar Agricole (p173)
THOMAS WINZ/LONELY PLANET IMAGES ©

Sun-Thu, to 2am Fri & Sat; 🛜; Ⓜ Castro St) You haven't done the Castro till you've lolly-gagged on the sun-drenched patio at the Flore – everyone winds up here sooner or later. Weekdays present the best chance to meet neighborhood regulars, who colonize the tables outside. Weekends get packed. Great happy-hour drink specials, like two-for-one margaritas. Pretty good food, too. Wi-fi weekdays only.

### Blackbird
Gay Bar

Map p166 (📞 415-503-0630; www.blackbirdbar.com; 2124 Market St; 🕐 3pm-2am Mon-Fri, noon-2am Sat & Sun; Ⓜ Church St) The Castro's lounge-bar draws a mix of guys in tight T-shirts and their gal-pals. The look is sleek and clean, but not overstyled. We dig the macabre news clippings on the walls. The cocktails are strong and there's a good selection of wines and craft beers by the glass. Bartenders provide eye candy. Ideal spot to begin a Castro pub crawl, but it gets packed weekends.

### 440 Castro
Gay Bar

Map p166 (📞 415-621-8732; www.the440.com; 440 Castro St; 🕐 noon-2am; Ⓜ Castro St) The most happening bar on the street, 440 Castro draws bearded, gym-fit 30-something dudes – especially for Thursday's 'CDXL', when go-go boys twirl – and an odd mix of Peter Pans for Monday's underwear night.

### Moby Dick
Gay Bar

Map p166 (📞 415-861-1199; www.mobydicksf.com; 4049 18th St; 🕐 2pm-2am Mon-Fri, noon-2am Sat & Sun; Ⓜ Castro St) The name overpromises, but not for the giant fish tank behind the bar, which provides a focal point for shy boys who would otherwise look at their shoes. Weekdays it's a mellow spot for pool, pinball and meeting neighborhood 20-to-40-somethings.

### Twin Peaks Tavern
Gay Bar

Map p166 (📞 415-864-9470; www.twinpeakstavern.com; 401 Castro St; 🕐 noon-2am Mon-Fri, 8am-2am Sat & Sun; Ⓜ Castro St) Don't call it the glass coffin. Show some respect: Twin Peaks was the first gay bar in the world with windows opening to the street.

The jovial crowd skews (way) over 40, but they're not chicken hawks (or they wouldn't hang here), and they love it when happy kids show up and join the party. Ideal for a tête-à-tête after a film at the Castro, or for cards, Yahtzee or backgammon (BYO).

### Churchill
Bar

Map p166 (www.churchillsf.com; 198 Church St; Ⓜ Church St) Another gay bar bites the dust and goes straight(-ish), but you'd never know from the stylin' decor – a mash-up of recycled wood, nautical rope strung across the ceiling, vintage blown-glass lanterns and tufted sofas that evoke 1940s cool and dockworker hot, making this the best-looking bar in the 'hood.

### Badlands
Gay Bar

Map p166 (📞 415-626-9320; www.badlands-sf.com; 4121 18th St; Ⓜ Castro St) The Castro's long-standing dance bar gets packed with gay college boys, their screaming straight girlfriends and chicken hawks. If you're over 30, you'll feel old. Weekends, expect a line.

## ✪ Entertainment

## The Mission

### Roxie Cinema
Cinema

Map p156 (📞 415-863-1087; www.roxie.com; 3117 16th St; admission $6-10; Ⓜ & Ⓡ 16th St Mission) A little neighborhood nonprofit cinema with major international clout for helping distribute and launch indie films stateside, and for showing controversial films and documentaries banned elsewhere. Film buffs should monitor this calendar, because tickets to film festival premieres, rare revivals and the raucous annual Oscars telecast sell out fast – but if the main show is sold out, check out documentaries in the teensy **Little Roxy** next door instead.

### Elbo Room
Live Music

Map p156 (📞 415-552-7788; www.elbo.com; 647 Valencia St; admission $5-15; 🕐 5pm-2am; Ⓜ & Ⓡ 16th St Mission) Funny name, because there isn't much to speak of upstairs on show nights with crowd-favorite funk, dancehall dub DJs and offbeat indie bands like Uni and Her Ukelele. Come any night for $2 pints from 5pm to 9pm at the chilled downstairs bar (admission free).

### Make-Out Room
Live Music

Map p156 ( 415-647-2888; www.makeoutroom.com; 3225 22nd St; cover free-$10; 6pm-2am; M & 24th St Mission) Velvet curtains and round booths help you settle in for the evening's entertainment, which ranges from punk-rock fiddle to '80s one-hit-wonder DJ mash-ups and the painfully funny Mortified readings, when the power of margaritas convinces grown men to read aloud from their teenage journals. Booze is a bargain, but the bar is cash only.

### Amnesia
Live Music

Map p156 ( 415-970-0012; www.amnesiathebar.com; 853 Valencia St; admission free-$10; 5:30pm-2am; M Valencia St; 16th St Mission) A closet-sized boho dive with out-sized swagger, serving cold Belgian beer and red-hot jazz to ragtag hipsters. Just to keep the crowds guessing, musical acts range from bluegrass to gypsy punk, plus Tuesday open mics, random readings and cinema shorts; check the calendar or just go with the flow.

## SoMa

### Slim's
Live Music

Map p160 ( 415-255-0333; www.slims-sf.com; 333 11th St; tickets $11-28; 5pm-2am; M Market St) Guaranteed good times by Gogol Bordello, Tenacious D, the Expendables and AC/DShe (a hard-rocking female tribute band) fit the bill at this midsized club owned by R&B star Boz Skaggs – but at any moment, legends like Prince and Elvis Costello might show up to play sets unannounced. Shows are all ages, though shorties may have a hard time seeing once the floor starts bouncing. Come early to score burgers and fries with balcony seating; credit cards accepted, with $20 minimum.

## Detour:
# Bottom of the Hill

Quite literally at the bottom of Potrero Hill, **Bottom of the Hill** (Map p156; 415-621-4455; www.bottomofthehill.com; 1233 17th St; admission $5-12; shows begin 9-10pm Tue-Sat; 16th St) is definitely out of the way but always top of the list for seeing fun local bands, from notable alt-rockers like Deerhoof to newcomers worth checking out by name alone (Yesway, Stripmall Architecture, Excuses for Skipping). The big smokers' patio is ruled by a cat that enjoys music more than people – totally punk rock. Anchor Steam on tap, but it's a cash-only bar; check the website for lineups.

### Mezzanine
Live Music

Map p160 ( 415-625-8880; www.mezzaninesf.com; 444 Jessie St; admission $10-40; M Market St; Powell St) Big nights come with bragging rights at the Mezzanine, with the best sound system in SF bouncing off the brick walls and crowds hyped for breakthrough hip-hop and R&B shows by Wyclef Jean, Quest Love, Method Man, Nas and Snoop Dogg. Mezzanine also hosts throwback new-wave nights and books classic alt bands like the Dandy Warhols and Psychedelic Furs; check the calendar.

### Yerba Buena Center for the Arts
Live Music

Map p160 (YBCA; 415-978-2787; www.ybca.org; 700 Howard St; tickets free-$35; M & Powell St) Rock stars would be jealous of art stars at YBCA openings, which draw overflow crowds of impeccably hip art groupies coat-checking their skateboards and shaggy faux furs to see live hip-hop by Mos Def, 1960s smut film festivals, spontaneous light shows set to the music of unrehearsed bands and Vik Muniz' documentary on making art from trash. Most touring dance and jazz companies perform at YBCA's main theater (across the sidewalk from the gallery).

## AsiaSF
Nightclub

Map p160 ( ☎ 415-255-2742; www.asiasf.com; 201 9th St; per person from $35; ☺7-11pm Wed & Thu, 7pm-2am Fri, 5pm-2am Sat, 7-10pm Sun, reservation line 1-8pm; Ⓜ & Ⓡ Civic Center) First ladies of the world, look out: these dazzling Asian ladies can out-hostess you in half the time and less than half the clothes. Cocktails and Asian-inspired dishes are served with a tall order of sass and one little secret: your servers are drag stars. Every hour, the ladies get up on the red bar and work it like a runway on fire. Gaggles of girlfriends squeal and blushing straight businessmen play along, but once the inspiration and drinks kick in, everyone mixes it up on the downstairs dance floor. The three-course 'Menage à Trois Menu' runs $39, cocktails around $10 and, honey, those tips are well earned.

## Hotel Utah Saloon
Live Music

Map p160 ( ☎ 415-546-6300; www.hotelutah .com; 500 4th St; shows $5-10; ☺11:30am-2am Mon-Fri, 2pm-2am Sat & Sun; Ⓜ4th St) The ground-floor bar of this Victorian hotel became ground zero of the underground scene in the '70s, when upstarts Whoopi Goldberg and Robin Williams took the stage – now it's a sure bet for Monday night open mics, indie-label debuts and local favorites like Riot Earp, Saucy Monkey and the Dazzling Strangers. Back in the '50s the bartender graciously served Beats,

grifters and Marilyn Monroe, but snipped the ties of businessmen when they leaned across the bar; now you can wear whatever, as long as you're buying, but there's a $20 credit-card minimum.

# The Castro

## Castro Theatre
Theater, Cinema

Map p166 ( ☎ 415-621-6120; www.thecastro theatre.com; 429 Castro St; adult/child $10/7.50; Ⓜ Castro St) The Spanish-Moorish exterior of the city's grandest cinema, opened in 1922, yields to a mishmash of styles inside, from Italianate to Asian. The Mighty Wurlitzer organ rises from the orchestra pit before evening performances, and the audience cheers as the organist plays classics from the Great American Songbook. If there's a cult classic on the bill, such as *Whatever Happened to Baby Jane,* expect audience participation. Otherwise, the crowd is well behaved and rapt. Note: sound echoes in the balcony.

The Castro (p164)
ROBERTO GEROMETTA/LONELY PLANET IMAGES ©

### Café du Nord/Swedish American Hall
Live Music

Map p166 (☎415-861-5016; www.cafedunord .com; 2170 Market St; cover varies; Ⓜ Church St) You never know what's doing at Café du Nord, a former basement speakeasy, with bar and showroom. Rockers, chanteuses, comedians, raconteurs and burlesque acts perform nightly, and the joint still looks like it must've in the '30s. The hall upstairs, with balcony seating and Scandinavian woodwork, hosts miscellaneous events. Check the online calendar.

## 🔓 Shopping

### The Mission

### Adobe Books & Backroom Gallery
Bookstore, Art

Map p156 (www.adobebooksbackroomgallery .blogspot.com; 3166 16th St; ⏲11am-midnight; Ⓜ & Ⓡ16th St Mission) Come here for every book you never knew you needed used and cheap, plus zine launch parties, poetry readings and art openings. To get to the Backroom Gallery, first you have to navigate the obstacle course of sofas, cats, art books and German philosophy. But it's worth it: artists who debuted here have gone on to success at international art fairs and Whitney Biennials.

### Gravel & Gold
Housewares, Gifts

Map p156 (www.gravelandgold.com; 3266 21st St; ⏲noon-7pm Tue-Sat, to 5pm Sun; Ⓜ & Ⓡ24th St Mission) Get in touch with your roots and back to the land, without ever leaving sight of a Mission sidewalk. Gravel & Gold celebrates the 1960s to '70s hippie homesteader movement with every fiber of its being and its hand-dyed smocked dresses – which you can try on among psychedelic murals behind a patched curtain, of course. The proud purveyor of rare vintage artifacts like silk-screened Osborne Woods peace postcards and limited-edition books on DIY Mendocino shingle-shack architecture, Gravel & Gold also answers to a higher California calling: getting a whole new generation excited about the organic connections between art and nature.

### Needles & Pens
Gifts, Books

Map p156 (www.needles-pens.com; 3253 16th St; ⏲noon-7pm; Ⓜ & Ⓡ16th St Mission) Do it

Needles & Pens

SABRINA DALBESIO/LONELY PLANET IMAGES ©

yourself or DIY trying: this scrappy zine/craft/how-to/art gallery delivers the inspiration to create your own magazines, rehabbed T-shirts or album covers. Nab Jay Howell's *Punks Git Cut* comic illustrating failed fighting words, Nigel Peake's pen-and-ink aerial views of patchworked farmland, and alphabet buttons to pin your own credo onto a handmade messenger bag.

## Mission Statement
Clothing, Accessories

Map p156 (www.missionstatementsf.com; 3458 18th St; ☺noon-7pm Wed-Mon; Ⓜ18th St; Ⓡ16th St Mission) Finally: locally designed, fashion-forward clothing and accessories that keep real bodies and real budgets in mind. Sofie Ølgaard's silk minidresses make anyone look leggy, Vanessa Gade's circle-chain necklaces bring a touch of infinity to low necklines and Estrella Tadao's reconstructed '70s men's suit jackets with zip-up lapels fend off SF fog.

## Good Vibrations
Clothing, Accessories

Map p156 (☎415-522-5460; www.goodvibes.com; 603 Valencia St; ☺10am-9pm Sun-Thu, to 11pm Fri & Sat; Ⓜ & Ⓡ16th St Mission) 'Wait, I'm supposed to put that where?' The understanding salespeople in this worker-owned cooperative are used to giving rather, um, explicit instructions, so don't hesitate to ask. Margaret Cho is on the board, so you know they're not shy here. Check out the antique vibrators in the museum display by the door, and imagine getting up close and personal with the one that looks like a floor waxer – then thank your stars for modern technology.

## Paxton Gate
Gifts

Map p156 (www.paxton-gate.com; 824 Valencia St; ☺11am-7pm; ⓂValencia St; Ⓡ16th St Mission) Salvador Dalí probably would've shopped here for all his taxidermy and gardening needs. What with puppets made with animal skulls, terrariums sprouting from lab specimen jars and teddy-bear heads mounted like hunting trophies, this place is beyond surreal. The new **kids' shop** down the street

(766 Valencia St) maximizes playtime with volcano-making kits, sea-monster mobiles and solar-powered dollhouses.

## Room 4
Clothing, Accessories

Map p156 (☎415-647-2764; www.room4.com; 904 Valencia St; ☺1-7pm Mon-Fri, noon-7pm Sat, noon-5pm Sun; Ⓜ Mission St; Ⓡ16th St Mission) Spare yourself years of arduous thrifting and head to this tiny treasure-box boutique for the good stuff: trippy green-and-orange-swirled enamel dishes, free-form driftwood lamps, creepy portraits of big-eyed toddlers in the rain, and Pendleton plaid wool shirts and brass trucker belt buckles with unisex appeal.

# SoMa

## SFMOMA Museum Store
Books, Gifts

Map p160 (www.sfmoma.org/museumstore; 151 3rd St; ☺10am-6:30pm Mon-Wed & Fri-Sun, to 9:30pm Thu; Ⓜ Market St, Montgomery St; Ⓡ Montgomery St) Design fetishists may have to be pried away from the glass shelves and display cases, which brim with cereal bowls that look like spilt milk, Pantone color-swatch espresso cups and watches with a face to match Mario Botta's black-and-white SFMOMA facade.

## Jeremy's
Clothing, Accessories

Map p160 (www.jeremys.com; 2 South Park St; ☺11am-6pm Mon-Wed & Fri, 11am-8:30pm Thu, noon-6pm Sun; Ⓜ Townsend St) No South Park excursion would be complete without swapping stories about your all-time-best bargains from Jeremy's. Runway modeling, window displays and high-end customer returns translate to jaw-dropping bargains on major designers for men and women. Men's stuff gets picked over faster, but you could score a skinny Prada suit at half off if you work fast.

## Branch
Housewares

Map p160 (www.branchhome.com; 345 9th St; ☺9:30am-5:30pm Mon-Fri; Ⓜ10th St) When you're looking for original home decor with a sustainable edge, it's time to Branch out. Whether you're in the market for a cork chaise lounge, beech-wood-fiber bath towel or a tiny bonsai in a reclaimed breath-mint tin, Branch has you covered – and yes, they ship.

**Gama-Go**  Clothing, Accessories
Map p160 (www.gama-go.com; 335 8th St; ⏱noon-6pm Mon-Fri, to 5pm Sat & Sun; Ⓜ & Ⓡ Civic Center) Every one of SF-designer Gama-Go's products seems calibrated to hit the fascination nerve: a hand-shaped cleaver called the Karate Chopper, T-shirts with a roaring powder-blue yeti, and a tape measure disguised as a cassette tape. Gama-Go is distributed nationally, but here in the showroom you'll find 70% off last season's lines and score 15% off all purchases from noon to 2pm daily.

## The Castro

**Sui Generis**  Clothing, Accessories
Map p166 (www.suigenerisconsignment.com; men's shop 2231 Market St, women's shop 2265 Market St; Ⓜ Castro St) Emerge with confidence from his-and-her designer-consignment boutiques knowing you won't spot another person working your new look. The well-curated collection of contemporary and vintage clothing skews dressy. Best for those who fit runway-model sizes, but with relatively fat wallets.

**Cliff's Variety**  Housewares
Map p166 (www.cliffsvariety.com; 479 Castro St; Ⓜ Castro St) None of the hardware maestros at Cliff's will raise an eyebrow if you express a dire need for a jar of rubber nuns, silver body paint and a case of cocktail toothpicks, though they might angle for an invitation. The window displays at Cliff's, a community institution since 1936, are a local landmark.

**Under One Roof**  Gifts, Housewares
Map p166 (www.underoneroof.org; 518a Castro St; Ⓜ Castro St) All the fabulous gifts under this roof are donated by local designers and businesses, so AIDS service organizations get 100% of the proceeds from your etched San Francisco–skyline martini glasses and adorable Jonathan Adler vase. Those sweet sales clerks are volunteers, so show them love for raising $11 million to date.

**Worn Out West**  Accessories
Map p166 (582 Castro St; Ⓜ Castro St) Left your gear at home? Pick up leathers, original-cut Levi's 501s, cock rings and tank tops at this old-school-Castro used-clothing store and dress like a local. Good fetish wear at great prices. Not much for gals, alas.

## 🏃 Sports & Activities

**AT&T Park**  Baseball
Map p160 (📞415-972-2000; http://sanfrancisco .giants.mlb.com; AT&T Park; tickets $5-135; Ⓜ N) The San Francisco Giants, SF's 2010 World Series–winning National League baseball team, plays 81 home games from April to

AT&T Park
ERIC BRODER VAN DYKE/SHUTTERSTOCK ©

# Detour:
# San Francisco 49ers

The **49ers** (📞415-656-4900; www.sf49ers.com; Candlestick Park; tickets $25-100; **M**T & shuttle buses) were the dream team of the National Football League (NFL) during the 1980s and early '90s, but the team languished in the early part of the 21st century, finishing at the very bottom of the heap in the 2004 season. But in 2011 they came roaring back to life, finishing 13-3 for their best regular season since 1997 and playing in the NFC Championships (they lost) for the first time since that same year. Fan loyalty has not flagged, but the team keeps threatening to leave San Francisco, perhaps as a ploy to get voters to approve a bond measure to build a new, updated stadium closer to the city instead of old Candlestick Park. Book tickets through www.ticketmaster.com, and factor in $20 to park in the stadium lot, due to recent car break-ins during games.

October in this ballpark, which changes its name with every telecom merger. The Giants pack huge crowds and often make the play-offs, with superstitious practices that might seem eccentric elsewhere but endear them to SF: the entire team has been known to sport bushy beards and the pitcher to wear women's underwear on winning streaks. Games are frequently sold out, but season-ticket holders often sell unwanted tickets through the team's Double Play Ticket Window on the website.

On nongame days a behind-the-scenes **tour** (📞415-972-2400; tickets $12.50; ⏰10:30am & 2:30pm) includes visits to the clubhouse, dugout and field. There's also a miniature replica of the field, the world's largest baseball glove and a kids' play structure in that hideous giant Coca-Cola bottle that pretends to be a sculpture. Bonus: on the east side of the park, you can stand at the archways along the waterfront promenade and watch a few innings for free.

## City Kayak
Kayaking

Map p160 (📞415-357-1010; www.citykayak.com; South Beach Harbor; kayak rentals per hr $35-65, 3hr lesson & rental package $59, tours $65-75;

**M**Embarcadero) You haven't seen San Francisco until you've seen it from the water, and the next best thing to Sir Francis Drake's ship the *Golden Hind* is a kayak. Newbies can venture calm waters near the Bay Bridge, and experienced paddlers might hit the choppy waters beneath the Golden Gate Bridge or take a moonlight tour with all-inclusive rentals. First-timers can take lessons and head out alone or with an escorted tour; check the website for details.

## Yerba Buena Center Ice Skating & Bowling
Ice Skating, Bowling

Map p160 (📞415-820-3532; www.skatebowl.com; 750 Folsom St; skating adult/child $8/6 plus $3 skate rental, bowling per game $5.50-9 plus $3 shoe rental; ⏰bowling 10am-10pm Sun-Thu, to midnight Fri & Sat; **M** & **R**Powell St) Built on the rooftop of the Moscone Convention Center, the ice skating and bowling center is a huge draw for families. Unlike most rinks, this one is bright and naturally lit with walls of windows; the bowling alley has just 12 lanes but serves beer. Check the website or call for skating times.

# The Haight & Hayes Valley

**You don't come out here to see the sights.** Because, really, there are hardly any. These two laid-back neighborhoods are where people live, shop and eat. But the Haight will claim you as its own, whether you're a hippie born too late, a punk born too early or a weirdo passing as normal. Since its heyday during the Summer of Love, it's specialized in skateboarding, street musicians, potent coffee, radical literature and retail therapy for rebels.

Savvy eateries along Divisadero St south of Geary Blvd are attempting to attract a foodie crowd. East of Divisadero, the Lower Haight has better bars, candy-colored mansions ringing Alamo Square and a pot-club kind of mellow only occasionally disrupted by gang activity northeast of Fillmore and Haight Sts.

To the east of Alamo Square lies creative-chic Hayes Valley, where resident Zen monks wander past Victorian storefronts showcasing cutting-edge local designers and upstart chefs.

Bound Together Anarchist Book Collective (p186)

# The Haight & Hayes Valley Highlights

## Alamo Square (p193)

Did these Painted Ladies make a deal with the devil? They're survivors of the 1906 earthquake and fire, yet Alamo Square's ageless Victorians are always ready for their close-ups in vacation shots of Postcard Row. For the best seat in town, nab a hilltop picnic table with views Downtown, past mansions with turrets and cupolas – and see if you can tell your Queen Annes from your Sticks.

## Bar Hopping (p196)

Request a pint of mead or a light Serbian summer brew and you'd get laughed out of most bars – but at Toronado, they thought you'd never ask. Take your pick from more than 100 craft beers, seasonal ales and house-brewed mead. The Alembic's team of able mixologists serves up fashionable artisanal cocktails, and over in Hayes Valley, Smuggler's Cove satisfies thirsty pirate types with flaming rum drinks. Toronado (p196)

## Hayes Valley Boutiques (p200) ③

The attack of the killer sales rack begins innocently enough. Perhaps you came to Hayes Valley for some other reason – but once these clever Victorian boutiques pull you in, suddenly you're knee-deep in ankle boots, corsetry, carpets and luggage. A fabulous alternative to Downtown department stores, these shops are the very reason to bring an empty suitcase. Polanco (p201)

## ④ Haight Street (p188)

The place to be during the Summer of Love, Haight St is host to a different sort of scene these days: boutiques, cafes and bars have sprung up where psychedelic drugs and music once ruled. If you want to indulge your inner flower child, you can still score a bong, shop for vintage duds or peace out with the kids who panhandle along the sidewalks.

## ⑤ Buena Vista Park (p188)

'Buena Vista' means 'Good View' – and that pretty much sums up what we love about this lofty park that springs up suddenly and dramatically from the relatively flat surrounding earth, peaking at 575 feet. Make it to the top (you're in luck – there are stairs) and you're rewarded with panoramic views and a cardio workout that's earned you the snack of your choice upon descent.

# The Haight & Hayes Valley Walk

*Cover Haight history from the 1860s and meander aimlessly through the Summer of Love. This neighborhood has been the address of rock stars, authors and outcasts, whose homes are still here even though they're long gone.*

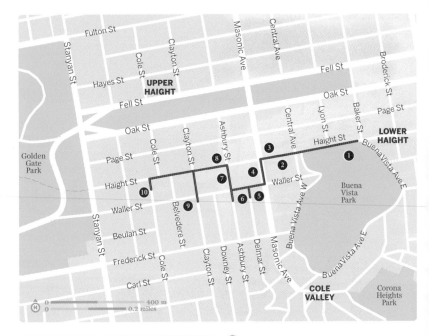

## WALK FACTS
- **Start** Buena Vista Park
- **Finish** 635 Cole St
- **Distance** 1.3 miles
- **Duration** 90 minutes

## ❶ Buena Vista Park

Start your trip back in time with panoramic city views that inspired Victorians to make scandalously bold romantic moves c 1867, and that moved surviving San Franciscans to tears after the fire of 1906. (p188)

## ❷ Bound Together Anarchist Book Collective

Across Haight St, you may recognize Emma Goldman and Sacco and Vanzetti in the *Anarchists of Americas* mural – if you don't, staff can provide you with some biographical comics by way of introduction.

## ❸ Magnolia Brewpub

Heading west on Haight St, you can't miss this corner microbrewery and organic eatery (p192) named after a Grateful Dead song, which hippies may dimly recognize as the site of the infamous Drogstore Café. Pull up a seat at the communal table for a bite and/or a sampler of beer – with any luck, Arrogant Bastard will be on tap.

### ④ 1235 Masonic Ave

You might once have glimpsed the Symbionese Liberation Army in disguise at this address, where the SLA is believed to have held Patty Hearst, the kidnapped heiress turned revolutionary bank robber.

### ⑤ 32 Delmar St

Turning right off Masonic Ave onto Waller St, you'll notice a narrow lane leading uphill. No 32 was the site of the 1978 Sid Vicious overdose that finally broke up the Sex Pistols. Under new ownership, this building betrays no trace of its rock 'n' roll past.

### ⑥ Grateful Dead House

Pay your respects to the former flophouse of Jerry Garcia, Bob Weir and Pigpen, plus sundry Deadheads, at 710 Ashbury St. In October 1967, antidrug cops raided the house and arrested everyone in it (Garcia wasn't home).

### ⑦ 635 Ashbury St

Down the block from the house of the Dead, this is one of many known SF addresses for Janis Joplin, who had a hard time hanging onto leases in the 1960s – but, as she sang in her rendition of Kris Kristofferson and Fred Foster's 'Me & Bobby McGee': 'Freedom's just another word for nothin' left to lose.'

### ⑧ 4:20 Clock

At the corner of Haight and Ashbury, you'll notice that the clock overhead always reads 4:20, better known in 'Hashbury' as International Bong-Hit Time.

### ⑨ Haight Ashbury Food Program

Back on Waller St, swing by the nonprofit that serves up hot meals and fresh starts to anyone in need. With a helping hand or modest donation, visitors can help the Food Program keep the spirit of the Summer of Love alive.

### ⑩ 635 Cole St

This apartment building once housed Charles Manson, the cult leader behind the 'Helter Skelter' murder of Sharon Tate – but on the corner, the rainbow *Evolution* mural serves to lighten the mood.

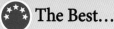 The Best...

### PLACES TO EAT

**Jardinière** Sustainable food made by a star chef. (p194)

**Bar Jules** Lovable neighborhood bistro. (p194)

**Rosamunde Sausage Grill** The best food bargain in the whole neighborhood. (p189)

**Zuni Cafe** New takes on old favorites in a dramatic Market St space. (p195)

### PLACES TO DRINK

**Smuggler's Cove** Rum drinks and a tiki theme. (p197)

**Toronado** Take your pick from the extensive beer selection. (p196)

**Alembic** Artisan cocktails paired with artisan bar bites. (p196)

**Hôtel Biron** Not a hotel, but a wine bar and art gallery. (p197)

### PLACES TO UNLEASH YOUR INNER FREAK

**Haight St** The preferred address of the Summer of Love. (p188)

**Noc Noc** DJs, happy hour and scavenged furnishings. (p196)

**Rebel Bar** Fun-house southern biker-bar disco. (p198)

Bar Jules (p194)

# Discover the Haight & Hayes Valley

## 🔁 Getting There & Away

○ **Bus** Number 21 heads from Downtown west through Hayes Valley along Hayes St, 49 runs up Van Ness Ave along the eastern edge of Hayes Valley and 5 passes along the north side. Market St buses 6 and 71 run up Haight St to Golden Gate Park, passing the south end of Hayes Valley. The 22 links the Lower Haight to the Mission and Potrero Hill to the south, and Japantown, Pacific Heights and the Marina to the north. Number 24 connects the Haight to the Castro and Pacific Heights via Divisadero.

○ **Streetcar** The N line runs between Downtown and Ocean Beach through the Lower Haight, passing the Upper Haight to the north.

○ **BART** Civic Center BART is four blocks east of Hayes Valley.

Victorian houses on Haight St
ROBERTO GEROMETTA/LONELY PLANET IMAGES ©

## ◎ Sights

### The Haight

**Haight St**                                      Street
Map p190 (Haight St btwn Fillmore & Stanyan Sts; Ⓜ Haight St) Was it the fall of 1966 or the winter of '67? As the Haight saying goes, if you can remember the Summer of Love, man, you probably weren't there. The fog was laced with Nag Champa incense and burning draft cards, entire days were spent contemplating Day-Glo Grateful Dead posters and the corner of Haight and Ashbury Sts became the turning point of a generation.

Since the '60s, Haight St has been divided into two major splinter factions: between Golden Gate Park and Divisadero St is the **Upper Haight**, which is what most people are referring to when they wax nostalgic about the Summer of Love. And to the east between Divisadero and Webster Sts is the **Lower Haight**, which has its share of grit but remains a magnet for its cafes, bars and shops.

**Buena Vista Park**              Park
Map p190 (Haight St btwn Central Ave & Baker St; Ⓜ Haight St) True to its name, this park founded in 1867 offers sweeping views of the city beyond century-old cypresses to the Golden Gate Bridge as rewards for hiking up the steep hill. When SF went up in flames in 1906, this was where San Franciscans found refuge and watched the town smolder; on your way downhill, take Buena Vista Ave W to spot Victorian mansions that date from that era. Hanging around after the park closes at sunset for boozing or cruising is risky, given recent criminal activity at night.

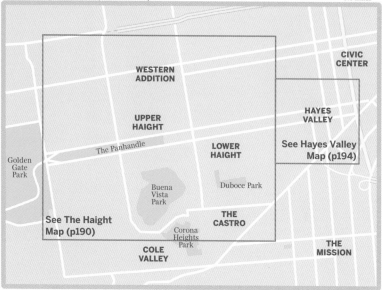

## Hayes Valley

### Zen Center                    Historic Building

Map p194 (☎415-863-3136; www.sfzc.org; 300 Page St; ⏱9:30am-12:30pm & 1:30-5pm Mon-Fri, 8:30am-noon Sat; ⓜHayes St) No, this isn't a spa, but an active spiritual retreat (since 1969) for the largest Buddhist community outside Asia. The graceful landmark building was designed by Julia Morgan, California's first licensed female architect, better known as chief architect of Hearst Castle and the Chinatown YWCA (see p111). The center is open to the public for visits, meditation (see the website for the meditation schedule) and Zen workshops, and also offers overnight stays by prior arrangement for intensive meditation retreats.

## Eating

## The Haight

### Rosamunde Sausage
### Grill                              Sausages $

Map p190 (☎415-437-6851; 545 Haight St; sausages $4-6; ⏱11:30am-10pm; ⓜHaight St)

Impress a dinner date on the cheap: load up classic Brats or duck-fig links with complimentary roasted peppers, grilled onions, whole-grain mustard and mango chutney, and enjoy with your choice of 100 beers at Toronado (p196), next door.

###  Three Twins
### Ice Cream                        Ice Cream $

Map p190 (☎415-487-8946; www.threetwins icecream.com; 254 Fillmore St; cones $2.25-3.25; ⏱noon-10:30pm Mon-Thu, 11am-11pm Fri & Sat, to 10:30pm Sun; ⓜHaight St) Lower Haight's kids, locavores and pot-club regulars agree: Three Twins has the finest seasonal, certified-organic ice creams in town. Fall means cardamom, winter is an excuse for Meyer lemon cookie, spring brings honey orange blossom and summer is all about Strawberry Je Ne Sais Quoi, with a dash of balsamic vinegar.

### Ragazza                          Pizza $$

Map p190 (☎415-255-1133; www.ragazzasf .com; 311 Divisadero St; pizzas $13-18; ⏱5-10pm Mon-Thu, to 10:30 Fri & Sat; 🖋🍴; ⓜDivisadero St) 'Girl' is what the name means, as in, 'Oooh, *girl,* did you try the nettle

**189**

# The Haight

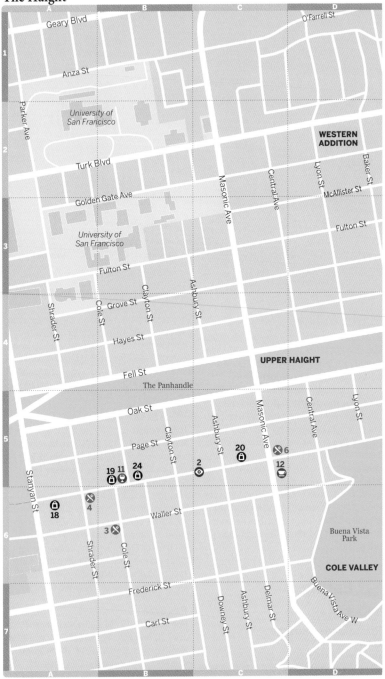

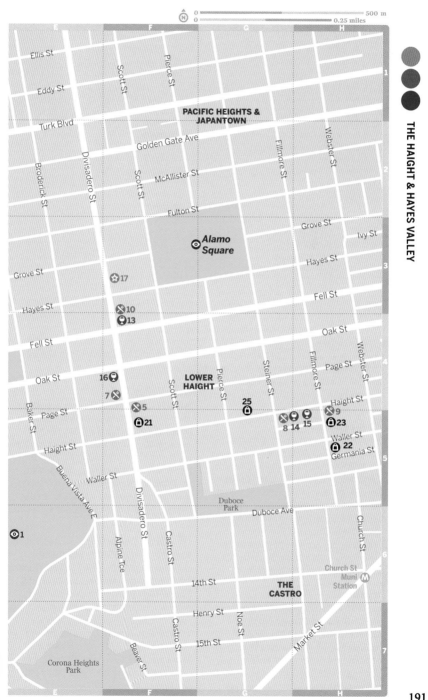

# The Haight

## ◎ Top Sights
Alamo Square.................................................F3

## ◎ Sights
1 Buena Vista Park ....................................E6
2 Haight St .................................................C5

## ✕ Eating
3 Cole Valley Cafe ....................................B6
4 Escape from New York Pizza ...............A6
5 Little Chihuahua....................................F4
6 Magnolia Brewpub.................................C5
7 Ragazza....................................................F4
8 Rosamunde Sausage Grill ...................G5
9 Three Twins Ice Cream .........................H5
10 Ziryab .......................................................F3

## ◎ Drinking & Nightlife
11 Alembic ...................................................B5
12 Coffee to the People..............................C5

13 Madrone ..................................................F4
14 Noc Noc ...................................................H5
15 Toronado .................................................H5
16 Vinyl Wine Bar ........................................F4

## ✿ Entertainment
17 Independent............................................F3

## 🛍 Shopping
18 Amoeba Music.........................................A6
19 Loyal Army Clothing ..............................B5
20 Piedmont Boutique.................................C5
21 Prairie Collective ...................................F5
22 Revolver...................................................H5
23 Upper Playground ..................................H5
24 Wasteland................................................B5
25 Xapno.......................................................G5

pizza?!' Since it comes with Boccalone pancetta, portobello mushrooms and nutty provolone, you definitely should. Locally cured, humanely raised pork is the breakout star of many Ragazza pies, from the Amatriciana with pecorino, bacon and egg to the Calabrian chili with cauliflower and pork belly.

## 🗹 Magnolia Brewpub
Californian, American $$
Map p190 ( 🗹 415-864-7468; www.magnoliapub .com; 1398 Haight St; mains $11-20; ⏱ noon-midnight Mon-Thu, to 1am Fri, 10am-1am Sat, 10am-midnight Sun; Ⓜ Haight St) Organic pub grub and samplers of homebrews keep the conversation flowing at communal tables, while grass-fed Prather Ranch burgers satisfy stoner appetites in the side booths – it's like the Summer of Love all over again, only with better food.

## Ziryab
Middle Eastern $$
Map p190 ( 🗹 415-522-0800; www.ziryabgrill .com; 528 Divisadero St; mains $10-16; ⏱ 4-11:30pm Mon-Thu, noon-12:30pm Fri & Sat, noon-11pm Sun; 🗹; Ⓜ Divisadero St) Banish all traumatic memories of dry chicken *shwarmas* (kebabs) with this succulent, organic poultry rolled in flatbread and sealed by hummus with a tantalizing whiff of curry. The vegan lentil soup is so robust it'll make your voice drop an octave, and the hookahs on the front porch provide solace to smokers rendered furtive by SF's antismoking laws.

## Cole Valley Cafe
Cafe $
Map p190 ( 🗹 415-668-5282; www.colevalleycafe .com; 701 Cole St; sandwiches $5-6; ⏱ 6:30am-8:30pm Mon-Fri, to 8pm Sat & Sun; 🗹🗹🗹; Ⓜ Haight St) Powerful coffee and chai, free wi-fi, chocolate-chip pumpkin cake and hot gourmet sandwiches – go for the lip-smacking thyme-marinated chicken with lemony avocado spread, or smoky roasted eggplant with peppers and pesto.

## 🗹 Little Chihuahua
Mexican $
Map p190 ( 🗹 415-255-8225; www.thelittle chihuahua.com; 292 Divisadero St; tacos/burritos $4/7; ⏱ 11am-11pm Mon-Fri, 10am-11pm Sat & Sun; Ⓜ Haight St) Who says sustainable, organic food has to be expensive or French? Charbroiled tomatillos, sustainable fish, Niman Ranch meats and organic veggies add up to sensational tacos, washed down with $3 draft beer or housemade organic *agua fresca* (fruit drink).

DIANA MAYFIELD/LONELY PLANET IMAGES ©

## ✓ Don't Miss
## Alamo Square

San Franciscans seldom miss an opportunity to show off, as you can see from the outrageous Victorian homes ringing Alamo Square Park. When San Franciscans struck it rich in the Gold Rush, they upgraded from Downtown tenements to grand houses embellished to the eaves with woodwork and gilding. These ornaments served a practical purpose: rows of houses were hastily constructed using a similar template, and citizens needed to know which stairs to stumble up after long, Barbary Coast nights.

Since Alamo Square homes were built on bedrock away from Downtown, several were spared San Francisco's 1906 earthquake and fire. But modern real-estate magnates consider Gold Rush tastes garish enough to bring down property values, so many of SF's 'Painted Ladies' have been painted in a marketable bland beige. The pastel, cookie-cutter Painted Ladies of famed **Postcard Row** on Alamo Square's east side literally pale in comparison with the colorful characters along the north side of the park, and along parallel McAllister and Golden Gate Sts. Here you'll spot true Barbary Coast baroque: facades bedecked with fish-scale shingles, swaged stucco garlands and gingerbread trim dripping from peaked roofs.

### NEED TO KNOW
Map p190; btwn Hayes & Scott Sts; admission free; Ⓜ Hayes St

---

**Escape from New York Pizza**                    Pizza $
Map p190 ( 📞 415-668-5577; www.escapefrom newyorkpizza.com; 1737 Haight St; slices $3-4;

🕐 11:30am-midnight Sun-Thu, to 2am Fri & Sat; 🅿️ 👫 ; Ⓜ Haight St) The Haight's obligatory midbender stop for a hot slice. Pesto with roasted garlic and potato will send you

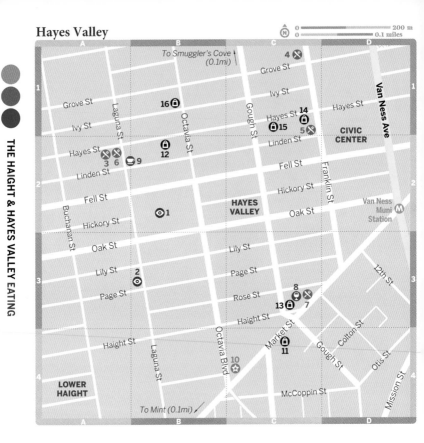

blissfully off to carbo-loaded sleep, but the sundried tomato with goat cheese, artichoke hearts and spinach will recharge you to go another round.

# Hayes Valley

### Jardinière                    Californian $$$

Map p194 (☎415-861-5555; www.jardiniere .com; 300 Grove St; mains $19-37; ⏲5-10:30pm Tue-Sat, to 10pm Sun & Mon; Ⓜ Van Ness) Her formidable reputation as Iron Chef, Top Chef Master and James Beard Award winner precedes her, but star chef Traci Des Jardins is better known at her namesake restaurant Jardinière as a champion of sustainable, salacious California cuisine. She has a way with California's organic vegetables, free-range meats and sustainably caught seafood that's probably illegal in other states, lavishing braised oxtail

ravioli with summer truffles and stuffing crispy pork belly with salami and fig. Go Mondays, when $45 scores three decadent courses with wine pairings.

### Bar Jules                    Californian $$

Map p194 (☎415-621-5482; www.barjules.com; 609 Hayes St; mains $10-26; ⏲6-10pm Tue, 11:30am-3pm & 6-10pm Wed-Sat, 11am-3pm Sun; Ⓜ Hayes St) Small, local and succulent is the credo at this corridor of a neighborhood bistro. The short daily menu thinks big with flavor-rich, sustainably minded offerings like local duck breast with cherries, almonds and arugula, a local wine selection and the dark, sinister 'chocolate nemesis.' Even with reservations, waits are a given – but so is simple, tasty food.

# Hayes Valley

### ◎ Sights
| | |
|---|---|
| 1 Hayes Valley Farm | B2 |
| 2 Zen Center | B3 |

### ✕ Eating
| | |
|---|---|
| 3 Bar Jules | A2 |
| 4 Jardinière | C1 |
| 5 Nojo | C1 |
| 6 Suppenküche | A2 |
| 7 Zuni Cafe | C3 |

### ◎ Drinking & Nightlife
| | |
|---|---|
| 8 Hôtel Biron | C3 |
| 9 Momi Toby's Revolution Café | A2 |

### ◎ Entertainment
| | |
|---|---|
| 10 Rebel Bar | C4 |

### ◎ Shopping
| | |
|---|---|
| 11 Flax | C4 |
| 12 Flight 001 | B2 |
| 13 Gangs of San Francisco | C3 |
| 14 Lotus Bleu | C1 |
| 15 Polanco | C1 |
| 16 Reliquary | B1 |

Reservations and fat wallets are handy, but the see-and-be-seen seating is a kick and the food is beyond reproach: Caesar salad with house-cured anchovies, crispy wood-brick-oven-roasted free-range chicken with horseradish mashed potatoes, and mesquite-grilled organic-beef burgers on focaccia (pile of shoestring fries $6 extra, and recommended).

### 🍃 Nojo
Japanese $$

Map p194 ( ☎ 415-896-4587; www.nojosf .com; 231 Franklin St; small plates $4-12; ⏱ 5-10pm Wed, Thu, Sun & Mon, to 11pm Fri & Sat; Ⓜ Hayes St) Everything you could possibly want skewered and roasted at happy hour, except maybe your boss. The house specialty is Japanese *izakaya* (bar snacks), especially grilled chicken yakitori (kebabs), panko-crusted anchovies and spicy beef heart slathered with earthy soy-based sauce. Plates are tasting-portion size, and you'll need that room for the house sundae: Humphry Slocombe black sesame and white miso ice creams with rice crackers.

### Suppenküche
German $$

Map p194 ( ☎ 415-252-9289; www.suppenkuche .com; 525 Laguna St; mains $10.50-20; ⏱ dinner 5-10pm daily, brunch 10am-2:30pm Sun; Ⓜ Hayes St) Feast on housemade Bratwurst

**Zuni Cafe** Californian, American $$$
Map p194 ( ☎ 415-552-2522; www.zunicafe.com; 1658 Market St; mains $14-29; ⏱ 11:30am-11pm Tue-Thu, to midnight Fri & Sat, 11am-11pm Sun; Ⓜ Market St) Gimmickry is for amateurs – Zuni has been turning basic menu items into gourmet staples since 1979.

---

# A Wild Idea: Hayes Valley Farm

After the 1989 earthquake damaged the freeway on-ramp at Fell St, a 2-acre stretch of asphalt was left to crumble into urban blight – until a group of renegade community gardeners began the wildest urban permaculture experiment in the West. With labor donated by neighbors and support ranging from Project Homeless Connect to the mayor, asphalt has been pulled up, the soil certified lead-safe and organic compost laid down.

The nonprofit **Hayes Valley Farm** (Map p194; ☎ 415-863-3136; www.hayesvalleyfarm .com; entry 450 Laguna St at Fell St; ⏱ noon-5pm Sun, Wed & Thu; Ⓜ Hayes St) is subject to future city development plans, and there have been some setbacks, as when community beehives (key for pollination) were vandalized. Visitors are welcome three days a week, and there's no need to call ahead to volunteer. Just show up Sundays, Wednesdays and Thursdays by 12:30pm and, after a brief orientation, community farmers will put you to work.

# Triple Threat: Vinyl Wine Bar

Combine three food trends – gourmet food trucks, wine on tap and pop-up restaurants – swirl vigorously, and voilà: **Vinyl Wine Bar** (Map p190; ☎415-621-4132; www.facebook.com/vinylwinebar; 359 Divisidero St; ◷5:30-11pm Mon-Thu, to midnight Fri-Sun; **M**Divisadero St). It all started as a creative work-around: people drink more wine with food, but the former cafe venue didn't have a restaurant license. Trucked-in culinary options ranging from fresh pasta to soul food draw diverse foodie crowds and tantalizing pairing possibilities. Care for an Austrian Grüner Veltliner with those grits? Or maybe you'd prefer to blend your own wine to accompany that asparagus ravioli in sheep's milk sauce?

sausages and spaetzle (dumplings) oozing with cheese, and toast your new friends at the unvarnished communal table with a 2L glass boot of draft beer – then return to cure inevitable hangovers with Sunday brunches of inch-thick 'Emperor's Pancakes' studded with brandied raisins.

## Drinking & Nightlife

## The Haight

### Toronado                                      Pub
Map p190 (www.toronado.com; 547 Haight St; ◷11:30am-2am; **M**Haight St) Glory hallelujah, beer lovers: your prayers have been heard. Be humbled before the chalkboard altar that lists 50-plus beers on tap and hundreds more bottled, including spectacular seasonal microbrews. Bring cash, come early and stay late, with a sausage from Rosamunde (p189) next door to accompany ale made by Trappist monks.

### Alembic                                        Bar
Map p190 (www.alembicbar.com; 1725 Haight St; ◷noon-2am; **M**Haight St) Haight St's spiffiest, tiniest bar has hammered-tin ceilings, rough-hewn wood floors and 250 choices of specialty hooch – plus throngs of artisan bourbon drinkers and cocktail research historians proudly standing behind the 'No Red Bull/No Jägermeister' sign. Bar snacks here aren't elementary

peanuts, but advanced-degree artisan cheeses, pickled quail eggs and iced duck hearts.

### Coffee to the People                          Cafe
Map p190 (1206 Masonic Ave; ◷6am-8pm Mon-Fri, to 9pm Sat & Sun; 🛜 📶; **M**Haight St) Coffee breaks here may induce flashbacks, what with the radical bumper stickers on the tables, hippie macramé on the walls, shelves of consciousness-raising books and enough fair-trade espresso to revive the Sandinista movement.

### Madrone                                        Bar
Map p190 (☎415-241-0202; www.madronelounge.com; 500 Divisadero St; ◷5pm-2am Tue-Sat, 6pm-2am Sun & Mon; **M**Divisadero St) A changing roster of DJs and giggling cuties come as a surprise in a Victorian bar decorated with rotating art installations and a tree-trunk bar, a bomb-shaped disco ball and an absinthe fountain. But nothing tops the jaw-dropping mash-ups at the Saturday-monthly Prince vs Michael Jackson party, when the place packs.

### Noc Noc                                        Bar
Map p190 (☎www.nocnocs.com; 557 Haight St; ◷5pm-2am; **M**Haight St) Who's there? Nearsighted graffiti artists, anarchist hackers moonlighting as electronica DJs and other characters straight out of an R Crumb comic, that's who. Happy hour is from 5pm to 7pm daily, but be warned: those sake cocktails will knock-knock you off your scavenged steampunk stool.

# Hayes Valley

### Smuggler's Cove
Bar

off Map p194 (www.smugglerscovesf.com; 650 Gough St; 🕓5pm-2am; Ⓜ Van Ness) Yo-ho-ho and a bottle of rum...or wait, make that a Dead Reckoning tawny port cocktail with Angostura bitters, Nicaraguan rum and vanilla liqueur, unless someone wants to share the flaming Scorpion Bowl? Pirates are bedeviled by choice at this shambling Barbary Coast shipwreck of a tiki bar, hidden speakeasy-style behind a tinted door.

### Hôtel Biron
Bar

Map p194 (www.hotelbiron.com; 45 Rose St; 🕓5pm-2am; Ⓜ Market St) An oenologist's dream walk-in closet that serves as a wine bar, with standout Californian, Provençal and Tuscan vintages, and a ceiling made of corks. The vibe is French underground, with exposed-brick walls, surreally romantic art, a leather couch and just a few tables for two. Barkeeps let you keep tasting until you find what you like; pair with decadent cheese plates.

### Momi Toby's Revolution Café
Cafe

Map p194 (528 Laguna St; 🕓7:30am-10pm Mon-Thu, to 11pm Fri, 8am-10pm Sat & Sun;

## Detour: Karaoke at the Mint

Die-hard singers pore over giant books of 30,000 tunes in every genre at mixed-straight-gay karaoke bar the **Mint** (off Map p194; ☎415-626-4726; www.themint.net; 1942 Market St; 🕓noon-2am; Ⓜ Market St), where big voices rattle pennies in the basement of the US mint just uphill. Coinage won't get you far here, though: standard karaoke-jockey tip is $1 a song. Billy Idol is fair game for a goof, but only serious belters take on Barbra.

Ⓜ Hayes St) For once, a cafe that's not an internet port. Dig the boho scene, with artists on both sides of the counter, swilling coffee and wine. Bask in the sun at outdoor tables, or snag a window

Jardinière (p194)

THE HAIGHT & HAYES VALLEY DRINKING & NIGHTLIFE

seat inside and mingle with locals over leisurely happy hours (4pm to 7pm daily).

## ⭐ Entertainment

### Independent                          Live Music
Map p190 ( ☎ 415-771-1421; www.theindependent sf.com; 628 Divisadero St; tickets $13-20; ⏱ box office 11am-6pm Mon-Fri, to 9:30pm show nights, doors 7:30pm or 8:30pm; M Divisadero St) One of the city's coolest live-music venues, the Independent showcases funky soul acts (Nikka Costa, Sergent Garcia), indie dreamers (Kimya Dawson, Blonde Redhead) and cult rock (Meat Puppets, Ted Nugent), plus such wacky events as the US Air Guitar Championships. Ventilation is poor, but drinks are cheap.

### Rebel Bar                              Gay Club
Map p194 ( ☎ 415-431-4202; 1760 Market St; ⏱ 5pm-3am Mon-Thu, to 4am Fri, 11am-4am Sat & Sun; M Market St) Fun-house southern biker-bar disco, complete with antique mirrored walls, signature Hell's Angel cocktail (Bulleit bourbon, Chartreuse and OJ) and all those exposed pipes (ahem). Rebel looks badass, but it's SF all the way: bartenders are flirty, there's vinegary Carolina-style BBQ at the in-house pop-up restaurant and the crowd is not above bouncing to Gaga.

## 🔒 Shopping

### The Haight
#### Amoeba Music                          Music Store
Map p190 (www.amoeba.com; 1855 Haight St; ⏱ 10:30am-10pm Mon-Sat, 11am-9pm Sun; M Haight St) Enticements are hardly necessary to lure the masses to the West Coast's most eclectic collection of new and used music and video, but Amoeba offers listening stations, a free music zine with uncannily accurate reviews, a free concert series that recently starred Elvis Costello and Shonen Knife, and a foundation that's saved more than 1000 acres of rainforest.

## Prairie Collective    Gifts, Accessories

Map p190 (www.prairiecollective.com; 262 Divisadero St; ⊙11am-6pm Wed-Mon, noon-4pm Sun; M Haight St) Three local designers are heading back to nature while putting down roots in a San Francisco storefront with mellow pups-in-residence Bernie and Lil' Boy. Studio Choo's wildflower arrangements burst from antique medicine bottles, Magpie & Rye's tree-trunk bowls and macramé-covered pebble paperweights usher the outdoors into offices, and vintage flour sacks find new purpose in life thanks to found-design specialists the Cloak and Cabinet Society.

## Piedmont Boutique    Clothing, Accessories

Map p190 (www.piedmontsf.com; 1452 Haight St; ⊙11am-7pm; M Haight St) 'No food, no cell phones, no playing in the boas,' says the sign at the door, but inside, that last rule is gleefully ignored by cross-dressers, cabaret singers, strippers and people who take Halloween dead seriously. All the getups are custom-designed in-house and built to last – so, like certain escorts, honey, they're not as cheap as they look.

## Loyal Army Clothing    Clothing, Accessories

Map p190 (www.loyalarmy.com; 1728 Haight St; ⊙11am-7pm Mon-Sat, 11:30am-7pm Sun; ; M Haight St) Food with high self-esteem is a recurring theme on this San Francisco designer's cartoon-cute tees, totes and baby clothes. A bag of chips says 'All that and me!', while California rolls brag to nigiri sushi 'That's how we roll!' and a butter pat on pancakes squeals 'I'm a hot mess!' But the most popular character is the San Francisco fogbank: most of the clouds are silver and smiling, but there's always one that has fangs.

**Wasteland** Clothing, Accessories
Map p190 (www.wastelandclothing.com; 1660 Haight St; ⏱11am-8pm Mon-Sat, noon-7pm Sun; Ⓜ Haight St) The catwalk of thrift, this vintage superstore adds instant style with barely worn Marc Jacobs smocks, '70s Pucci maxi-skirts and a steady supply of go-go boots. Hip occasionally verges on hideous with fringed sweaters and patchwork suede jackets, but at these prices you can afford to take fashion risks.

**Revolver** Clothing, Accessories
Map p190 (www.revolversf.com; 136 Fillmore St; ⏱noon-8pm; Ⓜ Haight St) Entering this boutique is like wandering into the bedroom of some stoner-dandy Western novelist, with easy pieces in natural, nubby fabrics strewn across wooden crates, and clocks made from linen-bound antique books ticking noisily on the walls.

**Upper Playground** Clothing, Accessories
Map p190 (☎415-861-1960; www.upperplay ground.com; 220 Fillmore St; ⏱noon-7pm; Ⓜ Haight St) Blend into the SF scenery with locally designed 'Left Coast' hoodies, geek-chic tees featuring the state of California stuffed into a tube sock, and collegiate pennants for city neighborhoods (the Tenderloin totally needs a cheering section). Men's gear dominates, but there are women's tees, kids' tees in the back room and slick graffiti art in **Fifty24SF Gallery** next door.

**Xapno** Gifts, Clothing
Map p190 (☎415-863-8199; www.xapno.com; 678 Haight St; ⏱11am-7pm Tue-Thu & Sun, 10am-9pm Fri & Sat; Ⓜ Haight St) Antique typewriter ribbon tins, bracelets locally made from pocket-watch faces, succulents dripping from hanging nautilus shells: such unusual gifts lead grateful recipients to believe you've spent weeks and small fortunes in San Francisco curiosity shops. But Xapno regularly stocks rare finds at reasonable prices and will wrap them for you, too. Hours are erratic.

# Hayes Valley

**Reliquary** Clothing, Accessories
Map p194 (☎415-431-4000; www.reliquarysf .com; 537 Octavia Blvd; ⏱11am-7pm Tue-Sat, noon-6pm Sun; Ⓜ Hayes St) Earthy and urbane is not an oxymoron but a lifestyle choice achievable through years of

Loyal Army Clothing (p199)

SABRINA DALBESIO/LONELY PLANET IMAGES ©

# Gangs of San Francisco T-Shirts

Watch out, because Laureano Faedi, owner of **Gangs of San Francisco** (Map p194; ☏ 415-621-2431; www .gangsofsanfrancisco.com; 66 Gough St; ☺noon-6pm Tue-Sat, to 4pm Sun; Ⓜ Hayes St) is about to get all historical on your T-shirt – and if that sounds quaintly threatening, wait until you see his logos. The Brazil-born SF silk screener has unearthed insignia for every thuggish clique to claim an SF street corner, from the San Francisco Vigilance Committee – known for conducting kangaroo trials and swift hangings during SF's Gold Rush era – to the Richmond Beer Town Brawlers, who malingered near Golden Gate Park c 1875–96.

meditation and/or a shopping spree at Reliquary. Half the stock is well-traveled vintage – ikat silk kimonos, Santa Fe woolen blankets, silver jewelry banged together by Humboldt hippies – and the rest are cult American designs like Court denim, Majestic tissue-tees and Claire Vivier pebble-leather clutches.

## Flight 001                   Accessories
Map p194 ( ☏415-487-1001; www.flight001.com; 525 Hayes St; ☺11am-7pm Mon-Sat, to 6pm Sun; Ⓜ Hayes St) Having a nice flight in the zero-legroom era is actually a possibility with the in-flight assistance of Flight 001. Clever carry-ons built to fit international size regulations come with just the right number of pockets for rubber alarm clocks, travel Scrabble sets and the first-class Jet Comfort Kit with earplugs, sleep mask, booties, neck rest, candy and cards.

## Polanco          Accessories, Housewares
Map p194 ( ☏ 415-252-5753; 393 Hayes St; ☺noon-6pm Mon, 11:30am-6:30pm Tue-Sat, 1-6pm Sun; Ⓜ Hayes St) Contemporary folk art by Mexican and Chicano artists mixes traditional techniques and new ideas at Polanco, from Artemio Rodriguez' woodcuts of Day of the Dead skeletons sporting Mohawks to Gabriel Mendoza's surrealist *retratos* (portraits) of professionals literally consumed by their work. Don't miss the Oaxacan devil masks embedded with actual goat's horns, or the Frida Kahlo–esque earrings of silver hands cupping tiny hearts.

## Flax                        Art Supplies
Map p194 ( ☏415-552-2355; www.flaxart .com; 1699 Market St; ☺9:30am-7pm Mon-Sat; ☺; Ⓜ Market St) People who swear they lack artistic flair suddenly find it at Flax, where an entire room of specialty papers, racks of plump paint tubes in luscious colors and a wonderland of hot-glue guns practically make the collage for you. Art projects for kids start here, and the vast selections of pens and notebooks are novels waiting to happen.

## Lotus Bleu                   Housewares
Map p194 ( ☏415-861-2700; www.lotusbleu design.com; 325 Hayes St; ☺11am-6pm Tue-Fri, to 7pm Sat, noon-5pm Sun; Ⓜ Hayes St) French whimsy, Vietnamese design and San Franciscan psychedelic color keep eyes open wide in this compact design boutique packed from basement to rafters with fuchsia felt bull's-eye pillows, French laminated-canvas totes and lacquer breakfast trays.

# Golden Gate Park & the Avenues

Outdoor adventures and ethnic eateries urge everyone to 'Go West.' San Franciscans would prefer to keep this part of the city to themselves. All those Golden Gate Bridge postcards and talk of Downtown restaurants are diabolical ploys to direct your attention away from the western stretch of the city.

Golden Gate Park is the city's glorious wild streak, with bonsai forests, redwood groves, pagan altars and bison paddocks that make New York's Central Park look entirely too staid. If the park had decent espresso and burritos, people might never leave.

After populist millionaire Adolph Sutro built a public railway out to Ocean Beach in the 1890s, modest tract homes sprang up along the north side of the park, where transplanted immigrant communities thrived. South of Golden Gate Park, the Sunset District offers top-value ethnic restaurants and surf hangouts.

Coastal Trail (p212)

# Golden Gate Park & the Avenues Highlights

## Coastal Trail (p212)

Bundle up and bring your binoculars: this 9-mile trek along San Francisco's windswept Pacific Coast leads from abandoned missile silos haunted by hawks and hang gliders to smooch-inspiring sculpture at a war-memorial museum. (Start midway at the Sutro Baths for a shorter hike that's still long on coastal drama.) This trail is an essential link in a planned 1200-mile coastal hiking trail from Mexico to Oregon. Sutro Baths (p213) and Cliff House (p213)

**1**

**2**

## Legion of Honor (p212)

Inside this marble-clad replica of Paris' Legion d'Honneur is a world-class collection of arts and crafts, from Monet water lilies to John Cage soundscapes, ancient Iraqi ivories to R Crumb comics. Rodin's *The Thinker* is the star of the legacy of Legion benefactor 'Big Alma' de Bretteville Spreckels – except at 4pm on weekends, when pipe-organ recitals steal the show in the Rodin gallery.

## Outdoor Activities (p208)

At over 1000 acres, Golden Gate Park has plenty of room for everybody to get outside and play. Of course there are the requisite tennis courts and jogging paths, but the park also gives unsung sports their due. There's a lawn bowling club, a model-yacht marina, 18 holes of disc golf, a big-band shell for Lindy-hopping, and blacktop reserved for Sunday roller disco. Skateboarder in Golden Gate Park (p208)

## Ocean Beach (p213)

Toes curl at their first encounter with the frigid Pacific, but they'll be back for more. Beachcombers strike it rich in sand dollars on the south end of the beach, while surfers and sea lions brave wicked waves around Seal Rock to the north. By day, puppies and kids have the run of the place; by night, bonfires keep bikers and Beat poetry readers warm.

## Multi-Ethnic Eat Streets (p217)

Follow your nose and you can find several continents' worth of ethnic cuisine in the Avenues. Whether you want to try something entirely new or relive memories of travels past, you can find all manner of fare on Irving, Geary or Clement Sts: Middle Eastern stuffed grape leaves, organic Moroccan, traditional dim sum, wildly inventive sushi, sizzling-hot Szechuan, Irish pub fare or Burmese tea-leaf salad. Aziza (p217)

# Golden Gate Park & the Avenues Walk

*This end-to-end tour of Golden Gate Park takes in all our favorite sites, including formal gardens, fabulous museums, Victorian architecture and grazing bison. If the nearly 4 miles seems a little long, you can always rent a bike.*

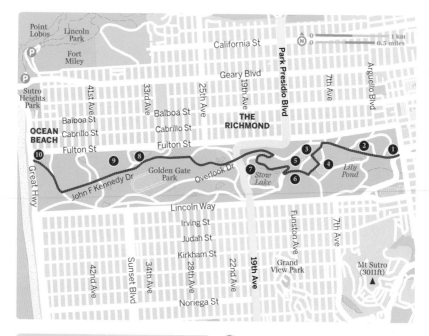

## ① McLaren Lodge
The former home of Park Superintendent John McLaren, this substantial looking Moorish-Gothic building constructed in 1896 is the headquarters of the SF Recreation and Parks Department.

## ② Conservatory of Flowers
Even if you don't come inside to see the orchids, water lilies and carnivorous plants, pass by to marvel at this 1878 Victorian greenhouse (p211) built of wood and glass and surrounded by lively formal flower gardens.

## ③ MH de Young Museum
Some folks grumbled when this copper-clad building (p209) was unveiled in 2005, but the idea of a building that will oxidize over time to blend in with the park has won over many critics. Take the elevator up to the free look-out tower for city views.

### 4 California Academy of Sciences

Two words: wildflower roof. Unlike the de Young, this museum (p209) got nothing but praise when it opened in 2008, thanks to the innovative, environmentally friendly design by Renzo Piano.

### 5 Japanese Tea Garden

Designed by Makoto Hagiwara for the 1894 Midwinter International Exposition, the 5 acres of formal Japanese gardens (p210) are punctuated with Buddha statues, bridges, a teahouse and rumors that this is where fortune cookies were invented.

### 6 Botanical Garden

You can cram a lot of plants into 55 acres, and if you have time, wandering the footpaths will give you the opportunity to acquaint yourself with thousands of well-tended plants from all around the world. (p210)

### 7 Stow Lake

A favorite with paddleboaters and casual walkers, **Stow Lake** (p211) surrounds an island (accessible by a stone bridge) where you can see a man-made waterfall and a pagoda.

### 8 Spreckels Lake

If you're lucky, you'll see a fleet of diminutive free-sail model yachts out on the water, though there won't be anyone aboard: **Spreckels Lake** is home of the San Francisco Model Yacht Club.

### 9 Bison Paddock

Promoting bison population growth and general goodwill toward the furry beasts, this paddock operated by the San Francisco Zoo gives you the chance to see these rare creatures straight out of the Old West.

### 10 Dutch Windmill

It's nearly another mile to the **Dutch Windmill**, which was built in 1903 to supply water to the park and sits beside the **Queen Wilhelmina Tulip Garden**. But it might be worth the effort to say you traversed the entire length of Golden Gate Park, all the way out to the Pacific Ocean.

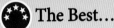 **The Best...**

## PLACES TO EAT

**Aziza** Cal-Mediterranean cuisine from a Food Network chef. (p217)

**Namu** Local, organic, Korean-inspired soul food. (p217)

**Kabuto** Join the throngs for innovative sushi. (p217)

**Thanh Long** Vietnamese by the beach – try the crab. (p220)

## PLACES TO DRINK

**Beach Chalet** Microbrews, ocean views. (p221)

**Trouble Coffee** Wake up with an espresso near the ocean. (p221)

**Social** Modernist version of a brewpub. (p221)

**Plough & the Stars** Irish pub with live music. (p222)

## URBAN WILDLIFE SIGHTINGS

**Bison** From the Old West to Golden Gate Park. (p207)

**Bank swallows** Tiny birds that burrow at Fort Funston. (p217)

**White alligator** Albino alligator gets star status. (p209)

**Snowy plover** Skittering shorebirds. (p216)

Dutch Windmill, Golden Gate Park
RICHARD CUMMINS/LONELY PLANET IMAGES ©

# ☑

## Don't Miss
# Golden Gate Park

When San Franciscans refer to 'the park,' there's only one that gets the definite article: Golden Gate Park. Mayor Frank McCoppin's park project seemed impossible in 1866. Even Frederick Law Olmstead, architect of New York's Central Park, was daunted by the prospect of transforming 1017 acres of dunes into park, so San Francisco's green scheme fell to young, tenacious civil engineer William Hammond Hall. Today, everything San Franciscans hold dear is here: free spirits, free music, redwoods, Frisbee, protests, fine art, bonsai and buffalo.

Map p214

☎ 415-831-2700

www.sfrecpark.org

btwn Stanyan St & Great Hwy, Fulton St & Lincoln Way

admission free

☉ sunrise-sunset

Ⓜ Stanyan, Irving, Fulton Sts

# MH de Young Museum

The oxidized copper building keeps a low profile, but there's no denying the park's star attraction: the **MH de Young Museum** (Map p214; ☎415-750-3600; www.famsf.org/dey oung; 50 Hagiwara Tea Garden Dr; adult/child $10/ free, discount with Muni ticket $2, 1st Tue of month free; ⏱9:30am-5:15pm Tue-Sun, to 8:45pm Fri mid-Jan–Nov; Ⓜ9th Ave). The collection features African masks and Meso-American sculpture alongside California crafts and American painting. Its new home designed by Swiss architects Herzog & de Meuron (of Tate Modern fame) is equally daring. The seemingly abstract pattern on the facade is drawn from aerial photography of the park, and clever light wells illuminate surprises around every corner.

The 144ft **tower** is the one architectural feature that seems incongruous with the park, but it offers spectacular views on clear days to the Pacific and Golden Gate Bridge. Access to the tower viewing room is free, and worth the wait for the elevator.

Upstairs, don't miss 19th-century Oceanic ceremonial oars and stunning Afghani rugs from the 11,000-plus textile collection. Blockbuster basement shows range from Queen Nefertiti's treasures to Balenciaga's sculptural gowns, but even more riveting are main-floor installations.

# California Academy of Sciences

Leave it to San Francisco to dedicate a glorious four-story monument entirely to freaks of nature: **California Academy of Sciences** (Map p214; ☎415-379-8000; www .calacademy.org; 55 Music Concourse Dr; adult/child $30/25, discount with Muni ticket $3; ⏱9:30am-5pm Mon-Sat, 11am-5pm Sun; Ⓜ9th Ave). The Academy's tradition of weird science dates from 1853, with thousands of live animals and 46 scientists now under a 2½-acre wildflower-covered roof. Butterflies flutter through the glass rainforest dome, a rare **white alligator** stalks a swamp and Pierre the Penguin paddles in his tank in the African Hall. In the basement aquarium, kids duck inside a glass bubble to enter an eel forest, find Nemos in the tropical-fish tanks and befriend starfish in the aquatic petting zoo.

1 **MH DE YOUNG MUSEUM**
When I bring people to the park for the first time, the first place I take them is the de Young's top-floor observation tower. In addition to the museum's superb collection, the 360-degree views from here are awe-inspiring. Past the greenness of the park, you can see from the Panhandle all the way to the ocean – the end of the continent.

2 **CALIFORNIA ACADEMY OF SCIENCES**
You see the wavy green roof from the top of the de Young, and when you go there you realize what a fantastic vantage point it has as well. The roof was specifically designed to attract butterflies and insects. It's also the world's largest LEED-platinum-certified museum, and the building contains so many architectural and engineering feats.

3 **CONSERVATORY OF FLOWERS**
I tell everyone that the Conservatory has the best oxygen in San Francisco. It's a Victorian-era greenhouse – the first building erected in the park – and it's a literal jungle inside, with exhibits of tropical, carnivorous and aquatic plants. On a cool day, your glasses fog over when you walk into the humid environment.

4 **JAPANESE TEA GARDEN**
The garden was recently renovated and feels very authentic now. The trees are maintained bonsai-style, and the rocks and plants in the green garden are symbolically placed. It has very traditional and beautiful statues and a pagoda, plus wooden bridges and koi ponds, and cherry trees that flower in spring. It's a very spiritual place to many people.

5 **BOTANICAL GARDEN**
The botanical collection is very unique because of San Francisco's climate. A visit here is like walking through a global garden because we can grow plants from temperate zones around the world. The redwood grove seems like nature's cathedral – the towering trees disappear into the clouds on foggy days and make you feel dwarfed by their size.

ROBERTO GERMETTA/LONELY PLANET IMAGES ©

JUDY BELLAH/LONELY PLANET IMAGES ©

# Botanical Garden

Travel around the world inside the 70-acre **San Francisco Botanical Garden** (Map p214; ☎ 415-661-1316; www.strybing.org; 1199 9th Ave; admission $7; ⏰ 9am-6pm Apr-Oct, 10am-5pm Nov-Mar; Ⓜ 9th Ave). Almost anything grows in the microclimates of this corner of Golden Gate Park, from South African savannah grasses to Japanese magnolias, New Zealand cloud-forest mosses to Mexican cacti. The Mediterranean fragrance garden is designed to be touched, smelled and tasted, and the California native-plant section explodes with color when wildflowers bloom in early spring. Don't miss the redwood grove, lily pond with giant koi or the lake where blue egrets pose for photos. Free tours take place daily; for details, stop by the bookstore inside the entrance. Last entry is one hour before closing.

## Hungry?

The **Academy Café** (☎ 415-876-6121; www.academycafesf.com; California Academy of Sciences; mains $6-13; ⏰ 9:30am-5pm Mon-Fri, 10am-5pm Sat-Sun) offers the most reliable food inside the park, but inexpensive, tasty alternatives line 9th Ave between Lincoln Way and Judah St in the Sunset, and are just a couple of blocks away on Balboa St between 5th and 8th Sts in the Richmond.

# Japanese Tea Garden

Inchworm-backed bridges, five-tiered pagodas and miniature waterfalls offer photo ops galore in the **Japanese Tea Garden** (Map p214; www.japaneseteagardensf.com; Hagiwara Tea Garden Dr; adult/child $7/5, Mon, Wed & Fri before 10am free; ⏰ 9am-6pm Mar-Oct, to 4:45pm Nov-Feb; Ⓜ 9th Ave). Since 1894 this 5-acre garden has blushed with cherry blossoms in spring, turned flaming red with maple leaves in fall and lost all track of time in the meditative Zen Garden. Green tea and fortune cookies – legendarily invented for this garden's inauguration – are served in the open-air tea pavilion year-round.

But the signature attraction is the 100-year-old **bonsai grove** tended for decades by landscape designer Makoto Hagiwara, whose family returned from WWII Japanese American internment camps to discover their prized miniature evergreens had been sold. The Hagiwaras spent two decades tracking down the trees and returned them to their rightful home. Free tours cover the garden's history Mondays and Saturdays at 9:30am.

## Conservatory of Flowers

Inside San Francisco's **Conservatory of Flowers** (Map p214; 415-666-7001; www.conservatoryofflowers.org; Conservatory Dr West; adult/child $5/3; sunrise-sunset), a recently restored 1878 Victorian greenhouse, orchids command center stage like opera divas, lilies float contemplatively in ponds and carnivorous plants give off odors that smell exactly like insect belches.

## Stow Lake

A park within the park, **Stow Lake** (Map p214; www.sfrecpark.org/StowLake.aspx; sunrise-sunset; M 9th Ave) offers steep hikes up a picturesque island called **Strawberry Hill**, with red-tailed hawks circling overhead. **Huntington Falls** tumble down the 400ft hill into the lake, near a romantic Chinese pavilion that fairly begs for soap-opera scenes. Pedal boats, rowboats and bicycles are available at the 1946 **boathouse** (Map p214; 415-752-0347; per hr paddleboats/canoes/rowboats $24/20/19, tandem bicycles $15, bicycles $8; rentals 10am-4pm).

### Wild Nights at the Academy

The penguins nod off to sleep, but night owls roam after-hours events at the California Academy of Sciences. Kids may not technically sleep during **Academy Sleepovers** (www.calacademy.org), but they might kick off promising careers as research scientists. At over-21 NightLife Thursdays, rainforest-themed cocktails are served and strange mating rituals may be observed among shy internet daters. Book ahead online.

# Discover Golden Gate Park & the Avenues

## 🔂 Getting There & Away

○ **Bus** Numbers 1 and 38 run from Downtown to the Richmond. Buses 5 and 21 head from Downtown along the north edge of Golden Gate Park, while number 2 runs the length of Clement St past the Legion of Honor. Bus 71 hooks around Golden Gate Park on the Sunset side.

○ **Streetcar** The N line runs from Downtown, through the Sunset to Ocean Beach.

## ◎ Sights

### The Richmond

**Golden Gate Park**  Park

Golden Gate Park includes the following sights: MH de Young Museum (p209), California Academy of Sciences (p209), San Francisco Botanical Garden (p210), Japanese Tea Garden (p210), Conservatory of Flowers (p211) and Stow Lake (p211).

**Coastal Trail**  Landmark

Map p214 ( ☼ sunrise-sunset; Ⓜ Judah St) Suit up and hit your stride on the 9-mile Coastal Trail, starting at Fort Funston, crossing 4 miles of sandy Ocean Beach, wrapping around the Presidio and then ending at Fort Mason. Casual strollers can pick up the trail near Sutro Baths, head around Land's End for a peek at Golden Gate Bridge and then duck into the Legion of Honor at Lincoln Park.

**Legion of Honor**  Museum

Map p214 ( ☏ 415-750-3600; http://legionofhonor.famsf.org; 100 34th Ave; adult/child $10/6, discount with Muni ticket $2, 1st Tue of month free; ☼ 9:30am-5:15pm Tue-Sun; Ⓜ Clement St) Never doubt the unwavering resolve of a nude model. This marble-clad replica of Paris' Legion d'Honneur was a gift to San Francisco from Alma de Bretteville Spreckels, a larger-than-life sculptor's model who married well and donated her fortune to create this monumental tribute to Californians killed in France in WWI. The museum is a bit of a schlep, especially by public transit, but it's worth it for its special exhibitions and its dramatic location on a bluff overlooking

Cliff House
THOMAS WINZ/LONELY PLANET IMAGES ©

the bay and Golden Gate Bridge. Wander into Lincoln Park for the best views. Don't miss rotating shows from the Legion's Achenbach Foundation for Graphic Arts, a major modern collection of 90,000 works on paper.

### Lincoln Park                    Park
Map p214 (Clement St; ☽sunrise-sunset; Ⓜ Clement St) John McLaren took time out from his 56-year job as Golden Gate Park's superintendent to establish lovely Lincoln Park, the official western terminus of the cross-country Lincoln Hwy. A partially paved path with a couple of flights of stairs covers rugged coastline from the Legion of Honor to the Cliff House, part of the 9-mile Coastal Trail. Terrific views of the Golden Gate and low-tide sightings of coastal shipwrecks are highlights of the 45-minute (1.4-mile) hike around Land's End; pick up the trailhead north of the Legion of Honor.

### Sutro Baths                    Park
Map p214 (www.nps.gov/prsf; ☽sunrise-sunset; Ⓜ 48th Ave) Hard to imagine from these ruins, but Victorian dandies and working stiffs converged here for bracing baths and workouts in itchy wool rental swimsuits. Mining magnate Adolph Sutro built hot and cold indoor pools to accommodate 10,000 unwashed masses in 1896, but the masses apparently preferred dirt, and the place was finally closed in 1952. Head through the sea-cave archway at low tide for end-of-the-world views of Marin Headlands.

### FREE Cliff House        Notable Building
Map p214 ( ☎415-386-3330; www.cliffhouse .com; 1090 Point Lobos Ave) Populist millionaire Adolph Sutro imagined this place as a working-man's paradise, and in 1863 it was a much-needed escape from Downtown tenements. After an 1894 fire, Sutro rebuilt the Cliff House as a palatial eight-story Victorian resort with art galleries, dining rooms and an observation tower. It miraculously survived the 1906 earthquake, only to be destroyed by fire the following year. The 1909 stark neoclassical replacement built by Sutro's daughter Emma remained popular for its saloon and restaurant.

In 2004, a $19-million face-lift turned the Cliff House into an upscale (read: overpriced) restaurant with all the charm of a fast-food outlet. But two popular attractions remain: sea lions barking on Seal Rock and the **Camera Obscura** (Map p214; ☎415-750-0415; www.giantcamera.com; 1096 Point Lobos Ave; adult/child $3/2; ☽11am-sunset), a Victorian invention that projects the sea view outside onto a parabolic screen.

## The Sunset
### Ocean Beach                    Beach
Map p214 ( ☎415-561-4323; www.parks conservancy.org; ☽sunrise-sunset; Ⓜ 48th Ave) Bikinis, Elvis sing-alongs and clambakes are not the scene here – think more along the lines of wet suits, pagan rituals and toasted marshmallows. Bonfires are permitted in the artist-designed fire pits, but follow park rules about fire maintenance

## Free Concerts

Hear that echo across Golden Gate Park? It's probably a concert, and very likely free. Opera divas, indie acts, bluegrass greats and hip-hop heavies take turns rocking SF gratis, from the wintry days of June through golden October afternoons. Most concerts are held in Sharon Meadow or Polo Fields on weekends; for upcoming events, consult the calendar (http://events.sfgate.com /san-francisco-ca/events/golden+gate+concert+schedule).

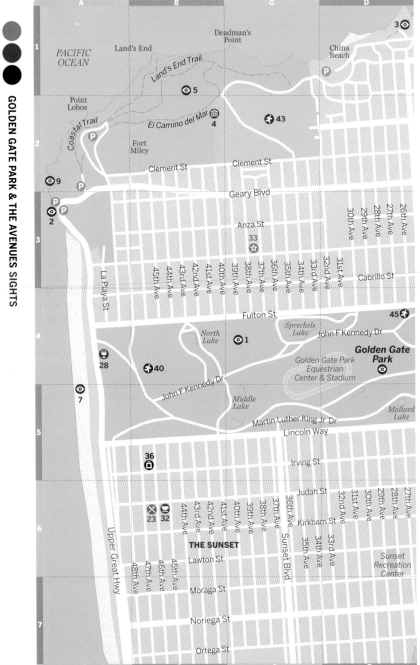

PACIFIC
OCEAN

Land's End

Deadman's
Point

China
Beach

3

Point
Lobos

Coastal Trail

5

El Camino del Mar
4

43

9

Fort
Miley

Clement St

Clement St

2

Geary Blvd

Anza St

33

La Playa St

45th Ave
44th Ave
43rd Ave
42nd Ave
41st Ave
40th Ave
39th Ave
38th Ave
37th Ave
36th Ave
35th Ave
34th Ave
33rd Ave
32nd Ave
31st Ave

30th Ave
29th Ave
28th Ave
27th Ave
26th Ave

Cabrillo St

Fulton St

North
Lake

1

Spreckels
Lake

45

John F Kennedy Dr

28

40

John F Kennedy Dr

Golden Gate
Park

Golden Gate Park
Equestrian
Center & Stadium

7

Middle
Lake

Mallard
Lake

Martin Luther King Jr Dr

Lincoln Way

36

Irving St

Judah St

23  32

Kirkham St

THE SUNSET

Lawton St

Upper Great Hwy

48th Ave
47th Ave
46th Ave
45th Ave
44th Ave
43rd Ave
42nd Ave
41st Ave
40th Ave
39th Ave
38th Ave
37th Ave
36th Ave
35th Ave
34th Ave
33rd Ave
32nd Ave
31st Ave
30th Ave
29th Ave
28th Ave
27th Ave

Sunset Blvd

Sunset
Recreation
Center

Moraga St

Noriega St

Ortega St

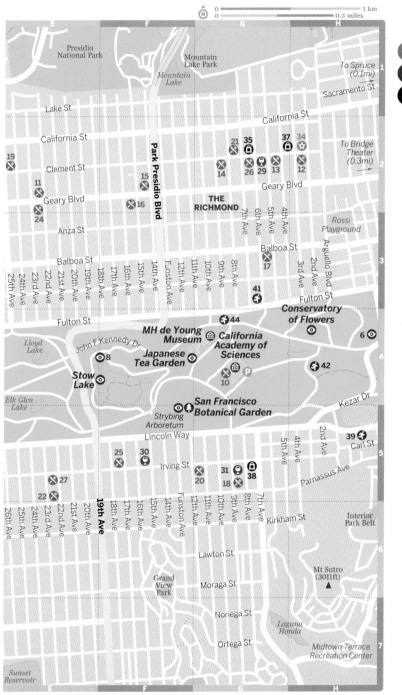

# Golden Gate Park & The Avenues

### ◎ Top Sights
California Academy of
  Sciences.............................................G4
Conservatory of Flowers.................H4
Golden Gate Park.............................D4
Japanese Tea Garden .....................F4
MH de Young Museum.........................G4
San Francisco Botanical
  Garden.............................................F5
Stow Lake...........................................F4

### ◎ Sights
1 Bison Paddock ...............................C4
Camera Obscura.........................(see 2)
2 Cliff House .......................................A3
3 Coastal Trail....................................D1
4 Legion of Honor.............................B2
5 Lincoln Park.....................................B1
6 McLaren Lodge ..............................H4
7 Ocean Beach ..................................A5
8 Stow Lake Boathouse ..................F4
9 Sutro Baths.....................................A2

### ✴ Eating
10 Academy Café ...............................G4
11 Aziza ................................................E2
12 B Star Bar .......................................H2
13 Burma Superstar ..........................G2
14 Halu..................................................G2
15 House of Bagels ............................F2
16 Kabuto.............................................F2
17 Namu ...............................................G3
18 Nanking Road Bistro ....................G5
Outerlands...................................(see 32)
19 PPQ Dungeness Island..................E2
20 San Tung..........................................G5
21 Spices...............................................G2

22 Sunrise Deli ....................................E5
23 Thanh Long .....................................B6
24 Ton Kiang Restaurant....................E2
25 Underdog.........................................F5
26 Wing Lee .........................................G2
27 Yum Yum Fish ................................E5

### ◉ Drinking & Nightlife
540 Club .........................................(see 26)
28 Beach Chalet ..................................A4
29 Bitter End.......................................G2
30 Hollow .............................................F5
31 Social................................................G5
32 Trouble Coffee ...............................B6

### ◎ Entertainment
33 Balboa Theater ..............................C3
34 Plough & the Stars ........................H2

### ⬤ Shopping
General Store.................................(see 32)
35 Green Apple Books ........................G2
36 Mollusk............................................B5
Park Life.........................................(see 34)
37 Seedstore ........................................G2
38 Wishbone..........................................G5

### ✚ Sports & Activities
39 Circus Center Trapeze...................H5
40 Golden Gate Municipal Golf
  Course.............................................B4
41 Golden Gate Park Bike &
  Skate...............................................G3
42 Lawn Bowling Club.........................H4
43 Lincoln Park Golf Course...............C2
44 Lindy in the Park............................G4
45 San Francisco Disc Golf.................D4

and alcohol (not allowed) or you could get fined. On rare sunny days the waters may beckon, but only hard-core surfers and sea lions should brave these riptides. At the south end of the beach, beachcombers may spot sand dollars and the remains of a 19th-century shipwreck. Stick to paths in the fragile dunes, where skittish, knock-kneed snowy plover shorebirds shelter in winter.

**Fort Funston**                         Park
( ☏ 415-561-4323; www.parksconservancy .org; Skyline Blvd; Ⓜ Judah St) Grassy dunes up to 200ft high at Fort Funston give

you an idea of what the Sunset looked like before it was paved over in the 20th century. In this defunct military installation, you'll find 146-ton WWII guns pointing out to sea and abandoned Nike missile silos near the parking lot. Nuclear missiles were never launched from Ft Funston, but on any sunny, breezy day, flocks of hang gliders launch and land here. If you're driving, cycling or walking here, follow the Great Hwy south and turn right on Skyline Blvd; the park entrance is past Lake Merced, on the right-hand side.

# Fort Funston's Plucky Little Cliff-Dwellers

Fort Funston is a refuge for the smallest birds in North America: **bank swallows**. They may be little, but they throw all .3oz to .7oz of themselves into their work, burrowing holes 4ft deep into Fort Funston's sandstone cliffs to provide safe havens for their tiny chicks. Heftier females are highly desirable mates, since they can handle their share of the heavy lifting of nest building and hauling insects to feed chicks. These plucky little birds are endangered in California, but as many as a couple of hundred bank swallows have been spotted recently in Fort Funston's cliffs, alongside starlings that squat in old nests. Bring binoculars from April to June, and you may spot chicks finding their wings.

# Eating

## The Richmond

**Aziza**  Moroccan, Californian $$
Map p214 ( 415-752-2222; www.aziza-sf.com; 5800 Geary Blvd; mains $16-29; 5:30-10:30pm Wed-Mon; ; Geary Blvd) Mourad Lahlou's inspiration is Moroccan and his produce organic Californian, but his flavors are out of this world: Sonoma duck confit melts into caramelized onion between flaky layers of pastry *basteeya* (meat pie), while sour cherries rouse slow-cooked local lamb shank from its barley bed. Chef Mourad has his own Food Network show and is opening a restaurant Downtown, but he continues to pioneer Moroccan-California crossroads cuisine at Geary and 22nd – and pastry chef Melissa Chou's Moroccan mint tea Bavarian deserves its own landmark.

**Namu**  Korean, Californian $$
Map p214 ( 415-386-8332; www.namusf.com; 439 Balboa St; small plates $8-16; 6-10:30pm Sun-Tue, to midnight Wed-Sat, brunch 10am-3pm Sat & Sun; Balboa St) SF's unfair culinary advantages – top-notch organic ingredients, Silicon Valley inventiveness and deep roots in Pacific Rim cuisine – are showcased in Namu's Korean-inspired soul food. Don't miss the complimentary housemade kimchi, ultra-savory shiitake mushroom dumplings and Namu's original take on *bibimbap*: organic vegetables and a Sonoma farm egg served sizzling on rice in a stone pot, with optional (and recommended) marinated Marin Sun Farms grass-fed steak.

**Kabuto**  Californian, Sushi $$
Map p214 ( 415-752-5652; www.kabutosushi .com; 5121 Geary Blvd; sushi $6-10; 11:30am-2:30pm & 5:30-10:30pm Tue-Sat, 5:30-10:30pm Sun; Geary Blvd) Strict Tokyo traditionalists and seafood agnostics alike squeal over the innovative sushi served in this converted vintage hot-dog drive-in. Every night there's a line out the door to witness sushi chef Eric top nori-wrapped sushi rice with foie gras and olallieberry reduction, *hamachi* (yellowtail) with pear and wasabi mustard, and – eureka! – the '49er oyster with sea urchin, caviar, a quail's egg and gold leaf, chased with rare sake. Reserve ahead; seats groups up to four.

**Ton Kiang Restaurant**  Dim Sum $$
Map p214 ( 415-387-8273; www.tonkiang.net; 5821 Geary Blvd; dim sum $3-7; 10am-9pm Mon-Thu, to 9:30pm Fri, 9:30am-9:30pm Sat, 9am-9pm Sun; ; Geary Blvd) The reigning champion of dim sum runs laps around the competition, pushing trolleys laden with fragrant, steaming bamboo baskets. Choose some on aroma alone, or ask for the *gao choy gat* (shrimp and chive dumplings), *dao miu gao* (pea tendril and shrimp dumplings) and *jin doy* (sesame balls) by name. A running tally is kept at your table, so you could conceivably quit

while you're ahead of the $20 mark – but wait, here comes another cart...

###  Spruce    Californian $$$

off Map p214 ( 📞415-931-5100; www.sprucesf .com; 3640 Sacramento St; mains $14-30; 🕐11:30am-2:30pm Mon-Fri, 5-10pm Sun-Thu, 5-11pm Fri & Sat; Ⓜ California St) VIP all the way, with Baccarat crystal chandeliers, tawny leather chairs and your choice of 1000 wines. Ladies who lunch dispense with polite conversation, tearing into grass-fed burgers on house-baked English muffins loaded with pickled onions, zucchini grown on the restaurant's own organic farm and an optional slab of foie gras. Want fries with that? Oh yes you do: Spruce's are cooked in duck fat.

### Spices    Chinese $

Map p214 ( 📞415-752-8884; www.spices restaurantonline.com; 294 8th Ave; mains $7-13; 🕐11am-11pm; Ⓜ Geary Blvd) The menu reads like an oddly dubbed Hong Kong action flick, with dishes labeled 'fire-burst!!' and 'stinky!', but the chefs can call zesty pickled Napa cabbage with chili oil, silky ma-po tofu and brain-curdling spicy chicken whatever they want – it's definitely worthy of exclamation. When you head toward the kitchen for the bathroom, the chili aroma will make your eyes well up – or maybe that's just gratitude. Cash only.

### PPQ Dungeness Island    Seafood $$$

Map p214 ( 📞415-386-8266; 2332 Clement St; crab mains $20-30; 🕐11am-10pm Wed-Mon; 🚻; Ⓜ Geary Blvd) Dungeness crab season lasts most of the year in San Francisco, which means now is a fine time to enjoy one whole atop garlic noodles or dredged in peppercorn-laced flour and lightly fried, for a market price of about $20 per person. Ignore everything else on the menu, and put that bib to work.

### House of Bagels    Bakery $

Map p214 ( 📞415-752-6000; www.houseofbagels .com; 5030 Geary Blvd; bagels $1-3; 🕐6am-6pm; Ⓜ Geary Blvd) New Yorkers believe that

218

**Left:** Fort Funston (p216); **Below:** Wing Lee

(LEFT) ROBERTO GEROMETTA/LONELY PLANET IMAGES ©; (BELOW) SABRINA DALBESIO/LONELY PLANET IMAGES ©

while SF has better weather and produce, they have better bagels – at least until they try the poppy seed bagel (boiled, not steamed, then baked) with lox schmear (cream cheese spread) at this mainstay of SF's Russian Jewish neighborhood.

### Halu
Japanese $$

Map p214 ( ☎ 415-221-9165; 312 8th Ave; yakitori $2.50-4, ramen $10-11; ⏰ 5-10pm Tue-Sat; Ⓜ Geary Blvd) Between the rare Beatles memorabilia plastering the walls and adventurous foods drifting by on skewers, dinner at this snug five-table joint feels like stowing away on the Yellow Submarine. Ramen is respectably toothsome, but the house specialty is yakitori, small bites crammed onto sticks and barbecued. Get anything wrapped in bacon – scallops, quail eggs, *mochi* rice cake – and if you're up for offal, have a heart.

### Burma Superstar
Burmese $$

Map p214 ( ☎ 415-387-2147; www.burmasuperstar.com; 309 Clement St; mains $9-22; ⏰ 11am-3:30pm & 5-10pm Mon-Thu, to 10:30pm Sat & Sun; Ⓜ Geary Blvd) Yes, there's a wait, but do you see anyone walking away? Blame it on creamy, fragrant catfish curries and *la pat,* a traditional Burmese green-tea salad tarted up with lime and dried shrimp. Reservations aren't accepted, so ask the host to call you at the cafe across the street, and enjoy a glass of wine – or if you can't wait for that tea salad, head down the street to its casual small-plates sister restaurant, **B Star Bar** (Map p214; 127 Clement St).

### Wing Lee
Dim Sum $

Map p214 ( ☎ 415-831-7883; 501 Clement St; dim sum $1.60-3.50; ⏰ 10am-5pm; Ⓜ Geary St) How do you feed two famished surfers for $10? Just Wing Lee it. Line up with small bills and walk away loaded with shrimp and leek dumplings, BBQ pork buns (baked or steamed), chicken *shu mai* (open-topped dumplings), pot stickers

219

and crispy sesame balls with a chewy red-bean center. Fluorescent-lit lunch tables aren't made for dates, but these dumplings won't last long anyway.

# The Sunset

### Thanh Long
Vietnamese $$

Map p214 ( 415-665-1146; www.anfamily.com /restaurants/thanhlong_restaurant; 4101 Judah St; mains $10-18; 5-9:30pm Tue-Thu & Sun, to 10pm Fri & Sat; ; Judah St) Since 1971 San Franciscans have lingered in the Sunset after sunset for two reasons, both at Thanh Long: roast pepper crab and garlic noodles. One crab serves two (market price runs $34 to $40) with noodles ($9), but shaking beef and mussels make a proper feast. The wine list offers good-value local pairings, especially Navarro's dry gewürztraminer.

### Sunrise Deli
Middle Eastern $

Map p214 ( 415-664-8210; 2115 Irving St; dishes $4-7; 9am-9pm Mon-Sat, 10am-8pm Sun; ; Judah St) A hidden gem in the fog belt, Sunrise dishes up what is arguably the city's best smoky baba ghanoush, *mujeddrah* (lentil-rice with crispy onions), garlicky *foul* (fava bean spread) and crispy falafel, either to go or to enjoy in the old-school cafe atmosphere. Local Arab American hipsters confess to passing off the Sunrise's specialties as their own home cooking to older relatives.

### Yum Yum Fish
Japanese, Sushi $

Map p214 ( 415-566-6433; www.yumyumfish sushi.com; 2181 Irving St; sushi $1-8; 10:30am-7:30pm; ; Judah St) Watch and learn as Yum Yum's sushi chef lovingly slices generous hunks of fresh sashimi, preparing a platter to order with your special *maki* needs in mind. Rolls can be made specially for vegans for as little as a dollar per order, and if you want sustainable sushi, bring your **Seafood Watch Card** (www .seafoodwatch.org) and order accordingly.

### Nanking Road Bistro
Chinese $

Map p214 ( 415-753-2900; 1360 9th Ave; mains $7-12; 11:30am-10pm Mon-Fri, noon-10pm Sat & Sun; ; Irving St) Northern regional Chinese food is underrepresented in historically Cantonese SF, but the breakaway stars of Nanking Road's menu are clamshell *bao* (bun) folded over crispy Beijing duck and a definitive *kung pao* chicken lunch special ($7), with the right ratio of chili to roast peanuts. Chinese opera characters stare you down from massive paintings as though to ensure you finish your vegetables – with caramelized eggplant and smoky dry-braised string beans, that's not hard.

### San Tung
Dim Sum $

Map p214 ( 415-242-0828; www.santungrestaurant .com; 1031 Irving St; mains $8-13; 11am-9:30pm Thu-Tue; Irving St) When you arrive at 5:30pm on a Sunday and the place is already packed, you might think you've hit a family dinner rush – but

Beach Chalet

# Detour: Outerlands

When windy Ocean Beach leaves you feeling shipwrecked, drift into this beach-shack bistro for organic California comfort food. Lunch at **Outerlands** (Map p214; ☎ 415-661-6140; www.outerlandssf.com; 4001 Judah St; sandwiches & small plates $8-9; ⏱ 11am-3pm & 6-10pm Tue-Sat, 10am-2:30pm Sun; Ⓜ Judah St) means open-faced sandwiches on crusty house-baked bread – pastrami brisket with pickled slaw is a menu mainstay – or the $9 grilled artisan cheese combo with seasonal housemade soup, especially if it's pumpkin or leek. Dinners get fancy, with slow-cooked pork shoulder slouching into green-garlic risotto and almond financiers with cherry-tarragon coulis. Arrive early and sip wine outside until seats open up indoors.

no, it's this crowded *all* the time. Blame it on the dry braised chicken wings – tender, moist morsels that defy the very name – and housemade dumplings and noodles. You'll be smacking your lips with the memory when the bill comes: a three-course meal for two for $20.

## Underdog
Sausages $

Map p214 ( ☎ 415-665-8881; www.underdog organic.com; 1634 Irving St; hot dogs $4-5; ⏱ 11:30am-9pm; 🖊🚼; Ⓜ Irving St) For cheap, organic meals on the run in a bun, Underdog is the clear winner. The roasted garlic and Italian pork sausages are USDA certified–organic, and the smoky veggie chipotle hot dog could make dedicated carnivores into fans of fake meat.

# 🍷 Drinking & Nightlife

## Beach Chalet
Brewery, Bar

Map p214 (www.beachchalet.com; 1000 Great Hwy; ⏱ 9am-10pm Sun-Thu, to 11pm Fri & Sat; Ⓜ 48th Ave) Pacific sunsets are even more impressive when glimpsed through a pint glass of the Beach Chalet's microbrewed beer. If there's a wait, wander downstairs to see 1930s Works Progress Administration (WPA) frescoes highlighting San Francisco history and the development of Golden Gate Park. There's live music on Tuesdays and Fridays.

## 📝 Trouble Coffee
Cafe $

Map p214 (www.troublecoffee.com; 4033 Judah St; ⏱ 7am-8pm Mon-Fri, 8am-8pm Sat, 8am-5pm Sun; Ⓜ Judah St) Coconuts are unlikely near blustery Ocean Beach, but here comes trouble with the 'Build Your Own Damn House' $8 breakfast special: coffee, thick-cut cinnamon-laced toast and an entire young coconut. The hewn-wood bench out front is permanently damp from surfers' rears, but house-roasted 'The Hammer' espresso at the reclaimed wood counter indoors breaks through any morning fog.

## 540 Club
Bar

Map p214 (www.540-club.com; 540 Clement St; ⏱ 11am-2am; Ⓜ Geary St) Unless you're a master criminal, this is the most fun you'll ever have inside a bank. Look for the neon pink elephant over the archway, and enter the converted savings-and-loan office to find minor mayhem already in progress, thanks to absinthe, $2 PBR, Punk Rock BBQ and Catholic School Karaoke (see website for events). Under vaulted ceilings, bartenders pull a dozen brews on tap – including bitter Guinness, blond Leffe and wheat Hoegaarden – to loosen you up for friendly games of darts or pool.

## Social
Brewery

Map p214 (www.socialkitchenandbrewery.com; 1326 9th Ave; ⏱ 5pm-midnight Mon-Thu, to 2am Fri, 11:30am-2am Sat, to midnight Sun; Ⓜ Irving St) In every Social situation, there are a the pool tables and dartboard on the balcony.

# Detour: Hollow

Between simple explanations and Golden Gate Park, there's **Hollow** (Map p214; ☎415-242-4119; www.hollowsf.com; 1493 Irving St; ⏱8am-5pm Mon-Fri, 9am-5pm Sat & Sun; Ⓜ Irving St): an enigma wrapped in a mystery inside an espresso bar. House coffee is made with SF's cultish Ritual roasts, and the secret ingredient in the cupcakes is Guinness – but that doesn't begin to explain those shelves. Magnifying glasses, galvanized tin pails, deer antlers and monster etchings are inexplicably for sale here, obsessive-compulsively organized into a kind of shelf haiku. There are only a couple of marble tables, so expect a wait among like-minded eccentrics.

couple of troublemakers – specifically L'Enfant Terrible, a dark Belgian ale with an attitude, and bitter but golden Rapscallion. This snazzy, skylit modern building looks like an architect's office but tastes like a neighborhood brewpub, which just happens to serve addictive lime-laced brussels-sprout chips – but hey, hogging the bowl is anti-Social.

**Bitter End** Pub
Map p214 (441 Clement St; ⏱4pm-2am Mon-Fri, 11am-2am Sat & Sun; Ⓜ Geary Blvd) Don't be bitter if tricky Tuesday-night trivia games don't end with decisive wins – near-victories are fine excuses for another beer or alcoholic pear cider at this local haunt with proper creaky wood floors, Irish bartenders and passable pub grub. Sore losers can always challenge trivia champs to a friendly grudge match at

## ☆ Entertainment

**Bridge Theater** Cinema
off Map p214 (☎415-267-4893; www.landmark theatres.com; 3010 Geary Blvd; adult/child $10.50/8) One of SF's last single-screen theaters, the Bridge screens international independent films, from yakuza gangster thrillers to film-festival sensations.

**Balboa Theater** Cinema
Map p214 (☎415-221-8184; www.balboa movies.com; 3630 Balboa St; adult/child $10/7.50; Ⓜ Balboa St) First stop, Cannes; next stop, Balboa and 37th, where Russian documentaries split the bill with art house darlings like Woody Allen. Film-makers vie for marquee spots at this 1926 neighborhood movie palace, which has just one screen and a director who also programs for Telluride Festival.

**Plough & the Stars** Bar
Map p214 (☎415-751-1122; www.theploughand stars.com; 116 Clement St; ⏱3pm-2am Mon-Thu, 2pm-2am Fri-Sun, showtime 9pm; Ⓜ Geary Blvd) Bands who sell out shows from Ireland to Appalachia and headline San Francisco's Hardly Strictly Bluegrass Festival (see p41) turn up to jam on weeknights, taking breaks to clink pint glasses at long union-hall-style tables. Mondays are compensated for no live music with an all-day happy hour, plus free pool and blarney from regulars; expect modest cover charges for Friday and Saturday shows.

## 🔒 Shopping

**Park Life** Art, Books
Map p214 (☎415-386-7275; www.parklifestore .com; 220 Clement St; ⏱11am-8pm; Ⓜ Geary Blvd) Is Park Life a design store, an art gallery or an indie publisher? All of the above, with limited-edition scores that include piggy-bank lamps with fluorescent-

## Summer Movie Madness

Weekends in summer, the **Bridge Theater** (off Map p214; ☎415-267-4893; www .landmarktheatres.com; 3010 Geary Blvd; ticket $13) hosts Midnight Mass, featuring camp, horror and B-grade movies such as *Showgirls* and *Mommie Dearest,* with each screening preceded by a drag show spoofing the film. Local celeb Peaches Christ wrangles the always-raucous crowd; reserve ahead.

At the **Balboa Theater** (Map p214; ☎415-221-8184; www.balboamovies.com; 3630 Balboa St; tickets $15-20; Ⓜ Balboa St), summertime brings the occasional superhero flick and lots of classic ballet, dance, opera, jazz and Shakespeare performances screened in their entirety.

BYO blanket to outdoor Friday movie nights in summer at the Beach Chalet (p221), where admission is free with your purchase of house-brewed beer.

coil tails, artist-designed statement tees with drawn-on pockets or bold semi-colons, and Park Life's own publications on graffiti artist Andrew Schoultz.

### Green Apple Books
Bookstore

Map p214 ( ☎415-387-2272; 506 Clement St; ⏱10am-10:30pm Sun-Thu, to 11:30pm Fri & Sat; Ⓜ Geary Blvd) Blissed-out booklovers emerge blinking into the sunset after an entire day browsing three floors of new releases, used titles and staff picks more reliable than *New York Times* reviews. Local favorites are easy to spot in the local interest section – look for the local author tag. Don't miss the fiction and music annex two doors down.

### Mollusk
Outdoor Gear

Map p214 ( ☎415-564-6300; www.mollusksurf shop.com; 4500 Irving St; ⏱10am-6:30pm; Ⓜ Judah St) The high-impact store sign painted by Tauba Auerbach before she hit the Whitney Biennial is the first hint that this is the source of West Coast surfer cool. Visits by celebrity shapers (surfboard makers) yield limited-edition boards you won't find elsewhere, and signature Mollusk T-shirts and hoodies by local artists buy you nods of recognition on Ocean Beach.

### General Store
Gifts, Accessories

Map p214 ( ☎415-682-0600; 4035 Judah St; ⏱11am-7pm Mon-Fri, 10am-7pm Sat & Sun;

Ⓜ Judah St) Anyone born in the wrong place or time to be a NorCal hippie architect can still look the part, thanks to a) beards and b) General Store. Pine-lined walls showcase handcrafted recycled-leather boots, antique turquoise neck-laces, brass bicycle bells, egg-shaped terrariums and vintage how-to books.

### Wishbone
Gifts

Map p214 (www.wishbonesf.com; 601 Irving St; 11:30am-7pm Mon, Tue & Thu-Sat, to 6pm Sun; Ⓜ Irving St) Certain gifts never fail to please: explode-in-your-mouth Pop Rocks candy, smiling toast coin purses and blue ribbons that proclaim 'Computer Whiz!' Gifts here will gratify hip parents, from a bath towel that doubles as a pirate's cape to the onesie silkscreened to look like a BART card.

### Seedstore
Clothing

Map p214 (www.seedstoresf.com; 212 Clement St; ⏱11am-7pm Mon-Fri, to 8pm Sat, to 6pm Sun; Ⓜ Geary St) Less like enter-ing a store than raiding the wardrobe of a modern spaghetti western star. The old-timey shingle hung over the door is misleading: no gardening supplies are sold here, but you will find Joe's Jeans, Superdry military-style jackets, BB Dakota riding pants, filmy Free People peasant blouses and vintage Navajo-pattern cardigans.

SABRINA DALBESIO/LONELY PLANET IMAGES ©

# 🏃 Sports & Activities

### Golden Gate Park
### Bike & Skate
Cycling, Skating

Map p214 (📞415-668-1117; www.goldengatepark bikeandskate.com; 3038 Fulton St; skates per hr $5-6, per day $20-24, bicycles per hr $3-5, per day $15-25, tandem bicycles per hr/day $15/75, discs $6/25; ⏱10am-6pm; MFulton St) Besides bicycles and skates (both quad-wheeled and inline), this little rental shop just outside the park rents disc putters and drivers for the nearby free Frisbee golf course. Call ahead to confirm it's open if the weather looks iffy.

### Golden Gate
### Municipal Golf Course
Golf

Map p214 (📞415-751-8987; www.goldengate parkgolfcourse.com; 47th Ave & Fulton St, Golden Gate Park; adult/child Mon-Thu $15/5, Fri-Sun $19/7; ⏱6am-8pm; 👫; MFulton St) Golden Gate Park has a challenging nine-hole, par-27 course built on sand dunes, with some 100yd drop-offs, 180yd elevated greens and Pacific views. No reservations are taken, but it's busiest before 9am weekdays and after school. On weekend afternoons, bide your time waiting with excellent clubhouse wood-fired BBQ sandwiches (their secret: Anchor Steam beer in the sauce). Equipment rentals and practice range available; kids welcome.

### Lincoln Park Golf Course
Golf

Map p214 (📞415-221-9911; www.lincolnparkgc .com; 34th Ave & Clement St, Lincoln Park; Mon-Thu $37, Fri-Sun $41, cart $26; ⏱sunrise-sunset; MClement St) For game-sabotaging views, the hilly, 18-hole Lincoln Park course wraps around Land's End and the Legion of Honor to face Golden Gate Bridge. This course has the most iconic SF vistas, so watch out for daydreaming hikers and brides posing for wedding pictures – fore!

### Harding Park Municipal
### Golf Course
Golf

(📞415-664-4690; www.harding-park.com; 99 Harding Rd at Skyline Blvd; 9-hole course Mon-Thu $26, Fri-Sun $31, 18-hole course Mon-Thu $150, Fri-Sun $170; ⏱6:30am-7pm; MSkyline Blvd) San Francisco's bargain public course is a lush 18-hole landscape par-tially shaded by cypress trees beside the ocean, plus the Jack Fleming nine-hole course, where walk-ins are welcome. Cart is included with 18-hole greens fees or costs $14 with nine holes; call to reserve tee times.

## Circus Center Trapeze
*Circus*

Map p214 (☎415-759-8123, ext 810 for trapeze enrolment; www.circuscenter.org; 755 Frederick St; 2hr workshop $45; 🚼; M Irving St) If you've ever dreamed of running away and joining the circus, indulge your fantasy at this circus-arts school, where adults and kids learn everything from contortionist tricks to the flying trapeze. Serious pupils with red-rubber noses attend the school's Clown Conservatory, the only clown-training school in the US.

## Lawn Bowling Club
*Lawn Bowls*

Map p214 (☎415-487-8787; http://sflb.files forfriends.com; Bowling Green Dr, Golden Gate Park; M Stanyan St) Pins seem ungainly and bowling shirts unthinkable once you've joined the sweater-clad enthusiasts on America's first public bowling green. Free lessons are available from member volunteers at noon on Wednesdays and Saturdays; call to confirm volunteer availability. Flat-soled shoes are mandatory, but otherwise people dress for comfort and the weather – though all-white clothing has been customary at club social events since 1901.

## FREE Lindy in the Park
*Dance*

Map p214 (www.lindyinthepark.com; John F Kennedy Dr btwn 8th & 10th Ave; ⏲11am-2pm Sun; 🚼; M Fulton St) Sundays swing at the free Lindy-hopping dance party in Golden Gate Park, at the outdoor band shell between the MH de Young Museum and the California Academy of Sciences (weather permitting). All are welcome; dancers range from first-timers to semi-professionals, hipsters to grandparents. Free half-hour lessons begin at noon, but you can always just watch or wing it.

## FREE San Francisco Croquet Club
*Croquet*

(☎415-928-5525; www.croquetworld.com /sfcc.html; Stern Grove, 19th Ave & Wawona St; 🚼; M 19th Ave) Croquet is not just for mad queens and chichi garden parties anymore. These folks are hard core about their wickets, but nonmembers can join free sessions on the first three Saturdays of the month, and kids are always welcome.

## FREE San Francisco Disc Golf
*Disc Golf*

Map p214 (www.sfdiscgolf.org; Marx Meadow Dr at Fulton St btwn 25th & 30th Ave; M Fulton St) If you love to throw Frisbees, head to the tranquil woods of Golden Gate Park to find a permanent 18-hole disc golf course, enjoyed by cultish veterans and reckless beginners. You can rent a bag of flying saucers at Golden Gate Park Bike & Skate and limber up for tournaments, which kick off Sundays from 8:30am to 10am.

# Day Trips

## Napa Valley (p228) & Sonoma Valley (p231)

Fancy-pants Napa put America on the world's viticulture map, but historic Sonoma retains its folksy ways. In California's Wine Country expect pastoral landscapes and great wine.

## Muir Woods & Muir Beach (p232)

The world's tallest trees lord over the primordial forest and rugged seacoast, just across the Golden Gate in Marin County.

## Sausalito & Tiburon (p233)

Picturesque towns, perfect for strolling, are a ferry ride away in Marin County. Linger bayside, glass of wine in hand.

Muir Woods (p232)

# Napa Valley

The most glamorous stretch of farmland in America, Napa Valley is famous for cabernet sauvignon, star chefs and small towns with huge reputations. Tiny Yountville has more Michelin-starred eateries per capita than anywhere else in America. St Helena – the Beverly Hills of Napa – is where traffic always jams, but there's great strolling if you can find parking. Folksy Calistoga – Napa's least gentrified town – marks the valley's north end, home to hot-spring spas and mud-bath emporiums that use volcanic ash from adjacent Mt St Helena. Hwy 29 slows to a standstill summer weekends; come midweek if possible.

## Getting There & Away

**Car** To Napa: take Hwy 101 to Hwy 37 east. At the 121/37 split take Hwy 121 north, which veers east toward Napa. At Hwy 29, turn north. From Downtown, the Bay Bridge is quicker, but less scenic: take I-80E to Hwy 37 west (exit 33), then go north on Hwy 29. Alternatively, to reach Calistoga and bypass the lower and midvalley, take Hwy 101 to Mark West Springs Rd (exit 494/River Rd) and keep winding east into Porter Creek Rd and Petrified Forest Rd.

**Ferry & Bus** Possible, but slow: take the Vallejo ferry (p282), then bus 10 Napa Valley Vine (www.nctpa.net).

## Need to Know

○ **Area Code** ☎707

○ **Location** 50 miles northeast of San Francisco

○ **Napa Valley Welcome Center** (☎707-260-0107; wwww.legendarynapavalley.com; 600 Main St; ◷9am-5pm)

# ◉ Sights

When visiting wineries, call ahead for bookings whenever possible – by local law, some wineries require advance reservations and must cap their daily number of visitors. Book one appointment and plan your day around it. Go north on Hwy 29, then return southward on parallel-running Silverado Trail. Napa can be done as a day trip, but you'd be smart to stay at least one night. The sights listed are in south to north order.

### di Rosa Art + Nature Preserve
Art Gallery

(☎707-226-5991; www.dirosapreserve.org; 5200 Carneros Hwy 121; ◷gallery 9:30am-3pm Wed-Fri, by appointment Sat) When you notice scrap-metal sheep grazing Carneros vineyards, you've spotted di Rosa Art + Nature Preserve, one of the best collections of Northern California art. Reservations recommended for tours, covering everything from Tony Oursler's grimacing video projections in the wine cellar to million-dollar Robert Bechtel abstracts hung on the living-room ceiling.

### Vintners' Collective
Tasting Room

(☎707-255-7150; www.vintnerscollective.com; 1245 Main St, Napa; tasting $25; ◷11am-6pm) Ditch the car and chill in downtown Napa at this supercool tasting bar – inside a former 19th-century brothel – that represents 20 high-end, boutique wineries too small to have their own tasting rooms.

### Twenty Rows
Winery

(☎707-287-1063; www.twentyrows.com; 880 Vallejo St, Napa; tasting $10; ◷11am-5pm Tue-Sat) Downtown Napa's only working winery crafts light-on-the-palate cabernet sauvignon for a mere $20 a bottle. Taste in the barrel room – essentially a chilly garage with plastic picnic tables – with fun dudes who know their wines.

### Hess Collection
Winery, Art Gallery

(☎707-255-1144; www.hesscollection.com; 4411 Redwood Rd, Napa; tasting $10; ◷10am-4pm) Blue-chip art and big reds are the pride of Hess Collection, a winery/gallery northwest of downtown Napa that pairs monster cabs with art by megamodernists like Francis Bacon and Robert Motherwell.

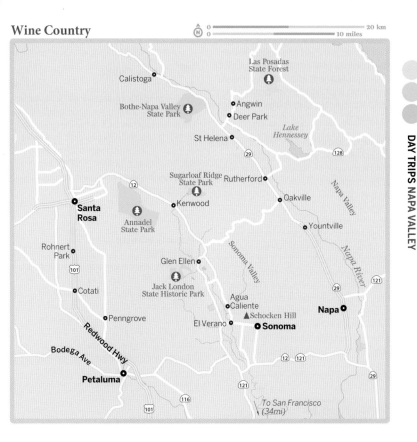

## Darioush
Winery

( ☎707-257-2345; www.darioush.com; 4240 Silverado Trail, Napa; tasting $18-35; ⏰10:30am-5pm) Stone bulls glower from atop pillars lining the driveway of Darioush, a jaw-dropping, over-the-top winery styled after the ancient Persian temples of Persepolis; it's known for monumental merlots, shiraz and cabernet. Very fancy.

## Castello di Amorosa
Winery

( ☎707-967-6272; www.castellodiamorosa.com; 4045 Hwy 29, Calistoga; tasting $10-15, tour adult/child $32/22; ⏰by appointment; 👪) It took 14 years to build this near-perfect recreation of a 12th-century Italian castle, complete with moat, hand-cut stone walls, catacombs, frescoes hand-painted by Italian artisans and torture chamber filled with period equipment. Trust us, take the tour (bring a sweater). Make reservations.

## Old Faithful Geyser
Landmark

( ☎707-942-6463; www.oldfaithfulgeyser.com; 1299 Tubbs Lane, Calistoga; adult/child $10/3; ⏰9am-6pm; 👪) Calistoga's miniversion of Yellowstone's Old Faithful shoots boiling water 60- to 100ft into the air every 30 minutes. The vibe is pure roadside Americana kitsch, with folksy hand-painted interpretive exhibits, picnicking and a little petting zoo with llamas. It's 2 miles north of town, off Silverado Trail.

# 🍴 Eating

Napa is the outpost of San Francisco's food scene; plan to have a lingering lunch or dinner. Make reservations whenever possible; even on weekdays in winter, many restaurants sell out. Most Napa restaurants don't serve late – average visitors get too drunk during the daytime to stay up for a 9pm table. There's a **farmers market** (www.sthelena farmersmkt.org; Crane Park, off Grayson Ave; ◷7:30am-noon May-Oct) Friday mornings in St Helena.

### French Laundry                Californian $$$
(☎707-944-2380; www.frenchlaundry.com; 6640 Washington St, Yountville; prix fixe menu $270; ◷dinner daily, lunch Sat & Sun) A high-wattage culinary experience on par with the world's best, Thomas Keller's French Laundry is ideal for marking lifetime achievements – a 40th birthday, say, or a Nobel Prize. Book exactly two months (to the day) ahead: call at 10am sharp, or log onto www.opentable.com at precisely midnight. If you can't score a reservation, console yourself at Keller's nearby note-perfect French brasserie, **Bouchon** (☎707-944-8037; www.bouchonbistro.com; 6354 Washington St, Yountville; ◷11:30am-midnight), which is (much) easier to book

and makes perfect roast chicken and *steak-frites*.

### 🖉 Oxbow Public Market                Market $
(www.oxbowpublicmarket.com; 610 & 644 1st St, Napa; ◷9am-7pm Mon-Sat, 10am-5pm Sun) A gourmet food court á la the Ferry Building in SF, Oxbow showcases local, sustainably produced artisanal food, such as Hog Island oysters (six for $15), Pica Pica's Venezuelan cornbread sandwiches ($8) and Three Twins certified-organic ice cream ($4 for a single waffle cone). Come hungry and plan to graze.

### Bounty Hunter Wine Bar                American $$
(www.bountyhunterwine.com; 975 1st St, Napa; dishes $14-24; ◷11am-10pm; 🖑) Inside an 1888 grocery store with pressed-tin ceilings and trophy heads on the walls, Bounty Hunter has an Old West vibe, a fitting backdrop for superb barbecue, made with house-smoked meats, and a standout whole chicken roasted over a can of Tecate beer. Great for a no-fuss meal in downtown Napa. Ten local beers and 40 wines by the glass.

### Gott's Roadside/ Taylor's Automatic Refresher                Burgers $$
(☎707-963-3486; www.gottsroadside .com; 933 Main St, St Helena; dishes $8-15; ◷10:30am-9pm; 🖑) Wiggle your toes in the grass at this 1950s drive-in diner with 21st-century sensibilities: burgers are of all-natural Niman Ranch beef or lean *ahi* tuna, with optional sides of chili-dusted sweet-potato fries. To avoid hunger-inducing waits,

Darioush (p229)

avoid peak meal times or call ahead for takeout to beat the line.

# Sonoma Valley

There are three Sonomas: the town, which is in the valley, which is in the county. Think of them as Russian dolls. The town of Sonoma makes a great jumping-off point for exploring Wine Country – it's only an hour from San Francisco and has a marvelous sense of place, with 19th-century historical sights lining the state's largest town square.

## Getting There & Away

**Car** From San Francisco to downtown Sonoma, take Hwy 101 to Hwy 37 east. At the split take Hwy 121 north, then Hwy 12 to Sonoma town and valley. One hour.

**Bus** From San Francisco, take Golden Gate Transit (☑511 or 415-923-2000; www .goldengatetransit.org) to Petaluma (90 minutes), then connect with Sonoma County Transit (☑511, 707-576-7433; www.sctransit .com) to downtown Sonoma (30 minutes). Service is infrequent: call for assistance booking the right connections.

## Need to Know

○ **Area Code** ☑707

○ **Location** 45 miles north-northeast of San Francisco

○ **Sonoma Valley Visitors Bureau** (☑707-996-1090; www.sonomavalley.com; 453 1st St E; ☻9am-5pm)

# ◎ Sights

More casual and less commercial than Napa, Sonoma Valley has 70 wineries around Hwy 12 – and unlike Napa, most welcome picnicking. You don't usually need appointments to taste, but call ahead for tours. If you don't feel like driving, find multiple tasting rooms around Sonoma Plaza.

**Sonoma Plaza**     Square
(Bordered by Napa, Spain & 1st Sts) Century-old trees cast sun-dappled shade on the plaza, a great spot for a picnic with a bottle of Sonoma wine. Historic buildings line the plaza's north side.

**Jack London State Historic Park**     Historic Site
(☑707-938-5216; www.jacklondonpark.com; 2400 London Ranch Rd, Glen Ellen; parking $8; ☻10am-5pm Thu-Mon; ♿) Up Hwy 12 in Glen Ellen, obey the call of the wild at Jack London State Historic Park, where adventure-novelist Jack London moved

## Sleeping in Wine Country

Most lodging in Wine Country costs well over $200. Motels near the freeway cost $60 to $100 in high season. The following are good midrange choices.

**Avia Hotel** (☑707-224-3900; www .aviahotels.com; 1450 1st St, Napa; r $149-249; ❄ @ ☏) Downtown Napa's newest hotel opened in 2009 and feels like a big-city hotel, with business-class-fancy rooms, styled in retro-'70s chic.

**El Bonita Motel** (☑707-963-3216, 800-541-3284; www.elbonita.com; 195 Main St, St Helena; $119-179; ❄ @ ☏ ⋇) Book well ahead to score a room at this sought-after motel with up-to-date rooms, hot tub and sauna.

**Sonoma Chalet** (☑707-938-3129; www.sonomachalet.com; 18935 5th St W, Sonoma; r without bath $125, r with bath $140-180, cottages $195-225) Beautiful old farmstead surrounded by rolling hills, with rooms in a Swiss-chalet-style house adorned with country-Americana bric-a-brac. We especially love the free-standing cottages. No air-con in rooms with shared bath.

in 1910 to build his dream house – which burned down on the eve of completion in 1913. Miles of **hiking trails** (some open to mountain bikes) weave through the park's 1400 hilltop acres.

### Gundlach-Bundschu
Winery

(☏707-938-5277; www.gunbun.com; 2000 Denmark St; tasting $10; ☺11am-4:30pm) Down a country road from downtown, Gundlach-Bundschu dates to 1858 and looks like a storybook castle. Perched in a park-like setting, above a reclaimed-water lake, the solar-powered winery produces legendary tempranillo; riesling and gewürztraminer are the signatures.

### Benziger
Winery

(☏888-490-2739; www.benziger.com; 1883 London Ranch Rd, Glen Ellen; tasting $10-20, tram tour adult incl tasting/child $15/5; ☺10am-5pm; ) If you're new to wine, Benziger provides an excellent crash course in winemaking on its worthwhile (nonreserveable) open-air **tram tour** (☺half-hourly, 11:30am-3:30pm) through biodynamic vineyards, which includes a tasting afterward.

## Eating

### Fremont Diner
American $

(☏707-938-7370; 2698 Fremont Dr/Hwy 121; mains $8-11; ☺8am-3pm Mon-Fri, 7am-4pm Sat & Sun; ) Lines snake out the door on weekends at this farm-to-table roadside diner, where you order at the counter, then snag a table – outdoors or inside – and feast on ricotta pancakes with real maple syrup, chicken and waffles, oyster po' boys and finger-licking barbecue.

### Cafe la Haye
American $$$

(☏707-935-5994; www.cafelahaye.com; 140 E Napa St, Sonoma; mains $19-29; ☺dinner Tue-Sat) Tops for earthy New American cooking, made with produce sourced from within 60 miles. The tiny room is cheek-by-jowl and service borders on perfunctory, but the clean simplicity and flavor-packed cooking make it foodies' first choice. Reservations essential.

### Fig Cafe & Winebar
Californian $$

(☏707-938-2130; www.thefigcafe.com; 13690 Arnold Dr, Glen Ellen; mains $15-20; ☺5:30-9pm daily, 10am-2:30pm Sat & Sun) Sonoma's take on soul-satisfying comfort food – organic salads, Sonoma duck cassoulet and free corkage on Sonoma wines – in a converted living room in the little town of Glen Ellen.

### El Dorado Kitchen Corner Cafe
Cafe $$

(☏707-996-3030; www.eldoradosonoma.com; 405 1st St W, Sonoma; dishes $9-15; ☺7am-10pm; ) Biodynamic salads and gargantuan pastrami sandwiches with parmesan-dusted truffle fries are big enough to split in this sunny corner cafe, but order your own soft-serve ice cream topped with BR Cohn olive oil and sea salt.

# Muir Woods & Muir Beach

Coastal redwoods are the tallest living things on earth and exist only on the California coast, from Santa Cruz to just over the Oregon border. Only 4% of the original forest remains, but you can explore a glorious old-growth stand within 30 minutes of San Francisco.

### Getting There & Away

**Car** Head north on Hwy 101 across the Golden Gate Bridge, exit at Hwy 1 and continue north along Hwy 1/Shoreline Hwy to Panoramic Hwy (a right-hand fork). Follow that for about 1 mile to Four Corners, where you turn left onto Muir Woods Rd (there are plenty of signs).

**Ferry & Bus** On weekends and holidays (when the parking lot at Muir Woods overflows) Marin

Transit (📞511; www.marintransit.org; round-trip adult/child $3/1; ⊙weekends & holidays late May-Sep) operates bus 66, a 40-minute shuttle from the Sausalito Ferry Terminal, timed to connect with four ferries from San Francisco.

### Need to Know

○ **Area code** 📞415

○ **Location** 15 miles from downtown San Francisco

## ◉ Sights

### Muir Woods National Monument
Nature Reserve

Map p234 (📞415-388-2595; www.nps.gov/muwo; adult/child under 16 $5/free; ⊙8am-sunset) The closest stand of coastal redwoods to San Francisco, the old-growth forest dates back to time immemorial. To beat the crowds, come early in the day, late afternoon or midweek; otherwise the parking lot fills up and you'll need to take a shuttle. Even at busy times, a short hike will get you out of the densest crowds and onto trails with huge trees and stunning vistas.

### Muir Beach
Beach

Map p234 The turnoff to Muir Beach from Hwy 1 is marked by the north coast's longest row of mailboxes (mileage-marker 5.7, just before Pelican Inn). Immediately north there are superb coastal views from the **Muir Beach Overlook**; during WWII, scouts kept watch from the surrounding concrete lookouts for invading Japanese ships. You'd do well to bring a sweater: chances are it'll be chilly.

## ✕ Eating

### Pelican Inn
Pub, Inn

Map p234 (📞415-383-6000; www.pelicaninn.com; 10 Pacific Way; lunch $12-17, dinner $17-34; 🛜) Hikers, cyclists and families come for pub lunches at the Tudor-style timbered restaurant and cozy bar, perfect for a pint, game of darts and warming-up fireside. The British fare is respectable, but it's the setting that's magical.

# Sausalito & Tiburon

Sausalito is the first town over the Golden Gate. Perched above Richardson Bay, it's known for galleries, window-shopping and picture-postcard vistas of SF and Angel Island. And it's often sunnier than San Francisco. However cute, Sausalito

Fig Cafe & Winebar
JERRY ALEXANDER/LONELY PLANET IMAGES ©

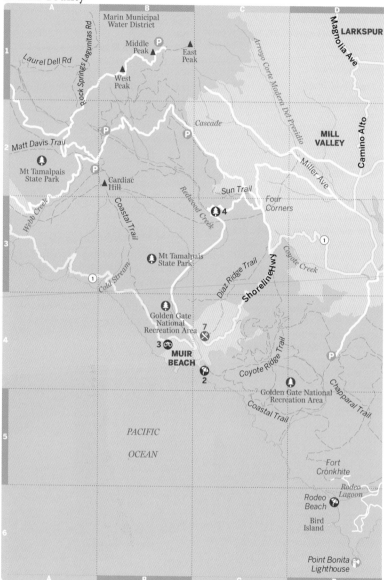

becomes a victim of its charm on summer weekends, when day-trippers jam the sidewalks, shops and restaurants.

With its tiny Main St, Tiburon isn't at the forepoint of most tourists' minds, so

the town has retained more of its original character than Sausalito. Browse shops on Main St, grab a bite to eat and you've done Tiburon. Friday nights May through

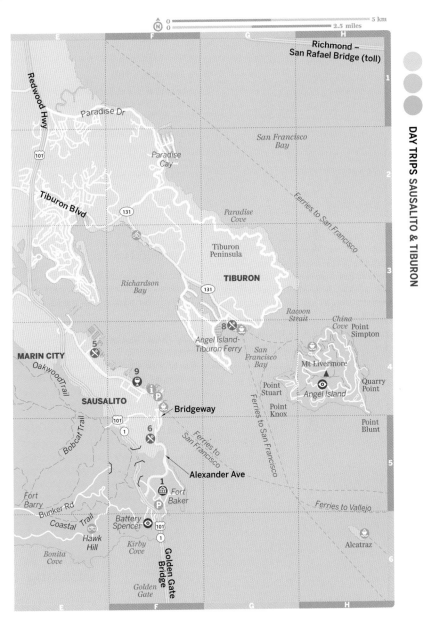

October, Tiburon throws its Main St block party, kicking off at 6pm.

## Getting There & Away

**Ferry** Golden Gate Ferry (☎415-455-2000; www.goldengateferry.org; one-way $9.25) sails to Sausalito from the Ferry Building. Blue & Gold Fleet (☎415-705-8200; www.blueandgoldfleet .com; Pier 41; one-way $10.50) sails to Sausalito from Fisherman's Wharf and to Tiburon from Fisherman's Wharf *and* the Ferry Building. Bicycles ride free.

## Marin County

### ⊙ Sights

1 Bay Area Discovery Museum...............F5
2 Muir Beach..............................................C4
3 Muir Beach Overlook.........................B4
4 Muir Woods National
   Monument .........................................C3

### ⊗ Eating

5 Fish .........................................................E4
6 Golden Gate Market ............................F5
7 Pelican Inn ...........................................C4
8 Sam's Anchor Cafe.............................G4

### ⊖ Drinking

9 Wellingtons Wine Bar.........................F4

**Car** To Sausalito: immediately over the Golden Gate, take Alexander Ave (exit 442). Alternatively, take the Sausalito exit (445A) and drop into town from the north. To Tiburon: take Tiburon Blvd/E Blithedale Ave (exit 450) and follow Tiburon Blvd east and south into town.

**Bus** Golden Gate Transit (☎415-455-2000; www.goldengatetransit.org; fare $4.25) bus 10 operates daily to Sausalito from Downtown; commute bus 8 operates weekdays between San Francisco and Tiburon.

### Need to Know

○ **Area code** ☎415

○ **Location** By car, Sausalito is 10 miles north of San Francisco and Tiburon is 17 miles northeast.

○ **Sausalito Visitors Center** (☎415-332-0505; www.sausalito.org; 780 Bridgeway Blvd; ⊙11:30am-4pm Tue-Sun)

○ **Tiburon Peninsula Chamber of Commerce** (☎415-435-5633; www.tiburonchamber.org; 96b Main St)

## ⊙ Sights

Sausalito's main strip is Bridgeway Blvd, along the waterfront. The ferry terminal marks the town center.

### Bay Area Discovery Museum
Museum

Map p234 (☎415-339-3900; www.baykids museum.org; adult/child $10/8; ⊙9am-4pm Tue-Fri, 10am-5pm Sat & Sun; ⊕) Just under the north tower of the Golden Gate Bridge, at East Fort Baker, this excellent hands-on activity museum is specifically designed for children. Permanent, multilingual exhibits include a wave workshop, small underwater tunnel and large outdoor play area with a shipwreck to romp around.

## ⊗ Eating & Drinking

### Fish
Seafood $$

Map p234 (☎415-331-3474; 350 Harbor Dr, Sausalito; mains $13-25; ⊙11:30am-8:30pm; ⊕) This kid-friendly dockside joint at

Sausalito marina
GLENN VAN DER KNIJFF/LONELY PLANET IMAGES ©

the end of Harbor Dr hooks locals with sustainable, line-caught fish and picnic-table, bayside seating. Sustainability and organics have their price, but it's worth it – especially come salmon season. Chow down on seafood sandwiches, oysters and Dungeness crab rolls. Cash only.

### Sam's Anchor Cafe          Seafood $$
Map p234 (☎415-435-4527; 27 Main St, Tiburon; dishes $15-25; 🚼) Everyone wants an outdoor table, but you can't reserve the bay-front patio at this ever-popular seafood and burger shack – the town's oldest restaurant. Watch for seagulls swooping in to steal your fries.

### Golden Gate Market          Grocery $
Map p234 (☎415-332-3040; 221 2nd St, Sausalito; ⏱8am-9pm Mon-Sat, 9am-7pm Sun) Grab deli sandwiches, cheese and wine for picnics at this grocery/deli/liquor store on the town's south side.

### Wellingtons Wine Bar          Bar
Map p234 (☎415-331-9463; www.wellington swinebar.com; 1306 Bridgeway, at Turney St, Sausalito; ⏱4-10pm; 🅿🛜) Cozy up with a glass of wine, before catching the ferry home, at this dockside wine bar and pub with drop-dead vistas across San Francisco Bay. Friendly crowd, great service – you'd not be the first to miss your boat for the fun you're having.

# San Francisco
# In Focus

**San Francisco Today**   **240**
Find out what's top of mind at the moment, including the green movement, social media and gay marriage.

**History**   **242**
From the Gold Rush to earthquakes, from Beat poets to dot-coms, discover the past that shapes the city's present.

**Family Travel**   **248**
Bringing the kids along on vacation? You'll never hear 'I'm bored' in kid-friendly San Francisco.

**Food & Drink**   **250**
Whatever you're craving, you'll find it here, from local specialties to creative cocktails, plus every type of ethnic cuisine.

**Arts & Architecture**   **254**
Creative expression is a cultural imperative, and it's waiting around every corner.

**Hills & Fog**   **259**
Always a rebel, San Francisco differentiates itself even through its weather and topography.

**GLBT SF**   **263**
If you're gay, lesbian, bisexual or transgender, you'll feel right at home in San Francisco.

**Cable Cars**   **265**
Putter your way up and down the city's famous hills in a wonderfully outdated mode of transportation.

Wild parrots, Telegraph Hill (p107)
PHOTOGRAPHER: THOMAS WINZ/PHOTOLIBRARY/GETTY IMAGES ©

# San Francisco Today

Pride Parade (p41)

> *You can blame SF for any number of temptations: chocolate bars, martinis, online shopping and LSD*

**politics** (% of population)

84
**Democratic**

14
**Republican**

2
Other

**if San Francisco were 100 people**

42 would be Caucasian
33 would be Asian
15 would be Hispanic/Latino
6 would be African American
4 would be Other

**population per sq mile**

San Francisco

USA

= 90 people

## Green City, USA

In 2011, San Francisco was named North America's greenest city, and you'll notice that distinction when it comes to choosing what to eat, where to sleep and how to get around town. Pretty much anything you might want to do in San Francisco, you can do with a green conscience – just look for the designation in this book. Businesses must compost and recycle by law here, so only ones that have gone above and beyond standard SF practices earn a designation. These include San Francisco city-certified green businesses, LEED-certified green attractions, all-hybrid-car taxi services, and restaurants and bars with a verifiable commitment to using ingredients from organic local farms or foraged ingredients.

## Social-Mediated SF

If you're not on Twitter, Facebook, Yelp, Google+, Yahoo Groups or LinkedIn, are you sure you still have a pulse? San Francisco will

fountains back into active service – and if there's a video store that hasn't yet been converted into a medical marijuana dispensary, it's only a matter of time. All those herbal clubs and saloons do help explain the near-ubiquity of food trucks and pop-up restaurants throughout the city, doing a brisk business in cupcakes and curries.

Yet despite their many indulgences and slacker reputations, San Franciscans still hold more patents per capita than any other US city, and they read more books and rack up many more degrees than other Americans. The city has been working up quite a reputation for compassion, too, creating new models for AIDS care, family homeless shelters and more nonprofits than any other US city.

LEE FOSTER/LONELY PLANET IMAGES ©

try to convince you that you must use one of these Bay Area–based social-media platforms in order to validate your existence. After all, a lot of local jobs depend on it.

But there is already a backlash afoot in this technological hub. In a city where telecommuters have turned public spaces into satellite offices for the past decade, cafes have begun removing electrical outlets and unplugging wi-fi routers, and boutiques and restaurants are posting signs saying 'No phone calls. No excuses.' Conversations are happening offline and off the cuff, and early adopters are now returning social media to its initial use: as a place to briefly touch base and make plans to meet in person.

## Extravagant Indulgence

Lately, San Francisco's saloon revival has been putting spittoons and absinthe

## Always a Bridesmaid

San Francisco was the first city to authorize same-sex marriages back in 2004 – but some 4036 honeymoons were abruptly ended when their marriages were legally invalidated by the state. Court battles ensued, and California voters narrowly passed 2008's California Proposition 8 measure to legally define marriage as between a man and a woman. Countersuits were initiated, arguing that limiting marriage rights runs contrary to civil rights protections in California's constitution.

Meanwhile, New York passed a law allowing gays to marry in June 2011. But star-crossed San Francisco couples aren't all booking flights. Many are awaiting the results of the Supreme Court challenge to Proposition 8 that would set a nationwide precedent and could start the maddest dash for white tulle San Francisco has ever seen.

**241**

# History

Fort Point (p62)

RICHARD CUMMINS/LONELY PLANET IMAGE

*Native Californians had found gold in California long before 1849, but it hardly seemed worth mentioning, as long as there were oysters for lunch and venison for dinner. Once word circulated, San Francisco was transformed almost overnight from bucolic trading backwater to Gold Rush metropolis. One hundred and fifty years of booms, busts, history-making hijinks and low-down dirty dealings later, San Francisco remains the wildest city in the west.*

## Cowboys on a Mission

When Spanish cowboys brought 340 horses, 302 head of cattle and 160 mules to settle Mission San Francisco in 1776, there was a slight hitch: the area had already been settled by Native Americans for over 14,300 years. Since there was enough shellfish and wild foodstuffs to go around, the arrival of Captain Juan Bautista de Anza and his crew was initially met with no apparent resistance – until they began to demand more than dinner.

### 1776

Captain Juan Bautista de Anza establishes Mission Dolores with cattle, settlers and guns.

The new arrivals expected the local Ohlone to build them a mission. Without immunity to European diseases, many Native Californians who had been conscripted to build the 1776 mission didn't survive to see the end result – some 5000 Ohlone and Miwok are buried under Mission Dolores.

The mission settlement never really prospered. The sandy, scrubby fields were difficult to farm, fleas were a constant irritation and the 20 soldiers who manned the local Presidio army encampment were allotted one scanty shipment of provisions per year. Spain stopped sending supplies long before the colony was lost to Mexico, who promptly surrendered the troublesome backwater to the US.

## Gold Fever

Mexico could not have had worse timing: within days of signing away California in the Treaty of Guadalupe Hidalgo, gold was discovered in the Sacramento River. San Francisco ballooned from a population of 800 to 100,000, due to the influx of prospectors between 1847 and 1849, and California was fast-tracked for statehood in 1850. Most of the early prospectors (called '49ers, after their arrival date) were men under the age of 40, and to keep them entertained – and fleece the gullible – some 500 saloons, 20 theaters and numerous venues of ill repute opened within five years in the lawless harbor known as the 'Barbary Coast.'

In 1848, each prospector earned an annual average of about $300,000 in today's terms, but by 1865 it had dipped to $35,000. Panic ensued after gold was discovered in Australia, and irrational resentment turned on Australians and

## Emperor Norton of San Francisco

The Gold Rush made paupers into kings, but it also made one man a penniless emperor. Within months of his arrival in San Francisco in 1849, Joshua Norton made a fortune, lost it all and then disappeared. In 1859 he returned, wearing gold-braided military attire and proclaiming himself 'Emperor of the United States and Protector of Mexico.' Local newspapers published Emperor Norton's proclamations, including a decree outlawing the nickname 'Frisco' and imposing a penalty of $25 (payable to him, naturally). Police saluted him in the streets, and some establishments accepted banknotes issued by the 'Imperial Government of Norton.'

**1846**
After the Mexican–American War breaks out, Mexico cuts its losses and dumps unruly California.

**1848**
SF tabloids publish rumors of gold in the Sierras, kicking off the Gold Rush.

**1873**
When a nervous driver backs out, Andrew Hallidie successfully steers the first cable car downhill.

Chinese dockworkers. Ordinances passed in 1870 restricted housing and employment for anyone born in China, and the 1882 Chinese Exclusion Act barred Chinese from immigration and citizenship until 1943. Anti-Asian sentiment was a windfall for local robber barons, who recruited Chinese San Franciscans on the cheap to do the dangerous, dirty work of dynamiting through the Sierras and building railways to mining claims.

## Up from the Ashes

Anxious to distract attention from the waterfront and attract legitimate businesses, San Francisco built a beaux arts Civic Center in the early 20th century. These grand plans were destroyed in under a minute on April 18, 1906, when an earthquake estimated at a terrifying 7.8 to 8.3 on today's Richter scale struck. For 47 seconds, the city emitted unholy groans as streets buckled, windows popped and brick buildings keeled over. Firefighters couldn't pass through rubble-choked streets to put out blazes, and fires raged for three days. When the smoke lifted, the devastation was clear: as many as 3000 people were dead or missing, and 100,000 were left homeless. Some survivors fled San Francisco, but those who stayed rebuilt the city at an astounding rate of 15 buildings per day. Most of the Barbary Coast had burned, and the city rebuilt the ragged pirate piers into a major port.

## Rocking the Boat

WWII brought a shipbuilding boom, but not everyone benefited from wartime expansion. Two months after the Japanese attack on Pearl Harbor, President Franklin Delano Roosevelt signed Executive Order 9066, ordering 120,000 Japanese Americans into internment camps. The San Francisco–based Japanese American Citizens League challenged the measure and, after a historic 40-year effort, won reparations and set key precedents for the Civil Rights movement.

WWII sailors discharged in San Francisco for insubordination and homosexuality soon found themselves at home among the bohemian coffeehouses and anarchic alleyways of North Beach. When the rest of the country took a sharp right turn with McCarthyism in the 1950s, rebels and romantics headed for the Left Coast, where jazz broke down barriers in desegregated clubs and José Sarria led gay bar–patrons in nightly choruses of 'God Save Us Nelly Queens.' San Francisco became America's home of free speech and free spirits, and soon everyone who was anyone was getting arrested: Beat poet Lawrence Ferlinghetti for publishing Allen Ginsberg's epic poem *Howl*, African American Jewish anarchist Bob Kaufman for taunting police in rhyme, comedian Lenny Bruce for uttering the F word onstage and burlesque dancer Carol Doda for going topless.

### 1906
A massive earthquake levels entire blocks of SF; fires finish off most of what's left.

### 1910
Angel Island immigration station opens, subjecting 175,000 Asian arrivals to interrogation, deprivation and imprisonment.

### 1915
As host of the Panama-Pacific International Exposition, SF becomes a showplace for new technology, art and ideas.

# Flower Power

It wasn't ribald jokes, stripteases, gay bars or even uncompromising poetry that would pop the last button of conventional morality in San Francisco. No, this would be a job for the CIA. The federal agency inadvertently kicked off the psychedelic era when a CIA operation tested psychoactive drugs – intended to create the ultimate soldier – on writer Ken Kesey, who promptly introduced LSD to the masses at the legendary 1966 San Francisco Acid Tests. At the January 14, 1967, Human Be-In event in Golden Gate Park, tripmaster Timothy Leary urged a crowd of 20,000 hippies to dream a new American dream, and 'turn on, tune in, drop out.'

For weeks, months, even a year or two, depending on who you talk to and how stoned they were at the time, San Francisco was the place where it seemed possible to make love, not war. There were draft-card-burning protests in Golden Gate Park and free food, love and music in the Haight until 1969, when the assassinations of Bobby Kennedy and Martin Luther King Jr brought a sudden chill to the Summer of Love.

Harvey Milk Civil Rights Academy (p150)

### 1937
After four years of labor in treacherous Pacific tides, the Golden Gate Bridge is complete.

### 1967
The Summer of Love begins with the burning of draft cards and Allen Ginsberg streaking.

### 1969
Native American activists claim Alcatraz as reparation for broken treaties; the protest lasts 19 months.

## Pride

As the fog settled in over the Haight, San Francisco gays ditched hetero hippie communes for sunny Victorians in the Castro and proceeded to make history to a funky disco beat. The Castro was triumphant when local entrepreneur Harvey Milk became the nation's first openly gay elected official in 1977. But the celebration was short lived. Less than a year after he was elected, Milk and then-Mayor George Moscone were assassinated by former City Supervisor Dan White.

By the 1980s the city was preoccupied with a strange illness appearing in local hospitals. The gay community was hit hard by the virus initially referred to as GRID (Gay-Related Immune Deficiency). A social stigma became attached to the virus, compounding a grim prognosis with patient isolation. But San Francisco health-care providers and gay activists rallied to establish standards for care and prevention of the pandemic now known as HIV/AIDS, and vital early interventions made possible through local fund-raisers saved untold lives around the world.

Another item on the community's political agenda was (and remains) same-sex marriage, authorized by San Francisco Mayor Newsom in time for Valentine's Day 2004. In 2008, California voters voided 4037 same-sex marriages with Proposition 8, which limited marriage rights to heterosexual couples. Prop 8 was judged unconstitutional in 2010; unless the decision is overturned on appeal to the US Supreme Court, same-sex couples may again be permitted to marry in California in the near future.

## Geeking Out

Industry dwindled steadily in San Francisco after WWII, but the brains of military-industrial operations found work in Silicon Valley. At San Francisco's first West Coast Computer Faire in 1977, 21-year-old Steve Jobs and 26-year-old Steve Wozniak introduced the Apple II, the first personal computer with a then-staggering 4KB of RAM, 1MHz microprocessor and a retail price of US$1298 (about $4300 today). Skeptics were stumped when it came to the idea of networking capabilities: what would consumers do with a computer network?

## The Best...
## Beat
## Hangouts

1 City Lights (p121)

2 Beat Museum (p106)

3 Vesuvio (p119)

4 Li Po (p119)

5 Bob Kaufman Alley (p111)

### 1977

Harvey Milk fatefully says: 'If a bullet should enter my brain, let that bullet destroy every closet door.'

### 1989

The Loma Prieta earthquake hits 6.9 on the Richter scale in 15 seconds, killing 41. Postquake Marina apartment building

DAVID RYAN/LONELY PLANET IMAGES ®

# The Twinkie Defense

On November 27, 1978, enraged former City Supervisor Dan White – still smarting over Mayor George Moscone's decision not to reinstate him into the job he'd resigned from a couple of weeks earlier – climbed in a window of City Hall with a loaded gun and assassinated Moscone and City Supervisor Harvey Milk.

The facts of the case were never disputed: White had killed two men and confessed immediately; he had even intended to kill two more people. So the city was stunned when White was convicted only of voluntary manslaughter and given a meager seven-year sentence. White's attorneys had swayed the jury with a defense of depression and 'diminished capacity,' but a passing mention of a snack-food binge would forever label the argument the 'Twinkie Defense.'

After the announcement of the verdict, peaceful protesters took to the street, but as night fell the situation intensified into what would come to be known as the White Night riots. California eventually abolished the diminished capacity defense and, a year after his 1984 release, White committed suicide.

By the mid-1990s an entire dot-com industry had boomed in SoMa warehouses. When venture-capital funding dried up, multimillion-dollar sites shriveled into online oblivion. Yet San Francisco managed to retain its talent pool, and it still has more entrepreneurs with advanced degrees than any other US city. It's a self-selecting community that can live with the risk of earthquakes and a volatile economy based on technology and tourism, and more people keep opting in each year.

**2000**
After the NASDAQ index peaks at double its 1999 value, the dot-com bubble pops.

**2010**
Number of active users of Bay Area–based Twitter, Facebook, Yelp and FourSquare tops 700 million.

**2013**
America's Cup to be held in San Francisco.

# Family Travel

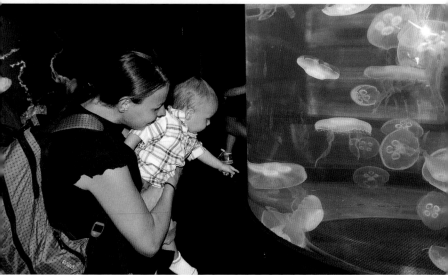

Aquarium of the Bay (p56)

LEE FOSTER/LONELY PLANET IMAGES

*Census data reveals that San Francisco has the least number of children per capita of any US city. (According to SF SPCA data, approximately 19,000 more dogs live here than children.) But San Francisco never shirks its duties as a playground for all ages: it's packed with attractions designed for kids, from outdoor activities and kid-friendly museums to weird and wonderful delights that are uniquely San Francisco.*

## Fun for All Ages

Adults think San Francisco is meant for them, but kids know better. There's a certain storybook quality to this city that kids can relate to: wild parrots squawking indignantly at passersby on Telegraph Hill, murals in hidden alleys awaiting discovery, slumbering sea lions nudging one other off the docks and into the water at Pier 39 with a comical *sploosh!* Golden Gate Park includes a butterfly-filled rainforest dome and penguins at the California Academy of Sciences, miniature forests at the Japanese Tea Garden, and paddleboats and tandem bikes at Stow Lake.

## Child-Friendly Attractions

To kids, San Francisco is one big carnival ride. Uphill journeys become big adventures on San Francisco's historic cable cars, and a ferry ride can make a grand day out. Alcatraz simultaneously fascinates kids and creeps them out, and it can keep them on their best behavior for hours. When spirits and feet begin to drag, there's plenty of ice cream and kid-friendly meals to pick them back up, plus toy stores to bribe them up that last hill. Except for a few swanky restaurants that toddlers probably wouldn't appreciate anyway, most places are fairly kid-friendly. To find the best kid-friendly attractions in the city, look for the 👫 symbol throughout this book.

## The Marina & Fisherman's Wharf

For entertainment options aimed specifically at kids, make a beeline to the waterfront. In the Marina, kids squeal their way through the Tactile Dome at the Exploratorium and burn off energy flying kites at Crissy Field. For vacation photo ops, check out the city's historic ships, the charming old carousel at Pier 39 and 19th-century arcade games at Musée Mécanique.

## Creative Kids

A rest in the Poet's Chair at City Lights may inspire a haiku, but arts workshops are also available at the Cartoon Art Museum and 826 Valencia. The Cartoon Art Museum also features original Spiderman cover drawings. San Francisco also has the high-tech Children's Creativity Museum, where kids can make their own music videos.

## Museums

Kids are highly encouraged to explore art in San Francisco, with free admission for kids aged 12 and under at the San Francisco Museum of Modern Art (SFMOMA), Asian Art Museum, Legion of Honor, MH de Young Museum, Museum of the African Diaspora and Contemporary Jewish Museum.

## Playgrounds

Combine sightseeing with playtime at playgrounds located in Chinatown's historic Portsmouth Square and Old St Mary's Park, or head to the best-equipped playground in town at Golden Gate Park, where there are swings, monkey bars, play castles with slides, and steep hillside slides for daredevil older siblings.

# Food & Drink

Cowgirl Creamery (p83)

ROBERTO GEROMETTA/LONELY PLANET IMAGES

*San Francisco cuisine has been called a lot of names lately – organic, locavore, seasonal, sustainable... While chefs work hard to make sure their food lives up to those descriptors, the local fare still answers to the same name it has been called for 160 years: damn tasty. You won't go thirsty here, either: wine and cocktails are as much a part of the culture as hills and fog.*

## Key Ingredients

During the Gold Rush, San Francisco was transformed almost overnight into a global culinary capital with the help of two secret ingredients: competition and dirt. Miners from around the world craved the flavors of home, and fortunes were made and lost speculating on local tastes for specialties such as Japanese rice and Australian wines. Imports took months to arrive by ship, so chefs increasingly looked to local sources. Turns out that almost anything can and does grow in California's fertile Central Valley to the south of San Francisco; rocky, sandy coastal pastures to the north are prime grazing territory for livestock; and rocky hillsides and volcanic *terroir* (earth) yield fine wines in nearby Sonoma and Napa counties.

# SF Cuisine

Clever SF chefs are making the most of the city's three distinct advantages: its Pacific Rim location, population of adventurous eaters and local produce. In 1971, Berkeley chef Alice Waters pioneered California cuisine, making the most of the Bay Area's seasonal, sustainably produced bounty. Within 200 miles of San Francisco, chefs can now find premium organic produce, free-range meats, hormone-free dairy products and sublime wines. The city's signature fresh flavors come from raw ingredients that don't lose flavor or nutrients during weeks (or months) of transit and warehousing. Add local, sustainably harvested seafood to the mix and it seems like a no-fail recipe for success.

But what a chef does with those ingredients can make or break a restaurant in San Francisco, where there is one restaurant for every 28 people. That's 10 times as many restaurants per capita as any other city in North America. Stiff competition has created a culture of picky eaters who demand both consistency and innovation – not to mention value for their money. For even a $10 meal, San Francisco diners expect inventive combinations of fresh, seasonal ingredients; for $50, they expect to know where the organic dry-farmed tomatoes were grown, when the fish was caught, and everything but the pet nickname of the cow. Menus at even low-end San Francisco restaurants are meticulously detailed and heavily footnoted, sharing credit with the farms that grow key ingredients and noting which ingredients are organic and sustainably sourced. Mock if you must, but people have been known to move here for the food.

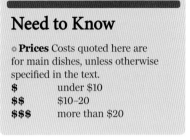

## Need to Know

○ **Prices** Costs quoted here are for main dishes, unless otherwise specified in the text.

| | |
|---|---|
| $ | under $10 |
| $$ | $10–20 |
| $$$ | more than $20 |

## Specialties

When San Franciscans idly discuss moving to New York or London for a change of pace, inevitably the objection is raised: 'Yeah, but where would you find decent Mexican food, dim sum, oysters, salami, vegetarian food, sourdough bread and artisan ice cream – all within walking distance?' Point taken. Instead of booking ahead for your SF feast, you can just head to a major culinary strip and take your pick of restaurants offering local specialties. Here's what you'll find where:

**Burritos, vegetarian fare and artisan ice cream** Follow your nose to taquerías around 16th and Valencia and 24th and Mission. Tucked in among the Mexican mainstays between 16th and 30th streets you'll find artisan ice creameries and inspired Indian, Middle Eastern and California-cuisine vegetarian options.

**Dim sum and then some** Venture beyond Chinatown to the Richmond and inner Sunset, especially upper Geary between 15th and 30th Aves for traditional dim sum and organic Moroccan, and around 9th and Irving for dim sum, bakeries and curry. For more eclectic dining choices, Clement St in the Richmond offers standout Burmese, Szechuan and Vietnamese options; in the Sunset at Irving around 19th, the choices range from Middle Eastern to Japanese, and Judah around 48th offers organic California cuisine.

**Fresh sourdough bread and seafood** Head for the Embarcadero and the Piers, especially in and around the Ferry Building.

**Italian specialties** For spicy salami, fresh focaccia, seafood cioppino (stew) and gelato, hit North Beach along upper Grant and around Washington Square Park.

## Opening Hours

Most restaurants are open seven days a week in San Francisco, though some close Sunday and/or Monday night. To feed caffeine needs, cafes open as early as 6am or 7am and tend to stay open until 8pm. Lunch starts at noon and runs until 3pm. Evening dining starts around 7pm, with restaurants open for happy hour around 5:30pm; last service is usually 9:30pm on weekdays and 10pm on weekends.

## Reservations

Most restaurants take reservations for both lunch and dinner, so call ahead if you can – even if it's the same day. You also could just show up and try your luck – many restaurants set seats aside for walk-ins or offer meals at the bar. Restaurants that don't take reservations frequently subject customers to a long wait (20 minutes or more), so get your name on the waiting list and make yourself comfortable.

Holidays excepted, you should be able to get reservations at most restaurants with a couple days' notice. A few restaurants require reservations well in advance – namely Michael Mina, Gary Danko, Slanted Door, Kabuto or anywhere in Napa.

## Tipping

As elsewhere in the USA, tipping is customary. Servers expect at least 15% of the check total before tax, unless something went horribly wrong with the service, and diners give up to 10% more if the service is exceptional. Keep in mind that servers get paid minimal wages, and tips are what pay the rent. Many restaurants add an automatic 18% service charge for parties of six or more, so if you're traveling with an entourage, check before you tip. Tipping is optional at coffee bars and places where you order at the counter, but a tip (50¢ to $1 per coffee) is appreciated by busy baristas.

Some restaurants have started tacking on a 4% surcharge to cover city-mandated employee health care. If you're offended, don't take it out of the tip; that only hurts the server.

# The Best...
# San Francisco Treats

**1** Thai curry peanut butter ice cream at Humphry Slocombe (p168)

**2** Carnitas, no rice, spicy pickles at La Taqueria (p165)

**3** Leek and shrimp dumplings at City View (p117)

**4** Sustainable sushi at Tataki (p133)

**5** Organic black-bean chili at Greens (p68)

# Wash it Down

So how do you wash down a bite of bliss? You're spoiled for pairing suggestions in San Francisco, where your server might recommend cocktails custom-muddled by the resident mixologist, seasonal Anchor Steam microbrews or dusty-boots cowboy cabernets from Napa Valley. Tips are expected: $1 per beer and $1 to $2 for wine or a cocktail, even when your bartender seems curt. San Franciscans don't mind bossy bartenders, as long as the pours are generous.

## Beer

Blowing off steam took on a new meaning during the Gold Rush, when entrepreneurs, trying to keep up with the demand, started brewing beer faster at higher temperatures. When a keg was tapped, an effervescent mist was released – hence the name of San Francisco brewery Anchor Steam, which brews its signature amber ale locally using vintage 1896 copper distillery equipment. Local microbrews remain the drink of choice at many bars and restaurants, but the best selection can be found on tap at Toronado and Zeitgeist.

## Cocktails

San Franciscans are hardly traditionalists, except when it comes to cocktails. Flashy flaming drinks and vodka martinis fizzled out with the dot-com boom: now local boozehounds prefer their cocktails hand-muddled and seasonal, with obscure Kentucky bourbons or gin from San Francisco distilleries Junipero and 209 Gin. Restaurants offer cocktail pairing suggestions from resident mixologists, who pore over recipes from 1930s speakeasies for inspiration.

Thanks to SF's resident research historians of drink, you can now get a gin martini served with a twist and a dash of bitters, in a nod to its 19th-century origins. Legend has it that the martini was invented in San Francisco when a local lush needed a drink to tide him over on a trip across the bay to Martinez. (A likely story...but hey, we'll drink to that.) *Caffè corretto* (coffee 'corrected' with liquor) is another beloved tradition in foggy North Beach, while classic margaritas (tequila, lime, Cointreau, ice and salt) come in seasonal fruit variations ideal for balmy Mission nights.

## Wine

San Francisco wine lists weren't always so extensive. Grapes have been grown around San Francisco since its Mission days, producing sacramental wine and swill for soldiers – which turned out to be a strategic military error. On one wine-soaked Sonoma night in 1846, a group of frontier rabble-rousers decided to seize the state government from Mexican authorities. To everyone's surprise, they succeeded, and California history was made along with Sonoma's Wine Country reputation. Some 130 years later, neighboring Napa Valley kicked off another revolution at the 1976 Paris Tasting, aka the 'World Cup of Wine,' when Stag's Leap cabernet sauvignon and Chateau Montelena chardonnay beat home-*terroir* French favorites.

## Classic SF Cocktails

- **Irish coffee** Buena Vista Cafe, Fisherman's Wharf (p70)
- **Caffè corretto** Tosca Cafe, North Beach (p118)
- **Habañero-chili cosmos** Elixir, the Mission (p170)
- **Mint julep** Alembic, the Haight (p196)

# Arts & Architecture

Concert in Yerba Buena Gardens (p163)

RICHARD CUMMINS/LONELY PLANET IMAGES

*Between its skyscrapers and Victorians, San Francisco is held together by fog and creativity. Despite its small size, SF has consistently been rated one of the top five US cities for the caliber and number of its fine artists, musicians, dancers and independent filmmakers, and its architecture reflects a mishmash of styles that reaches into both the past and the future.*

## Music

You'll have to excuse San Francisco DJs if they seem schizophrenic: only an extremely eclectic set can cover SF's varied musical tastes. Classical, bluegrass, Latin music, and Chinese and Italian opera have survived fires and earthquakes in San Francisco. Music trends that started in the Bay Area never really went away.

If San Francisco history had a soundtrack, it would start with opera and bluegrass, then segue into cool West Coast jazz: Dave Brubeck with Paul Desmond on saxophone. Spoken-word jazz splinters off into folk – think Bob Dylan and Joan Baez during their West Coast affair. Next thing you know, amps are blown by Jimi Hendrix, Janis Joplin wails herself hoarse and Grace Slick hits ear-splitting notes to clear the air. The song remains the same with the Grateful Dead for decades, until the Dead Kennedys wage aural anarchy and the Sex Pistols split up onstage in Japantown. The reverb of '70s funk meets Mission salsa and disco in the Castro, until synthesizers take over: '80s anthems ensue. Grunge trickles down from Seattle in the '90s and stomps power pop. Now you'll hear remixes, with jazz-inflected hip-hop and pop punk.

## Performing Arts

If you don't see it here, you might not catch it anywhere: SF's independent cinemas and theaters specialize in sleeper hits, strangely captivating one-offs and cult classics. Check for half-price theater tickets at the Union Square kiosk, or last-minute tickets to film festivals and dance performances on Craigslist – but if you can't score a seat, there's always the street theater of San Francisco's street fairs, protests and parades.

Before San Francisco was a foodie town, or a tech town, or even much of a town at all, it was the West Coast's home for theater. Major productions destined for Broadway and London open at the American Conservatory Theater, with breakthrough productions by Tony Kushner (*Angels in America*), Robert Wilson and William S Burroughs (*Black Rider*), Tom Stoppard (*Arcadia*) and David Mamet (*Oleanna, November*). For better or for worse (depending on how likely a tune is to haunt you) San Francisco is the proving ground for musicals such as *Rent* and *Phantom of the Opera*.

But it's not just great theatre you'll find here. From burlesque to ballet and all shades of modern, San Francisco's gotta dance. The nation's oldest professional ballet company, San Francisco Ballet, was formed in 1933 with George Balanchine setting the tone, and it produced the nation's first full-length productions of *Nutcracker Suite* and *Swan Lake*. Widely credited with originating modern dance, Isadora Duncan

### The Best... Way-Off-Broadway Theater

1 Magic Theatre (p71)

2 Castro Theatre (p177)

3 Beach Blanket Babylon (p120)

4 BATS Improv (p72)

## Our Fave 'Hollywood North' Directors

○ **Francis Ford Coppola** *The Godfather* auteur's American Zoetrope headquarters is North Beach's Columbus Tower.

○ **George Lucas** Never mind the Presidio-based director's *Star Wars* prequels – *American Graffiti* (1973), *Star Wars* (1977) and *Raiders of the Lost Ark* (1981) were hugely influential.

○ **Sean Penn** The director and Academy Award–winning actor (for 2008's *Milk*) is a sometime Columbus Tower tenant.

○ **Sofia Coppola** Produces variable films with consistent dreamlike qualities, including *Virgin Suicides* (1999) and *Lost in Translation* (2003).

○ **Wayne Wang** The indie director of *Chan is Missing* (1982), *Smoke* (1995) and *Because of Winn Dixie* (2006) is also headquartered in Columbus Tower.

(1877–1927) was born west of Union Square, and an alley off Taylor St between Post and Geary Sts bears her name. Today, Oberlin Dance Collective combines raw, Western physicality with modern San Francisco ingenuity.

## Visual Arts

While global art trends are making many art scenes look eerily alike, SF continues its homegrown tradition of rough-and-ready-made '50s Beat collage, '60s psychedelic Fillmore posters, earthy '70s funk and beautiful-mess punk, and '80s graffiti culture. Today, street artists and graduates from SF's distinguished art schools fill risk-taking arts venues Downtown and in the Mission. Art collectors stock up in SF, where world-class collections such as di Rosa Art + Nature Preserve have surprisingly affordable works from local galleries.

## The Best... SF Literary Scenes

1 LitQuake (p41)

2 Edinburgh Castle (p95)

3 Make-Out Room (p176)

4 Cartoon Art Museum (p158)

## Literature

If San Francisco didn't exist, writers would have to make it up. Set an unlikely story in San Francisco and somehow it seems believable. Where else could poetry fight the law and win? Yet when Beat poet Lawrence Ferlinghetti and bookseller Shig Murao were arrested for 'willfully and lewdly' publishing Allen Ginsberg's incendiary *Howl and Other Poems,* they won a landmark 1957 free-speech court case for City Lights. Without poetic will and, let's be honest, a certain amount of lewdness, Bay Area bookstores would look mighty barren – or worse, boring.

Today you can hardly throw a pebble in this town without hitting a writer, though it might get you cursed in verse. San Francisco has more writers per capita than any other US city, buys more books per capita than any other North American burg and hoards three times the national average of library books. Despite pronouncements of their imminent demise in the internet age, books remain wildly popular here in the capital of new technology.

Many San Franciscans seem like characters in a novel, and the reverse is also true. After a few days here, you might feel like you've seen Armistead Maupin's bright-eyed, corn-fed Castro newbies, Dashiell Hammett's mysterious redheads and Amy Tan's American-born daughters explaining slang to their Chinese-speaking moms. Ambrose Bierce and Mark Twain set the San Francisco standard for sardonic wit early on, but recently, Bay Area graphic novelists such as Daniel Clowes have added a twist to this tradition with finely drawn, deadpan behavioral studies.

People watching rivals reading as a preferred San Francisco pastime, and close observation of antics that would seem bizarre elsewhere pays off in stranger-than-fiction nonfiction – hence Hunter S Thompson's gonzo journalism and Joan Didion's core-shaking truth telling.

San Francisco's literary scene isn't confined to books and iPads; it's also fertile soil for homegrown zines. The most successful local zine of all, *McSweeney's,* is masterminded by Dave Eggers, who used the proceeds from his memoir *A Heartbreaking Work of Staggering Genius* to start McSweeney's publishing and 826 Valencia, a nonprofit writing program for teens. *McSweeney's* also publishes an excellent map of literary San Francisco, so you can get out there and walk the talk.

# Architecture

In San Francisco, most buildings are low enough for even a middling superhero to leap in a single bound. The Transamerica Pyramid and Ferry Building clocktower are helpful pointers to orient newcomers, and Coit Tower adds emphatic punctuation to the city skyline – but San Francisco's low-profile buildings are its highlights. A trip across town will bring you face to facade with the region's Spanish and Mexican heritage, East Asian influences, Victoriana, California Arts and Crafts and high modernist architecture.

## Mission & Makeshift SF

Not much is left of San Francisco's original Ohlone style, beyond the grass memorial hut you'll see in the graveyard of the Spanish Mission Dolores and the wall of the original presidio (military post), both built in adobe with conscripted Ohlone labor. During the Gold Rush, buildings were slapped together from ready-made sawn timber components, sometimes shipped from the East Coast or Australia. In those Barbary Coast days, City Hall wasn't much to look at, at least from outside: it was housed in the bawdy Jenny Lind Theater in Portsmouth Square.

## The Best...
# Low-Profile Landmarks

1 California Academy of Sciences (p209)

2 Zen Center (p189)

3 MH de Young Museum (p209)

4 Chinese Historical Society of America (p111)

IN FOCUS ARTS & ARCHITECTURE

## Victoriana

As San Francisco boomed, rows of houses were built with a similar underlying floor plan, but with eye-catching embellishments and paint jobs. The city's signature architectural style was labeled 'Victorian,' but demure Queen Victoria would surely blush to see the eccentric architecture perpetrated in her name in San Francisco. Local 'Painted Ladies' have candy-jar color palettes, lavish gingerbread woodworking dripping off steeply peaked roofs, and gilded stucco garlands swaging huge, look-at-me bay windows. Some proved surprisingly sturdy: several upstanding Victorian row houses remain in Pacific Heights.

The 1906 earthquake and fire destroyed many of the city's 19th-century treasures and much of its kitschy excess. But Victorian-era styles can still be spotted: long-windowed brick Italianates, gabled Gothic Revivals and exuberant Queen Annes, lavished with balconies, towers, turrets, chimneys, bay windows and gables. Bodacious Queen Annes survive around Alamo Square Park and Pacific Heights. Some Victorian mansions are now B&Bs, so you too can live large in swanky San Francisco digs of yore.

## Pacific Polyglot Architecture

This Pacific Rim city also felt a pull in other stylistic directions. Mission St movie-palace facades and Sansome St banks incorporated Spanish and Aztec design influences from Mexico. The 1920s also brought the mission revival style, a nostalgic look back at the state's Hispanic heritage.

Julia Morgan became the first licensed female architect in California and rose to fame with precocious postmodern landmarks incorporating wildly different cultural traditions, from her over-the-top Spanish-Gothic-Greek Hearst Castle to her tastefully restrained pagoda-topped brick Chinese Historical Society of America. Distinctive Chinatown deco became a cornerstone of Chinatown's redevelopment initiative after the 1906 quake, when a forward-thinking group of merchants consulted with a cross

257

section of architects to produce a crowd-pleasing, modern chinoiserie look that would attract tourists. (It worked.)

Meanwhile, Berkeley-based architect Bernard Maybeck reinvented England's Arts and Crafts movement with the down-to-earth California bungalow – a small, simple, single-story design derived from summer homes favored by British officers serving in India. California Arts and Crafts style can be spotted in Berkeley Craftsman cottages and earthy ecclesiastical structures.

## Modern Skyline

Once steel-frame buildings stood the test of the 1906 earthquake, San Francisco began to think big with its buildings. Willis Polk was among the city's busiest architects, defining Downtown with his Hallidie Building at the Powell St cable car turnaround. The city hoped to rival the capitals of Europe and commissioned architect Daniel Burnham to build a grand City Hall in the classicizing beaux arts or 'city beautiful' style.

San Francisco became a forward-thinking port city in the 1930s, with Streamline Moderne apartment buildings that looked like ocean liners and its signature art deco Golden Gate Bridge. But except for Coit Tower, most new buildings kept a low profile. Until the 1960s, San Francisco was called 'the white city' because of its low, unbroken swaths of white stucco.

As engineers figured out how to retrofit and reinforce buildings for earthquakes, the Financial District became a forest of glass boxes, with the pointed exception of the Transamerica Pyramid. Recent high-rise construction has sprung up in South of Market (SoMa), as San Francisco braces itself for booms in biotech and social media. Amid Victorian-prefab row houses in San Francisco neighborhoods, you might also spot some of the sleek, architect-designed ecoprefab homes innovated in the Bay Area during the 1990s. Detractors debate the clash in styles, but this is San Francisco: eclectic is what we do here.

Victorian houses and Transamerica Pyramid (p81), designed by William Pereira

# Hills & Fog

Buena Vista Park (p188)

*Seen from space, San Francisco's defining features are surely the Golden Gate Bridge and the city's 47 hills – but astronauts who orbit any closer might also hear the people atop them, gasping in unison. If the climb doesn't take your breath away at hilltop parks, the Golden Gate vistas surely will. Luckily, the fog is there to cool you off after a rigorous sightseeing workout.*

## Peak Experiences

### Hilltop Parks

The city wasn't exactly planned, with sailors abandoning their ships in the harbor to swim ashore during the Gold Rush. But among the early arrivals were naturalist John Muir, the founder of the Sierra Club and Muir Woods, and William Hammond Hall, champion of Golden Gate Park, who saw beauty and not just gold in these hills. Thanks to them and other like-minded conservationists, virtually every hilltop in San Francisco has a precious green toupee it wouldn't be seen without; these hilltop parks give the city its natural charm.

San Francisco voters backed the 1867 creation of Buena Vista Park, and the staggering peak still offers the city's most sweeping panoramas, along with Pacific Heights' Alta Vista Park. Drivers gunning down Lombard St miss spectacular photo ops of the Golden Gate Bridge through the wind-swept pines of Sterling Park. Watch a sunset here, and you'll see what inspired poet and park namesake George Sterling to gush: 'Homeward into the sunset/Still unwearied we go/Till the northern hills are misty/With the amber of afterglow.'

### Next-Level Landmarks

Scandal, artistic masterpieces, enlightenment and a stiff drink await your arrival at the summit of San Francisco's hills. Scenic greenery prevented 1906 fires from devastating Russian Hill, preserving the quaint cottage at 29 Russell St where Jack Kerouac wrote *On the Road* and held up his end of a love triangle. Coit Tower has controversial murals capped with crowd-pleasing panoramas, while Diego Rivera Gallery murals show the Mexican maestro hard at work, capturing a sweeping SF cityscape. On Nob Hill, Grace Cathedral is illuminated from within by Keith Haring's AIDS Memorial altar of angels taking flight – the artist's last work before his death by AIDS in 1990. Across from Grace Cathedral, Top of the Mark offers your choice of 100 martinis with a view over foggy hilltops that'll make you misty.

### Stairway Walks

Instead of declaring your love for SF on a T-shirt, shout it from a hilltop – even if it does involve a bit of a climb. Whenever possible, take the stairs. On Telegraph Hill, Filbert St Steps are flanked with surreal statuary and wild parrots, while the flowering staircases that lead to Ina Coolbrith Park make a perfumed, romantic climb. With its cottage-lined stairway and leafy canopy, Macondray Lane was the model for mysterious 'Barbary Lane' in Armistead Maupin's *Tales of the City*. And never mind the motorists: walking lets you stop and smell the roses along zigzagging Lombard St.

### The Easy Way Up

Top-of-the-world views don't always have to be earned the hard way in San Francisco. Instead of trudging up stairs, elevators whisk you straight to the viewing platform of Coit Tower, SFMOMA's rooftop sculpture garden and cafe, and the wildflower-covered roof of the California Academy of Sciences. Downtown public roof gardens let you picnic with a view, and cable cars offer uphill thrills with your commute.

## The Best... Hilltop Parks

1 Telegraph Hill (p107)

2 Sterling Park (p131)

3 Buena Vista Park (p188)

4 Ina Coolbrith Park (p129)

## Foggy Days

Once you've watched the fog lurching into town like a pirate on shore leave, it's hard to imagine San Francisco without it. Minus these mists, the entire San Francisco Bay would be missing its standout scenery: lighthouses wouldn't be necessary and giant redwoods wouldn't survive the hot sun. Finicky native NorCal ferns would refuse to sprout from the cliffs along Hwy 1 or from shoe planters atop Alamo Square. Sourdough bread starter (technically, *lactobacillus sanfrancisco*) wouldn't start, and pinot noir grapes would shrivel into raisins. Worse yet, if San Francisco enjoyed warm California sunshine all day, every day, it might start to look like LA.

The foggy fact of the matter is, no sweeping San Francisco vista is complete without a case of the goose bumps. Sunny days suit most cities just fine, but San Francisco saves its most dramatic view of Golden Gate Bridge for foggy days. When fog swirls

# SF's Green Outlook

It's not always easy being green, even in San Francisco. Since local real-estate prices remain among the highest in the US, there's always the fear that San Francisco's scenic hilltop living rooms will be swallowed up by private development. But a motley coalition of neighborhood councils, dog walkers, parrot feeders, parents, kite fliers, conservationists and lollygaggers have actively protected San Francisco's urban green spaces for over a century. San Franciscans successfully lobbied for the preservation of Golden Gate Park in the 19th century and recently convinced the US military to hand over a military base for use as public parkland in the Presidio.

Nature has lavished the city with hilltop parks, gardens and top-notch produce – and the city does its best to repay the favor, with mandatory composting citywide and thoughtful everyday conservation efforts. All around you in San Francisco you'll notice wild ideas in action, with support ranging from green-certified businesses to the Green Party (a power player in city politics). Rooftop vegetable gardens have taken off, and defunct freeway ramps were converted into the nonprofit Hayes Valley Farm. There's even a buzz about public beekeeping, to encourage healthy cross-pollination in urban plant life.

This is one town where you can eat, sleep and cavort sustainably; just look for 🌿 icons throughout this book. All these measures help make San Francisco a livable, breathable city – that urban claustrophobia you get surrounded by New York skyscrapers or Los Angeles freeways isn't a problem here. From the bottom of its heart to the top of its green hills, San Francisco thanks you.

around the towers, romantics and photographers rejoice – and you'll swear you see the ghost of Alfred Hitchcock at misty Fort Point, rubbing his hands with glee.

## Microclimates

Armies of glam rockers with dry-ice machines can't create the moody, misty effects San Francisco comes by naturally. On sunny summer afternoons, the city skyline can vanish into clouds within an hour. There are two secrets to San Francisco's amazing disappearing act: geography and microclimates.

To understand how fog moves inland, first you need to picture California's geography. The vast agricultural region in the state's interior, the Central Valley, is ringed by mountains, like a giant bathtub. As this inland valley heats up and the warm air rises, it creates a deficit of air at surface level, generating wind that gets sucked through the only opening it can find: the Golden Gate. Suddenly the misty air hovering over the chilly Pacific gets pulled into the bay, and ta-da: the city disappears behind a misty veil.

Rolling fog moves fast, and it's unpredictable: gusty wind is the only indication that it's coming. But even when the fog swallows beaches in the Presidio, the sun is probably still shining in the Mission. Hills block fog, especially at times of high atmospheric pressure, as often happens in summer. When forecasters refer to the Bay Area's 'microclimates,' this is what they mean. These alternating pockets of fog and sun may support different flora, ranging from windswept Presidio pines to Mission palm trees.

Now you know why jackets are a permanent style statement in San Francisco. In July it's not uncommon for inland areas to reach 100°F (38°C), while the mercury

at the coast barely reaches 70° (21°C). Even across the city, temperatures can vary by 15 degrees or more. When the fog has worn out its welcome in the Avenues and the Haight, take a bus to the Castro or the Mission – and when the fog reaches the Mission, hop BART to sunny Berkeley across the bay.

## Misty-Eyed Sunsets

Surfer hangouts, bargain gourmet meals and unforgettable sunset views over the velvety fog are all good reasons to linger in the Avenues after the fog has sneaked into Golden Gate Park. Above the east end of the park are the side-by-side 922ft and 904ft Twin Peaks, formerly known as El Pecho de la Chola (the Breasts of the Indian Girl), which are ideal vista points. Climb either one (by car, preferably) to watch the fog roll in from the ocean around sunset and see the Oakland Hills glitter with golden after-noon light across the bay. To drive to Twin Peaks, head southwest on Market St as it climbs steeply uphill (it becomes Portola Ave) and then turn right on Twin Peaks Blvd.

## Top Places for Fog-Watching

- Facing the Golden Gate Bridge from the dock alongside Crissy Field.
- Looking down on the city from atop Corona Heights.
- Overlooking Golden Gate Park from the MH de Young Museum tower.
- While eading poetry on a hillside bench at Sterling Park.
- While sprawling naked on Baker Beach...brrrrr.

Golden Gate Bridge (p58)

# GLBT SF

Pride Parade (p41)

RICK GERHARTER/LONELY PLANET IMAGES ©

*It doesn't matter where you're from, who you love or who's your daddy: if you're here and you're queer, you're home. San Francisco is the mothership of gay culture, America's pinkest city and the easiest place in the US to be out of the closet. Singling out the best places to be out and about in San Francisco is almost redundant.*

## Where to Be Gay in the Bay

In San Francisco, you don't need to trawl the urban underworld for a gay scene. Here 'mos are mainstream, and hetero norms need not apply. Remember, this is where gay marriage first became legal in the US. If you're giving aggressive gaydar, the scene will find you. Drag shows are popular with San Franciscans of all persuasions, though you'll never need a professional reason to cross-dress – next to baseball, gender-bending is SF's favorite sport.

To get the latest on the GLBT scene, check the *Bay Area Reporter* (BAR; www .ebar.com) for news and listings, and pick up the *San Francisco Bay Times* (www .sfbaytimes.com), which also has good resources for transsexuals.

## Nightlife

Party boys cruise the Castro by day and South of Market (SoMa) by night. The intersection of 18th and Castro Sts is the heart of the gay scene, and there are bars a-go-go, but most are predictably middlebrow. Dancing queens and slutty boys head to SoMa, the location of most thump-thump clubs and sex venues. Weeknights, it's trickier to find the party – most guys stay home and the main cruising action is online. At clubs with outdoor patios, expect clouds of pot smoke: SF is stoner central.

Back in the pre-1960s days of police raids, bars would euphemistically designate Sunday afternoons as 'tea dances,' appealing to gay crowds to make money at an otherwise slow time. The tradition makes Sunday one of the busiest times for SF's gay bars, though now you can also find your choice of gay bars open any day of the week.

## Women

So where are all the hot chicks into hot chicks? To join the party, scan our Mission listings or just head to Valencia St – the funkier outer fringe where the Castro hits the Mission, and the preferred 'hood of bad-ass dykes, alt-chicks and cute femmes, where you can flirt the day away in cafes, thrift shops, bookstores and arts venues. Many gay bars host regular ladies' nights: expect grrrls galore Fridays at the Stud and Saturdays at the EndUp.

## The Best... Gay Hangouts

1 Pride Parade (p41)

2 Castro Theatre (p177)

3 Mission Dolores Park (p155)

4 Cafe Flore (p174)

5 GLBT History Museum (p164)

## Party Planning

Find out where the party's happening on the weekend through these SF resources:

**Craigslist** (www.craigslist.org) Click on women-seeking-women or men-seeking-men to search for roving parties or post a query.

**Betty's List** (www.bettyslist.com) Parties, fund-raisers, power lesbian mixers.

**Get Your Girl On** (http://gogetyourgirlon.com) Find concerts and parties for (who else?) girls.

**Juanita More** (www.juanitamore.com) The drag superstar throws fierce parties attended by hot boys, especially for Pride.

**Honey Soundsystem** (www.honeysoundsystem.com) Roving queer DJ collective stirs the pot with insane dance parties.

# Cable Cars

California St cable car (p267)

THOMAS WINZ/LONELY PLANET IMAGES ©

*A creaking hand brake seems to be the only thing between you and a cruel fate as your 15,000lb cable car picks up speed downhill, careening toward oncoming traffic. But Andrew Hallidie's 1873 contraptions (avoid calling them 'trolleys' or be branded an outsider) have held up miraculously well on San Francisco's breakneck slopes, and groaning brakes and clanging brass bells only add to the carnival-ride thrills.*

## History

Legend has it that the idea of cable cars occurred to Hallidie in 1869, as he watched a horse carriage struggle up Jackson St – until one horse slipped on wet cobblestones and the carriage went crashing downhill. Such accidents were considered inevitable on San Francisco's steep hills, but Hallidie knew better. His father was the Scottish inventor of wire cable, which Hallidie had put to work hauling ore out of mines during the Gold Rush. If hemp-and-metal cable could haul rocks through High Sierras snowstorms, surely it could transport San Franciscans through the fog.

The 'wire rope railway' wasn't a name that inspired confidence, and skeptical city planners granted the inventor just three months to make his contraption operational by August 1, 1873. Hallidie only missed his deadline by four hours when his cable car was

# Need to Know

○ **Operating hours** Cable car lines operate from about 6am to 1am daily, with scheduled departures every three to 12 minutes; for detailed schedules, see http://transit.511.org.

○ **Cost** If you're planning to stop en route, get a Muni Passport (p280); one-way tickets cost $6, with no on-and-off privileges.

○ **Boarding** The Powell St and California St cable car turnarounds usually have queues, but they move fast. To skip the queue, head further up the line and jump on when the cable car stops. Cable cars may make rolling stops, especially on downhill runs. To board on hills, act fast: leap onto the baseboard and grab the closest leather hand strap.

○ **Stops** Cable cars stop at almost every block on the California St and Powell-Mason lines, and every block on the north–south stretches of the Powell-Hyde line; detailed transit maps are available free online at www.sfmuni.com or at the Powell St turnaround kiosk for $3.

○ **Child safety** This Victorian transportation is certainly not childproof. You won't find car seats or seat belts on these wooden benches; kids love the open-air seating in front, but holding small children securely inside the car is safer.

○ **Accessibility** Cable cars are not accessible for people with disabilities.

○ **Signage** To help distinguish the two Powell lines, Powell-Mason is signed in yellow and Powell-Hyde in red.

poised on Jones St ready for the descent. The cable car operator was terrified, and Hallidie himself is said to have grabbed the brake and steered the car downhill.

By the 1890s, 53 miles of track crisscrossed the city. Hallidie became a rich man, and even ran for mayor. Defamed as an opportunistic Englishman despite his civic contributions and US citizenship, he lost. He remained a lifelong inventor, earning 300 patents and becoming a prominent member of the California Academy of Sciences.

## Technology & Operation

Today the cable car seems more like a steampunk carnival ride than modern transportation, but it remains the best way to conquer San Francisco's highest hills. Cable cars still can't move in reverse, and require burly gripmen to lean hard on hand-operated brakes to keep them from careening downhill. The city receives many applicants for this job, but 80% fail the strenuous tests of upper-body strength and hand-eye coordination, and rarely reapply.

Although cables groan piteously with uphill effort, they seldom fray and have rarely broken in more than a century of near-continuous operation. The key to the cable car's amazing safety record is the cable grip wheel: clips click into place and gradually release to prevent cables from slipping. To watch this clever Victorian technology in action, visit the Cable Car Museum.

### Lines

Powell-Hyde cars offer the most scenic route; Powell-Mason cars take a fairly direct north–south route; and the historic California line is the east–west route.

# San Francisco's Cable Cars

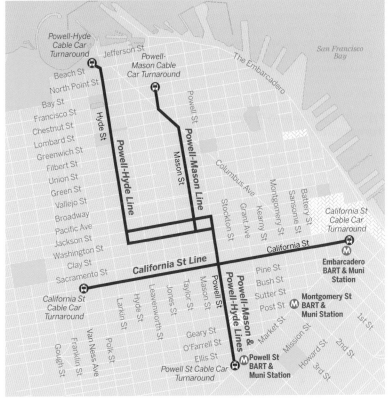

## Powell-Hyde Cable Car

The ascent up Nob Hill feels like the world's longest roller-coaster climb – but on the Powell-Hyde cable car, the biggest thrills are still ahead. This cable car bobs up and down hills, with the Golden Gate Bridge popping in and out of view on Russian Hill. Instead of riding all the way to the waterfront, hop off the cable car at the top of Lombard St and zigzag your way down.

## Powell-Mason Cable Car

The Powell-Hyde line may have multimillion-dollar vistas, but the Powell-Mason line is the quickest way to get to Fisherman's Wharf. Instead of taking the scenic route, it climbs straight up Nob Hill and delivers you just a few blocks from Pier 39.

## California St Cable Car

History buffs and crowd-shy visitors prefer San Francisco's oldest cable car line: the California St cable car, which has been in operation since 1878. This divine ride west heads through Chinatown, climbs Nob Hill and stops at Van Ness before heading back toward the Ferry Building.

## Powell St Cable Car Turnaround

At Powell and Market Sts, you'll spot cable car operators gripping trolleys and slooowly turning them around by hand on a revolving wooden platform. Cable cars can't go in reverse, and this 'turnaround' is where the Powell-Mason and Powell-Hyde lines end and begin. Tourists line up here to secure a seat, with street performers and doomsday preachers as entertainment – or not. Locals hop on further uphill.

## Friedel Klussmann Cable Car Turnaround

The Powell-Hyde turnaround at Fisherman's Wharf is named after the gardener who rallied her ladies' garden club in 1947 against the mayor's scheme to replace Powell cable car lines with buses – the mayor lost to the 'Cable Car Lady' by a landslide. In 1952, Klussmann campaigned to rescue the insolvent California line. Upon her death in 1986, cable cars citywide were draped in black.

# The Best...
# Cable Car
# Stop Offs

1 Union Square (p84)

2 Sterling Park (p131)

3 Lombard St (p132)

4 Grace Cathedral (p133)

# Survival Guide

## SLEEPING 270

Where to Stay 271

Best Places to Stay 272

## TRANSPORT 278

Getting to San Francisco 278

Getting Around San Francisco 279

Tours 283

## DIRECTORY 283

Business Hours 283

Electricity 284

Emergencies 284

Medical Services 284

Money 284

Public Holidays 285

Safe Travel 286

Taxes & Refunds 286

Telephone 286

Time 286

Tourist Information 286

Travelers with Disabilities 286

Visas 287

Four-wheel bicycle in Golden Gate Park (p208)

PHOTOGRAPHER: SABRINA DALBESIO/LONELY PLANET IMAGES ©

# Sleeping

San Francisco is the birthplace of the boutique hotel. You'll find standard-issue chains with good-value rates, four-stars with upmarket comforts and a few palatial five-stars with top-flight luxuries, but it's the little places that stand out – elegant Victorians on neighborhood side streets, artsy downtowners with intimate bars and cozy small inns that smell of freshly baked cookies.

## Accommodation Types

### Hotels

Large hotels abound Downtown and are usually part of a national chain. The decor may be uninspiring, but the quality is fairly consistent, and you may be able to take advantage of amenities like business centers and on-site gyms.

### Boutique Hotels

The boutique trend started here, but the term has become so overused that it's nearly meaningless. Usually, the term refers to upmarket hotels with fewer than 100 rooms, unique decor and service standards that distinguish them from cookie-cutter chains or other small hotels.

### Motels

No interstate highway means no preponderance of cheap, soulless chain motels. But there are a few independent, converted motels that offer relatively inexpensive lodging with retro appeal.

### B&Bs

At a bed and breakfast you can expect personalized service, a homier environment and, of course, breakfast.

### Hostels

If you really just need a place to sleep and don't mind a dorm situation, hostels are the cheapest way to go.

## Costs

Rates in SF fluctuate wildly. Some hotels have internet specials not available by telephone. When booking online, know that 'best rate' does not necessarily mean the lowest available rate. When in doubt, call the hotel directly.

Although bright, friendly hostels and budget hotels have opened up around town, rooms are never truly cheap in SF: expect to pay at least $65 at a budget hotel or for a private hostel room, and over $100 at any midrange hotel – plus a hefty 15.5% room tax. Prices run higher from June to August, and drop September to May. If you're staying awhile, ask about weekly rates. On weekends and holidays, rates for business and luxury hotels decrease, but increase for tourist hotels.

## When to Book

Chain hotels routinely overbook when there's a big convention in town. If you haven't chosen dates yet, check the convention calendar (www.sanfrancisco.travel/meeting-planners), which shows the expected bed count for upcoming conventions. The city has 33,000 total rooms; if the calendar says a convention (such as Oracle) will require over 10,000 beds, choose other dates or expect to pay a premium.

## Useful Websites

**Lonelyplanet.com** (http://hotels.lonelyplanet.com) For more accommodation reviews by Lonely Planet authors; you can also book online here.

**Priceline** (www.priceline.com) Clearinghouse for midrange to upscale lodging.

**Topaz Hotel Services** (www.hotelres.com) Hotels in the Bay Area and Wine Country.

# Where to Stay

| NEIGHBORHOOD | FOR | AGAINST |
| --- | --- | --- |
| THE MARINA & FISHERMAN'S WHARF | Near the northern waterfront; good for kids; lots of restaurants and nightlife at the Marina. | Fisherman's Wharf is all tourists; parking at the Marina and Wharf is a nightmare. |
| DOWNTOWN & CIVIC CENTER | Biggest selection of hotels; near all public transportation, including cable cars; walkable to many sights, shopping and theaters. | Downtown quiet at night; Civic Center feels rough – the worst area extends three blocks in all directions from Eddy and Jones Sts; parking is expensive. |
| NORTH BEACH & CHINATOWN | Culturally colorful; great strolling; lots of cafes and restaurants; terrific sense of place. | Street noise; limited choices and transport; next-to-impossible parking. |
| NOB HILL, RUSSIAN HILL & FILLMORE | Stately, classic hotels atop Russian and Nob Hills; good nightlife and shopping in Japantown and Pacific Heights. | The Hills are steep and hard on the out-of-shape; parking difficult; slightly removed from major sights. |
| THE MISSION, SOMA & THE CASTRO | Parts of SoMa are close to major Downtown sights; great nightlife and restaurants, especially for GLBT travelers in the Castro; flat terrain makes walking easier. | Limited choice; distance from major tourist sights; gritty street scene in both SoMa and the Mission. |
| THE HAIGHT & HAYES VALLEY | Lots of bars and restaurants; Hayes Valley near cultural sights; the Haight near Golden Gate Park. | Limited public transportation in the Haight; gritty street scene at night on major thoroughfares; parking difficult. |
| GOLDEN GATE PARK & THE AVENUES | Quiet nights; good for outdoor recreation; easier parking. | Very far from major sights; foggy and cold in summer; limited transportation. |

# Best Places to Stay

| NAME | | REVIEW |
|------|--|--------|
| **ARGONAUT HOTEL** $$$ | The Marina & Fisherman's Wharf | Built as a cannery in 1908, it has century-old wooden beams, exposed brick walls and an over-the-top nautical theme. |
| **TUSCAN INN** $$ | The Marina & Fisherman's Wharf | Way more character than a chain, with spacious rooms done in bold colors and mixed patterns; afternoon wine hour. |
| **HOTEL DEL SOL** $$ | The Marina & Fisherman's Wharf | A revamped 1950s motor lodge in the Marina with a colorful tropical theme plus a (rare) heated outdoor pool. |
| **COVENTRY MOTOR INN** $ | The Marina & Fisherman's Wharf | Highest overall quality-to-value ratio, with spacious, well-maintained (if plain) rooms and extras like air-con and parking. |
| **MANDARIN ORIENTAL** $$$ | Downtown & Civic Center | Asian-accented classical decor, sumptuous beds and, oh, those vistas: every room has a sweeping, unobstructed view. |
| **PALACE HOTEL** $$$ | Downtown & Civic Center | A monument to turn-of-the-20th-century grandeur, aglow with century-old crystal chandeliers and stunning glass ceilings in the Garden Court. |
| **HOTEL PALOMAR** $$$ | Downtown & Civic Center | Crocodile-print carpets, stripy persimmon-red chairs, chocolate-brown wood and cheetah-print robes in the closet. Hugh Hefner would approve. |
| **HOTEL MONACO** $$$ | Downtown & Civic Center | Maintains its playful spirit, though rooms are a touch dated. Still, we love the bold fabrics and the opulent lobby. |
| **INN AT UNION SQUARE** $$$ | Downtown & Civic Center | Traditionalists love the conservative chintz decor and personalized service; best for older travelers who appreciate quiet. |
| **ORCHARD GARDEN HOTEL** $$ | Downtown & Civic Center | No need to trade comfort for conscience at this all-green-practices hotel: rooms have unexpectedly luxe touches. |
| **HOTEL REX** $$ | Downtown & Civic Center | Common areas conjure NY's Algonquin in the 1920s. Sunny, compact rooms feature hand-painted lampshades and works by local artists. |
| **GALLERIA PARK** $$ | Downtown & Civic Center | Exuberant staff and rooms styled with contemporary art, luxe amenities and handsome furnishings in soothing jewel tones. |
| **WHITE SWAN INN** $$ | Downtown & Civic Center | Evoking the English countryside, this romantic inn is styled with cabbage-rose wallpaper, flannel bedspreads and Colonial-style furniture. |

| PRACTICALITIES | BEST FOR... |
|---|---|
| ☎415-563-0800, 866-415-0704; www.argonauthotel.com; 495 Jefferson St; r $205-325; P❄🛜♿; M Jones & Beach Sts | Tons of atmosphere. |
| ☎415-561-1100, 800-648-4626; www.tuscaninn.com; 425 North Point St; r $169-229; P❄@🛜♿; M Beach & Mason Sts | Decor and waterfront location. |
| ☎415-921-5520, 877-433-5765; www.thehoteldelsol.com; 3100 Webster St; d $149-199; P❄@🛜🏊♿; M Fillmore & Lombard Sts | Retro-style family fun. |
| ☎415-567-1200; www.coventrymotorinn.com; 1901 Lombard St; r $95-145; P❄🛜♿; M Chestnut & Buchanan Sts | Great value. |
| ☎415-276-9888, 800-622-0404; www.mandarinoriental.com/sanfrancisco; 222 Sansome St; r $295-375, ste from $875; ❄@🛜; M & 🚋Montgomery St; 🚠California St | Five-star service. |
| ☎415-512-1111, 800-325-3535; www.sfpalace.com; 2 New Montgomery St; r $199-329; ❄@🛜🏊; M & 🚋Montgomery St | Historical charm. |
| ☎415-348-1111, 866-373-4941; www.hotelpalomar-sf.com; 12 4th St; r $199-299; ❄@🛜; M & 🚋Powell St | Sexy luxury. |
| ☎415-292-0100, 866-622-5284; www.monaco-sf.com; 501 Geary St; r $199-269; ❄@🛜; M Geary & Taylor Sts | Quirky style. |
| ☎415-397-3510, 800-288-4346; www.unionsquare.com; 440 Post St; r $229-289, ste $309-359; ❄@🛜; M & 🚋Powell St; 🚠Powell-Hyde, Powell-Mason | Proximity to shopping and theaters. |
| ☎415-399-9807, 888-717-2881; www.theorchardgardenhotel.com; 466 Bush St; r $179-249; ❄@🛜; M Sutter & Stockton Sts | Sustainable travel. |
| ☎415-433-4434, 800-433-4434; www.jdvhotels.com; 562 Sutter St; r $169-279; P❄@🛜; M & 🚋Powell St; 🚠Powell-Hyde, Powell-Mason | Artful travelers. |
| ☎415-781-3060, 800-738-7477; www.jdvhotels.com; 191 Sutter St; r $189-229; ❄@🛜; M & 🚋Montgomery | Downtown boutique charmer. |
| ☎415-775-1755, 800-999-9570; www.jdvhotels.com; 845 Bush St; r $159-199; P@🛜; M Bush & Jones Sts | Anglophiles. |

| **HOTEL ABRI $$** | Downtown & Civic Center | Snazzy rooms with bold black-and-tan motifs, pillow-top beds, feather pillows, iPod docking stations, flat-screen TVs and rainfall showerheads. |
| --- | --- | --- |
| **STEINHART HOTEL & APARTMENTS $** | Downtown & Civic Center | A glorious early-20th-century building with high ceilings, swank art deco furnishings and studios with kitchenettes or full kitchens. |
| **HOTEL TRITON $$** | Downtown & Civic Center | Every room is different. Some are tiny, but all have an aggressively whimsical design, ecofriendly amenities and shag-worthy beds. |
| **HOTEL DIVA $$** | Downtown & Civic Center | Favored by midbudget fashionistas and traveling club kids, the industrial-chic design conveys a sexy urban look. |
| **GOLDEN GATE HOTEL $$** | Downtown & Civic Center | Like an old-fashioned *pensione* (boardinghouse) with kindly owners and simple rooms with mismatched furniture, inside a 1913 Edwardian hotel. |
| **CRESCENT HOTEL $$** | Downtown & Civic Center | Some sexy details, like smoked mirrors and white-vinyl headboards, but lumpy pillows and small baths keep rates low. |
| **PHOENIX HOTEL $$** | Downtown & Civic Center | Minor celebs and Dionysian revelers are drawn to this vintage 1950s motor lodge with basic rooms dolled up with tropical decor. |
| **HOTEL METROPOLIS $** | Downtown & Civic Center | Ignore the streetwalkers outside; the Metropolis has fresh-looking rooms with standard-issue Ikea-like furniture and good amenities (although tiny baths). |
| **FITZGERALD HOTEL $** | Downtown & Civic Center | Upgrade from hostel to hotel at this 1910 property styled with a quirky mishmash of scuffed furniture from fancier boutiques. |
| **WASHINGTON SQUARE INN $$$** | North Beach & Chinatown | Decidedly European, with tasteful rooms and a few choice antiques. The least-expensive rooms are tiny, but what an address. |
| **HOTEL BOHÈME $$** | North Beach & Chinatown | Our favorite boutique hotel is a love letter to the Beat era, with moody color schemes that nod to the 1950s. |
| **SAN REMO HOTEL $** | North Beach & Chinatown | Rooms are simple, with shared baths and mismatched turn-of-the-century furnishings. Think reputable, vintage boardinghouse. |
| **PACIFIC TRADEWINDS HOSTEL $** | North Beach & Chinatown | San Francisco's smartest-looking all-dorm hostel has a blue-and-white nautical theme, fully equipped kitchen and spotless glass-brick showers. |

📞415-392-8800, 866-823-4669; www.hotel-abri.com; 127 Ellis St; r $149-229; ✳️ @ 📶; Ⓜ& ®Powell St — Up-to-date sensibility.

📞415-928-3855, 800-533-1900; www.steinharthotel .com; 952 Sutter St; studio per week $595-665, 1-bedroom apt per week from $1325; 📶; Ⓜ Sutter & Leavenworth Sts — Week or longer stays.

📞415-394-0500, 800-800-1299; www.hotel-tritonsf .com; 342 Grant Ave; r $169-239; ✳️ @ 📶; Ⓜ & ®Montgomery St — Unique rooms.

📞415-885-0200, 800-553-1900; www.hoteldiva .com; 440 Geary St; r $159-229; ✳️ @ 📶; Ⓜ Geary & Mason Sts — Party weekend.

📞415-392-3702, 800-835-1118; www.goldengatehotel .com; 775 Bush St; r with/without bath $165/105; @ 📶; Ⓜ Sutter & Powell Sts; 🚋Powell St — Location plus value.

📞415-400-0500; www.crescentsf.com; 417 Stockton St; r $139-179; @ 📶; Ⓜ Sutter & Stockton Sts — Hip cats on a budget.

📞415-776-1380, 800-248-9466; www.jdvhospitality .com; 601 Eddy St; r incl breakfast $119-169; Ⓟ 📶 🏊; Ⓜ Eddy & Polk Sts — Rocker crash pad.

📞415-775-4600, 800-553-1900; www.hotel metropolis.com; 25 Mason St; r $89-125; Ⓟ @ 📶; Ⓜ & ®Powell St — Good digs at great prices.

📞415-775-8100, 800-334-6835; www.fitzgeraldhotel .com; 620 Post St; s $89-119, d $99-139; @ 📶; Ⓜ Post & Taylor Sts — Budget travel.

📞415-981-4220, 800-388-0220; www.wsisf.com; 1660 Stockton St; r incl breakfast $179-329; @ 📶; Ⓜ Columbus Ave & Union St — The over-40 set.

📞415-433-9111; www.hotelboheme.com; 444 Columbus Ave; r $174-194; @ 📶; Ⓜ Stockton St & Columbus Ave — Vibrant street scene.

📞415-776-8688, 800-352-7366; www.sanremo hotel.com; 2237 Mason St; d $65-99; @ 📶; Ⓜ Columbus Ave & Francisco St; 🚋Powell-Mason — Old-fashioned charm.

📞415-433-7970, 888-734-6783; www.sanfrancisco hostel.org; 680 Sacramento St; dm $29; @ 📶; Ⓜ Sacramento & Kearny Sts — Great service, fun staff.

| HOTEL DRISCO $$$ | Nob Hill, Russian Hill & Fillmore | A stately 1903 apartment-hotel tucked between mansions. The location is convenient to the Marina; anywhere else requires bus or taxi. |
|---|---|---|
| MARK HOPKINS INTERCONTINENTAL $$ | Nob Hill, Russian Hill & Fillmore | Glistening marble floors reflect glowing crystal chandeliers in the lobby of the 1926 Mark Hopkins, a San Francisco landmark. |
| HOTEL TOMO $$ | Nob Hill, Russian Hill & Fillmore | Japanese pop culture informs the Tomo's aesthetic, with minimalist furniture and anime-style murals in each room. |
| HOTEL MAJESTIC $$ | Nob Hill, Russian Hill & Fillmore | This 1902 hotel holds a torch for traditional elegance, though with frayed edges. Small standard rooms are a good value. |
| INN SAN FRANCISCO $$ | The Mission, SoMa & the Castro | A stately inn occupying an elegant 1872 Italianate-Victorian mansion, impeccably maintained and packed with period antiques. |
| HOTEL VITALE $$$ | The Mission, SoMa & the Castro | An ugly exterior disguises a fashion-forward hotel enhanced by up-to-the-minute luxuries. Excellent spa with rooftop hot tubs. |
| MOSSER HOTEL $$ | The Mission, SoMa & the Castro | This older, tourist-class hotel has tiny rooms, tinier baths, stylish details and rates that are usually a bargain. |
| PARKER GUEST HOUSE $$ | The Mission, SoMa & the Castro | The Castro's most stately gay digs occupy two side-by-side Edwardian mansions. Details are elegant and formal, but never froufrou. |
| BECK'S MOTOR LODGE $ | The Mission, SoMa & the Castro | Its placement at the center of the Castro makes this motor lodge the de-facto gay favorite. Rear-facing units are quieter. |
| PARSONNAGE $$$ | The Haight & Hayes Valley | This 23-room Italianate-Victorian retains gorgeous original details, including rose-brass chandeliers and marble fireplaces. Convenient to transportation. |
| CHATEAU TIVOLI $$ | The Haight & Hayes Valley | A glorious Victorian mansion near Alamo Square full of soul and character, with gabled roofs, domed turrets and cornices. |
| RED VICTORIAN BED, BREAKFAST & ART $$ | The Haight & Hayes Valley | The Summer of Love lives on at the tripped-out Red Vic, with individually decorated rooms and a hippie vibe. |
| HAYES VALLEY INN $ | The Haight & Hayes Valley | Like a European *pensione*, this inn has simple, small rooms with shared baths and staff who want to mother you. |
| SEAL ROCK INN $$ | Golden Gate Park & the Avenues | Rooms need updating (think 1970s rumpus-room style), but most sleep up to four. All have refrigerators; some have kitchens. |

☏415-346-2880, 800-738-7477; www.jdvhotels.com; 2901 Pacific Ave; r $209-299; @ 🛜; MDivisadero & Jackson Sts

Elegant simplicity.

☏415-392-3434, 800-327-0200; www.markhopkins .net; 999 California St; r $179-339; ✳ @ 🛜; 🚋California St

Timeless Nob Hill elegance.

☏415-921-4000, 888-822-8666; www.jdvhotels.com /tomo; 1800 Sutter St; r $119-189; P ✳ @ 🛜 ♿; MSutter & Buchanan Sts

Families and anime nuts.

☏415-441-1100, 800-869-8966; www.thehotel majestic.com; 1500 Sutter St; r $100-175; @ 🛜; MSutter & Gough Sts

Old-school vibe.

☏415-641-0188, 800-359-0913; www.innsf.com; 943 S Van Ness Ave; r $175-285, with shared bath $120-145, cottage $335, all incl breakfast; P @ 🛜; MMission & 20th Sts

Victorian elegance.

☏415-278-3700, 888-890-8688; www.hotelvitale .com; 8 Mission St; d $239-379; ✳ @ 🛜; M & 🚋Embarcadero

Smart style and great views.

☏415-986-4400, 800-227-3804; www.themosser .com; 54 4th St; r $129-159, with shared bath $69-99; @ 🛜; M & 🚋Powell St

Conventioneers on a budget.

☏415-621-3222, 888-520-7275; www.parker guesthouse.com; 520 Church St; r incl breakfast $149-229; P @ 🛜; MChurch & 18th Sts

GLBT visitors with style.

☏415-621-8212, 800-227-4360; www.becksmotor lodge.com; 2222 Market St; r $95-135; 🛜; 🚋Castro St

Casual digs in the Castro.

☏415-863-3699, 888-763-7722; www.theparsonage .com; 198 Haight St; r $200-250; @ 🛜; MHaight & Laguna Sts

Formal breakfast and bedtime brandy.

☏415-776-5462, 800-228-1647; www.chateautivoli .com; 1057 Steiner St; r $140-200, r without bath $100-130, ste $250-290; 🛜; MFillmore St & Golden Gate Ave

Antique-laden, TV-free rooms.

☏415-864-1978; www.redvic.net; 1665 Haight St; r $149-229, without bath $89-129, incl breakfast; 🛜; MHaight & Cole Sts

Flower children.

☏415-431-9131, 800-930-7999; www.hayesvalleyinn .com; 417 Gough St; s $80-105, d $84-120, incl breakfast; @ 🛜; MHayes & Gough Sts

Amazingly reasonable prices.

☏415-752-8000, 888-732-5762; www.sealrockinn .com; 545 Point Lobos Ave; s $129-167, d $139-177; P 🛜 ⛱ ♿; M48th & Point Lobos Aves

Families, beach access.

# Transport

## Getting to San Francisco

Service from three Bay Area airports makes getting to San Francisco quick and convenient. Bargain fares can be found online year-round, but don't forget to factor in additional transit time and costs to get to SF if you're flying into San Jose or Oakland instead of San Francisco.

Flights, tours and rail tickets can be booked online at lonelyplanet.com/bookings.

### ✈ Air

### San Francisco International Airport

One of the busiest airports in the country, **San Francisco International Airport** (SFO; www.flysfo.com) is 14 miles south of downtown off Hwy 101 and accessible by BART.

GETTING TO/FROM
SAN FRANCISCO
INTERNATIONAL AIRPORT

**BART** (Bay Area Rapid Transit; www.bart.gov; one-way $8) Offers a fast, direct 30-minute ride to/from downtown San Francisco. The SFO BART station is connected to the International Terminal; tickets can be purchased from machines inside the station entrance.

**BusSamTrans** (www.samtrans.com; one-way $5) Express bus KX takes about 30 minutes to reach Temporary Transbay Terminal in the South of Market (SoMa) area.

**Airport Shuttles** (one-way $14-17) Depart from baggage-claim areas, taking 45 minutes to most SF locations. Companies include **SuperShuttle** (☎ 800-258-3826; www.supershuttle.com), **Quake City** (☎ 415-255-4899; www.quakecityshuttle.com), **Lorrie's** (☎ 415-334-9000; www.gosfovan.com) and **American Airporter Shuttle** (☎ 415-202-0733; www.americanairporter.com).

**Taxi** Taxis to downtown San Francisco cost $35 to $50, departing from the yellow zone on the lower level of SFO.

**Car** The drive between the airport and the city can take as little as 20 minutes, but give yourself an hour during morning and evening rush hours.

### Oakland International Airport

Travelers arriving at **Oakland International Airport** (OAK; ☎ 510-563-3300; www.oaklandairport.com), 15 miles east of Downtown, will have a little further to go to reach San Francisco.

GETTING TO/FROM
OAKLAND INTERNATIONAL
AIRPORT

**BART** The cheapest way to get to San Francisco from the Oakland Airport. AirBART shuttles (adult/child $3/1) run every 10 to 20 minutes to the Coliseum station, where you can catch BART to downtown SF ($3.80, 25 minutes).

**Taxi** Taxis leave curbside from Oakland airport and average $25 to Oakland and $50 to $70 to SF.

**SuperShuttle** (☎ 800-258-3826; www.supershuttle.com) Offers shared van rides to downtown SF for $25 to $30.

### Norman y Mineta San Jose International Airport

Fifty miles south of downtown San Francisco, **Norman y Mineta San Jose International Airport** (SJC; ☎ 408-501-0979; www.sjc.org) is a straight shot into the city by car via Hwy 101. The VTA Airport Flyer (bus 10; tickets $2; from 5am to midnight) makes a continuous run between the Santa Clara Caltrain station (Railroad Ave and Franklin St) and the airport terminals, departing every 15 to 30 minutes. From Santa Clara station, Caltrain (one-way $9; 90 minutes) runs several trains every day to the terminal at 4th and King Sts in SF.

### 🚌 Bus

Until the new terminal is complete in 2017, SF's intercity hub remains the **Temporary Transbay Terminal** (Map p160; Howard & Main Sts,

SoMa). From here you can catch the following buses:

**AC Transit** (www.actransit.org) Buses to the East Bay.

**Golden Gate Transit** (www.goldengatetransit.org) Northbound buses to Marin and Sonoma counties.

**Greyhound** ( ☎ 800-231-2222; www.greyhound.com) Buses leave daily for Los Angeles ($57, 8 to 12 hours), Truckee near Lake Tahoe ($33, 5½ hours) and other destinations.

**SamTrans** (www.samtrans.com) Southbound buses to Palo Alto and the Pacific coast.

## 🚌 Train

Easy on the eyes and carbon emissions too, train travel is a good way to visit the Bay Area and beyond.

**Caltrain** (Map p160; www.caltrain.com; cnr 4th & King Sts) Caltrain connects San Francisco with Silicon Valley hubs and San Jose.

**Amtrak** ( ☎ 800-872-7245; www.amtrakcalifornia.com) Amtrak serves San Francisco via its stations in Oakland and Emeryville (near Oakland). Amtrak offers rail passes good for seven days of travel in California within a 21-day period (from $159). Amtrak runs free shuttle buses from its stations in Emeryville and Oakland's Jack London Sq to San Francisco's Ferry Building and Caltrain station.

⬤⬤⬤

# Getting Around San Francisco

When San Franciscans don't have somewhere else to be right quick – and even when they do – most people walk, cycle or take Muni instead of a car or cab.

## 🚌 Bus, Streetcar & Cable Car

**Muni** (Municipal Transit Agency; www.sfmuni.com) operates bus, streetcar and cable car lines. Buses and streetcars are referred to interchangeably as Muni and marked in this book with Ⓜ while cable cars are marked with 🚟. Muni spares you the costly hassle of driving and parking in San Francisco, and it's often faster than driving during rush hour.

### Schedules

For fastest routes and the most exact departure times, consult http://transit.511.org. Arrival times can also be viewed on digital displays or guesstimated by consulting schedules posted inside bus shelters.

### System Maps

A detailed Muni Street & Transit Map is available free online (www.sfmuni.com) and at the Powell Muni kiosk ($3).

### Tickets

Standard fare for buses or streetcars is $2; tickets can be bought on board buses and streetcars (exact change required) and at underground Muni stations. Cable car tickets cost $6 per ride, and can be bought at cable car turnaround kiosks or on board from the conductor. Hang onto your ticket even if you're not planning to use it again: if you're caught without one by the transit police, you're subject to a $100 fine.

### Transfers

At the start of your Muni journey, free transfer tickets are available for additional Muni trips within 90 minutes (not including cable cars or BART). After 8:30pm, buses issue a Late Night Transfer good for travel until 5:30am the following morning.

# Climate Change & Travel

Every form of transport that relies on carbon-based fuel generates $CO_2$, the main cause of human-induced climate change. Modern travel is dependent on aeroplanes, which might use less fuel per kilometer per person than most cars but travel much greater distances. The altitude at which aircraft emit gases (including $CO_2$) and particles also contributes to their climate change impact. Many websites offer 'carbon calculators' that allow people to estimate the carbon emissions generated by their journey and, for those who wish to do so, to offset the impact of the greenhouse gases emitted with contributions to portfolios of climate-friendly initiatives throughout the world. Lonely Planet offsets the carbon footprint of all staff and author travel.

## Buses Around the Bay

Three public bus systems connect San Francisco to the rest of the Bay Area. Most buses leave from clearly marked bus stops; for transit maps and schedules, see the bus system websites.

**AC Transit** (www.actransit.org) Offers East Bay services from the Temporary Transbay Terminal. For public transportation connections from BART in the East Bay, get an AC Transit transfer ticket before leaving the BART station, and then pay an additional 75¢ to $1.

**Golden Gate Transit** (www.goldengatetransit.org) Connects San Francisco to Marin (tickets $2 to $3.25) and Sonoma counties (tickets $9.25 to $10.25), but be advised that service can be slow and erratic.

**Samtrans** (☎800-660-4287; www.samtrans.com) Runs buses between San Francisco and the South Bay, including services to/from SFO. Buses pick up/drop off from the Temporary Transbay Terminal and other marked bus stops within the city.

### Discounts & Passes

#### MUNI PASSPORTS

A **Muni Passport** (1-/3-/7-days $14/21/27) allows unlimited travel on all Muni transportation, including cable cars. It's sold at the Muni kiosk at the Powell St cable car turnaround on Market St, SF's Visitor Information Center (p286), the TIX Bay Area kiosk at Union Square (p84) and from a number of hotels.

#### CLIPPER CARDS

Downtown Muni/BART stations issue the **Clipper Card**, a reloadable transit card with a $5 minimum that can be used on Muni, BART, AC Transit, Caltrain, SamTrans, and Golden Gate Transit and Ferry (not cable cars). Clipper Cards automatically deduct fares and apply transfers – only one Muni fare is deducted in a 90-minute period.

#### FAST PASS

**Monthly Muni Fast Pass** (adult/child $62/21) offers unlimited Muni travel for the calendar month, including cable cars. Fast Passes are available at the Muni kiosk at the Powell St cable car turnaround.

### Streetcar

Muni Metro streetcars run from 5am to midnight on weekdays, with limited schedules on weekends. The L and N lines operate 24 hours, but aboveground Owl buses replace streetcars between 12:30am and 5:30am. The F-Market line runs vintage streetcars aboveground along Market St to the Embarcadero, where they turn north to Fisherman's Wharf. The T line heads south along the Embarcadero through SoMa and Mission Bay, then down 3rd St. Other streetcars run underground below Market St Downtown.

### Cable Car

In this age of seat belts and air bags, a rickety cable car ride is an anachronistic thrill. There are seats for about 30 seated passengers, who are often outnumbered by passengers clinging to creaking leather straps. For more on cable car maps, service and history, see p265. The following are the key cable car routes:

**California St** Runs east to west along California St, from the Downtown terminus at Market and Davis Sts, through Chinatown and Nob Hill to Van Ness Ave.

**Powell-Mason** Runs from the Powell St cable car turnaround past Union Square, turns west along Jackson St and then descends north down Mason St, Columbus Ave and Taylor St toward Fisherman's Wharf. On the return trip it takes Washington St instead of Jackson St.

**Powell-Hyde** Follows the same route as the Powell-Mason line until Jackson St, where it turns down Hyde St to terminate at Aquatic Park; coming back it takes Washington St.

### 🚊 BART

Throughout this book, venues readily accessible by **BART** (Bay Area Rapid Transit; www .bart.gov; ⏱4am-midnight Mon-Fri, 6am-midnight Sat, 8am-midnight Sun) are denoted by 🚇 followed by the name of the nearest BART. The fastest link between Downtown and the Mission District also offers transit to SF airport, Oakland ($3.20) and Berkeley ($3.75). Four of the system's five lines pass through SF before terminating at Daly City or SFO. Within SF, one-way fares start at $1.75.

### Tickets

BART tickets are sold at BART stations, and you'll need a ticket to enter and exit. If your ticket's value is less than needed to exit, use an Addfare machine to pay the appropriate amount. The Clipper Card can be used for BART travel.

### Transfers

At San Francisco BART stations, a 25¢ discount is available for Muni buses and streetcars; look for transfer machines before you pass through the turnstiles.

### 🚕 Taxi

Fares start at $3.50 at the flag drop and run about $2.25 per mile. Add at least 10% to the taxi fare as a tip ($1 minimum). Credit cards are often accepted, but confirm before getting into the cab.

The following taxi companies have 24-hour dispatches:

**DeSoto Cab** ( 📞 415-970-1300)

**Green Cab** ( 📞 415-626-4733; www.626green.com)

**Luxor** ( 📞 415-282-4141)

**Yellow Cab** ( 📞 415-333-3333)

### 🏍 Car & Motorcycle

If you can, avoid driving in San Francisco: traffic is a given, street parking is harder to find than true love and meter readers are ruthless. If you're driving a stick shift (manual transmission), you'd better have your hill-start technique down pat.

### Traffic

Try to avoid driving during rush hours: 7:30am to 9:30am and 4:30pm to 6:30pm, Monday to Friday. Before heading to any bridge, airport or other traffic choke point, call 📞 511 for a traffic update.

### Parking

Parking is tricky and often costly, especially Downtown. Ask your hotel about parking, and inquire about validation at restaurants and entertainment venues.

#### GARAGES

Downtown parking garages charge from $2 to $8 per hour and $25 to $50 per day, depending on how long you park and whether you require in-and-out privileges. The most convenient Downtown parking lots are at the Embarcadero Center, at 5th and Mission Sts, under Union Square and at Sutter and Stockton Sts; for more public parking garages, see www.sfmta.com.

#### PARKING RESTRICTIONS

Parking restrictions are indicated by the following color-coded sidewalk curbs:

**Blue** Disabled parking only; identification required.

**Green** Ten-minute parking zone from 9am to 6pm.

**Red** No parking or stopping.

## ℹ Crossing the Bridge

Unlike the Bay Bridge, the Golden Gate Bridge provides access to cyclists and pedestrians.

Pedestrians take the eastern sidewalk (open 5am to 9pm in summer, to 6pm in winter). Dress warmly. From the parking area and bus stop (off Lincoln Blvd), a pathway leads past the toll plaza, then it's 1.7 miles across. If walking the 3.4 miles round-trip seems too much, bus to the north side via Golden Gate Transit, then walk back.

By bicycle, follow the 49-mile Dr signs along Lincoln Blvd, through the Presidio, to the parking lot right before the toll plaza. Facing the snack bar, go right, toward the flower beds, then follow the bicycle path that crosses under the roadway to the western sidewalk, reserved for bicycles only.

**White** For picking up or dropping off passengers only.

**Yellow** Loading zone from 7am to 6pm.

TOWING VIOLATIONS

Desperate motorists often resort to double-parking or parking in red zones or on sidewalks, but parking authorities are quick to tow cars. If this should happen to you, you'll have to retrieve your car at **Autoreturn** (☎ 415-865-8200; www.autoreturn.com; 450 7th St, SoMa; ☺ 24hr; Ⓜ 27, 42).

## Rental

Typically, a small car might cost $50 to $60 a day or $175 to $300 a week, plus 9.5% sales tax. Unless your credit card covers car-rental insurance, you'll need to add $10 to $20 per day for a loss/damage waiver. Most rates include unlimited mileage; with cheap rates, there's often a per-mile charge above a certain mileage.

Booking ahead usually ensures the best rates, and airport rates are generally better than those in the city. As part of SF's citywide green initiative, rentals of hybrid cars and low-emissions vehicles from rental agencies at SFO are available at a discount.

To rent a motorcycle, contact **Dubbelju** (☎ 415-495-2774; www.dubbelju.com; 689a Bryant St; Ⓜ 27); rates start at $99 per day.

Major car-rental agencies include:

**Alamo Rent-a-Car** (☎ 415-693-0191, 800-327-9633; www.alamo.com; 750 Bush St, Downtown; ☺ 7am-7pm; Ⓜ 2, 3, 4, 76; 🚋 Powell-Mason, Powell-Hyde)

**Avis** (☎ 415-929-2555, 800-831-2847; www.avis.com; 675 Post St, Downtown; ☺ 6am-6pm; Ⓜ 2, 3, 4, 76)

**Budget** (☎ 415-292-8981, 800-527-0700; www.budget.com; 321 Mason St, Downtown; ☺ 6am-6pm; Ⓜ 2, 3, 4, 38)

**Dollar** (☎ 800-800-5252; www.dollarcar.com; 364 O'Farrell St, Downtown; ☺ 7am-7pm; Ⓜ 2, 3, 4, 38)

**Hertz** (☎ 415-771-2200, 800-654-3131; www.hertz.com; 325 Mason St, Downtown; ☺ 6am-6pm Mon-Thu, to 8pm Fri & Sat; Ⓜ 2, 3, 4, 38)

**Thrifty** (☎ 415-788-6906, 800-367-2277; www.thrifty.com; 350 O'Farrell St, Downtown; ☺ 7am-7pm; Ⓜ 2, 3, 4, 38)

## Car Share

Car sharing is a convenient alternative to rentals that spares you pick-up/drop-off and parking hassles: reserve a car online for an hour or two, or all day, and you can usually pick up/drop off your car within blocks of where you're staying.

**Zipcar** (☎ 866-494-7227; www.zipcar.com) rents Prius Hybrids and Minis by the hour for flat rates starting at $7 per hour, including gas and insurance, or per day for $70; a $25 application fee and $50 prepaid usage are required in advance.

## 🚢 Boat

The opening of the Bay Bridge in 1936 and the Golden Gate Bridge in 1937 spelled the near demise of ferry services across the Bay, but with the revival of the Embarcadero and reinvention of the Ferry Building as a gourmet dining destination, commuters and tourists alike are taking the scenic way across the bay after leisurely Ferry Building meals.

### East Bay

**Blue & Gold Fleet Ferries** (☎ 415-705-8200; www.blueandgoldfleet.com) operates ferries from the Ferry Building, Pier 39 and Pier 41 at Fisherman's Wharf to Jack London Sq in Oakland (one-way $6.25). Ticket booths are located at the Ferry Building and Piers 39 and 41.

### Marin County

**Golden Gate Transit Ferries** (☎ 415-455-2000; www.goldengateferry.org; ☺ 6am-9:30pm Mon-Fri, 10am-6pm Sat & Sun) runs regular ferry services from the Ferry Building to Larkspur and Sausalito (one-way adult/child $9.25/4.50). Transfers are available to Muni bus services, and bicycles are permitted.

**Blue & Gold Fleet Ferries** also provides service to Tiburon or Sausalito (one-way $10.50).

### Napa Valley

Get to Napa car-free via **Vallejo Ferry** (☎ 877-643-3779; www.baylinkferry.com; adult/child $13/6.50) with departures from Ferry Building docks about every hour from 6:30am to 7pm weekdays, and every two hours from 11am to 7:30pm on weekends. Bicycles are permitted. From the Vallejo Ferry Terminal, take Napa Valley Vine bus 10 to downtown Napa, Yountville, St Helena or Calistoga.

# Cycling Around the Bay Area

o **Within SF** Muni has racks that can accommodate two bicycles on some of its commuter routes, including 17, 35, 36, 37, 39, 53, 56, 66, 76, 91 and 108.

o **Marin County** Bicycles are allowed on the Golden Gate Bridge, so getting north to Marin County is no problem. You can transport bicycles on Golden Gate Transit buses, which usually have free racks available (first-come, first-served). Ferries also allow bicycles aboard when space allows.

o **Wine Country** To transport your bicycle to Wine Country, take Golden Gate Transit or the Vallejo Ferry. Within Sonoma Valley, take Arnold Dr instead of busy Hwy 12; through Napa Valley, take the Silverado Trail instead of Hwy 29 to avoid manic drivers U-turning for wineries. The most spectacular ride in Wine Country is sun-dappled, tree-lined West Dry Creek Rd in Sonoma's Dry Creek Valley.

o **East Bay** Cyclists can't use the Bay Bridge, so you'll need to take your bicycle on BART. Bicycles are allowed on BART at all hours, but during rush hours some limits apply. During rush hours, you can also travel with your bicycle across the bay via the **Caltrain's Bay Bridge Bicycle Commuter Shuttle** (☎510-286-0876; tickets $1; ⏱6:20-8:30am & 3:50-6:15pm Mon-Fri), which operates from the corner of Folsom and Main Sts in San Francisco and MacArthur BART station in Oakland.

## ◎ Bicycle

San Francisco is fairly bicycle-friendly, but traffic Downtown can be dangerous; cycling is best east of Van Ness Ave. Bicycles can be carried on BART, but not in the commute direction during weekday rush hours. If you're bringing your own, bicycles can be checked in boxes on Greyhound buses for $20 to $30; boxes cost $10. On Amtrak, bicycles can be checked as baggage for $5.

●●●●

## Tours

**Chinatown Alleyway Tours** (☎415-984-1478; www

.chinatownalleywaytours.org; adult/child $18/5; ⏱11am Sat & Sun) Neighborhood teens lead two-hour tours for up-close-and-personal peeks into Chinatown's past (weather permitting). Book five days ahead or pay double for Saturday walk-ins; cash only.

**Fire Engine Tours** (☎415-333-7077; www.fireenginetours.com; Beach St at the Cannery; adult/child $50/30; ⏱tours depart 1pm) Hot stuff: a 75-minute ride in an open-air vintage fire engine over Golden Gate Bridge. Dress warmly in case of fog.

**Public Library City Guides** (www.sfcityguides.org)

Volunteer local historians lead free tours by neighborhood and theme: Art Deco Marina, Gold Rush Downtown, Pacific Heights Victorians, North Beach by Night and more. See website for upcoming tours.

# A-Z

## Directory

●●●●

# Business Hours

Standard business hours are as follows. Nonstandard hours are listed in specific reviews.

**Banks** 9am to 4:30pm or 5pm Monday to Friday (occasionally 9am to noon Saturday).

**Offices** 8:30am to 5:30pm Monday to Friday.

**Restaurants** Breakfast 8am to noon, lunch noon to 3pm, dinner 5:30pm to 10pm; Saturday and Sunday brunch 10am to 2pm.

**Shops** 10am to 6pm or 7pm Monday to Saturday and noon to 6pm Sunday.

# Electricity

120V/60Hz

120V/60Hz

Electric current in the USA is 110V to 115V, 60Hz AC. Outlets may be suited for flat two-prong or three-prong plugs. If your appliance is made for another electrical system, pick up a transformer or adapter at Walgreens (p284).

# Emergencies

### Police, Fire & Ambulance
(  emergency 911, non-emergency 311)

### San Francisco General Hospital (  emergency room 415-206-8111, main hospital 415-206-8000; www.sfdph.org; 1001 Potrero Ave; M Potrero Ave)

### Drug & Alcohol Emergency Treatment
(  415-362-3400)

### Trauma Recovery & Rape Treatment Center (  415-437-3000; www.traumarecoverycenter.org)

# Medical Services

Before traveling, contact your health-insurance provider to find out what types of medical care they will cover outside your hometown (or home country). Overseas visitors should acquire travel insurance that covers medical situations in the US, where nonemergency care for uninsured patients can be very expensive. For nonemergency appointments at hospitals, you'll need proof of insurance or cash. Even with insurance, you'll most likely have to pay up front for nonemergency care, and then wrangle with your insurance company afterwards in order to get reimbursed.

# Emergency Rooms

### Davies Medical Center
(  415-565-6000; cnr Noe & Duboce Sts; 24hr; M 6, 22, 24, 71, J, N) Offers 24-hour emergency services.

### San Francisco General Hospital (  emergency 415-206-8111, main hospital 415-206-8000; www.sfdph.org; 1001 Potrero Ave; 24hr; M 9) Provides care to uninsured patients; no documentation required beyond ID.

### University of California San Francisco Medical Center (  415-476-1000; www.ucsfhealth.org; 505 Parnassus Ave; 24hr; M 6, 24, 71, N) Leading medical advances nationwide.

## Pharmacies

### Walgreens (  415-861-3136; www.walgreens.com; 498 Castro St at 18th St; 24hr; M 24, 35, F) Pharmacy and over-the-counter meds; dozens of locations citywide (see website).

# Money

US dollars are the only accepted currency in San Francisco. Debit/credit cards are accepted widely, but bringing a combination of cash, cards and traveler's checks is wise.

## ATMs

Most banks have ATMs, which are open 24 hours a day, except in areas where street crime has proved a problem (such as near the BART stop at 16th and Mission Sts). For a nominal service charge, you can withdraw cash from an ATM using a credit card.

## Changing Money

Though there are exchange bureaus located at airports, the best rates are generally at banks in the city. For the latest exchange rates, visit the currency converter website www.xe.com.

**American Express** (AmEx; ☎ 415-536-2600; www .americanexpress.com /travel; 455 Market St; ⏰ 8:30am-5:30pm Mon-Fri, 9:30am-3:30pm Sat; Ⓜ & Ⓡ Embarcadero) Traveler's checks are still a handy cash backup in case your ATM and credit cards inexplicably stop working; the shop exchanges money as well.

**Bank of America** (☎ 415-837-1394; www.bankamerica .com; downstairs, 1 Powell St; ⏰ 9am-6pm Mon-Fri, to 2pm Sat; Ⓜ & Ⓡ Powell St) Though any bank can exchange currency, this branch of the Bank of America is the most centrally located and convenient.

## Traveler's Checks

In the US, traveler's checks in US dollars are virtually as good as cash; you don't have to go to a bank to cash them, as many establishments will accept them just like cash. The major advantage of traveler's checks in US dollars over cash is that they can be replaced if lost or stolen.

# Practicalities

### NEWSPAPERS & MAGAZINES

○ **San Francisco Bay Guardian** (www.sfbg.com) SF's free, alternative weekly covers politics, theater, music, art and movie listings.

○ **San Francisco Chronicle** (www.sfgate.com) Main daily newspaper with news, entertainment and event listings online (no registration required).

○ **SF Weekly** (www.sfweekly.com) Free weekly with local gossip and entertainment.

### RADIO

For local listening in San Francisco and online via podcasts and/or streaming audio, check out these stations:

○ **KQED** (88.5FM; www.kqed.org) National Public Radio (NPR) and Public Broadcasting (PBS) affiliate offering podcasts and streaming video.

○ **KALW** (91.7FM; www.kalw.org) Local NPR affiliate: news, talk, music, original programming.

○ **KPOO** (89.5FM; www.kpoo.com) Community radio with jazz, R&B, blues and reggae.

○ **KPFA** (94.1FM; www.kpfa.org) Alternative news and music.

# Public Holidays

A majority of shops remain open on public holidays (with the exception of July 4, Thanksgiving, Christmas and New Year's Day), while banks, schools and offices are usually closed. For information on festivals and events, see p40. Holidays that may affect business hours and transit schedules include the following:

**New Year's Day** January 1

**Martin Luther King Jr Day** Third Monday in January

**Presidents' Day** Third Monday in February

**Easter** Sunday (and Good Friday and Easter Monday) in March or April

**Memorial Day** Last Monday in May

**Independence Day** July 4

**Labor Day** First Monday in September

**Columbus Day** Second Monday in October

**Veterans Day** November 11

**Thanksgiving** Fourth Thursday in November

**Christmas Day** December 25

## Safe Travel

Keep your city smarts and wits about you, especially at night in the Tenderloin, SoMa and the Mission. The Bayview-Hunters Point neighborhood south of Potrero Hill along the water is plagued by a high crime rate and frequent violence, and is not particularly suitable for wandering tourists. After dark, Mission Dolores Park, Buena Vista Park and the entry to Golden Gate Park at Haight and Stanyan Sts host drug deals and casual sex hookups.

Panhandlers are a reality in San Francisco. You will likely be asked for spare change. A simple 'I'm sorry' is always a polite response if you don't want to part with your money. (Many argue that dollars stretch further when donated to a local shelter or nonprofit.)

## Taxes & Refunds

SF's 9.5% sales tax is added to virtually everything, including meals, accommodations and car rentals. Groceries are about the only items not taxed, and unlike European Value Added Tax, sales tax is not refundable. There's also a 15.5% hotel-room tax to take into consideration when booking a hotel room.

## Telephone

The US country code is 🕿1, and San Francisco's city code is 🕿415. To make an international call from the Bay Area, call 🕿011 + country code + area code + number. When dialing another area code, the code must be preceded by 🕿1. Phonecards are available at most markets, convenience stores and pharmacies.

## Area Codes in the Bay Area

**East Bay** 🕿510

**Marin County** 🕿415

**Wine Country** 🕿707

## Cell Phones

Most US cell phones besides the iPhone operate on CDMA, not the European standard GSM – make sure you check compatibility with your phone service provider.

## Operator Services

**International operator** 🕿00

**Local directory** 🕿411

**Long-distance directory information** 🕿1 + area code + 555-1212

**Operator** 🕿0

**Toll-free number information** 🕿800-555-1212

## Time

San Francisco is on Pacific Standard Time (PST), three hours behind the East Coast's Eastern Standard Time (EST) and eight hours behind Greenwich Mean Time (GMT/UTC). Summer is Daylight Saving Time in the US.

The following table shows time differences from SF to major cities.

| San Francisco | noon |
| --- | --- |
| Chicago | 2pm |
| New York City | 3pm |
| London | 8pm |
| Moscow | midnight |
| Hong Kong | 4am the following day |
| Sydney | 7am the following day |

## Tourist Information

**San Francisco Visitor Information Center** (Map p160; 🕿 415-391-2000, events hotline 415-391-2001; www.onlyinsanfrancisco.com; lower level, Hallidie Plaza, Market & Powell Sts; ⌚9am-5pm Mon-Fri, to 3pm Sat & Sun; Ⓜ & Ⓡ Powell St) provides practical information for tourists, publishes glossy tourist-oriented booklets and runs a 24-hour events hotline.

For further tourist information, check out the following websites:

**Lonely Planet** (www.lonelyplanet.com)

**SFGate.com** (www.sfgate.com)

**SFist** (www.sfist.com)

# Travelers with Disabilities

All Bay Area transit companies offer travel discounts for disabled travelers and wheelchair-accessible service. Major car-rental companies can usually supply hand-controlled vehicles with one or two days' notice. For visually impaired people, major intersections emit a chirping signal to indicate when it is safe to cross the street. For the hearing impaired, many local TV stations include subtitles. Check the following resources:

**San Francisco Bay Area Regional Transit Guide** (www.transit.511.org /disabled/index.aspx) Covers accessibility for people with disabilities.

**Muni's Street & Transit** (www.sfmta.com) Details which bus routes and streetcar stops are wheelchair-friendly.

# Visas
## Canadians

Canadian citizens currently only need proof of identity and citizenship to enter the US – but check the US Department of State for updates, as requirements may change.

## Visa Waiver Program

The Visa Waiver Program (VWP) allows nationals from 36 countries to enter the US without a visa, provided they are carrying a machine-readable passport. For the updated list of countries included in the program and current requirements, see the **US Department of State** (http://travel.state.gov/visa) website. Citizens of VWP countries need to register with the **US Department of Homeland Security** (http://esta.cbp.dhs.gov) three days before their visit.

## Visas Required

You must obtain a visa from a US embassy or consulate in your home country if you meet the following qualifications:

○ Do not currently hold a passport from a VWP country.

○ Are from a VWP country, but don't have a machine-readable passport.

○ Are from a VWP country, but currently hold a passport issued between October 26, 2005, and October 25, 2006, that does not have a digital photo on the information page or an integrated chip from the data page.

○ Are planning to stay longer than 90 days.

○ Are planning to work or study in the US.

## Work Visas

Foreign visitors are not legally allowed to work in the USA without the appropriate working visa. The most common, the H visa, can be difficult to obtain. It usually requires a sponsoring organization, such as the company you will be working for in the US.

The following are different visa types

**H** For temporary workers.

**L** For employees in intracompany transfers.

**O** For workers with extraordinary abilities.

**P** For athletes and entertainers.

**Q** For international cultural-exchange visitors.

# Behind the Scenes

## Author Thanks

### MARIELLA KRAUSE

Thanks to coauthors Alison Bing and John A Vlahides, who tirelessly ate and drank their way around San Francisco, providing a true local perspective and a list of new places for me to check out in this fabulous city we live in. Your writing skills and wit made editing your sections a pleasure, and I quite literally could not have done it without you!

## Acknowledgments

Cover photographs: Front: Victorian houses facing Alamo Square, Walter Bibikow/AWL-images. Back: California St cable car in the Financial District, Sabrina Dalbesio/Lonely Planet Images ©.

Many of the images in this guide are available for licensing from Lonely Planet Images: www.lonelyplanetimages.com.

## This Book

This 2nd edition of *Discover San Francisco* was researched and written by Mariella Krause, Alison Bing and John A Vlahides. The previous edition was written by Alison Bing and John A Vlahides. This guidebook was commissioned in Lonely Planet's Oakland office, and produced by the following:

**Commissioning Editor** Suki Gear
**Coordinating Editor** Andi Jones
**Coordinating Cartographer** Mark Griffiths
**Coordinating Layout Designer** Carol Jackson
**Managing Editors** Anna Metcalfe, Angela Tinson
**Managing Cartographer** Alison Lyall
**Managing Layout Designers** Chris Girdler, Jane Hart
**Assisting Editor** Bella Li
**Assisting Cartographer** Valeska Cañas
**Cover Research** Naomi Parker
**Internal Image Research** Nicholas Colicchia
**Thanks to** Lucy Birchley, Laura Crawford, Sally Darmody, Janine Eberle, Ryan Evans, Larissa Frost, Liz Heynes, Lauren Hunt, Laura Jane, Yvonne Kirk, Kylie McLaughlin, Wayne Murphy, Trent Paton, Mazzy Prinsep, Jessica Rose, Mik Ruff, Jacqui Saunders, Laura Stansfeld, Gerard Walker, Clifton Wilkinson, Juan Winata

## SEND US YOUR FEEDBACK

We love to hear from travelers – your comments keep us on our toes and help make our books better. Our well-traveled team reads every word on what you loved or loathed about this book. Although we cannot reply individually to postal submissions, we always guarantee that your feedback goes straight to the appropriate authors, in time for the next edition. Each person who sends us information is thanked in the next edition, the most useful submissions are rewarded with a selection of digital PDF chapters.

Visit **lonelyplanet.com/contact** to submit your updates and suggestions or to ask for help. Our award-winning website also features inspirational travel stories, news and discussions.

Note: We may edit, reproduce and incorporate your comments in Lonely Planet products such as guidebooks, websites and digital products, so let us know if you don't want your comments reproduced or your name acknowledged. For a copy of our privacy policy visit lonelyplanet.com/privacy.

NOTES

# Index

See also separate subindexes for:

⊠ Eating p298

☺ Drinking & Nightlife p299

★ Entertainment p300

🔒 Shopping p301

🏃 Sports & Activities p302

**4:20 Clock 187**
**32 Delmar St 187**
**635 Ashbury St 187**
**635 Cole St 187**
**826 Valencia 21, 151, 155-8, 159, 249, 256**
**1235 Masonic Ave 187**

## A

accommodations 45, 231, 270-7
activities 40-1, *see also individual activities, individual neighborhoods,* Sports & Activities subindex
AIDS 41, 129, 133, 180, 246, 260
air travel 278
**Alamo Square 9, 24, 25, 184, 193, 257**
**Alcatraz 9, 13, 33, 44, 52-3, 248**
**Alta Vista Park 259**
alligators 14, 20, 207
ambulances 284
animals 14, 207, *see also individual animals*
**Aquarium of the Bay 15, 56**
**Aquatic Park 57**
**Aquatic Park Bathhouse 15, 42, 51, 56**
architecture 257-8, *see also individual buildings*
area codes 286

Sights 000
Map pages 000

Arnold, Carleigh 59
art galleries, *see* galleries
arts 254-6, *see also* film, literature, murals, music, theater
**Asian Art Museum 9, 16, 17, 35, 78, 86**
ATMs 284-5
**Audium 131**
Avenues, the 203-25, **214-15**
    accommodations 271, 276-7
    drinking & nightlife 207, 221-2
    entertainment 222, 223
    food 205, 207, 210, 217-221
    highlights 204-5, 208-11
    shopping 222-3
    sights 208-11, 212-16, 217
    sports & activities 224-5
    transportation 212
    walks 206-7

## B

**Baker Beach 28, 61-2, 262**
**Balmy Alley 18, 151, 159**
bank swallows 207, 217
Barbary Coast 42, 95, 105, 243, 257
BART 280-1
baseball 180-1
**Bay Area Discovery Museum (Sausalito) 236**
Beat movement 101, 106, 244, 246, 256, *see also* Ginsberg, Allen, Kaufman, Bob, Kerouac, Jack

**Beat Museum 105, 106-9, 246**
beer 119, 170, 174, 196, 252-3
**Benziger (Sonoma Valley) 232**
bicycling 73-4, 224, 283
bisexual travelers, *see* gay travelers, lesbian travelers
bison 14, 207
**Bison Paddock 207**
boat travel 74, 282-3
**Bob Kaufman Alley 18, 104-5, 111, 246**
books, *see individual authors,* Beat movement, literature
**Botanical Garden 207, 210**
bowling 181
**Buena Vista Park 30, 185, 186, 188, 259, 260**
bus travel 278-9, 279-80
business hours 252, 266, 283

## C

**Cable Car Museum 127, 133**
cable cars 9, 15, 33, 78, 248, 265-8, **267**
    history 243
    museums 127, 133
    planning 45, 279-80
    turnarounds 80, 84
cafes 39, 102, 188, 252
**California Academy of Sciences 9, 14, 20, 37, 207, 209-10, 211**
**California Historical Society Museum 163**

**Camera Obscura 213**
car travel 281-2
**Cartoon Art Museum 21, 158, 249, 256**
**Castello di Amorosa (Napa Valley) 229**
Castro, the 9, 22, 23, 147-81, **155, 166**
  accommodations 271, 276-7
  drinking & nightlife 151, 174-5, 264
  entertainment 149, 177-8
  food 151, 169-70
  highlights 148-9, 152-3
  shopping 180
  sights 152-3, 164
  sports & activities 180-1
  transportation 154
  walks 150-1
Castro Theatre 26, 148, 177, 255, 264
cathedrals, see churches & cathedrals
cell phones 44, 286
chemists 284
children, travel with 248-9
**Children's Creativity Museum 163, 249**
Chinatown 9, 18, 35, 101-23, **108-9**
  accommodations 271, 274-5
  drinking & nightlife 105, 119-20, 123
  entertainment 120
  festivals 40
  food 105, 117-18, 119, 251
  highlights 102-3
  shopping 122-3
  sights 107, 111-15
  tours 283
  transportation 106
  walks 104-5, 115
**Chinese Culture Center 111**
**Chinese Historical Society of America 111, 257**

**Chinese Telephone Exchange 113**
**Church of St Mary the Virgin 61**
churches & cathedrals 61, 64, 85, 112-13, see also individual churches & cathedrals
cinema, see film
**City Hall 85, 258**
City Lights 102, 104, 105, 121, 246, 256
Civic Center 77-99, **85, 92**
  accommodations 271, 272-5
  drinking & nightlife 81, 93, 95-6
  entertainment 96-8
  food 81, 85, 90, 91-3, 99
  highlights 78-9, 82-3
  shopping 98-9
  sights 82-3, 85, 86, 95
  transportation 84
  walks 80-1
**Clarion Alley 16, 151, 159**
**Cliff House 213**
climate 44, 65, 261-2
**Coastal Trail 30, 204, 212**
**Coit Tower 9, 21, 103, 107**
  architecture 257, 258
  murals 25, 260
  views 25
**Columbus Tower 109**
comedy 98, 120
**Commercial St 114**
**Conservatory of Flowers 206, 210, 211**
**Contemporary Jewish Museum 158-62, 249**
**Corona Heights 262**
costs 44-5, 251, 266, 270, 286
**Creativity Explored 155**
**Crissy Field 14, 49, 51, 61, 249, 262**
culture 240
currency 44
cycling 73-4, 224, 283

**D**
dance 255-6
dangers & annoyances 45, 286
**Darioush (Napa Valley) 229**
Dennis, Brent 209
**di Rosa Art + Nature Preserve (Napa Valley) 228, 256**
**Diego Rivera Gallery 128, 131-3, 260**
disabilities, travelers with 286-7
Downtown 77-99, **85**
  accommodations 271, 272-5
  drinking & nightlife 81, 93
  entertainment 96-8
  food 81, 85, 90, 91, 99
  highlights 78-9, 82-3
  shopping 98-9
  sights 82-3, 84, 86, 95
  transportation 84
  walks 80-1
**Dragon's Gate 9, 18, 113-15**
drinking & nightlife, see also individual neighborhoods, Drinking & Nightlife subindex
  cafes 39, 102, 188, 252
  saloons 29, 42, 81, 105, 118, 240
  speakeasies 9, 29, 96
drinks, see beer, wine
driving 281-2
drugstores 284
**Dutch Windmill 207**

**E**
El Pecho de la Chola 262
electricity 284
emergencies 284
Emperor Norton 243
entertainment, see also individual neighborhoods, music, Entertainment subindex
  comedy 98, 120
  film 40, 41, 43, 222, 255-6
  theater 26, 41, 255-6

environmental issues 240, 261, 279

events 40-1, 213

**Exploratorium 9, 20, 21, 48, 63, 249**

# F

**Fairmont Hotel 95**

farmers markets 12, 83

Feinberg, CJ 153

ferries 74, 282-3

**Ferry Building 9, 12, 13, 35, 81, 82-3**

festivals 40-1

**Filbert St Steps 25, 103, 107, 260**

Fillmore 125-45

accommodations 271, 276-7

drinking & nightlife 129

entertainment 139

food 129

highlights 126-7

sights 132

transportation 130

walks 128-9

**Fillmore St 127**

film 40, 41, 43, 222, 255-6

Financial District 86-90, 94-5

Fisherman's Wharf 33, 47-75, 249, **61, 66**

accommodations 271, 272-3

drinking & nightlife 51, 70

entertainment 71-2

food 51, 65-7, 68

highlights 48-9, 52-3, 54-7, 58-9

shopping 72-3

sights 52-3, 54-7, 58-9, 61

sports & activities 73-5

transportation 60

walks 50-1

**Flood Building 80**

fog 65, 259-62

food 12, 13, 83, 250-2, *see also individual neighborhoods,* Eating *subindex*

food trucks 12, 51, 68

football 181

**Fort Baker 59**

**Fort Funston 30, 207, 216, 217**

**Fort Mason Center 51, 60, 68**

**Fort Point 43, 59, 62-3, 261**

# G

**Galería de la Raza 158**

galleries 42, 128, 131-3, 155, 158, *see also individual galleries*

gardens, *see* parks & gardens

gay travelers 22, 263-4

Castro, the 9, 23

drinking & nightlife 140, 173, 175

entertainment 198

Pride Parade 22, 41, 264

sights 164

gay-rights movement 241, 246

**Ghirardelli Square 51, 57**

Ginsberg, Allen 43, 105, 244, 256

**Beat Museum 106**

City Lights 102, 121

**GLBT History Museum 164, 264**

**Glide Memorial United Methodist Church 85**

Gold Rush 243-4, 257

**Golden Gate Bridge 9, 11, 58-9, 281**

history 245

tours 283

views 25, 51, 262

**Golden Gate Park 9, 14, 19, 30, 37, 203-25, 214-15**

accommodations 271, 276-7

drinking & nightlife 207, 221-2

entertainment 222, 223

food 207, 210, 217-221

highlights 204-5, 208-11

history 259

shopping 222-3

sights 208-11, 212-16, 217, 248

sports & activities 224-5

transportation 212

walks 206-7

golf 75, 224

**Good Luck Parking Garage 115**

**Grace Cathedral 129, 133, 260, 268**

**Grant Ave 103**

Grateful Dead 26, 187, 254

**Gundlach-Bundschu (Sonoma Valley) 232**

# H

**Haas-Lilienthal House 130-1**

**Haight Ashbury Food Program 187**

**Haight St 21, 185, 187, 188**

Haight, the 9, 26, 183-201, **189, 190-1**

accommodations 271, 276-7

drinking & nightlife 184, 187, 196

entertainment 198

festivals 41

food 187, 189-94

highlights 184-5

shopping 198-200

sights 188, 193, 195

transportation 188

walks 186

Hammett, Dashiell 43, 80, 94, 256

**Harvey Milk Plaza 22, 23, 150, 164**

Hayes Valley 183-201, **189, 194**

accommodations 271, 276-7

drinking & nightlife 184, 187, 197-8

entertainment 198

Sights 000
Map pages 000

food 187, 194-6
highlights 184-5
shopping 9, 27, 35, 185, 200-1
sights 189, 193, 195
transportation 188
walks 186
**Hayes Valley Farm 42, 195, 261**
Hearst, Patty 187
**Hess Collection (Napa Valley) 228**
hiking 30, 232
hills 9, 30, 259-62
history 242-7
holidays 285
hospitals 284

**I**

ice skating 181
**Ina Coolbrith Park 30, 129, 133, 260**
itineraries 32-9

**J**

**Jack Kerouac Alley 18, 105, 106**
**Jack London State Historic Park (Sonoma Valley) 231-2**
Jackson Square 86-90, 94-5
**Japan Center 130**
**Japanese Tea Garden 9, 31, 37, 207, 210, 248**
Japantown **131, 134**
drinking & nightlife 138-9
entertainment 140-2
festivals 40
food 133-5
shopping 142-4
sights 130-1
sports & activities 145
Joplin, Janis 26, 121, 187, 254
**Justin Herman Plaza 81, 83**

**K**

Kaufman, Bob 244
**alley 18, 104-5, 111, 246**
kayaking 181
Kerouac, Jack 43, 104, 107
29 Russell St 128, 260
**alley 18, 105, 106**
**Konko Temple 130**

**L**

language 44
**Legion of Honor 17, 204, 212-13**
lesbian travelers 22, 263-4
Castro, the 9, 23
drinking & nightlife 140, 173, 175
entertainment 198
Pride Parade 22, 41, 264
sights 164
**Lincoln Park 30, 213**
literature 41, 43, 256, see also individual authors, Beat movement
**Lombard St 9, 19, 126, 128, 132, 268**
**Loof Carousel 163**
**Lotta's Fountain 81**

**M**

**Macondray Lane 18, 128-9, 133, 260**
magazines 285
Manson, Charles 187
Marina, the 47-75, 249, **61, 62-3**
accommodations 271, 272-3
drinking & nightlife 51, 70
entertainment 71-2
food 51, 67-9
highlights 48-9, 52-3, 54-7, 58-9
shopping 49, 72-3
sights 52-3, 54-7, 58-9, 60-1
sports & activities 73-5

transportation 60
walks 50-1
**Maritime Museum 51, 56**
**Mark Hopkins Hotel 129**
markets 12, 83
Martini, John 53
Maupin, Armistead 18, 128-9, 133, 256, 260
Maybeck, Bernard 64, 258
**McLaren Lodge 206**
media 240
medical services 284
**MH de Young Museum 17, 37, 206, 209, 257, 262**
Milk, Harvey 43, 246, 247
**plaza 22, 23, 150, 164**
**Mission Dolores 151, 154-5, 243, 257**
**Mission Dolores Park 150, 155, 264**
Mission, the 9, 16, 39, 147-81, **155, 156-7**
accommodations 271, 276-7
drinking & nightlife 29, 170-3
entertainment 149, 172, 175-6
festivals 40
food 148, 151, 156, 165-7, 251
highlights 148-9, 152-3
murals 16, 18, 22, 149, 151, 159
shopping 178-9
sights 152-3, 154-8, 159
sports & activities 180-1
transportation 154
walks 150-1
Miwok people 154, 243
mobile phones 44, 286
money 284-5
costs 44-5, 251, 266, 270, 286
taxes 45, 270, 286
tipping 44, 252, 270
motorcycle travel 281-2
**Muir Beach 232-3, 234-5**
**Muir Beach Overlook (Muir Beach) 233**

Muir, John 64, 259

Muir Woods 232-3, 259, **234-5**

**Muir Woods National Monument (Muir Woods) 233**

murals 164, 260

**Coit Tower 25, 107**

Mission, the 16, 18, 22, 149, 151, 159

**San Francisco Museum of Modern Art (SFMOMA) 153**

tours 44, 149

**Musée Mécanique 21, 50, 55, 249**

**Museum of Craft & Folk Art 163**

**Museum of the African Diaspora 162, 249**

museums 17, 37, 249, *see also individual museums*

music 43, 213, 254-5, *see also individual musicians*

festivals 40, 41, 42

San Francisco Opera 9, 26, 28, 79, 81, 97

San Francisco Symphony 9, 26, 28, 79, 81, 96

## N

Napa Valley 228-31, 253, **229**

**Napier Lane 107**

newspapers 285

nightlife, *see individual neighborhoods,* drinking & nightlife, Drinking & Nightlife subindex

Nob Hill 125-45, **131, 136-7**

accommodations 271, 276-7

drinking & nightlife 129, 139-40

entertainment 139, 140-2

food 129, 135-8

highlights 126-7

shopping 144-5

sights 131-3

sports & activities 145

transportation 130

walks 128-9

**Nob Hill Masonic Center 129**

North Beach 39, 101-23, **108-9**

accommodations 271, 274-5

drinking & nightlife 39, 102, 105, 118-19

entertainment 120

food 105, 115-17, 251

highlights 102-3

shopping 121-2

sights 106-11

transportation 106, 116

walks 104-5

Norton, Joshua 243

## O

Ocean Beach 9, 24, 30, 37, **205, 213-16**

Ohlone people 53, 154, 243, 257

**Old Faithful Geyser (Napa Valley) 229**

**Old St Mary's Cathedral 112-13**

**Old St Mary's Park 249**

**One Montgomery Terrace 95**

opening hours 252, 266, 283

**Orchard Garden Hotel 95**

## P

Pacific Heights 257, **131, 134**

drinking & nightlife 138-9

entertainment 140-2

food 133-5

shopping 142-4

sights 130-1

sports & activities 145

Painted Ladies 9, 24, 25, 184, 193, 257

**Palace Hotel 81**

**Palace of Fine Arts 51, 63-4**

parks & gardens 30, 95, 259-60, *see also individual parks & gardens*

parrots 14, 25, 83, 248, 260

pharmacies 284

**Pier 39 9, 33, 50, 51, 55**

sea lions 14, 15, 248

planning

basics 44-5

budgeting 44-5, 251, 266, 270, 286

children 248-9

festivals & events 40-1

itineraries 32-9

repeat visitors 42

resources 43, 45, 65, 264, 271

travel seasons 44-5

plover 207, 216

police 284

politics 240-1, 246

population 240

**Portsmouth Square 112, 249, 257**

**Powell St Cable Car Turnaround 84, 268**

Presidio, the 9, 28, 59, 261, **61, 70-1**

food 69-70

sights 61-4

Pride Parade 22, 41, 264

public holidays 285

## Q

**Queen Wilhelmina Tulip Garden 207**

## R

radio 285

**Redwood Park 79, 81, 91**

redwoods 79, 81, 91, 232-3

Richmond, the 212-13, 217-20

**Ross Alley 18, 114**

Russian Hill 125-45, **131, 136-7**

accommodations 271, 276-7

drinking & nightlife 129, 139-40

Sights 000
Map pages 000

entertainment 139, 140-2
food 129, 135-8
highlights 126-7
shopping 144-5
sights 131-3
sports & activities 145
transportation 130
walks 128-9

# S

safety 45, 286
sailing 74
**Saints Peter & Paul Church 104, 110-11**
saloons 29, 42, 81, 105, 118, 240
San Francisco 49ers 181
**San Francisco Art Institute 128**
**San Francisco Carousel 50, 56, 249**
**San Francisco Maritime National Historical Park 33, 48, 50-1, 55**
**San Francisco Museum of Modern Art (SFMOMA) 9, 17, 39, 42, 152-3, 260**
San Francisco Opera 9, 26, 28, 79, 81, 97
San Francisco Symphony 9, 26, 28, 79, 81, 96
Sausalito 233-7, **234-5**
sea lions 14, 15, 50-1, 55, 248
Sex Pistols 187, 255
Sherman, Amy 83
shopping 9, 27, 49, *see also individual neighborhoods,* Shopping *subindex*
SoMa 147-81, **155, 160-1**
accommodations 271, 276-7
drinking & nightlife 29, 151, 173-4, 264
entertainment 149, 176-7
food 151, 165, 167-9
highlights 148-9, 152-3
shopping 179-80
sights 152-3, 158-64

sports & activities 180-1
transportation 154
walks 150-1
**Sonoma Plaza (Sonoma Valley) 231**
Sonoma Valley 231-2, 253, **229**
spas 145
speakeasies 9, 29, 96
**Spofford Alley 114**
sports, *see individual activities, individual neighborhoods,* Sports & Activities *subindex*
**Spreckels Lake 207**
**SS Jeremiah O'Brien 33, 50, 55-6**
**Sterling Park 25, 30, 131, 260, 262, 268**
**Stow Lake 207, 211, 248**
**Stow Lake Boathouse 211**
streetcars 279-80
**Sue Bierman Park 81, 83**
Summer of Love 26, 43, 185, 186-7, 188, 245
**Sun Terrace 95**
Sunset, the 213-16, 220-1
sustainability 240, 261, 279
**Sutro Baths 213**
**Swedenborgian Church 64**
**Sycamore Alley 151**
Symbionese Liberation Army (SLA) 187

# T

**Tactile Dome 20, 21, 63, 249**
Tate, Sharon 187
taxes 45, 270, 286
taxis 281
technology 240, 246-7
**Telegraph Hill 9, 14, 25, 103, 107, 260**
telephone services 44, 270, 286
Tenderloin, the 29, 85, 91-3, 95-6, **92**
theater 26, 41, 255-6, *see also individual venues*

Tiburon 233-7, **234-5**
**Tien Hau Temple 114**
time 44, 286
tipping 44, 252, 270
tourist information 286
tours 44, 53, 59, 115, 149, 283-7, *see also individual neighborhoods*
train travel 279
**Transamerica Pyramid 79, 81, 91, 257, 258**
transportation 45, 265-8, 278-87
transsexual travelers, *see* gay travelers, lesbian travelers
traveler's checks 285
trekking 30, 232
**Twenty Rows (Napa Valley) 228**

# U

**Union Square 79, 80, 268, 88-9**
drinking & nightlife 93-4
food 90-1
sights 84
**USS Pampanito 33, 48, 55**

# V

vacations 285
vegetarian travelers 99, 251
Barney's Burgers 68
Greens 51, 60, 68, 252
Hodo Soy 83
Millennium 91-3
Mixt Greens 88-9
Yum Yum Fish 220
Vicious, Sid 187
Victorian houses 9, 24, 25, 184, 193, 257
vineyards 228, 229, 232
**Vintners' Collective (Napa Valley) 228**
visas 44, 287

# W

walking 30, 232, *see also individual neighborhoods*
**Walt Disney Family Museum 49, 64**
**Washington Square 104, 109**
**Wave Organ 21, 51, 60-1**
weather 44, 65, 261-2
websites 43, 45, 65, 264, 271
whale watching 74
wi-fi 44
wildlife 14, 207, *see also individual animals*
wine 253
   bars 51, 70-1, 94, 139, 171, 196, 197
   Napa Valley 228-31, 253, **229**
   stores 51, 70-1, 73
   Sonoma Valley 231-2, 253, **229**
wineries 228, 229, 232
**Women's Building 22, 151, 159**

# Y

Yerba Buena Center for the Arts 149, 176-7
**Yerba Buena Gardens 163-4**

# Z

**Zen Center 189, 257**

## Eating

4505 Meats 83

## A

A16 51, 67-8
Acquerello 129, 135
Anchor Oyster Bar 169
Aziza 37, 207, 217

Sights 000
Map pages 000

# B

B Star Bar 219
Bar Jules 187, 194
Barney's Burgers 68
Benkyodo 134
Benu 151, 167
Betelnut 51, 68
Bio 99
Bi-Rite 165
Bi-Rite Creamery 151, 165, 168
Blue Barn Gourmet 68-9
Bocadillos 88
Bouchon (Napa Valley) 230
Boudin Bakery 33, 67
Boulette's Larder 90
Boulevard 168
Bounty Hunter Wine Bar (Napa Valley) 230
Boxed Foods 91
Brenda's French Soul Food 93
Brioche Bakery 116
Bun Mee 135
Burma Superstar 219
Butler & the Chef 168-9

# C

Café Bastille 91
Cafe Claude 91
Café Jacqueline 116
Cafe la Haye (Sonoma Valley) 232
Cheese Plus 138
Chow 170
Cinecittá 116
Citizen's Band 168
City View 105, 117, 252
Coi 13, 42, 115
Cole Valley Cafe 192
Commonwealth 151, 165
Corner 42, 167
Cotogna 81, 87-8
Cowgirl Creamery 83
Cowgirl Creamery Sidekick 83
Crown & Crumpet 57, 65-7

# D

Delfina 13, 151, 165
Duc Loi 165

# E

Eagle Café 65
El Dorado Kitchen Corner Cafe (Sonoma Valley) 232
Emporio Rulli 99
Escape from New York Pizza 193-4

# F

Ferry Plaza Farmers Market 83
Fig Cafe & Winebar (Sonoma Valley) 232
Fish (Sausalito) 236-7
Forbes Island 33, 65
Frascati 137-8
Fremont Diner (Sonoma Valley) 232
French Laundry (Napa Valley) 44, 230

# G

Gary Danko 51, 65, 252
Ghirardelli Ice Cream 57, 67
Gitane 81, 90, 91
Golden Gate Market (Sausalito) 237
Golden Star 118
Gott's Roadside/Taylor's Automatic Refresher (Napa Valley) 230
Grandeho's Kamekyo II 67
Greens 51, 60, 68, 252
Grove 135

# H

Halu 219
Hapa Ramen 83
Hodo Soy 83
Hog Island Oyster Company 89-90
House of Bagels 218-19
House of Nanking 118
Humphry Slocombe 168, 252

## I

Ichi Sushi 166
In-N-Out Burger 67

## J

Jai Yun 105, 119
Jardinière 187
Johnny Foley's 90
Judy's Cafe 68
Juhu Beach Club 168

## K

Kabuto 207, 217, 252
Kara's Cupcakes 57, 69

## L

La Boulange 69
La Méditerranée 170
La Taqueria 16, 39, 151, 165, 252
Lefty O'Douls 90
Liguria Bakery 104, 116
Little Chihuahua 192

## M

Magnolia Brewpub 186, 192
Michael Mina 86, 252
Mijita 90
Millennium 91-3
Mission Beach Cafe 167
Mitchell's Ice Cream 168
Mixt Greens 88-9
Mocca on Maiden Lane 99
Molinari 105, 116-17

## N

Naked Lunch 117
Namu 12, 13, 83, 207, 217
Nanking Road Bistro 220
Nojo 195

## O

Off the Grid 68
Out the Door 83, 129, 133
Outerlands 42, 221
Oxbow Public Market
 (Napa Valley) 230

## P

Pelican Inn (Muir Woods)
 233
Pizzeria Delfina 129, 134
Plouf 91
PPQ Dungeness Island 218
Presidio Social Club 70

## R

Ragazza 189
Rainbow Grocery 165
Real Food 69
Recchiuti 83
Ristorante Ideale 39, 105,
 115-16
Rosamunde Sausage Grill
 187, 189
Rose's Café 68
Rotunda 99

## S

Sam's Anchor Cafe (Tiburon)
 237
San Tung 37, 220-1
Saporro-Ya 134-5
Sentinel 169
Shalimar 93
Slanted Door 35, 81, 83, 89,
 129, 252
Sons & Daughters 90-1
Sophie's Crepes 135
Spices 218
Spruce 218
Sunrise Deli 220
Suppenküche 195-6
Swan Oyster Depot 137
Swenson's Ice Cream 128

## T

Tartine 166-7
Tataki 129, 133, 252
Thanh Long 207, 220
Three Twins Ice Cream 189
Tiramisu 91
Tommy's Joynt 90
Ton Kiang Restaurant 217-18

Tony's Coal-Fired Pizza & Slice
 House 117
Tropisueño 169

## U

Udupi Palace 166
Underdog 221

## W

Warming Hut 69
Wing Lee 219-20

## Y

Yuet Lee 118
Yum Yum Fish 220

## Z

Za 138
Zero Zero 167-8
Ziryab 192
Zuni Cafe 35, 187, 195

## Drinking & Nightlife

15 Romolo 119
111 Minna 173
440 Castro 175
540 Club 221
1300 on Fillmore 129, 138, 139

## A

Alembic 184, 187, 196, 253
Amélie 129, 139

## B

Badlands 175
Bar Agricole 151, 173
Barrique 81, 94
Beach Chalet 207, 221, 223
Bigfoot Lodge 129, 139
Bitter End 222
Bix 81, 95
Blackbird 175
Bloodhound 29, 151, 173
Bourbon & Branch 29, 96
Buena Vista Cafe 51, 70, 253

Butter 174
Butterfly Bar 138

## C

Cafe Flore 174, 264
Caffe Trieste 104, 105, 118
California Wine Merchant 51, 70-1
Cat Club 151, 173
Church Key 119
Churchill 42, 175
Cinch 140
City Beer Store & Tasting Room 174
Coffee to the People 196
Comstock Saloon 29, 105, 118

## D

DNA Lounge 174
Doc's Clock 173
Dosa 138-9

## E

Edinburgh Castle 81, 95, 256
El Rio 171
Elixir 29, 151, 170, 253
EndUp 151, 173
EZ5 120

## H

Harlot 173
Harry's Bar 139
Heart 171
Hollow 222
Homestead 29, 171
Hôtel Biron 187, 197
House of Shields 174

## I

Irish Bank 93

## J

John's Grill 43, 94

## L

Latin American Club 172
Le Colonial 94
Li Po 105, 119-20, 246
Lush Lounge 95

## M

Madrone 29, 196
Medjool Sky Terrace 172
Mint 197
Moby Dick 175
Momi Toby's Revolution Café 197-8

## N

Noc Noc 187, 196

## O

Old Ship Saloon 81

## R

Rickhouse 29, 81, 93
Rickshaw Stop 96
Ritual Coffee Roasters 172
Rosewood 120
Ruby Skye 94

## S

Smuggler's Cove 29, 35, 184, 187, 197
Social 207, 221-2
Specs' 39, 105, 118
Stud 173

## T

Taverna Aventine 94
Tonga Room 126, 129, 139
Top of the Mark 129, 139-40, 260
Toronado 184, 187, 189, 196, 253
Tosca Cafe 39, 105, 118-19, 253
Trouble Coffee 207, 221
Tunnel Top 93
Twin Peaks Tavern 175

## V

Vesuvio 39, 105, 119, 246
Vinyl Wine Bar 196

## W

Wellingtons Wine Bar (Sausalito) 237

## Z

Zeitgeist 151, 170, 253

## ⭐ Entertainment

## A

Amnesia 176
AsiaSF 151, 177

## B

Balboa Theater 222, 223
BATS Improv 71-2, 255
Beach Blanket Babylon 26, 39, 120, 255
Bimbo's 365 Club 120
Boom Boom Room 129, 139, 141
Bottom of the Hill 151, 176
Bridge Theater 222, 223

## C

Café du Nord/Swedish American Hall 29, 178
Café Royale 81, 97
Castro Theatre 26, 148, 177, 255, 264
Cobb's Comedy Club 120

## D

Dance Mission 172

## E

Elbo Room 175
Encore Karaoke Lounge 141

## F

Fillmore Auditorium 129, 140

Sights 000
Map pages 000

**H**

Hotel Utah Saloon 177

**I**

Independent 198

**J**

Jazz Heritage Center 139

**M**

Magic Theatre 51, 71, 255
Make-Out Room 16, 176, 256
Metronome Dance Collective 172
Mezzanine 176

**P**

Pier 23 51, 71
Plough & the Stars 207, 222
Punch Line 98
Purple Onion 120

**R**

Rasselas 129, 139, 141
Rebel Bar 187, 198
Red Devil Lounge 141
Roccapulco Supper Club 172
Roxie Cinema 175
Rrazz Room 81, 97

**S**

San Francisco Opera 9, 26, 28, 79, 81, 97
San Francisco Symphony 9, 26, 28, 79, 81, 96
Sheba Piano Lounge 139
Slim's 176
Starlight Room 97
Sundance Kabuki Cinema 40, 142

**T**

Teatro Zinzanni 71

**V**

Viz Cinema 142

**Y**

Yerba Buena Center for the Arts 149, 176-7
Yoshi's 129, 139, 140

🔒 **Shopping**

101 Music 121

**A**

Adobe Books & Backroom Gallery 178
Al's Attire 121
Amoeba Music 198-9
Aria 121

**B**

Barneys 99
Bound Together Anarchist Book Collective 186
Branch 179

**C**

Chinatown Kite Shop 123
City Lights 102, 104, 105, 121, 246, 256
Clarion Music Center 123
Clary Sage Organics 142
Cliff's Variety 180
Cris 145
Crossroads 144

**D**

Double Punch 122

**E**

Eco Citizen 144
Eden & Eden 99
elizabethW 72

**F**

Far East Flea Market 123
Flax 201
Flight 001 201

**G**

Gama-Go 180
Gangs of San Francisco 201
General Store 42, 223
Golden Gate Fortune Cookie Company 18, 35, 122-3
Good Vibrations 179
Gravel & Gold 178
Green Apple Books 223

**H**

H&M 98
Hyde & Seek Antiques 145

**I**

Ichiban Kan 143

**J**

Jeremy's 179
Jonathan Adler 143-4

**K**

Katsura Garden 143
Kinokuniya Books & Stationery 130, 142-3
Kohshi 143

**L**

Lola of North Beach 122
Lotus Bleu 201
Loyal Army Clothing 199

**M**

Mingle 72
Mission Statement 179
Mollusk 42, 223
My Roommate's Closet 72-3

**N**

Needles & Pens 178
Nest 142
New People 143

**O**

Original Levi's Store 98

## P

Park Life 222-3
Past Perfect 72
Paxton Gate 179
Piedmont Boutique 199
PlumpJack Wines 73
Polanco 201
Prairie Collective 199

## R

Red Blossom Tea Company 123
Reliquary 200-1
Revolver 42, 200
Rock Posters & Collectibles 122
Room 4 179

## S

Seedstore 223
SFMOMA Museum Store 153, 179
Studio 144
Sui Generis 42, 180

## U

Uko 73
Under One Roof 180
Upper Playground 200

## W

Wasteland 200
Westfield San Francisco Centre 98
Wishbone 223
Worn Out West 180

## X

Xapno 200

## Z

Zinc Details 144

## Sports & Activities

Adventure Cat 74
AT&T Park 180-1
Blazing Saddles 73-4
Circus Center Trapeze 225
City Kayak 181
Golden Gate Municipal Golf Course 224
Golden Gate Park Bike & Skate 224
Harding Park Municipal Golf Course 224
House of Air 75
Kabuki Springs & Spa 127, 145
Lawn Bowling Club 225
Lincoln Park Golf Course 224
Lindy in the Park 225
Oceanic Society Expeditions 74
Presidio Golf Course 75
Red & White Fleet 74
San Francisco Croquet Club 225
San Francisco Disc Golf 225
Yerba Buena Center Ice Skating & Bowling 181